CREEK COUNTRY

CREEK

COUNTRY

THE CREEK INDIANS
AND THEIR WORLD

ROBBIE ETHRIDGE

The University of North Carolina Press

Chapel Hill and London

© 2003 The University of North Carolina Press
All rights reserved

Designed by April Leidig-Higgins
Set in Ehrhardt by Copperline Book Services, Inc.
Manufactured in the United States of America

The paper in this book meets the guidelines for
permanence and durability of the Committee on
Production Guidelines for Book Longevity of
the Council on Library Resources.

Library of Congress Cataloging-in-Publication Data
Ethridge, Robbie Franklyn, 1955–
Creek country: the Creek Indians and their world /
by Robbie Ethridge.
p. cm.   Includes bibliographical references and index.
ISBN 0-8078-2827-0 (cloth: alk. paper)
ISBN 0-8078-5495-6 (pbk.: alk. paper)
1. Creek Indians—History.   2. Creek Indians—
Land tenure.   3. Creek Indians—Government
relations.   I. Title.
E99.C9 E84 2003   976.004'973—dc21   2003011479

cloth   07 06 05 04 03   5 4 3 2 1
paper   07 06 05 04 03   5 4 3 2 1

For Nonie, in memory of our mother and father

CONTENTS

FIGURES

ACKNOWLEDGMENTS

First and foremost I would like to thank Charles Hudson, who directed my undergraduate honor's thesis, my master's thesis, and my Ph.D. dissertation, which was the first draft of this book. He also read many subsequent drafts as the manuscript progressed to completion. During the many years of our association, I have come to share his vision of what anthropology can be. He has been a great personal influence in my life, and my own work bears his imprint proudly. I would like to acknowledge two colleagues and friends who have been vital to this work. Maureen Meyers read more than her share of drafts, made several corrections, offered many suggestions, and generally kept me straight on the archaeology; she is the perfect combination of friend and colleague. My departmental colleague Jay Johnson has shown a kind of support rare in the academy, and I thank him deeply for it.

I would also like to acknowledge with gratitude those organizations that helped to fund this research: the American Philosophical Society Phillips Fund for Native American Studies, the Ethnohistory Project, the Coosawattee Foundation, Inc., Delta Kappa Gamma Society, and the University of Mississippi Faculty Summer Support Program. I would also like to thank the University of Georgia Research Foundation, Inc., for the encouragement and support that the foundation shows to UGA graduate students entering their professions through the Robert C. Anderson Memorial Award, which I received in 1999 based on this work when it was still in progress.

I would like to thank my editors at UNC Press, David Perry and Mark Simpson-Vos, for their commitment to this project and managing editor Ron Maner and his colleagues for seeing it through to completion. I would like to thank Gregory Waselkov and a second anonymous reader for their close reviews of the manuscript and for helping me see what *Creek Country* could be. I hope I have done their insights some justice here. Louis De Vorsey and Mark

Williams took the interest and time to look over the first draft and correct some important points, and I thank them. Thanks also to Stephanie Wenzel for copyediting and Jenni Rom for proofreading.

Although I am a cultural anthropologist, some of my most rewarding associations have been with southeastern archaeologists. In particular, I would like to thank Steve Kowalewski, David Hally, Dean Wood, Kay Wood, Dan and Rita Elliott, Tom Gresham, Chad Braley, Rob Benson, Tom Pluckhahn, Paul Webb, Joel Jones, John Chamblee, Thomas Foster, Jim Knight, Brett Riggs, Barnie Pavao-Zuckerman, Marvin Smith, John Worth, Ramie Gougeon, Betsy Reitz, Charlotte "Sammy" Smith, John O'Hear, Dave Moore, Chris Rodning, Rob Beck, Joel Dukes, and Marvin Jeter. I would also like to thank my ethnohistory colleagues, Tony Parades, Patricia Galloway, Steven Hahn, Josh Piker, Claudio Saunt, Greg O'Brien, Jamey Carson, Helen Rountree, Wendy St. John, and Katherine Braund, all of whom have generously shared manuscripts, sources, ideas, and lively email exchanges.

I would like to thank the staff at the Alabama State Archaeological Site Files, Eugene Futato in particular, for their prompt attention to a burdensome request. The folks at the Georgia State Archaeological Site Files deserve a special note of appreciation for all their help in providing information on Historic Period Indian sites and reports and for the use of their computer. John Chamblee, especially, was an invaluable help. Lucille McCook gave of her time to verify the botanical references. A very special thanks goes to Brian Davis at the University of Georgia Cartographic Services for his work on the first draft of the maps, to Paul Mitchell at the University of Mississippi Mineral Resources Institute for an additional one, and to Bill Nelson for the final versions of them. I would also like to thank Brooke Coward, my graduate teaching assistant, for her help in the niggling details of getting a final version ready.

This work involved much research at various archives and libraries. I would like to thank the staffs at the National Archives, the American Philosophical Society, the Historical Society of Pennsylvania, Independence National Historical Park, the Georgia State Department of Archives and History, the Library of Congress, the North Carolina Department of Archives and History, the University of North Carolina Library, the Indiana University Lilly Library, and the National Anthropological Archives.

As with any work that takes several years, I owe thanks to many friends and colleagues for their sustained support and interest. Thanks to Tina and Vic Chesnutt, Doug Hollingsworth, Paige West, J. C. Sayler, Jimmy Davidson, Jean Spencer, David Levitt, Beth Hale, Charles Ratliff, John McMahon, John Seawright, Dave McGivergan, William Gay, Greg Paulk, Nancy Feinstein,

Warren Roberts, Greg Keyes, Dan Hickerson, Jeff Jackson, Gabe Wroebel, Max Williams, Robert Thorne, Janet Ford, Ed Sisson, Vaughn Grisham, Gary Long, Elise Lake, Ann Johnson, Charles Wilson, Ted Ownby, Bob Brink-meyer, David and Marianne Wharton, Debra Cohen, Steve Brewer, Ann Fisher-Wirth, Peter Wirth, Brett and Marie Shadle, Scott Kreeger, Mathew Reed, Ann Abadie, Mary Hartwell Howorth, Ann O'Dell, Cliff Holley, Joe Ward, Bob Haws, Cliff Ochs, John Samonds, Kevin McCarthy, Sheila Skemp, Aileen Ajootian, Paula Temple, and Jan Murray. I would also like to thank my cohort of junior women faculty and staff at the University of Mississippi, who are some of the most intelligent, creative, supportive, and unusual women I've had the good fortune to fall in with. These are Kirsten Dellinger, Katie McKee, Laurie Cozad, Minjooh Oh, Marty McCarthy, Susan Ditto, Ethel Minor-Young, Annette Trefzer, Nancy Bercaw, Susan Grayzel, Theresa Levitt, Karen Raber, Debra Young, Lucille McCook, Karen Glynn, Susan Glisson, and Amy Randall.

I would like to thank my family: my husband, Denton Marcotte; my step-children, Ian and Shayla; my brother-in-law, Robert Duncan; and my nephew, Ryan Duncan. They have shown support, love, friendship, enthusiasm, inter-est, and most importantly, faith through it all. Finally, I would like to thank my sister, Nonie Duncan, who has been a source of strength for me in ways I cannot adequately express. This book is dedicated to her and in memory of our mother and father.

INTRODUCTION

This book is about a distant, lost world —the world of the Creek Indians at the close of the eighteenth century. I have attempted to portray this world through the surface of Creek life as lived by ordinary Creek men and women, and I have tried to understand something of the landscape in which they labored and loved, their jobs and tasks, their day-to-day affairs and concerns, and their towns and loyalties, as well as the larger historical forces at work that would eventually transform this world into an altogether different one.

But this was not a purely Indian world, nor had it been for almost 300 years. Creek life at the turn of the nineteenth century was so seamlessly stitched to that of frontier whites and blacks that it is difficult to separate Indian life from the life of others on the frontier. The territorial borders of Creek country never formed an impermeable boundary to people, goods, animals, plants, microbes, or ideas. In short, the lives of people in the American South at this time were thoroughly interwoven.[1] To portray Creek country in all its richness, detail, and complexity, then, requires telling something about Creek relationships with the others living in or near Creek country—other Indians, Africans, people of mixed parentage, and white Americans.

American Indians have played a central role in shaping the history of the nation, and they are deeply woven into the social fabric of much of American life. In the not-too-distant past they dominated the larger part of America geographically and militarily, and they played a vital role in its economy. However, only in the past few decades have Indians surfaced as more than just shadowy and tragic figures in history.[2] During the last three decades of the twentieth century, scholars of ethnohistory, of the "new Indian history," and of Native American studies forcefully demonstrated that to understand American history and the American experience, one must include American Indians.[3]

So why were Indians left out of history for so long?[4] There are many complicated reasons, of course. Perhaps the most pernicious is the well-documented construction of non-Western peoples, including American Indians, as Other —mystical, primitive, and ahistorical.[5] This conceptualization robs the Other of historical agency and effectively places people outside history. According to this paradigm, the Other is subject more to natural rather than historical processes.[6] This is one of the reasons why the study of non-Western peoples traditionally fell to anthropology and not history. Anthropology was decidedly ahistorical, if not antihistorical, for much of its history.[7] Thus, the Other and anthropology became subsumed under "natural history." To see that this conceptualization is still with us, one only has to look to natural history museums; these typically house the exhibits of the American Indians and other non-Western peoples.[8]

In the past several decades, however, scholars in anthropology and history, among other disciplines, have directed much attention to reconfiguring this conception of non-Western peoples, placing them into history, and understanding how historical processes have shaped, reshaped, and even created non-Western societies and, conversely, how non-Western societies have shaped, reshaped, and even created Western societies. Much of this work is showing that dividing history along Western/non-Western lines makes little sense. At least since contact between the Old and New Worlds, human history has comprised a single history, within a single world, composed of the interactions between all.[9] The structural elements of this single world have not changed significantly since contact. They are the elements of the modern world system wherein, on a global scale, all people participate to some degree in the modern economic system, in the colonial imperialism that underwrites this system, and in the buying and selling of commodities that fuels it.[10] At the end of the eighteenth century, Creek country was part of this modern world system, and the people, places, and historical and cultural forces within it formed a single world.[11]

Even though I emphasize that Indians have a history and are the products of that history, my purpose here is not to write a history of the Creeks. Other than a general overview of Creek life during the Historic Period (ca. 1540–

1840), I do not trace Creek life through time, nor do I render a narrative of events. Rather, this book is a snapshot in time, a kind of historical ethnography —a *histoire totale* that attempts to account for the regular events of regular people in daily life as well as the structural and historical underpinnings of their daily lives.[12] But one should not mistake this snapshot for all of Creek history. I have tried to capture Creek men and women in action during a particular time in a particular place, making both large and small decisions that affected historical outcomes, as well as those historical forces that undoubtedly weighed on their minds as they moved through their world. In other words, I have attempted to portray the Creeks as people, caught in history, shaping history, and negotiating their own moment in time.

The day-to-day human affairs played out in Creek country emerge from the archaeological and documentary records. The deeper meanings of their lives are notably obscure. In fact, the Creeks generally refused to discuss such things with whites.[13] And about such matters, archaeology cannot speak. On the surface, Creek life resembled that of frontier whites and blacks by the late eighteenth century. But underneath there were undoubtedly some fundamental differences. In times of personal crisis or in life's transitions—birth, marriage, illness, death, or revenge—Creek men and women likely invoked a worldview quite different from that of frontier whites and blacks. I have not attempted here to sketch even the outline of the deeper meanings in Creek life. That must wait for another work.[14]

Benjamin Hawkins and Reconstructing Creek Country, 1796–1816

Because the Creeks themselves left relatively few written documents, their lives (like the lives of all people from oral cultures) must be pieced together from the historical documents, through careful use of oral traditions, and from archaeological investigation. I have used all three in this book, but each presents challenges and limitations. In my research, I have examined significant documentary sources kept by a variety of literate people in Creek country: letters, journals, trade ledgers, account books, legal depositions, land deeds, military records, and census records, to name a few. These documents were written by Euro-American white males who were either in Indian territory or dealing with Indians for various reasons. Such documents are typically the resources for historians, and they have been used with great success in reconstructing aspects of the American past. But the information they contain on Indian life is often faulty and imprecise because there was an unevenness in the writers' access to and in their understanding of what they saw of Indian life.[15] Furthermore, the Creeks did not reveal some aspects of their lives to whites, and especially not to white elites and officials. Creek voices occasionally appear in the documents, but almost always in translation and as recorded by a Euro-American male.

In reconstructing Indian history, then, a more authentic Indian voice comes through oral traditions and archaeology. Oral traditions pose methodological problems that scholars are only now beginning to assess. Because of this, I have used oral traditions sparingly, and then not as literal renderings of past events or as explanations for past relationships and events but, rather, as later echoes of eighteenth-century social codes and beliefs.[16] Archaeology, on the other hand, has developed rigorous methods and interpretations for reconstructing the lives of people by examining their material remains. Because of the nature of material evidence, archaeology speaks best to the economic and material basis of life. Archaeology also gives us the spatial context of a people's life—how they situated themselves across a landscape and some sense of why they did so. Archaeology also is exceptional in delineating the long-term, persisting structures of life. However, archaeology cannot tell us everything, and it especially cannot speak definitively to the more intangible aspects of life that leave no material remains, particularly religious beliefs, ideologies, and opinions.

Much of my reconstruction of Creek life and Creek country is based on the letters, journals, and records of Benjamin Hawkins, the U.S. Indian agent to the Creeks from 1796 until his death in 1816.[17] Hawkins left a large volume of written correspondence and other documents on Creek life and Indian affairs in the South. The documents provide a rare window on a world about which we know so little. Although other scholars have put Hawkins's observations to excellent use, none has used the documents to reconstruct this world in all its detail and complexity, and I know of no other set of documents that provides such a view of this world. Certainly there were other Indian agents and literate people among the southern Indians, but none of them left such a detailed collection of documents, nor did they take such an especially ethnographic interest in the Indians.

My reliance on Hawkins also clarifies the chronological parameters of this book, 1796–1816, which cover Hawkins's tenure among the Creeks. But these parameters make sense in the Creek experience as well. The end of the eighteenth century was a time of critical transition for the Creeks. They found themselves in an economic and ecological crisis while squaring off with America over land issues. In fact, this transition brought Hawkins into Creek country in the first place, and it was this transition and the consequences of it that he witnessed and in which he participated.

There are problems with my use of Hawkins in this way, of course. By relying extensively on Hawkins, I run the risk of reconstructing his, and not the Creeks', version of Creek country. This is a thorny issue. Ethnohistorians have wrangled with such problems for some time, and the issue has vigorously resurfaced in recent years with the postcolonial critique.

I believe Hawkins's observations, tempered with the oral and archaeological record, can provide a reliable window on Creek society, however. In the first place, he entered Creek country at a time when the outsider/insider dichotomy was no longer accurate. By the end of the eighteenth century, Euro-Americans and Indians had been living together for more than 200 years. When Hawkins came among the Creeks, they did not see him as an exotic, undefinable creature; they understood him to be a white elite American, and they knew how to relate to him in that role. Nor were the Creeks exotic and undefinable to Hawkins. Indians figured much in the minds of white Americans at this time, and even Americans living in seaboard cities somewhat removed from Indian affairs had experience with Indians. Hawkins assuredly entered Creek country in a social division reserved for white elites, but this does not mean that he was outside this world. Rather, Hawkins, like the Creeks, Africans, Europeans, and others who lived there, was a part of Creek country.[18]

One must also remember that even though Hawkins brought his own biases, subjective responses, and preconceived ideas to Creek country, he did not create Creek country from whole cloth. There is some representation of Creek country through Creek eyes in Hawkins's writing, if only because Hawkins was reporting on Creek activities, Creek peoples, and Creek places. The task is to recover something of the Creeks' point of view of Creek country by examining the point of view that Hawkins has left us, while remembering that both existed in the same world.

Environmental historians have shown that the natural world always bears the imprint of the humans who inhabit it and that that imprint is a cultural consequence.[19] So, even if Hawkins's writings are necessarily the world as he understood it, we can "read" his version of the landscape of Creek country to understand the Creeks' cultural imprint on that landscape. I would argue one can do the same kind of reading for the social landscape. I can know where Creeks chose to place their towns because Hawkins gave such detailed descriptions of such. Likewise, I can locate natural resources that the Creeks identified as important, I can use Creek place-names collected by Hawkins to understand something about how the Creeks viewed the landscape, and so on.

Finally, this book contains a series of maps I constructed using information taken from Hawkins's writings, especially his *Sketch of the Creek Country in the Years 1798 and 1799*. These maps are unusual in that they depict Creek towns, places, and landscapes at a local level. I compiled these maps using information from Hawkins, but in effect they bring the reader into Creek country at ground level, so that the reader may imagine, for instance, what it was like for a Creek woman to walk with her sisters and cousins to the nearest stream to collect water. We can see how far the young women traveled, the gravelly spots in the path, what kinds of trees shaded their way, what inclines they had to climb, what squirrels dodged their steps, and what briars caught their skirts.[20] These maps do not contain everything that would have been salient to these Creek women as they wandered down to the river, but they can give us an approximation, which may be the best we can achieve.[21] Clearly the problems of evidence in reconstructing Indian history and the historic Indian perspective are many. Still, by reading Hawkins and the other evidence anthropologically, we can approach a fuller understanding of the Creek Indians and their world at this time.

CHAPTER ONE

BENJAMIN HAWKINS IN CREEK COUNTRY

I n 1774 a large rattlesnake slid into the camp of some Seminole traders and their families outside a small Indian town where Spalding's Lower Store was located on the St. John's River in northeastern Florida. A noisy commotion ensued as men, women, and children scattered out of the grove. Someone suggested calling for Puc Puggy. Puc Puggy, or "Flower Hunter," was the name the Lower Creeks had given to Philadelphia naturalist William Bartram, who was visiting the area as part of a scientific expedition in which he was assigned to document and collect specimens of the plants and animals of the present-day lower South.

Bartram, who had been in his quarters in the council house drawing some flowers, had heard the row and stepped out into the square ground to see what was happening. His friend "the old interpreter" met him there and informed him that a snake had taken possession of the camp and that they were calling for Puc Puggy. Bartram sent word that he wanted nothing to do with the creature, that his work "required application and quiet," and that he could not be disturbed. Presently three young men, "richly dressed and ornamented," approached Bartram and asked him to remove the snake. They explained that none of them had the courage or the freedom to do so. They reasoned that since he collected such things, perhaps he would be interested in this specimen; they added that he was welcome to it. Bartram agreed to see what he could do. In a footnote to this episode, Bartram explained that Creeks never killed rattlesnakes or any other snake because they were afraid that the living relatives of the dead snake would seek revenge. The party proceeded to the camp, where Bartram saw that "the dreaded and revered serpent leisurely traversed their camp, visiting the fire places from one to another, picking up fragments of their provisions and licking their platters." As Bartram approached the snake, it retracted into a large, defensive coil. Bartram threw a lightwood knot he was carrying at the rattler and hit it in the head. He then cut off its head and carried it "bleeding in my hand as a trophy of victory, and taking out the mortal fangs, deposited them carefully amongst my collections."

A while later Bartram was again roused by the calling of Puc Puggy. This time three young men, arm in arm, approached the council house and, flourishing their scratching instruments, informed Bartram that they had come to scratch him because he was "too heroic and violent, that it would be good for me to loose [sic] some of my blood to make me more mild and tame."[1] With that, they took hold of Bartram. He struggled, and within seconds one of the young men, who had earlier befriended Bartram, interposed. The young man told the other fellows that Bartram was his friend and a brave warrior. According to Bartram, the other young men instantly and without explanation changed their countenance, "whopped in chorus, took me friendly by the hand, clapped me on the shoulder and laid their hands on their breasts in token of sincere friendship, and laughing aloud, said I was a sincere friend to the Siminoles." The three young men then "joined arm in arm again and went off, shouting and proclaiming Puc-Puggy was their friend."[2]

Bartram and his Seminole friends, as this episode illustrates, lived side by side and participated in one another's lives. Even though this incident took place on the borderland between the Creek Confederacy and Seminole country and even though it took place among Lower Creeks who were, at this time, forging their own political and social alliance with other Indians and Africans to form the Seminoles, it reflects much about life in Creek country at the end of the eighteenth century. Indians, whites, and Africans lived together and blended their lives and ways according to mutually shared rules and roles. In this way, daily experiences usually made sense to all involved. But because this world was comprised of many elements, sometimes cultural nuances could be misunderstood or lost. Bartram understood that the Seminoles' desire to have him dispatch the rattlesnake was grounded in their ideas of revenge and their reverence for snakes. Conversely, the Seminoles understood Bartram's work habits and his collections, and they may have reckoned him to be a kind of medicine man, since healers were typically interested in plants. They may have also figured that since Bartram was not a Seminole, he would not have been subject to clan revenge and hence could kill the snake with impunity. The scratching, however, is perhaps a case of cultural misunderstanding. Certainly Bartram did not understand a painful scratching to be necessary to his spiritual well-being, and clearly he was somewhat suspicious of it. In fact, perhaps the young Seminole men wanting to scratch the heroism and violence out of Bartram were playing with the irony of Flower Hunter killing the deadly rattler; there could not have been a more mild-mannered man in Creek country than Bartram. Still, when Bartram refused to be scratched, although the young men may have wanted to do so as a joke, the young warriors were probably uneasy for Bartram's welfare because he was, in fact, now polluted and, hence, dangerous. Bartram, confused but not altogether wrong, concluded that the scratching was a ritual to satisfy the spirit of the slain rattlesnake.[3]

Bartram's visit among the southeastern Indians was not one of purely scientific curiosity. Bartram was one of many European naturalists, surveyors, and entrepreneurs sent into Creek country and elsewhere in the South to evaluate the land for its commercial potential. These men were the vanguard of troubling times for the southeastern Indians. At the time of Bartram's visit, southeastern Indians were deeply involved in the deerskin trade, and they had been for about a hundred years. The South had an enormous population of white-tailed deer, and Indian men were excellent hunters. The infrastructure necessary to the deerskin trade was already in place, only now that Indian men were no longer subsistence hunters, they had become commercial hunters, selling their peltries to European traders in exchange for European-manufactured items. The deerskin trade was one of the main economic activities in the interior South until the late eighteenth century. Many hundreds of thousands of deerskins were shipped out of Charleston, Savannah, Mobile, Pensacola, and New Orleans throughout the eighteenth century. A number of white traders became wealthy, some Indian families were also beginning to acquire wealth, and all Indian families relied on the trade for certain goods, especially firearms and ammunition, but also rum, cloth, metal tools, and other items manufactured in Europe expressly for the Indian trade.[4]

The trade system proved transforming. Not only did it lock the southeastern Indians into the global economy; it also required most Indians to learn new ways of making a living. Southeastern Indian men and women assuredly still farmed, hunted, and gathered wild plant foods, but within a new economic context. Most of the men had become commercial hunters, and the women now sold their surplus foods on the informal market. Indian men and women also entered new part-time occupations: guide, translator, mercenary, postal rider, slave catcher, horse thief, prostitute, and so on. Many traders married Indian women and raised large families of mixed-descent children, who would later constitute a rising class of elites as defined by Euro-American conceptions of wealth and property.[5]

One historical factor played into the deerskin trade that rendered favorable the position of the southeastern Indians, and especially the Creeks. At this time parts of the Southeast were claimed by three European rivals: England claimed much of the East coast; Spain, most of Florida; and France, much of the western territory. But none of these nations had a sufficient military to maintain and fortify its borders. In reality, these European colonies only controlled small toeholds on the coast; various Indian groups lived in and controlled almost all of the interior lands. The Creek Confederacy lay at the intersection of the three European claimants.

Therefore, the Europeans spent much time courting Indian alliances through trade agreements. The southeastern Indians, of course, understood this policy of trade and politics. Many Indian headmen, like Emperor Brims of the Creeks, were exceptionally shrewd and manipulated the system to the Indians' benefit. The Indians would play one European power off against another, and rarely would they give ironclad agreements to serve as soldiers and allies in frontier skirmishes. Rather, they claimed neutrality, to which the Europeans would respond with even more favorable trade conditions to ensure that they remained so. In essence, the southeastern Indians held the balance of power in their region during the eighteenth century because all of the European rivals had to deal with the Indians, and they had to deal with them as equals. In this way the southeastern Indians negotiated their place in the modern world economic system.[6]

During this time a "middle ground" was established between the autonomy of Indian groups before contact and the oppression of them as a people no longer useful to the economic machinery. This middle ground was not necessarily a zone of mutual cooperation. Rather, it was a zone in which Indians and Europeans met, for a while at least, on a level playing field where each group assumed itself to be the superior agent and, as such, fought over and negotiated contested power, resources, and influences, and in the process created a new world composed of these interactions as well as all the myriad friendlier and smaller ones.[7] This middle ground had begun to erode soon after Puc Puggy killed a rattlesnake on the St. John's.

The reasons for this erosion are multifaceted. For one, the population of white-tailed deer in the South appears to have seriously declined because of commercial hunting. For another, the American Revolution completely disrupted the southern Indian trade. White traders who had lived and worked among the Creeks for decades had close ties with England and took the Loyalists' side in the conflict. Afterward, in defeat, many of them had their property confiscated. Many fled to Europe or, in some cases, were hanged. Plus, the Treaty of Paris prohibited commercial arrangements between the United States and Britain, and transatlantic commerce came to a temporary halt. The lines of credit and banking between the former colonies and Britain, which had been fundamental to the Indian trade, deteriorated beyond repair.[8] The British trading houses in the territory now claimed by the United States were shut down. Only one British trade company still operated—that of Panton, Leslie, and Company (changed in 1805 to John Forbes and Company after William Panton's death)—in the port town of Pensacola in Spanish-held West Florida. Panton, Leslie, and Company remained the primary trade house in the South until 1830.[9] In place of the British trade system, the United States instituted the Factory System under the domain of the U.S. Treasury Department by which the government hoped to regulate the Indian trade. In addition, the southeastern Indians lost a valuable bargaining chip after the American Revolution in that their services were no longer needed for maintaining European-claimed frontier borders. France and Spain kept only a weak hold on their southern lands, and each would eventually cede or sell these lands to the United States. Britain continued fighting to regain its former colonies, kept up some intrigues, and courted Indian allies; but with the trade in decline, frontier defense and trade became separated.[10]

Just as the system began to falter, a major player emerged: Alexander McGillivray, the son of a Creek woman from the prestigious Wind clan and a well-to-do Scottish trader. McGillivray positioned himself as a strong and central leader of the Creeks by using the old strategy of playing the Europeans off one another while that was still feasible. But he held an unusual amount of influence and power for a late-eighteenth-century Creek headman. Although he tailored his leadership to the Creek clan-based and consensual form of government, much of his power base lay not in kinship but in his links to Panton, Leslie, and Company, through which he could bring economic pressures to bear on opponents and control Creek political bodies.[11]

The story of McGillivray's rise to power among the Creeks is full of unusual twists and turns and cannot be fully told here. He died in 1793 leaving a legacy of intrigue, duplicity, resentment, and harsh retaliations against the Georgians he had always hated. After his death, the situation between the Creeks and the State of Georgia became explosive. President George Washington knew that the Creeks mistrusted the federal government and that they deplored the Georgia government. The current Indian agent, James Seagrove, was ineffectual and terrified of the Indians, and he could not deal with the situation. In 1796 President Washington appointed Benjamin Hawkins as temporary agent to the southern Indians. Upon entering Creek country, Hawkins initially settled in the Lower Creek town of Coweta Tallahassee. In 1803, when his status was changed from temporary to permanent, Hawkins moved to the Flint River, just off the Lower Trading Path, where he built the Creek Agency.[12] Hawkins lived there with his wife, Lavina Downs, and his six daughters, Georgia, Muscogee, Cherokee, Carolina, Virginia, and Jeffersonia, and one son, Madison.[13]

At the time of his appointment in 1796, Hawkins was not a newcomer to Indian affairs. As a North Carolina senator he had served on committees appointed to investigate some Indian matters. He served as a U.S. commissioner in the 1785 Treaty of Hopewell with the Cherokees, as an unofficial observer at the negotiations for the 1790 Treaty of New York with the Creeks, and as a U.S. commissioner in the 1796 Treaty of Colerain with the Creeks.[14] Through these works he had garnered a reputation among government officials as being fair and just in his dealings with the Indians, and in fact, this was the very reason President Washington appointed him as Indian agent.[15]

Hawkins also had an interest in Indian life beyond that of negotiating treaties. He and his friend Thomas Jefferson exchanged letters on a wide array of topics on Indian life as well as on scientific farming, agricultural experiments, and gardening. Once in the South, Hawkins compiled numerous word lists in Choctaw, Cherokee, and Creek for Jefferson, who was intensely interested in Indian languages.[16] After attending the negotiations for the 1790 Treaty of New York, Hawkins sent a special envoy to Alexander McGillivray to inquire into Creek life and politics, the environment, and the "plan for civilization" to which McGillivray had referred in the treaty.[17]

At the time of Hawkins's appointment, the position of the southeastern Indians became even more threatened when land for growing cotton replaced deerskins as the most valuable commodity in the South. Eli Whitney invented the cotton gin in 1793. Before Whitney's invention, cotton growing had been confined to the tidewater South because only wealthy tobacco, indigo, and sugar planters had the land and the labor needed for growing cotton. With the invention of the cotton gin, however, slaves could remove cotton seeds relatively quickly instead of devoting long, tedious hours to removing the seed by hand.[18]

Concurrently with the invention of the cotton gin, a worldwide boom in

cotton occurred, raising cotton prices. With the gin now available, cotton became a very profitable enterprise, despite the investment of labor. Thus it was
that land became the natural resource most in demand. During the deerskin
trade era the southeastern Indians had been a necessary part of the global economic machinery. After the American Revolution, the Creeks as well as all of
the southern interior Indian societies found themselves not only unnecessary
to the American economy, but in fact, they had become impediments to the
system. Instead of deerskins and trade, the Americans needed land for cotton
production and its attendant agriculture, husbandry, and industry, and the
Creeks possessed much of the land in the lower South—land which they were
legendary in their refusal to relinquish.[19]

Before the American Revolution, British traders had understood the necessity of maintaining decent relations with the interior Indians, and in fact, their
fortunes and positions had depended on it. With their social, economic, and
political prominence in the colonial South, they managed to protect their own
interests by protecting, to some degree, those of the Indians. However, when
land replaced deerskins as the most valuable southern commodity, a new kind
of American leadership emerged in the South, one based in land speculation,
that had no desire to continue the Indian trade, and that had little interest in
keeping good relations with the Creeks or any other Indian group.[20]

These men kept constant pressure on the southern Indians for land cessions. During Hawkins's tenure, the Creeks made four major land cessions. In
the 1796 Treaty of Colerain, which confirmed the 1790 Treaty of New York,
the Creeks ceded the lands roughly between the Ogeechee and Oconee Rivers
in Georgia. The 1802 Treaty of Fort Wilkerson ceded a portion of land between the Oconee and Ocmulgee Rivers, and in the Treaty of 1805 (also known
as the Treaty of Washington), the Creeks sold the remaining section of land
between the two rivers, making the boundary between the Creek Confederacy
and Georgia roughly the Ocmulgee River (see fig. 1).[21]

Another method these leaders devised for divesting the Indians of their
land was the plan for civilization. The plan for civilization was official policy,
formulated by George Washington, Henry Knox, Thomas Jefferson, and other
statesmen, to assimilate Indians into American society. It was the culmination
of concepts derived from Enlightenment precepts, the ideas of certain northern philanthropic groups, the agrarian movement, and the philosophies of
Protestant sects, such as the Quakers.[22] The idea in the plan for civilization
was to provide the southern Indians with domesticated animals such as hogs,
cows, and sheep and manufactured implements of agriculture, especially the
plow, and to teach them to become herders and agriculturalists, growing cash

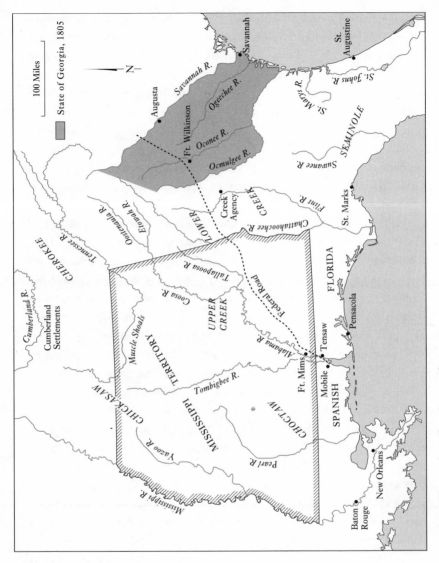

FIGURE 1. The southern frontier, ca. 1800

crops such as cotton and wheat and driving their herds to seaports or frontier markets. They would also engage in cottage industries such as cloth making. Through such changes, the thinking went, the southern Indians would become self-sufficient farmers who could clothe and feed themselves while participating in the market, exchanging agricultural and herd surpluses for manufactured items.[23] One of Hawkins's primary objectives in Creek country was to implement the plan for civilization.

The plan for civilization, although the more benevolent of the options publicly discussed, including extermination and expulsion, conspicuously ignored the fact that the southern Indians, who had been agriculturalists for millennia, were already more than capable of clothing and feeding themselves. Moreover, they were already experimenting with cash crops, and they had already diversified their market endeavors with cattle and hog ranching when the deerskin trade had begun to decline, and some even before then. Much of this ignorance derived from eighteenth-century Euro-American ethnocentrism. It also derived from Euro-American ideas on land use and so-called improvements, a concept elite agrarians understood to be the hallmark of proper stewardship of the land and of progress and civilization.[24]

The plan for civilization and Indian economic developments ultimately did not matter, however, because the hidden hand behind the plan for civilization was U.S. expansion. According to government reasoning, the plan for civilization, simply put, was a way of promoting expansion so "that the U.S. may be saved the pain and expense of expelling or destroying them [the Indians]."[25] The propaganda for the plan claimed that if the southern Indians were transformed into herders and commercial farmers, they would no longer rely on the hunt and therefore would not need as much hunting territory.[26] Thus, as whites needed more land, the Indians would be more willing to sell. The real agenda was to assimilate the Indians into American society, undermine their national sovereignty, and appropriate their lands in the process.

One may wonder why Hawkins, a man known for his fair and just approach to Indian affairs, was such a staunch advocate of a development plan designed to undermine Indian welfare.[27] His support of the plan only becomes clear within the larger public debate on Indian character occurring at that time in America and abroad. One camp in the debate depicted the Indians as wild, uncontrollable, ruled by passion, and inferior to whites. They were murderous, barbaric, and incapable of being civilized. This faction advocated extermination or expulsion. The opposing camp conceived of Indians as Noble Savages living in an idyllic but childlike and primitive state who needed the guiding hands of civilized men to advance into the modern world. These people advocated the plan for civilization and assimilation, and in the Northeast, some missionaries and philanthropists had already engaged in attempts to educate and convert the northern Indians.[28] Of course, both views were expansionistic.

Hawkins clearly weighed in on the latter side. He attributed to Creek men and women the same human traits and intelligence as any other people. He became close friends with many Creek men, especially the métis Tuckabatchee headman Oche Haujo, also known as Alexander Cornells, at whose death a stricken Hawkins wrote, "We have not his equal among us."[29] Even so, he was also ethnocentric and condescending. Hawkins was a man of his times; he was an Enlightenment thinker. Like many Enlightenment thinkers, he believed that Western civilization was the pinnacle of human achievement and that through science, human reason, and habits of thrift, sobriety, and hard work, humankind as a whole could be lifted to this higher plane. The plan for civilization appealed to Hawkins and other prominent Enlightenment intellectuals because it was based on many of the same principles, and they understood it to be the hand needed to guide the Indians to "civilization." Furthermore, Hawkins was a stalwart patriot. He believed deeply that America and the democratic principles upon which the country were founded were shining human advancements. To Hawkins, guiding the Indians along the path to U.S. citizenry was nothing less than an ultimate good.

Despite his ethnocentrism and condescension, Hawkins was, I have come to believe, a good man. His guiding principles were honesty and fairness in public and private concerns. He was not above playing a role in frontier intrigues, but generally he was honest and forthright. He insisted on Indian rights throughout his tenure as Indian agent, even in the face of stern and sometimes public criticisms from white government officials and even when Indian rights conflicted with official instructions from the War Department. I believe he genuinely liked the Creeks and cared about their welfare. Still, many questions about him must be examined.

For example, how well did Hawkins know and understand the Creeks? During his lifetime some men accused Hawkins publicly and privately of not knowing what the Creeks were up to. We can disregard these accusations, since most of these men were Georgia and Tennessee officials, land speculators, and others who were chagrined at Creek stubbornness regarding land cessions and who believed Hawkins should take a stronger stand for their interests. In the twenty-first century, anthropologists and ethnohistorians regard Hawkins's *Sketch of the Creek Country in the Years 1798 and 1799* as a reliable account of Creek life. My assessment is that Hawkins probably understood the Creeks better than any other literate non-Creek on the frontier. Surely white traders, white women, and former black slaves who married into Creek families understood Creek daily life more fully than Hawkins, but few of these people left written accounts.

Hawkins's writings mostly concern his office and duties, so the breadth of understanding that Hawkins demonstrates is more or less limited to the confines of his doing his job. For example, Hawkins knew the Creek political system and how to manipulate and to work within it. He knew and observed much about Creek agriculture because this, after all, was what he sought to change. He was also most likely fluent in Muskogean.[30] In other words, when Creek life intersected with his job, Hawkins showed a secure grasp and a deep understanding of Creek life.

There were, however, many areas of Creek life in which Hawkins does not seem to have been interested. For example, he rarely wrote about the Creek clan system, an inexplicable omission since the clan system was important to Creek life. Hawkins rarely wrote about the Creek belief system. Not a religious man himself, Hawkins did not think religious conversion essential to the plan for civilization. Even when two Moravian missionaries were sent to Creek territory, Hawkins, much to their lament, limited their work to the Creek Agency, and then only because they possessed much-needed carpentry skills.[31] Hawkins's inattention to Creek religious beliefs would create a serious blind spot when he encountered the millenarian movement behind the Red Stick War of 1813. One can only suppose that, for better or for worse, Hawkins did not view understanding the Creek clan system, the belief system, and other elements of Creek life as integral to getting his job done.

What did the Creeks think of Hawkins? This question may never be fully answered, since the Creeks themselves left only a few written documents. For the Creeks, Hawkins represented the U.S. government, a fact that automatically cast suspicion on him. George Stiggins, a well-to-do métis who wrote twenty years after Hawkins's death, stated that at first the Creeks distrusted Hawkins and his office. They believed he was a spy, and they frequently debated whether or not to kill him.[32] After several meetings and consultations with Hawkins, according to Stiggins, the Creeks "could not but admire his firm, honest, and candid deportment" and "loved him for his virtuous and disinterested greatness of mind, for he expressed to them his hopes and wishes for their welfare."[33] Twenty years after Hawkins's death, a Creek eulogy held him to have been "a gentlemen qualified by reputation and rectitude to fill the trust imposed on him."[34]

Even so, Creek opinion about Hawkins during his life was divided. Factions threatened Hawkins's life on at least three occasions. In the spring of

1798 some Coweta headmen roused Hawkins from his sleep at Coweta Talla-hassee and instructed him to flee because a group of warriors were en route to slay him. Hawkins refused to leave, and Coweta women and warriors guarded him through the night.[35] In 1799, after Hawkins had insisted on punishing some Creek horse thieves, the thieves openly threatened Hawkins's life.[36] That same year, British adventurer William Augustus Bowles, who was cam-paigning among the Seminoles and Creeks to garner British allies to oust the Americans from the South, issued a death warrant for Hawkins.[37] The war-rant stood for four years, until Bowles's arrest. Hawkins again refused to leave even though he was advised to do so; in his words, "I am not sensible of dan-ger, in other words, when I am resolved in doing what I conceive to be my duty, I never calculate on the dangers"[38]

Such episodes were almost inevitable, since in many ways the Creeks could not separate the man from his office. Hawkins represented America and its goals, which the Creeks knew to be expansionistic and antithetical to Creek self-determination. Hawkins likewise identified himself with his office and in-terpreted any threat to his person and opposition to the plan for civilization as reflecting anti-American sentiments. Conversely, Hawkins understood all those in favor of his reforms and his personal friends to be pro–American. As we shall see, Hawkins's interpretation was well founded, but some frontier episodes surely derived from other, more self-interested motives.[39] Regard-less, many Creeks did trust Hawkins to represent their interests to the U.S. government. Creek leaders refused to counsel with any federal, state, or mil-itary personnel unless Hawkins was in attendance. He was given the honorary high-ranking title of *isti atcagagi*, or "beloved man," denoting wisdom, ac-complishment, and trust.[40]

Hawkins's position as *isti atcagagi* bears scrutinizing. Some scholars have proposed that Hawkins stepped in to fill the power vacuum left after Alexan-der McGillivray died.[41] As a high-ranking federal official and representative of the United States, Hawkins held power. However, if his power can be mea-sured by how much influence Hawkins had among the Creeks, then one can see that his power was, in fact, quite limited. For instance, Hawkins on occa-sion bragged of his accomplishments among the Creeks. Among other things, Hawkins took credit for abolishing blood revenge. He also took credit for im-plementing a police system whereby certain towns assigned warriors as polic-ing agents. He even took credit for the National Council.[42] But blood revenge was never truly revoked. The police system largely conformed to Creek insti-tutions, plus the so-called police agents never wielded coercive power and were always subject to revenge according to the principles of blood revenge and retaliation. The National Council was probably a Creek institution in place long before Hawkins arrived. Hawkins often spoke of the success of the plan for civilization among the Creeks, and there can be no doubt that the economic developments chartered by the plan were moving along. But as mentioned above, the Creeks had begun these activities at least a decade before Hawkins's arrival. In fact, as this book demonstrates, on almost all counts Hawkins failed in what he attempted to achieve.

Creek life at the turn of the nineteenth century was in transition, but these changes were due not solely to Hawkins's presence but to larger forces at work and to Creek decisions and actions. Hawkins failed to change the Creeks because the power he held was very specific. His power was located in his position as the link between the Creeks and the U.S. government. Among the Creeks, Hawkins had little legislative, administrative, or coercive power, either in his office or in his person. In fact, Hawkins's leadership appears to have conformed somewhat to eighteenth-century Creek leadership, which was based on persuasiveness, leading by example, and building consensuses and coalitions. Hawkins, like other Creek headmen, could hardly force anyone to do anything.[43]

Hawkins had a certain amount of diplomatic power because he was the communications link between political bodies. He could speak for the United States, and when given license to do so, he could speak for the Creeks. When situations called for diplomatic solutions, Hawkins was usually a central figure in the talks and proceedings. Diplomacy was required regularly for large and small affairs. There were the obvious diplomatic negotiations such as treaty talks and trading arrangements. But Hawkins also intervened when conflicts and contested episodes occurred between regular folks. Everyone knew that minor infractions held real potential to become major offenses. An accusation of theft between a Creek and an American, for example, could lead to an international incident if not handled speedily and fairly. Creeks and Americans settled many disputes according to their own rules and regulations. Yet in countless incidents, both parties sought Hawkins as mediator. He represented the only international office on the frontier; hence, it made sense for people to use the office to settle disputes between Creeks and Americans. I believe that people also sought Hawkins because he was a fair man. As I demonstrate later, Hawkins took painstaking care to collect and assess the evidence in these disputes.

Any real power that Hawkins and his office held over the Creeks lay in the access to Euro-American goods, services, and influences. Creek leadership throughout the Historic Period hinged on similar access. Hawkins, like Creek leaders, could manipulate these things as leverage and often did so. Unlike that of Creek leaders, Hawkins's access was more direct and was countenanced by his position as U.S. Indian agent charged with implementing the plan for civilization. But Hawkins's access to goods and services was only remedial because the United States was not committed to the plan for civilization or to assimilation. Hawkins's power was limited by how far the United States would be willing to go to get things done according to a nonaggression model of expansion. However, in Creek eyes, even remedial access to goods, services, and influences was worth seeking in some cases. The Creeks pressured Hawkins for these things, which, of course, gave him some measure of leverage with them.

Still, the office of U.S. Indian agent, and hence Hawkins, represented the U.S. government. As such, the office and the office holder reflected the power and goals of the United States. The primary goal of the United States was westward expansion, and we must examine Hawkins, his office, and his work in terms of this goal. What we see throughout the nineteenth century is a shift in the balance of power between the United States and the Indian nations, and U.S. Indian policy grew increasingly brutal as this power differential increased. In the South the Indians' power base in the colonial playing field was linked to the deerskin trade and to competition among European nations. With the decline of the deerskin trade, their position was seriously undermined. When Hawkins came among the Creeks, the power of the United States as a nation was ascending but not yet secure. Hence, the official Indian policy in 1796 was one of assimilation and economic development. But in the South, as elsewhere, official policy began to change to one of expulsion and then of extermination as U.S. power waxed and Indian power waned.

Hawkins was caught in the middle of this transition. He supported westward expansion, but he advocated expansion in which Indians would become American citizens. He understood that it was his job as Indian agent to facilitate this process. He never advocated expulsion or extermination. When he became Indian agent, Hawkins did not face any moral crisis because U.S. policy, which it was his job to implement, squared well with his personal convictions. Yet as this policy became more demanding and unfair, his job became more difficult, and he became more disappointed and even disillusioned.

Facing the beginnings of what would become a crisis, the Creeks were readjusting their lives from commercial hunters to commercial farmers, ranchers, entrepreneurs, and landholders, hoping once again to make a place for themselves in their changing world. But these efforts were truncated by the question of land sales. The Creek Confederacy became seriously divided internally over the issues of land sales, the plan for civilization, and whether to negotiate the never-ending American demands for land or to defy them. In 1811 Tecumseh, the famous Shawnee warrior who was the military arm behind his prophet brother, Tenskwatawa, who advocated pushing the Americans into the sea and returning to native ways, visited the Creeks as part of his campaign for a pan-Indian uprising. Tecumseh's visit proved cataclysmic. A violent Creek civil war erupted, which gave the U.S. government the excuse for which it had been waiting to invade the Creek Confederacy. This was the Red Stick War of 1813–14.[44] The story told in this book stops two years after this war, with the death of Benjamin Hawkins. The Red Stick War was disastrous for the Creeks, as Hawkins had predicted.[45] The resultant Treaty of Fort Jackson, the fourth cession of land during Hawkins's tenure, was made by Andrew Jackson, who forced the Creeks to sign in 1814 and cut away two-thirds of Creek country.

With this treaty, Creek country as depicted in this book came to an end. The Creeks as a people, however, are not gone. In the first decades of the nineteenth century, they rallied as a nation in a unified effort to stop Indian Removal, but as we know, they failed. By the end of the 1830s the United States had forced a majority of Creeks to migrate to present-day Oklahoma, where the Muscogee (Creek) Nation now resides. Some Creeks remained in their homeland, and some of their descendants now form the Poarch Band of Creeks in present-day Alabama.[46] Certainly the Creeks of the nineteenth, twentieth, and twenty-first centuries retain cultural elements that existed in the late eighteenth century and perhaps even earlier. But much of Creek life has changed, and contemporary Creek Indians are modern people in a modern world. The late-eighteenth-century world of the Creek Indians is gone. But for a while Creek country was a distinct world with its own pattern of relations and places and people. I have endeavored to capture something of this world.

CHAPTER TWO

THE BEGINNINGS OF CREEK COUNTRY: A HISTORICAL OVERVIEW

T he Creeks had not always lived as they did when Benjamin Hawkins was among them. North American Indian life had undergone many transformations since the initial peopling of America some 12,000 years ago. In fact, anthropologists and historians are beginning to realize that the Indian polities most associated with the South—the Cherokees, the Creeks, the Choctaws, the Chickasaws, the Seminoles, and the Catawbas—did not exist prehistorically. Rather, they came into existence sometime in the late seventeenth and early eighteenth centuries in response to the contact between the Old and New Worlds.[1]

Undoubtedly, one of the major impacts of contact was the introduction of Old World diseases by the Spanish and French explorers of the sixteenth and early seventeenth centuries. During this time the chiefdoms of the Mississippian Period suffered a crippling loss of life from Old World diseases.[2] The consequences of this population collapse are not hard to see in the archaeological record. Some populations declined sharply, and some areas were abandoned altogether. The people ceased building mounds and ceremonial centers, and the level of ritual and artistic production declined sharply. Also, the elaborate status goods seen in late prehistoric graves disappear from the archaeological record in later times, suggesting a leveling of social status.[3] The people suffered an incalculable loss of knowledge and traditional practices. Old ways of minimizing the level of violence between and within chiefdoms undoubtedly broke down. Life in the Southeast must have become less predictable and palpably more hazardous. Assailed by Old World diseases and chaotic political and military finagling, the southeastern chiefdoms began their final decline, and the survivors found themselves facing unprecedented challenges.

Quite naturally, some of them tried to reorganize themselves in terms of their old beliefs and social arrangements. The old traditional ways were strongest in places where the Spanish and the French were dominant. The principal examples of such "traditionalist" societies were the Apalachees of present-day northern Florida, the Caddos of present-day western Louisiana and eastern Texas, and the Natchez of present-day Mississippi. None of these traditionalist societies had much staying power. The Apalachee were crushed in 1704 by English-sponsored Creek slaving raids. The Natchez were extirpated by 1730, after having revolted against the French colonists. The Caddoans lay far to the west of the English sphere of influence, and this gave them some insulation; but as the eighteenth century wore on, they gradually gave up their old-time ways. The traditionalist societies faded from history. The survivors dispersed, and some joined other societies in the Southeast that were forming along different lines, societies that may be termed "coalescent" societies.[4]

We still do not have an adequate vocabulary to describe the coalescent societies of the seventeenth and eighteenth centuries. They have been called confederacies, tribes, nations, and so on. Here, I will simply follow precedent and call them coalescent societies because they were all, in varying degrees, coalescences of people from different societies, cultures, and languages. The coalescent societies formed in areas where the English influence was the strongest, and in large part, the form they took was an adaptation to the new economic system ushered in by the English and Dutch—the global market system.[5]

The new economic system was a capitalist market system, and it was ushered in by a trade in dressed deerskins, but even more by a trade in enslaved Indians that enmeshed all of the natives in the Southeast.[6] Slavery was not unknown to the indigenous peoples of the eastern woodlands, and they practiced a version of it at the time of contact. Once slaves became a commodity to be bought and sold, however, a powerful new dynamic began shaping the lives of the southeastern Indians. The Indian slave trade in the South worked like this: European traders would give guns to a group of Indians on credit and ask to be paid in Indian slaves. The armed group would then raid an unarmed rival Indian group for slaves. The unarmed group, now vulnerable to Indian slave raiders, would then need guns and ammunition for protection, because bow-and-arrow Indians were at a disadvantage militarily to slave raiders armed with English-made guns. The Indians could not make their own guns, and they depended on the European trade for flintlock guns as well as for shot and powder. At this point, anyone needing guns had to become a slave raider. In this way, a cycle emerged that ensnared all native peoples who came into contact with it. The process snowballed until virtually all of the Indian groups in the Southeast both possessed firearms and owed enormous debts to English traders.[7]

Indian slave raiders captured Indian slaves by the thousands, mostly women and children, and sold them to English, French, and Dutch slavers who shipped them to the sugar plantations in the West Indies, although some certainly went to the new coastal plantations in Virginia, South Carolina, and French Louisiana as well as to New England. For most Indian groups, already seriously weakened by losses from disease, slaving was a serious blow. Wherever slaving penetrated, the same processes unfolded: many Indian groups moved to get away from slave raiders; some groups joined others in an effort to bolster their numbers and present a stronger defense; some groups became extinct when their numbers dwindled to nothing because of disease and slave raiding; and all those left became engaged in the slave trade. The result was the creation of a shatter zone of instability that covered the eastern woodlands. Slaving unleashed chaos and panic, because none could be sure that their neighbors would not turn on them as slave catchers. Some groups moved closer to the English and French colonies, where they became known as "settlement Indians" and "*petites nations*," respectively. Others united in alliance as slave catchers; these were the coalescent societies.[8]

Each coalescent society had certain mechanisms for admitting refugee groups under a political umbrella that, if nothing else, required mutual agreements that those in the alliance would not conduct slave raids against one another.[9] The slave trade gradually subsided after the Yamassee War of 1715, when the southeastern Indians, finally realizing the deleterious effects of the slave trade, arose in armed rebellion against the English traders. The Yamassee War failed to extricate the southeastern Indians from the modern world system, but it did succeed in diverting English trade interests from Indian slaves to deerskins. It was by this time more profitable to import slaves from Africa. However, the armed resistance of the Indians in the Yamassee War made some things very clear to the English. First, the Indian slave trade could be a dangerous enterprise. Second, despite the dependence of the southeastern Indians on English-made guns, Europeans had to respect them as a numerically superior military force. The Yamassee War forced the English to establish a more regulated trade in deerskins that ultimately gave the southeastern Indians a measure of political and economic power for most of the eighteenth century.[10]

So the Creek Confederacy, like the other southeastern coalescent societies, was originated by survivors of the collapse of the Mississippian world. In the eighteenth century, some social institutions among the Creeks probably resembled those of their former chiefdoms—institutions such as town councils, blood revenge, reciprocity, and matrilineality. These institutions had set rules governing polite behavior and proper courses of action in most situations.[11] These lower-level social institutions, in fact, proved to be highly adaptable. For example, the southeastern Indian domestic economy and division of labor was flexible enough to form linkages to the world economic system. The broad structural patterns of southeastern Indian households show some continuity from the Mississippi Period until the early nineteenth century. Reciprocity and redistribution became formalized in gift giving, wherein European and, later, American traders and officials lavished gifts on certain Indian men with whom they dealt. The Indian men, in turn, distributed these gifts among various people with whom they had connections.

The hierarchal political institutions of the old chiefdoms could not work when dealing with Europeans, and especially Europeans who held the key to needed guns, ammunition, and other goods. At first, Europeans attempted to work within the framework of the Indian political order, and the French and Spanish actually succeeded for a while. But, within the English sphere of influence, any vestiges of a hereditary elite quickly eroded. The English traders did not have to persuade an anti-English "chief" to their side. They would simply ally with another person in that society. Given the disunity of the coalescent societies, there were usually several men who could claim influence over some faction. The English chose to deal with whoever seemed most inclined to listen to their overtures, which, given the new opportunities for self gain, could be any number of people. An Indian man who had a modicum of influence over a particular faction could broker good trade deals and rise in prestige and authority. An Indian man's position was often tied to his access to European trade goods and his political and business savvy. The overall effect was at once a leveling of political power and a check on the rise of any one person to political prominence.[12]

Emperor Brims, one of the leading Apalachicola headmen, or *micos*, of the Creek Confederacy in the early eighteenth century, for instance, in no way resembled the *micos* of the Mississippian chiefdoms. Brims certainly was not carried around on a litter, nor did he and his family enjoy any special privileges other than meeting with English officials. He did not live in a temple atop a mound, and there was no evident ritual and symbolic separation between Brims and other Creek men. Among the Choctaws, Alibamon Mingo and Red Shoes became prominent headmen not because they were born into the position but because they were clever in dealing with Europeans.[13] Although some of southeastern Indian life during the Historic Period resembled life before contact, the political institutions at the chiefdom level had failed, and since these were the reigning institutions in Mississippian Period life, the southeastern Indians were forever changed.

The Formation of the Creek Confederacy

The coalescent societies—the Creeks, the Cherokees, the Chickasaws, the Choctaws, and the Catawbas, among others—have left the greatest mark on American history. These societies were strikingly different from the chiefdoms. In fact, less than 100 years after their formation into coalescent societies, the descendants of Mississippian peoples could not remember who had built some of the mounds, and they had little memory of the former significance of the mounds.[14] Many of them recounted myths that told of their migration from distant lands.[15]

As yet, scholars have only delineated the barest outlines of the formation of the coalescent societies. The archaeological and historical evidence indicates that refugees from fallen chiefdoms relocated and banded with other peoples. The Catawbas, who coalesced in the territory of old Cofitachequi, absorbed people from shattered societies in present-day North Carolina, South Carolina, and Piedmont Virginia. The Chickasaws coalesced near Tupelo, Mississippi, just north of the territory of the Mississippian Period province of Chicaza. Some of the Cherokee-speaking people continued to live in the mountains, where they became known as the Middle and Valley towns. Other Cherokee-speaking people—the Overhills—moved down to occupy choice agricultural lands on the Little Tennessee River that had been vacated by the northern allies of the paramount chiefdom of Coosa. The Choctaws coalesced in the great bend of the upper Pearl River, in Mississippi, in an area that previously had very little population, absorbing peoples from the Yazoo Basin and the east.

Archaeologists investigating the formation of the Creek Confederacy suggest that three protohistoric provinces formed the nuclei for people emigrating from their fallen chiefdoms. One was the Abihka province on the middle Coosa River in present-day northern Alabama; the second was the Tallapoosa province on the Tallapoosa River in present-day central Alabama; and the third was the Apalachicola province on the lower Chattahoochee River in present-day western Georgia.[16] The Abihka and Tallapoosa provinces eventually formed the Upper Creeks, and the Apalachicola province was the nexus of the Lower Creeks.

Of the Upper Creek provinces, the formation of the Abihka province is the best known. Archaeologists believe that Abihka was formed by the descendants of the paramount chiefdom of Coosa, who included the Coosas who lived on the Coosawattee River in present-day northwest Georgia; the Itabas who lived in the Etowah River valley near present-day Cartersville, Georgia; and the Ulibahalis (which included the Apicas) who lived along the Coosa River near present-day Rome, Georgia. When the Coosa chiefdom collapsed soon after contact, the survivors began a 200-year sojourn down the Coosa River. They eventually joined a local population (known only by their archaeological phase name—the Kymulga phase people) on the southernmost extremity of their former territory, near where Hawkins found the towns of Coosa and Aubecoochee (Abihka) in 1796.[17] Here they settled a few towns, with Abihka being the center of the province. They openly welcomed other refugees, specifically Natchez and some Shawnees.

The Tallapoosa River valley clearly had Mississippian Period chiefdoms, and the Tallapoosa province seems to have been formed out of local populations during the years of coalescence, although some Abihka people probably moved to this area and joined them. The archaeology is not yet clear enough to determine which local populations were involved in this or how much, if any, of their chiefdom trappings they retained after European contact. However, the similarity of ceramic types among the eighteenth-century towns in the lower Tallapoosa Valley suggests a close affiliation between the towns, and early European documents often referred to this collection of towns as the "Tallapoops." Hence scholars designate them as a single province. Clearly, Tuckabatchee was the head town of this province.[18] Sometime during the early eighteenth century, two other provinces emerged. The towns of Ocfuskee settled along the upper Tallapoosa. A group of Alabamas, originally from eastern Mississippi and joined by Koasatis from eastern Tennessee, settled several towns at the confluence of the Alabama, Coosa, and Tallapoosa Rivers.[19] The four provinces—the Abihkas, the Tallapoosas, the Ocfuskees, and the Alabamas—eventually became collectively known as the Upper Creeks.

The origins of the Apalachicola province and the Lower Creeks are a little better known.[20] Although he bypassed the lower Chattahoochee River valley altogether, when De Soto moved through the South, a Mississippian chiefdom was extant in the lower Chattahoochee River valley. Archaeologists suggest they were Hitchiti speakers, although this is not known for certain. Still, soon after De Soto, this polity collapsed, probably because of the devastations of European diseases. The few remaining people abandoned the earlier mound sites and settled in small villages; some might have moved downriver, closer to the chiefdom of Apalachee, in present-day north Florida, which was by now a part of the Spanish mission system. Apalachee was still functioning as a chiefdom throughout the Spanish period and hence probably attracted refugees. Archaeologists suggest that, in the numerous migrations that characterized the first sixty years after European contact, Muskogean speakers moved from present-day Alabama into the now abandoned area of the Chattahoochee Valley, and they either reoccupied former mound sites or built new mound centers. These new towns constituted Apalachicola. How many groups immigrated is not known, but they more than likely consisted of at least the ancestors of the eighteenth-century Cussetas and Cowetas. Those Hitchiti speakers who remained, although retaining some separate identity, loosely affiliated themselves with Apalachicola.[21]

By the early eighteenth century, mound construction had stopped on the Chattahoochee, and most of the towns of the Apalachicola province moved to the Ocmulgee River in present-day central Georgia to be closer to the English. Here the Apalachicola towns congregated around the confluence of the Towaliga and Ocmulgee Rivers; the Hitichi towns clustered around the confluence of Walnut Creek and the Ocmulgee River, near present-day Macon, Georgia. Together the two clusters became known to the English as Ochese Creek Indians, Ochese Creek being what early-eighteenth-century English colonists called the Ocmulgee River.[22] While on the Ocmulgee River, other immigrants joined the Ochese Creeks. In particular and among others, the Chiaha (Chehaw) moved from the Appalachian mountains of western North Carolina and affiliated themselves with the Hitchiti towns, and the Yuchi, probably also migrating from the Appalachians, eventually joined the Ocmulgee River settlements.

Following the Yamassee War of 1715, the Ochese Creeks began returning to the Chattahoochee River, where they took in additional refugees and became known as the Lower Creeks. With the Tallapoosas, Abihkas, Ocfuskees, and Alabamas now known collectively as the Upper Creeks, both divisions became known together as the Creek or Muskogee Confederacy.[23] The three original provinces of the Creek Confederacy retained some sort of political significance into the eighteenth century; but by the mid-eighteenth century, all of the provinces, although retaining some kind of township significance,

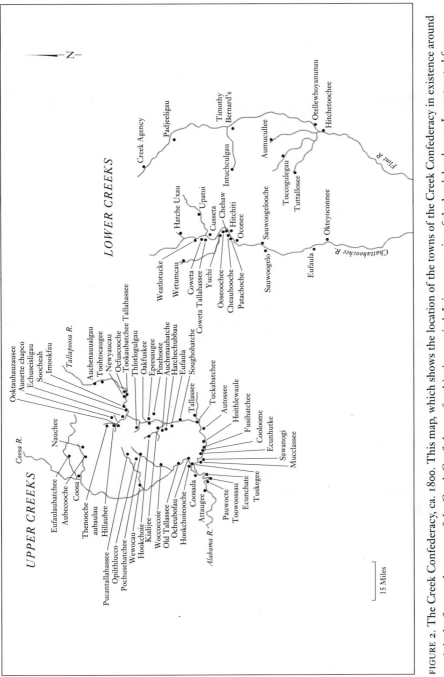

FIGURE 2. The Creek Confederacy, ca. 1800. This map, which shows the location of the towns of the Creek Confederacy in existence around 1796, is the first modern map of the Creek Confederacy for this time period. It is a composite of the local-level maps I constructed from Hawkins's writing; see Introduction, n. 20.

began to blur as the Creek Confederacy became a weak alliance of independent towns, divided along Upper and Lower divisions.[24]

The linguistic diversity of the eighteenth-century Creek Confederacy reflects this coalescence. Although the linguistic complexity has not yet been sorted out, we do know that most historic Creeks spoke one of several variants of Eastern Muskogean. Eastern Muskogean, a subgroup of the Muskogean language family, is further divided into Alabama (sometimes known as Alibamu); Koasati (which is somewhat similar to Alabama, and some linguists group the two as Alabama-Koasati); Muskogee (with two distinct dialects—Creek and Seminole); and Mikasuki (with two dialects—Hitchiti and Mikasuki). These Eastern Muskogean languages are mutually intelligible, except for Hitchiti.[25] Many non-Muskogean speakers also lived in the Creek Confederacy, most notably Yuchi, Shawnee, and Natchez speakers.[26] There is also some evidence that the towns of the Creek Confederacy were divided along either linguistic or refugee lines, with non-Muskogean speakers and refugee groups having a lesser role in public decisions.[27] Because of this kind of linguistic diversity, Hitchiti, Alabama, and Yuchi interpreters were often necessary at public meetings, and throughout the South, Indians, whites, and blacks used a pidgin known as Mobilian as a lingua franca.[28]

By the end of the eighteenth century, Indians still occupied and claimed much of the interior South, and the Creeks, in particular, owned a substantial portion of what later became the cotton belt. The exact boundary lines have never been worked out by historians, but we do have a general idea of where they fell (see fig. 1).[29] The Choctaws claimed land from present-day southern Louisiana into Mississippi and Alabama. Their northern boundaries, which reached about to present-day central Mississippi and west central Alabama, abutted Chickasaw lands in northern Mississippi and Creek lands in Alabama. The Chickasaws claimed territory from present-day central Mississippi into western Tennessee. The Cherokees lived in present-day western South and North Carolina, north Georgia, and most of Tennessee. The Seminoles claimed present-day north Florida and parts of present-day south Georgia.

Spain claimed La Florida (as present-day Florida was then known), which included a strip along the western Gulf coast to French-held Louisiana. But the Seminoles, who were especially antagonistic to settlers, really controlled the interior, and the area was sparsely occupied by whites. With the Louisiana Purchase in 1803, the United States acquired from France what became known as the Mississippi Territory, a tract encompassing all of the Choctaw and Chickasaw lands and most of the Creeks' western lands. The U.S. government recognized the Mississippi Territory as Indian lands but hoped eventually to acquire these lands from the Indians and to open them to American settlement. New Orleans, Mobile, and Pensacola were the major port cities. Outlying white settlements on ceded lands, such as Baton Rouge, Natchez, Tensaw, and Bigbe, bordered Indian territories upriver from the port cities. To the north, Tennessee had become a state in 1796, and Tennessee politicians and land speculators immediately began pressing the Cherokees for more lands.[30]

By the late eighteenth century, the territory of the Creek Confederacy ran from the Oconee River in present-day Georgia to the Tombigbee River in Alabama.[31] The Upper Creeks lived on the Tallapoosa, Coosa, and Alabama Rivers in present-day Alabama, and the Lower Creeks lived on the lower Chattahoochee and Flint Rivers in present-day Georgia. By this time, 73 towns, ranging in size from as few as 10 to 20 families to more than 200 families, comprised the Creek Confederacy—48 Upper Creek towns and 25 Lower Creek towns, in total about 15,000 to 20,000 people (see fig. 2).[32] This was Creek country.

CHAPTER THREE

THE LANDSCAPE OF CREEK COUNTRY

Creek country, in the late eighteenth century, comprised 62,130 square miles of the heartland of the American South.[1] One of the most salient features of these thousands of square miles, even today, is waterways. Waterways were obviously central to Creek life. In fact, the name "Muskogee" originally may have been an Algonkian word signifying "swamp" or "wet ground."[2] Rivers and streams had figured in southeastern Indian life since the Ice Age. Throughout the prehistoric and historic periods, people chose to live adjacent to waterways, at first, for hunting and access to river valley plant resources and, later, for good agricultural lands.[3] By the late eighteenth century, the major Lower Creek towns were primarily located on the lower Flint and Chattahoochee Rivers in present-day Georgia. The principal Upper Creek towns were situated on the Tallapoosa, Coosa, and upper Alabama Rivers in present-day Alabama (see figs. 1 and 2). Feeding these major waterways were secondary and tertiary streams, which eighteenth-century white travelers called creeks and branches, respectively, and which formed a web of waterways that crisscrossed Creek country.[4] Along these creeks and streams were the smaller Creek satellite towns and an increasing number of individual Creek farmsteads.

Although the significance of such to the Creeks is not recorded, the closeness of a town and its stream is reflected in the numerous instances where a town and a waterway shared the same name. These are too numerous to list, but some examples are the town of Coosa on the Coosa River; the early-eighteenth-century Creek town of Okmulgi on the present-day Ocmulgee River (the name translates as "bubbling or boiling water"); the Lower Creek village of Aumucullee on a creek of the same name (present-day Muckalee Creek; the name translates as "pour on me"); and the Upper Creek town of Fusihatchee, or "bird creek," which shared its name with the adjacent creek that flowed into the Tallapoosa.[5]

These rivers and most of the creeks still exist. In many cases their Creek names remain the same, but their appearance is certainly different.[6] Unlike today, in the eighteenth century, little soil runoff clouded southern streams. Without exception, literate white travelers who wrote about what they saw as they passed through Creek country eulogized these streams for their clarity and pure waters. The one river in the South that people described as murky ran far from Creek territory. This was the Mississippi River, which the Creeks called *wiogufki*, or "muddy water."[7] The Creeks, too, appreciated the purity of the waters in Creek country. For instance, the word "Chattahoochee" translates from the Muskogean as "stream with pictured rocks." The pebbles in the bed of the river apparently had natural discolorations and lines on them; people knew this because they could see the rocks from the surface of the river.[8] Other Creek stream names indicate the water's purity as well. One "beautiful little creek" near Tuckabatchee was called *wehuarthy*, or "sweet water."[9] Another was called *we-hem-tle*, or "good water."[10] The Creeks also understood their waters to be physically and spiritually purifying to humans. In a daily rite known as "going to water," Creek men and women bathed in nearby streams not only to wash off the dirt and grime of daily living but to ensure that they were pure spiritually as well. "Going to water" also figured in their medicinal practices, since they understood both pure bodies and spirits to be fundamental to good health.[11]

The headwaters of the rivers in Creek country generally are in the upland regions, known today by their physiographic province names of the Piedmont province (in present-day north Georgia), the Ridge and Valley province (in present-day north Alabama and western Tennessee and Georgia), the Appalachian Plateau (in present-day northwestern Alabama), and the Interior Low Plateaus (the very southern edge of which forms the corner of northwest Alabama) (see fig. 3). The rivers flow south into the Gulf of Mexico, gathering waters en route from their far-flung networks of secondary and tertiary streams. In their courses to the sea, the rivers dramatically change character at what geologists call the Fall Line. The Fall Line is a distinctive topographic line running roughly from present-day Providence, Rhode Island, through

Richmond, Virginia, to Raleigh, North Carolina, to Columbia, South Carolina, then southwest to present-day Montgomery, Alabama. At Montgomery the line curves to the northwest, loops around the Missouri boot hill, and then continues southwest to eastern Texas, encompassing the Mississippi River and its ancient floodplains (see fig. 3). The Fall Line demarcates the geological transition from the Piedmont, the Ridge and Valley, the Appalachian Plateau, and the Interior Low Plateaus to the Coastal Plain, the physiographic province that comprises much of the lower South.[12] The Fall Line transition is unmistakable to anyone traveling north-south in this area. Topographically, one passes rather quickly from the rolling hills of the Piedmont, the steep ridges and deep valleys of the Ridge and Valley, or the highlands of the Appalachian and Interior Low Plateaus to the flat lands of the Coastal Plain. The Coastal Plain once formed the sandy floor of an ancient sea; today, as in the eighteenth century, it is a relatively flat landscape underlain by sandy soils. The flatness slows their pace, and the rivers easily cut through the sandy sediments to form great meanders.

Above the Fall Line, in the uplands, the stream beds are relatively shallow and rocky, and the water flows rapidly downstream. Rivers run through thin channels and cut tight meanders on narrow valley floors. Occasionally the high ridges or hills come right to the river's edge, forming steep bluffs overlooking the water. Creek place-names say much about the streams above the Fall Line. For instance, the sound the swift waters make above the Fall Line gave many streams their names. The name of the small village of Wewocau on present-day Weoka Creek (a tributary of the Coosa River in northern Alabama) translates from the Muskogean as "roaring water."[13] The Lower Creeks had a similar name for a small town on the headwaters of Yuchi Creek, Wetumcau, which glosses as either "sounding water" or "rumbling water."[14] The small Upper Creek town of Sougohatche took its name from the nearby creek of the same name (present-day Soughatchee Creek), which made a distinctive rattling similar to the sound of the gourd rattles the Creeks used in their dances. *Sauga* is a gourd used for making rattles, and *saukas* means "I am rattling."[15] The Wehadkee Creek, in present-day Randolf County, Alabama, took its name from its appearance; the term glosses as "white water," which is also the Muskogean name for the ocean.[16]

Creek place-names also referenced a variety of topographical features common to these upland waterways. An Upper Creek town located in present-day Tallapoosa County, Alabama, named Chataksofka took its name from the deep falls nearby; the name glosses as "deep rock" or "rock deep down."[17] The name of the town of Oakfuskee translates as "in a point," which refer-

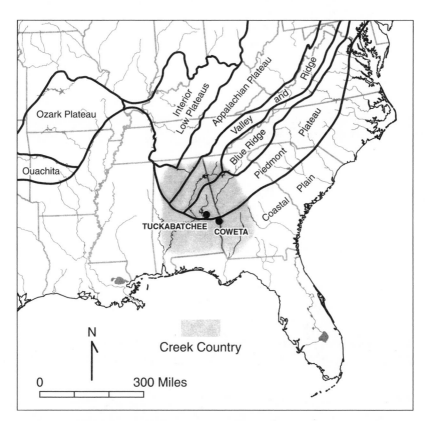

FIGURE 3. The physiographic provinces of Creek country

enced the point of land formed by a meander of the upper Tallapoosa River in which the town once stood.[18] The great curve in the upper Tallapoosa River where the last battle between Andrew Jackson's forces and the Red Sticks occurred was called *cholocco litabixee*, or "horse's flat foot."[19] Today it is called Horseshoe Bend.

Because of the sudden change in topography at the Fall Line, the rapid-flowing rivers and creeks break into wide falls and shoals and then continue at a more leisurely pace and within wider banks.[20] The Tallapoosa River at the Fall Line, for instance, takes a distinctive ninety-degree turn to the west and continues for about thirty miles before meeting the Coosa River. This stretch of the Tallapoosa has a wide, impressive river valley. Nowadays it is heavily farmed and mined, and it is the locus of Montgomery, the capital of Alabama. In the eighteenth century it was the center of the Upper Creek towns. In the eighteenth century both the Coosa and Tallapoosa flowed over lengthy, wide falls at the Fall Line. After this rushing, the rivers became "deep and quiet" before joining to form the Alabama River.[21] The Alabama River, the quintessential lazy southern river, cuts several great, looping, U-shaped meanders through the Coastal Plain to the Gulf of Mexico at Mobile Bay. The Alabama, in the late eighteenth century, was "remarkable for its gentle curves, pure waters, and good fish."[22] But the Alabama was not so remarkable as a site of human habitation. Other than four Creek towns near its formation at the juncture of the Tallapoosa and Coosa Rivers, there were no other towns on the Alabama River. The land is just too low, and large expanses of back swamps flank the river. The naturalist William Bartram, who traveled through much of Creek country in the 1770s, characterized the area as "one vast flat grassy savannah and Cane meadows, intersected or variously scrolled over with narrow forests and groves" and with longleaf pines "scattered" among the grasses.[23] There are few terraces above flood level, and any town within eight to nine miles of the river would have been regularly flooded.[24]

The Fall Line falls and shoals were wonderful places to fish. Even today, the freshwater ecosystems of the southeastern United States contain the greatest variety of freshwater fish in North America, and they are famous for their diversity of mollusks. There are more than 500 species of fishes in these streams, although today about 17 percent of these are considered imperiled.[25] The Creeks fished mostly in the spring and early summer, congregating from far and wide at favorite fishing spots. For instance, people flocked "in great numbers" to the Ocmulgee shoals to fish during "shad-catching" time (spring).[26] One can suppose that the town of Thlotlogulgau, on present-day Elkahatchee Creek, a tributary of the Tallapoosa right at the Fall Line, was a good fishing place. The town name translates as "fish ponds" and referred to the small, pondlike creek.[27] The waters just below the Tallapoosa falls, where Upahee Creek enters the river and where the town of Tallassee was located, were good fishing locations. Sturgeon (probably the American Atlantic sturgeon or the shovelnose sturgeon), trout, perch, rockfish, and red drum were abundant here.[28] (The scientific taxonomy for the plant and animal species referenced in the text is listed in the Appendix.) Although women usually did the fishing, Richard Thomas, one of Hawkins's white assistants, saw practically the whole town of Tuckabatchee turn out to fish at the Tallapoosa falls one June. According to Thomas, it took all the men, women, and children of the town to handle the 160-by-30-foot, cane-plaited net, with which "they caught a few."[29] At other sites, people reported catches of 100 to 200 fish per day with net fishing.[30] The Creeks also used a poison made of buckeye root mixed with clay to fish. Hawkins once heard of some Cherokees using this method of fishing on Limestone Creek (in present-day Alabama). The fish for eight miles downstream were killed, and sixty to eighty people took as many fish as they could carry.[31]

There is also some indication that these locations were not fished as common property. For instance, the Chattahoochee falls, in the late eighteenth-century, were a four-mile-long rocky shoal about 300 yards wide. The waters briefly separated at the falls and were forced into two channels by a series of rock islands. The eastern channel belonged to the Cowetas; the western channel belonged to the Cussetas. The fish taken here included shad, rockfish, trout, perch, catfish, suckers, and sturgeon.[32]

The Fall Line marked not only a topographic transition but a floral and faunal one as well. In fact, the Fall Line is a transition zone, or what ecologists refer to as an ecotone. An ecotone, as a transition zone, is unusually varied in plants and animals, because ecotones typically carry the flora and fauna of two or more zones, something ecologists refer to as an edge effect.[33] Archaeologists believe that the variety of wild foods at the Fall Line made it a popular place to live throughout the prehistoric and historic periods.[34] Late-eighteenth-century Creek towns were located mostly in the transitional ecotone of the Fall Line, although the Creeks claimed much more territory than just this.

Broadly speaking, Creek country encompassed sections of five physiographic provinces and four corresponding ecoregions: the Southeastern Conifer Forest ecoregion of the Coastal Plain, the transitional Southeastern Mixed Forest ecoregion of the Piedmont and Fall Line, and the Appalachian–Blue Ridge Mixed Mesophytic Forest and Appalachian Mixed Mesophytic Forest of, respectively, the Ridge and Valley and the Appalachian and Interior Low Plateaus physiographic provinces (see fig. 3). All four ecoregions lie within the Temperate Broadleaf and Mixed Forest Biome of eastern North America. Although accounts of the historic southern landscape emphasize the southern forest, none of these forest types was uniform. Not only was each forest different; but each had its own mosaic of vegetative and topographic features, and each included a great variety of nonforests ecosystems as well as forests ecosystems. It is difficult for the modern reader to envision the historic landscape of the South because, other than a few patches of old-growth forest, nothing in our experience matches these descriptions. Even these remaining old-growth forests may not resemble the eighteenth-century forests. Ecologists are beginning to understand that fire played a great role in southern ecosystems and, in fact, probably determined much of the species compositions of an ecosystem. Ecologists have determined the longleaf pine ecoregion of the Southeastern Conifer Forest to be a fire-dependent system. Recent studies also indicate that even the historic upland mixed forests coevolved with fire.

Fire, of course, is a natural occurrence, and there is every indication that forest fires occurred in the Historic Period as a result of lightning strikes. However, the Indians and, later, American farmers regularly set the woods on fire. Wandering through unmanaged or fire-suppressed contemporary southern forests, one cannot but notice the massive amounts of leaf and limb debris and the sometimes impenetrable tangles of briars, vines, and woody shrubs that compose the forest understory. In the eighteenth century and earlier, Indian women collected deadfall for firewood, thus clearing much of this debris, and the Indians also set fire to large areas of forest in order to burn off the leaf and small woody debris as well as the undergrowth.

As modern forest management is showing, burning has several beneficial ecological effects. Keeping the forest floor clear actually reduces the risk of catastrophic forest fires; when most fires occurred historically, then, they would have been low level, only singeing mature trees. Furthermore, forests that coevolved with fire have a floral and faunal species composition specific to that relationship. For instance, only fire-resistant trees grow in these forests, and the midstory and ground story are composed of flora that easily resprout after firing and that are actually rejuvenated by it. Likewise the fauna in a fire-dependent ecosystem must be able to tolerate and/or find refuge from low-level burns. Ground-nesting birds, for instance, are relatively few in these forests, compared with canopy nesters and cavity nesters.[35] Reptiles and amphibians that can quickly escape into underground or watery havens or that can climb quickly up a tall tree abound in these forests. Mole salamanders, who spend most of their time underground, for instance, thrive in the Southeast. Small mammals must be able to find refuge high in the trees, where the low flames do not reach, or in underground burrows. It is no fluke that squirrels of every variety permeate southern forests. Large mammals must necessarily be swift, like the white-tailed deer.[36]

The clear, open forests attracted many game animals, especially wild turkey, bear, and deer. The shoots of young plants fostered by burning are excellent deer browse; furthermore, the cleared understory made tracking easier.[37] The Indians, in effect, were creating a hunting reserve for deer and other animals. White frontier farmers also practiced burning for similar reasons, and accidental burning from unextinguished campfires as well as from lightning undoubtedly resulted in burned areas. Seasoned travelers could recognize areas that had been recently burned as well as those that had been burned some time in the past. We do not know the extent of the burned areas. Since Indi-

FIGURE 4. Basil Hall's drawing of a fire in the longleaf pine forest (Courtesy of the Lilly Library, Indiana University, Bloomington. This drawing is published in Captain Basil Hall, *Forty Etchings*, plate 24, "American Forest on Fire.")

ans and white hunters did not supervise the burning after the firing, one can suppose that areas varied from a few acres to large tracts of forest.[38] Basil Hall, an English aristocrat who passed through the longleaf forest in the late 1820s, drew a picture of a burning section of longleaf pine forest in the Coastal Plain from which "the volumes of smoke filled up the back ground completely, and deepened the general gloom in a very mysterious style" (see fig. 4).[39]

In addition to the clear floor, the trees of the southern forests were usually so tall and their branches so high that the result was open, parklike forests with high canopies and grassy and wildflower undergrowth. Philip Henry Gosse, a British naturalist who visited present-day Dallas County, Alabama, in the 1830s, claimed that the forests were so open and high that American hunters could "pursue their game on horseback at full speed through these sylvan recesses."[40] Gosse continued in his forest reverie:

> To walk in the forest alone is a high gratification. The perfect stillness and utter solitude, unbroken, commonly, by even ordinary woodland sounds and sights, tranquillize and sober the mind; the gloom has a solemn effect, for there is no light but what penetrates through the green leaves far above our head; the range of vision all around is limited by the innumerable straight and smooth trunks, exactly alike on every side, in which the fancy becomes lost. The devout spirit is drawn upward in such a scene, which imagination presently turns into a magnificent temple whose far distant roof is borne on uncounted columns; and indeed it is a glorious temple, one worthy of the Hand that reared it.[41]

Denser ground cover occurred in these forests, but only in specific areas. Midstory trees, shrubs, and vines grew mostly along stream edges and in the occasional forest clearing.[42] Forest glades were scattered, and some were undoubtedly formed in areas cleared by isolated tree falls or by large tornado swaths that snapped trees in half. Tornado, or "hurricane," tracks were common sights for travelers through Creek country. The Creeks called such places *hotali-huyana*, or wind passing.[43] Smaller clearings were created when a tree fell, either naturally or by human hand. Gosse described how slaves, attempting to retrieve honey from a beehive high in its branches, felled a giant longleaf pine tree: "At length it slowly bowed, groaned, cleft the air with a roar, and plunged with a deafening crash among the bushes and saplings, snapping its own stout limbs like glass, and scattering the moist earth far over the leaves on every side."[44] Mosses, ferns, and fungi found a habitat in the downed giants. Stream corridors, tree falls, and tornado paths interrupted the canopy, opened the forest floor to more sunlight, and hence allowed a denser understory of briars, shrubs, midstory trees, and flowering vines to grow.

A tremendous variety of animals and insects inhabited these forests. The Southeastern Mixed Forest ranks among the top ten ecoregions in the world in richness of amphibians, reptiles, birds, butterflies, and mammals.[45] Likewise, the Mixed Mesophytic Forest and the Appalachian–Blue Ridge Forest, taken together, form one of the world's richest temperate broadleaf forests, eclipsed only by the temperate flora of central China.[46] The longleaf pine forest ecoregion (Southeastern Conifer Forest) is likewise exceedingly rich. During the Ice Age, when glaciers and frigid temperatures covered most of North America, amphibians, reptiles, birds, and vascular plants found refuge at the lower latitudes of the Coastal Plain, creating an extremely old ecoregion with biodiversity that is "virtually unparalleled in North America."[47]

Mammals of every variety roamed through all of these southern forests types: white-tailed deer, beaver, otter, muskrat, red fox, grey fox, raccoon, squirrel, rabbit (eastern cottontail, marsh, and swamp, in particular), polecat, and so on.[48] Black bears, wildcats such as bobcats and mountain lions, and red wolves and grey wolves, all of which are nocturnal and reclusive by nature, were seldom seen, but everyone knew they were around because their foot-prints were in evidence in the soft soils or because they occasionally ransacked a camp for food.[49] A great variety of species of frogs, lizards, snakes, salaman-ders, and tortoises, among many other reptiles and amphibians, also found their homes here. Birds, simply put, abounded in all four forests types. It is not surprising that many of them, such as the pileated woodpecker, ivory-billed woodpecker, tufted titmouse, turkey vulture, bald eagle, sparrow hawk (or American kestrel), and great horned owl, among others, figured promi-nently in southeastern Indian beliefs.[50] Flocks of passenger pigeons, now ex-tinct, swarmed over the treetops, darkening the sky.[51] Flies, mosquitoes, ticks, gnats, and other pests bedeviled eighteenth-century southerners much like they still infuriate and exasperate twenty-first-century southerners. Gosse es-pecially disliked seed ticks, which, according to him, nestled in "any hollow or angle" of the body, where they would then "riot in impunity."[52] Bartram found horseflies intolerable:

> Next day we travelled but a few miles; the heat and the burning flies tor-
> menting our horses to such a degree, as to excite compassion even in the
> hearts of pack-horsemen. These biting flies are of several species, and their
> numbers incredible; we travelled almost from sun-rise to his setting, amidst
> a flying host of these persecuting spirits, who formed a vast cloud around
> our caravan so thick as to obscure every distant object; but our van always
> bore the brunt of the conflict; the head, neck and shoulders of the leading
> horses were continually in a gore of blood: some of these flies were near as
> large as humble [*sic*] bees; this is the *hipposbosca*.[53]

Although each of the forest types shared in much of the fauna and insects of the South, the vegetation in each had noticeable variations.[54] The mixed mesophytic forests of the uplands (the Appalachian–Blue Ridge and the Ap-palachian Mixed Mesophytic Forests) are underlain by some of the oldest ge-ologic formations in the world. These uplands were formed by great geologic events when ancient metamorphic rocks were thrust upward to the earth's crust millions of years ago. Today these uplands are relatively stable, and over time the peaks have eroded into today's rounded summits and ridges. Still, the topography here can be steep and craggy, with a lot of rock outcrops. The upland regions of Creek country, although comprising some of the most heavily populated areas during the Mississippian Period and before, were thinly populated by Creeks during the late eighteenth century.[55]

Today there are more than fifty genera of plants in these upland mesophytic forests. Modern ecologists report that before the massive logging of the early twentieth century, the forest cover here was dominated by the American chestnut, with a healthy population of oaks and tulip poplar. In addition to these tree types, today one can find blackgum, sweetgum, magnolia, hickory, walnut, elm, maple, and locust. The present-day forests are also home to a variety of shrubs, small trees, and flowering plants such as witch hazel, poison sumac, persimmon, holly, sassafras, mayapple, flowering dogwood, lady's slipper, several orchids, and jack-in-the-pulpit (also known as Indian turnip). Ferns, fungi, perennials, and annual herbaceous plants, shrubs, and small trees grow in and around the rock outcrops. In the early 1900s the chestnut nearly became extinct in the South because of the chestnut blight caused by the fungus *Cryphonectria parasitica*. There is also evidence that prehistoric Indians' use of fire affected these forests. Therefore, the modern mixed mesophytic forests in this region likely have a species composition different from that of the historic forests.[56]

Historic accounts of the mixed mesophytic forests of these uplands usually describe Cherokee country, north and east of Creek country.[57] However, Hawkins, en route to his new job, briefly passed through a part of the northern section of Creek country, and from his descriptions we can glean some idea of the upland forests of Creek country at this time. During his journey through this area, Hawkins specifically noted American chestnut, American beech, tulip poplar, white oak, black oak, post oak, hard-shelled hickory (perhaps shagbark hickory or shell-bark hickory), and scrub pine. He often commented on the stands of longleaf pine mixed with dwarf oaks that occurred on some ridges and hilltops, particularly in stony areas. Hawkins described the many rock outcrops he passed, most of which were covered with moss and many of which had large cedar (juniper) trees scattered about. He saw one river valley covered with black oak, and he described most of the trees as large. While still in Cherokee territory, just before entering Creek territory, he noticed some Cherokee women tapping maple trees (silver maple) along Limestone Creek. They used small wooden troughs and earthen pans to catch the sap and large ceramic pots as boilers.[58] Ginseng grew in and around the rock outcrops, and Indian men and women harvested it for its medicinal properties as well as to sell to frontier farmers.[59] Hawkins described the soils everywhere as "broken and stony," but he believed that the alluvial soils were still good for agriculture.[60]

In his movements through Creek country, Hawkins continually assessed areas for agricultural and commercial development potential. He judged the uplands as "not very inviting" because the river valleys were so narrow and they were abutted by "high and broken" lands.[61] Hawkins noted that the flood-plains had "good land for corn" and some good rangelands because of the river cane along the creeks.[62] About forty miles south of the Cherokee/Creek border lay the most northern Creek town, Auchenauualgau, or "cedar grove." Hawkins described Auchenauualgau as situated in good but "broken" soils, by which he most likely meant gravelly and stony. The town was located in a creek bottom and presumably in a cedar grove, since as we have seen, the Creeks often named their towns after local environmental features.[63] A few miles from there a "reedy glade" (probably switch cane) stood along the same stream. The trees surrounding this glade, consisting of southern red oak and post oak, were relatively small. Hawkins noted that the area probably con-tained iron ore, since the earth in places was remarkably black.[64] With his de-veloper's eye, Hawkins also observed that the "fine little creeks" of these up-lands would be good for running mills, and furthermore, the path from Etowah in Cherokee country to the Upper Creek town of Hillaubee passed nearby. On the whole, Hawkins concluded that the area around Auchenauualgau was "a country where the Indians might have desirable settlements."[65]

Like the uplands, the southern territory of Creek country also was sparsely populated. This was the Coastal Plain. The Coastal Plain during the late eigh-teenth century, as now, was famous for its longleaf pine ecosystem, which was once known as the Great Pine Barrens. This was a vast pine forest that swept through the Coastal Plain from Virginia through southern Georgia and north-ern Florida and into east Texas.[66] Travelers through the Coastal Plain were astonished at the extent of this pine forest and at the size of the pines. A seventy- or eighty-foot trunk, straight as a column, was not unusual. One traveler re-ported seeing pines measuring three fathoms, or arm's breadths, in circumfer-ence.[67] Basil Hall described it thus: "The ground was every where perfectly flat, and the trees rose from it in a direction so exactly perpendicular, and so entirely without lower branches, that an air of architectural symmetry was imparted to the forest, by no means unlike that of some gothic cathedrals."[68]

Plus, the longleaf forest sings. The needles of the longleaf pine are of such a length that, when the wind blows through them, they produce a distinctive

whistling sound. Bartram, in his typical style, described the longleaf song as a "solemn symphony of the steady Western breezes, playing incessantly rising and falling through the thick and wavy foliage."[69] Hall provided a rare sketch of the pine barrens in the early nineteenth century (see fig. 5). Hall grew bored with the longleaf forest because of the tiresome sameness for hundreds of miles, but Bartram, who was fascinated by everything in nature, found the forest to be pleasing, "rousing the faculties of the mind, awakening the imagination by its sublimity, and arresting every active, inquisitive idea, by the variety of the scenery."[70]

Bartram, unlike Hall, easily observed that the longleaf forest was not so monotonous, although one can understand Hall's complaint, since one could travel for weeks through this forest. Its historic extent is estimated at 90 million acres. Today, old-growth longleaf forest is restricted to a few small patches, although modern forest managers are cultivating longleaf pines in some managed areas. In total, contemporary longleaf pine covers only about 3 million acres.[71] As the name suggests, one of the dominant species in this forest is the longleaf pine, but the wiregrass understory is a second dominant species.[72] In fact, some ecologists refer to this as the longleaf pine/wiregrass ecoregion. As Bartram noticed so long ago, the original longleaf forest included quite a mosaic of ecological communities and habitats: sandhill longleaf forests, pine savannas, flatwoods, and hammocks.

The longleaf pine forest in Creek country resembled a savannah more than a forest. The large pines were widely scattered, with a grassy understory that consisted mostly of wiregrass but also contained a variety of other species, such as saw palmetto, gallberry, broomsedge, Indian grass, and panic grass.[73] An amazing variety of wildflowers also grew in this understory. Among the more than 3,000 species, two of the most unusual were the carnivorous Venus's-flytrap and the pitcher plant. In fact, pitcher plant bogs, which are now extremely rare, were a common, if unusual, feature of the historic longleaf forest. Even Bartram found that the pitcher plant "in any situation is a very great curiosity."[74] Bartram, who traveled extensively through the longleaf pine forest of present-day north Florida, recorded myriad flowers, shrubs, and grasses. In one short stretch of travel he noticed several species of pawpaw, including one with light green foliage and large, "perfectly white and sweet scented" flowers; the "beautiful little dwarf" calico bush; the gallberry; the butterfly pea; phlox; morning glories; the moonflower; verbena; ruellia; violets, and the atamasco lily, among others.[75]

The longleaf pine forest was also interspersed with hardwoods, especially in the alluvial river valleys and on hammocks, which are moderately fertile sections of higher ground. Hammocks contained hardwoods such as southern red oak, blackjack oak, water oak, blackgum, sweetgum, post oak, and black oak, all of which have thick barks and easily resprout after being burned.[76] Along the edges of rivers, low shrubs and small trees such as wild crabapples, yaupon, shining sumac, wild plums, flowering dogwoods, persimmon, sassafras, and wild strawberries grew in and around the hardwoods.[77] Flowering vines, such as the trumpet creeper, climbed thirty to forty feet up the large oak trees.[78] Nearer the coastal areas, where the longleaf pine and southern streams give way to tidal estuaries, swamps, and marshes, the forest became heavily interspersed with swamplands with river cane, cypress, tupelo, and sweetgum.[79]

Swamps are quite usual in the Coastal Plain as a whole because of the high water table, resulting in areas of standing water. The most famous swamp in the Coastal Plain is still the Okefenokee Swamp of present-day south Georgia; the Creeks called it Ecunfinocau, or "quivering earth."[80] The waters in these swamps, then as now, were still and dark, qualities again reflected in their names. The Creeks called one stream in present-day Laurens and Wheeler Counties, Georgia, *ochwalkee*, or "dirty water," and they referred to one dark stream in Pike County, Alabama, as *olustee*, or "black water."[81] These wetlands were home to an incredible number of waterfowl, including varieties of herons, cranes, storks, ibises, ducks, and geese. The bald eagle favored the cypress as a nesting tree because of its high, flat branches that formed a horizontal canopy high above the swamps.[82] The Carolina parakeet, now extinct, hovered among the cypress canopy cracking cypress cones for their seeds and nesting in hollow trees.[83] The ivory-billed woodpecker, with its great red crest, two-foot wing span, and distinctive double rap, flourished in the old-growth longleaf pine. It is now feared to be extinct. Many species of other birds also abounded: wrens, warblers, flycatchers, sparrows, bluebirds, American mourning doves, wild turkeys, and bobwhite quails.[84] Many other animals now on the endangered or threatened species list had homes in the longleaf ecosystem, including the flatwood salamander, striped newt, gopher frog, eastern indigo snake, eastern diamondback rattlesnake, Bachman's sparrow, brown-headed nuthatch, red-cockaded woodpecker, and pine snake, to name a few. The gopher tortoise, especially, is a keystone species in an old-growth longleaf forest. Its burrows provide safe haven for small animals from the low-level fires necessary to the ecology of the longleaf system.[85]

In the eighteenth century neither Creeks nor Americans considered the longleaf forest good for much except livestock raising, and that only in a limited way. The forest generally was considered just wild, and except for a few Lower Creek towns, the so-called pine barrens were mostly uninhabited.[86] Even travelers usually avoided the longleaf forest because it was considered more dangerous than elsewhere. For one thing, since there were few towns or villages for miles at a stretch, travelers could easily run short on supplies. Plus, the many swamps proved nearly impassable. Coastal Plain alligators, which sometimes could be found as far north as the Fall Line, were the stuff of folklore, and travelers confirmed the tales of twenty-foot alligators (the American alligator) in some Coastal Plain rivers and swamps. If this were not enough, mosquitoes and gnats infested the Coastal Plain, and wolves and other predators were a constant menace to humans. Perhaps more importantly, the pine barrens were a known hideout for mixed gangs of Indians, whites, and blacks, or banditti as they were called at the time, as well as other renegades who were quick to ambush and rob travelers. With the Treaty of Fort Jackson in 1814, Georgia acquired all of the longleaf forest in Creek territory and put the land up for sale through the lottery system. Even then, the longleaf forest was considered such a notorious wasteland that only a trickle of settlers opted for this land.[87] Its full commercial potential was not realized until the twentieth-century timber boom, which resulted in its dramatic reduction.

Almost all of the late-eighteenth-century Creek towns were located in the transitional ecoregion between the upland mesophytic forests and the Coastal Plain longleaf pine forest. This transitional zone was the Southeastern Mixed Forest ecoregion of the Piedmont and Fall Line, although in Alabama this regime stretched north along the river corridors to the foothills of the uplands. In this ecoregion the flora species composition can be quite variable, depending on underlying substrata, soils, and elevation. In the Historic Period, as now, the Southeastern Mixed Forest ecoregion that was part of Creek country was dominated by an oak-hickory-pine forest.

Generally speaking, the historic Southeastern Mixed Forest in Creek country consisted of longleaf pine and shortleaf pine and hardwoods such as black oak, southern red oak, post oak, white oak, tulip poplar, shagbark hickory, shell-bark hickory, and American chestnut. The river valleys held a mixed pine/hardwood forest with the same varieties of pine, hickory, oak, and chestnut, as well as other riparian trees such as walnut, American beech, maple, elm, southern magnolia, river birch, mulberry, sassafras, and persimmon.[88] The ratio of particular species of oaks, hickories, and pines during the Historic Period was probably different from that of today because of the dominating force of fire in shaping this ecosystem in the past. For instance, biologists comparing reconstructions of historic forests with contemporary old-growth forests (approximately 150 years old) find that the two do not match. One such study that compares a historic forest with a contemporary old-growth forest in present-day north Mississippi shows the historic forest to have consisted largely of post oak, black oak, and blackjack oak, with blackjack oak as one of the dominant tree types. Post oak and black oak are present in the contemporary old-growth patches, but blackjack oak is absent. Conversely, southern red oak, while present in the historic forest, was not particularly common, yet it is a dominant tree type in the contemporary old-growth patch. The contemporary old-growth patch has an "extraordinary abundance" of sweetgum, yet sweetgum is completely absent in the historic forest. Ecologists think that such differences between historic forests and contemporary old-growth forests occur because fires have been suppressed in the twentieth century as a part of forest management.[89]

Deciduous hardwood trees in the Southeastern Mixed Forest of the eighteenth century also looked different from today's 150-year-old trees. In areas not previously cleared and cultivated by prehistoric and historic Indians, the deciduous trees were very large.[90] They were sometimes 6, 8, or even 11 feet in diameter with branches spreading 100 feet from side to side. These trees reached to the sky on straight trunks with their limbs branching out only after 50 feet.[91] The "inexpressible grandeur" of these trees left many naturalists groping for words. Gosse declared that "many of the trees are of immense magnitude, and their trunks rise like pillars from the soft and damp soil, shooting upward in columnar majesty."[92] Bartram thought that no one would believe him about the magnificence of these trees when he lamented, "To keep within the bounds of truth and reality, in describing the magnitude and grandeur of these trees, I fear, fail of credibility."[93] To envision the full extent and productivity of these trees, consider the nut mast. When the nuts fell, usually in early fall to midwinter, the ground would be covered, sometimes up to several inches deep, in nuts.[94]

Stands of pure pines or pure hardwoods also occurred throughout the Southeastern Mixed Forest. Pure pine stands usually crowned the higher upland areas. But if place-names are any indication, groves of various tree species occurred throughout this ecoregion. For instance, a stream in Clay County, Alabama, was called Wesobulga, or "sassafras tree grove"; an Upper Creek town on the Coosa River was called Ocheubofau, which translates as "among hickory trees" or "hickory ground."[95] The Creek name for an oak grove was *tuckaumaupofau*.[96] Surely one of the most impressive groves was the area between the Alabama and Connecuh Rivers widely known as the Dogwoods. Flowering dogwood groves were common and distinctive enough for the Creeks to have a name for them: *ataphapulgus*. This particular grove, however, was especially large—eight miles wide and twenty miles long—and it was in an oak, American chestnut, and tulip poplar forest. Some of the dogwoods were as much as ten inches in diameter and twelve feet high, with interlocking branches.[97] According to a tired and hot Bartram, the whole was "one vast, shady, cool grove so dense and humid as to exclude the sunbeams and prevent the intrusion of almost every other vegetable, affording a most desirable shelter from the fervid sunbeams at noon-day."[98]

Most white travelers through Creek country noted tree types because this was the standard evaluation used for soil and land qualities. However, other midstory trees in the Southeastern Mixed Forest such as persimmon, sassafras, cherry, mulberry, and dogwood could be found, especially along stream edges and other areas where sunlight was more abundant.[99] Ground cover of vines, shrubs, wildflowers, and grasses also abounded in such areas. Bartram, in his wanderings through Creek country, noted many flowering shrubs such as the "very singular and beautiful" oak-leaved hydrangea, which grew in coppices on the banks of rivers and creeks. Golden St. John's-wort also grew along the banks of streams. On the banks of the Chattahoochee, near Yuchi Town, Bartram noted sassafras, red bay, pawpaw, white buckeye, and horse sugar.[100]

In addition, varieties of wild grasses were found in the "prairies" and "savannahs" that grew in the lower and moister parts of the Southeastern Mixed Forest. Although eighteenth-century literate travelers used these and other terms such as "glade" and "meadow" with little precision, a prairie usually referred to a large, open grassland, and a savannah usually referred to a mixed grassland/tree environment. In the Southeastern Mixed Forests, the savannahs differed from the forest proper only in that the oak, hickory, or pine trees were more widely spaced and the ground story of various types of grasses, some shrubs, and wildflowers was a more prominent feature.

Creek country held one of the largest prairies in the South: the grassy plains of the Black Prairie or Black Belt, or the *hiyucpulgee*, as the Creeks called them.[101] The Black Prairie is a twenty-mile-wide, sickle-shaped expanse running along the Fall Line from present-day central Alabama to northeast Mississippi. The Black Prairie is underlain by Selma chalk, which produces a deep black residual soil on which tall grasses thrive.[102] Bartram identified the key species as one of the tall species of the rosin weed, perhaps *Silphium terebinthinaceum*. This particular variety is no longer found in the Black Belt prairies; the key species today is *S. laciniatum*.[103] There were also coppices of post oaks in the Black Prairie wherever there were patches of sandy soil (probably the remnants of an earlier sediment formation).[104] Hawkins described these prairies as "waving, hill and dale," and the clumps of large post oaks divided the grassy expanse, giving the whole the appearance of being divided into fields.[105]

Certainly the most ubiquitous grass of the southern landscape was giant river cane and reed that grew in the active floodplains of the creeks and rivers. River cane, which the Creeks called *lap lako*, or "tall cane," and which is known today as "giant rive cane," is in the grass family (*Gramineae*), and it is related to bamboo.[106] White travelers frequently noted cane and reed in their accounts because they indicated especially fertile farmland and were indispensable horse fodder while on the trail. For the southern Indians, cane was also an important building and crafts material. Among other things, it was used as a construction material for buildings, for weaving baskets and mats, for musical instruments such as flutes, and for blowguns. The smaller variety was used for arrow shafts.[107] Cane is available year-round, and the Creeks harvested cane of suitable length and diameter as needed. Seeds of the smaller cane were also eaten.[108] By the late eighteenth century, cane, which remains green in the winter, was necessary forage for the growing Creek livestock population.

Giant river cane has a tall, rigid stalk with widely spaced knots and long, slender, lanceolate leaves, and it grows to about twenty-five feet. It is broadly tolerant of soils and wetness, hence its pervasiveness near southern streams throughout all of the forest types. Reed (today known as switch cane) is a smaller variety of cane, growing to about four feet in height. Reed has a more linear distribution along the length of secondary and tertiary streams, although Hawkins noted reed growing in patches "as cane" in a few areas along the upper Coosa River.[109] Cane and reed grew thickly together in the Coastal Plain swamps and on some creeks.[110] On the rivers, giant river cane grew in canebrakes, which were often two to three miles wide and took up hundreds, sometimes thousands, of acres. In fact, the Creeks distinguished canebrakes by size: a *coha-ålgi* was a "grove" or "clan" of cane, and a *coha-apat-i*, which glosses as "cane covering," referred to an extensive canebrake.[111] Certainly the 3,000-acre canebrake that Hawkins described in a bend of the Coosa River just before it joins the Tallapoosa was a *coha-apat-i*.[112] On the Chattahoochee River, a 1,000-acre canebrake was situated in a great bend of the river just below the Chehaw and Ooseoochee towns.[113] According to Bartram, these impressive canebrakes did not compare with one he saw on the Suwanee River in present-day Florida that he declared to be "the most extensive Cane brake . . . on the face of the whole earth."[114]

Canebrakes of giant river cane, which Hawkins once saw growing more than thirty-two feet tall, were so thick as to be impenetrable except with an ax.[115] Because of their impenetrability, canebrakes were a favored hideout for people. During the Red Stick War, for instance, American soldiers reported many women and children fleeing to nearby canebrakes when American troops approached their towns. In fact, the Creeks thought canebrakes superior to American forts, and they declared that they "would not give one swamp or cane brake for forty forts."[116] Because of the impenetrableness, only larger mammals, such as deer, bear, and cattle, find them good areas for foraging. Moderate- to small-sized birds use them for roosting.[117] Hawkins reported "the greatest collection" of crows he had ever seen roosting in a canebrake on the Tallapoosa River.[118] Canebrakes also make a distinctive noise when the wind blows through them; the Creeks called the sound *coha-haki*, or "cane noise."[119]

Hawkins described canebrakes as being on lowlands subject to flooding, indicating that cane grew in the primary quality soils on the active floodplain of the river valley. It is no surprise, then, that many Creeks cleared canebrakes for agricultural fields. The Chehaw and Ooseoochee had their fields in the canebrake just south of their towns.[120] In a meander of the Tallapoosa, just west of the Upper Creek town of Autossee, Hawkins noted a "rich cove" of land that had been a canebrake but was now under cultivation.[121] The Indian countryman Richard Bailey may have had his farm across the river from this canebrake, and the fields may have been Bailey's, not the Autossees'. A third of the 3,000-acre canebrake on the Coosa had once been the site of Creek agricultural fields, but when Hawkins visited the area, the fields were abandoned.[122] Hawkins also noticed that some islands at the Tallapoosa falls, just north of Tuckabatchee, were old fields margined by cane, which suggests the fields had been cut out of a canebrake.[123] Several other towns along the Tallapoosa located their cornfields in what Hawkins called "rich cane swamps."[124] The Alabama towns of Ecunchate, Toowoossau, and Pauwocte were located at a long, large meander in the Alabama River. The peninsula formed by the meander was a "rich cane swamp," and all three towns, although located across the river, had their fields in these swamps.[125]

Clearing a canebrake would not have been easy. Burning off the cane would not have been practicable, since cane is a fire-dependent species and burning actually increases cane growth.[126] Cane grows very quickly; in some cases it can sprout up to one and a half inches overnight.[127] Clearing a canebrake, then, required digging out the cane runners, which can form a thick mass. Once abandoned, these former canebrakes quickly reverted to cane. Cane is also a disturbance-driven species. Canebrakes on the major rivers appeared in the floodplains because of the regular flooding and scouring or in frequently flooded back swamps. Furthermore, archaeologists and ecologists believe that the amount of cane and reed in the Southeast during the Historic Period may have been a consequence of prehistoric and historic Indian agricultural and burning practices.[128] There is no doubt that cane and reed were abundant in Creek territory; white observers recorded its presence along the entire length of almost all streams and rivers. However, with the increasing number of livestock in Creek territory, cane and reed began to diminish, and it is still relatively rare today.

In the eighteenth and early nineteenth centuries, "Indian old fields" were also a well-known landscape type to historic travelers. As will be discussed later, Creek women rotated their fields, letting some lie in fallow for a number of years. These fallow fields were known as "old fields," but the term also applied to the sites of abandoned Indian towns and to any abandoned area of past agricultural activities. Since at least the Mississippian Period and perhaps earlier, the southeastern Indians had been moving and relocating their towns and agricultural fields.[129] Literate travelers often remarked on passing Indian old fields, and the more complete journals recorded passing as many as five or six in a day.[130] Setting the usual daily mileage at about twenty miles a day, in some travel one could pass an old field every four to five miles. Unfortunately, few bothered to describe these fields, which would give some indication as to how long they had been abandoned. Some of these fields would have been abandoned for almost a hundred years, some for a few decades or less. Old fields, then, would have been in many various stages of forest succession.

Some old fields were actual places on a map, such as the Cusseta Old Fields, the Apalachicola Old Fields, and the Ocmulgee Old Fields. The Cusseta Old Fields were situated on the eastern bank of the Chattahoochee River on a large, flat bluff, or "high flat," in eighteenth-century parlance. The town of Cusseta had once been located on this high flat, and at the time had been surrounded by agricultural fields. By the late eighteenth century, the town had been abandoned, and old fields reverting to pine forest stretched to the horizon. The people of Cusseta had relocated to the southern base of the bluff.[131] The Apalachicola Old Fields were the location of the Late Mississippian Period center of the Apalachicola province, located south of Cusseta. Ancient mounds and a plaza still stood there, and the old fields stretched along the low grounds of the Chattahoochee. According to a white trader who was showing Bartram around, some Creek families had continued to inhabit Apalachicola until about 1750, when they decided to leave because of the frequent flooding, because "they grew timorous and dejected, apprehending themselves to be haunted and possessed with vengeful spirits," and because they had been "repeatedly warned by apparitions and dreams to leave it."[132] Apparently these torments came from the ghosts of some traders slain there some years earlier.

The Ocmulgee Old Fields, located at the Fall Line of the Ocmulgee River near present-day Macon, Georgia, were not only the remnants of abandoned agricultural fields but also the remains of an abandoned town and trading fort from the early eighteenth century. The name stuck, and some vestiges of the old agricultural fields, "extensive, green, and open," were on the Ocmulgee floodplain.[133] James Adair, an eighteenth-century trader and writer, reported that every Indian knew of the Ocmulgee Old Fields. These old fields, too, were haunted. In fact, according to Adair, one could hear ghost warriors dancing at night. Adair claimed he never heard or saw the ghosts even though he had often camped there. His Chickasaw companions explained that was because he was an "obdurate infidel in that way."[134] Not all Indian old fields were so infamous or so old. In fact, most seem to have been of more recent origin, with small saplings of pines, tulip poplars, oaks, and American chestnuts and much underbrush.

Old fields, canebrakes, glades, groves, prairies, savannahs, swamps, hammocks, rivers, creeks, terraces, rock outcrops, coppices, longleaf pine forests, mesophytic mixed forests, and southeastern mixed forests—certainly Creek country was an environmental mosaic. It encompassed parts of virtually every ecosystem of the southeastern United States and hence shared in the richness and diversity of the flora and fauna typical of each. Or as Hawkins once put it, "The whole a very desirable country."[135] Most of this historical landscape is now gone, lost to ranching, cotton, timber, and other commercial enterprises. But even in the eighteenth century, Creek country was not a pristine wilderness, despite the rhetoric of the time. Rather, Creek country was a human-landscaped environment, and a human presence was everywhere in evidence, especially in the heart of Creek country.

CHAPTER FOUR

THE HEART OF CREEK COUNTRY

P erhaps one of the most striking features to a modern reader about Creek country is that this historic landscape was not all pristine forests, but it was an environmental mosaic clearly marked by and, in some cases, formed by a human presence. Nowhere is this more conspicuous than deep in the heart of Creek country, in the river valleys of the Chattahoochee and Tallapoosa Rivers where the Creek towns were located. By the end of the eighteenth century, the Chattahoochee and Tallapoosa River valleys had been occupied since the Paleo Indians moved into these areas at the end of the Ice Age, about 12,000 years ago. Considering the long human occupation, it should not be a surprise that these river valleys were actually highly landscaped environments.[1]

Still, many may find it surprising. For one, both native and nonnative Americans usually have strong ideas about the Indians' relationships to the land. Much of this belief is encapsulated in the concept of the so-called ecological Indian, or that Indian person who barely left his or her mark on the world out of respect and reverence for all things natural and who lived in harmony and balance with the natural world.[2] But much of this idea is stereotype. The eighteenth-century Creek Indians, for instance, assuredly had strong bonds to their land, and some of these were supernatural and reverential. They also had equally strong practical bonds to the land formed by their subsistence and commercial needs and certain political imperatives. Use of the environment, no matter how spiritually integrated or harmonious, still leaves an imprint and requires some kind of management. In other words, Indians had managed and changed their environments since they migrated to the New World, and the Creeks of the late eighteenth century were no different.

Although formed much earlier, the river valleys of most southern rivers stabilized at the end of the Ice Age, when the glaciers to the north melted. Much glacial water drained off the continent via southern rivers. This draining helped to entrench the rivers into a single channel and to form floodplain valleys, and the dynamics of floodplain rivers continually sculpted and re-sculpted the topography.[3] Bartram described some of this topography. In this passage Bartram, who had been traveling along the Fall Line on the Lower Trading Path, was in the Chattahoochee River valley, near present-day Columbus, Georgia, where the towns of Cusseta, Coweta, Coweta Tallahassee, Yuchi, Ooseoochee, and Chehaw were located. He described the Chattahoochee River valley thus:

> The land rises from the river with sublime magnificence, gradually retreating by flights or steps one behind and above the other, in beautiful theatrical order, each step or terrace holding up a level plain, and as we travel back from the river, the steps are higher, and the corresponding levels are more and more expansive; the ascents produce grand high forests, and the plains present to view a delightful varied landscape, consisting of extensive grassy fields, detached groves of high forest trees, and clumps of lower trees, ever-green shrubs and herbage; green knoll's with serpentine, wavy, glittering brooks crossing through the green plains.[4]

The topography Bartram described is what modern geologists refer to as river terracing that occurs in some alluvial river valleys. The flat land closest to the river is considered the active floodplain, and the steplike, slightly elevated lands are the terraces. Geologists refer to such terraces as first, second, and third terrace, and so on, with the first terrace being the one that rises first from the active floodplain. Terraces are former floodplains that have been built up through the repeated deposition of sediments in flooding intervals that are quite regular with floodplain rivers. They also form as the river cuts deeper and away from its outer banks. Over time, an active floodplain eventually builds to a height above regular flood stage; this would then be considered a terrace, and future flooding deposits would form a new active floodplain.[5]

Although Bartram does not mention it in this passage, the floodplains were the site of Creek agricultural fields, and their towns and households were located on the terraces, above the water level reached during yearly flooding.[6]

Literate late-eighteenth-century travelers often noted that the trees in these river valleys were usually smaller than those in the upland old-growth forests. The size of the trees probably reflects past clearing activities, undoubtedly for agricultural and garden fields.[7]

In addition, populated late-eighteenth-century river valleys appeared open and parklike due to frequent burning of the grounds. Unlike the burning of the hinterland forests, however, southeastern Indians set these fires in yards and surrounding areas to control insects, rodents, and other pests. It is also likely that they set the fires to stimulate growth that would attract deer, turkey, and other wild game to the vicinity as well as to generate the growth of berries, wild fruits, wild herbs, and other useful items that Creek women would collect.[8]

Gathering firewood also kept the grounds clean and open. Wood, hickory nuts, and giant river cane were the primary sources of fuel in Creek country. For wood, the Creeks did not fell trees; rather, Creek women collected the dead wood that fell to the ground.[9] The Creeks at Tuckabatchee told Hawkins that as the available firewood around a town became scarce, women had to walk farther and farther to collect firewood, until finally a whole town would move.[10] The archaeological evidence, however, belies this claim. The Historic Period Creek towns in the Chattahoochee and Tallapoosa River valleys had been occupied for at least 100 years and probably longer, and a recent archaeological study shows that fuelwood was not a factor in town relocations.[11] Only around Tuckabatchee did Hawkins note a dearth of fuelwood. Fuel was not a problem because, for one reason, with the commercial hunting of the eighteenth century, most people were scattered through the countryside during the coldest months.[12] This seasonal migration meant that at the time of peak consumption of fuel for heating, most people collected firewood from the hinterlands where they had their hunting camps. The yearly deadfall near the towns was sufficient for those who stayed home during the winter. During the warmer months, when hunting parties returned to the towns, fuel needs were lower, since it was only used for cooking and some blacksmithing.

Creek women kept a low fire continually burning in their house yards, where they usually had food cooking throughout the day. Also, after Hawkins had blacksmith shops built in Creek territory, Creeks needing the services of the smiths were required to provide their own fuel. Hawkins described the Creeks as "making coal," that is, charcoal, to bring to the blacksmith shops.[13] The Creeks had requested the blacksmith shops, but their needs for smithing were fairly limited at this time. Therefore it is unlikely that charcoal accounted for any large amount of wood consumption. Finally, using horses to collect wood in more distant areas undoubtedly relieved the burden on women when the supply around a town began to diminish.

Because Creek towns were primarily farming communities, one of the most obvious landscaped features in the Creek river valleys were their agricultural fields. Most Creek families did not farm separate, individual plots of land. Rather, a town opened a communal field, and the town council assigned each family one or more adjacent lots. These were not the orderly, rowed fields of Hawkins's scientific farming. Rather, Creek women, who were the farmers, practiced swidden agriculture, and these fields appeared to Euro-Americans as a tangled mass of vegetation, another indication for them that Indian farming techniques were "uncivilized." (Creek farming is discussed in detail in Chapter 7.) These fields typically ran along the active floodplains, in linear patterns along the riverbanks or in meander bends of streams. In swidden agriculture, farmers abandon fields when, for various reasons, they become difficult to farm. The farmers open new ones, and the abandoned fields are then left fallow to naturally regenerate the soils. In the documents, whites referred to fallow fields as "old fields," but they, of course, were of more recent origin than the old fields in the hinterlands. Hawkins noted many old fields in these populous river valleys.[14] In some cases, old fields bordered fields in active cultivation, giving the impression that Creek agricultural activities covered vast acres.

Each town had its own fields, and each town had corporate ownership of land, although the exact land boundaries of the towns are not known. Because late-eighteenth-century Creek towns varied in population, the acreage of their communal fields varied. Coweta, for instance, which was located just south of the falls of the Chattahoochee, on the western side of the river, had about 500 inhabitants at this time.[15] The fields of Coweta were on the same side of the river, about a quarter-mile south of the town, on a floodplain inside a slow curve of the Chattahoochee.[16] Figure 6 shows the location of Coweta and other landscape features of the eighteenth-century Chattahoochee River valley. Figure 6 is one in a series of figures designed to give a local view of the Creek towns and the surrounding landscape. The figures are drawn from U.S. Geological Survey topographic maps onto which I have plotted the location of Creek towns according to Hawkins's *Sketch of the Creek Country* and *Letters*, the Historic Indian archaeological site locations, and environmental information provided by Hawkins in his descriptions of Creek towns. Each map represents a section of a river and its valley as designated by a contour line. The contour line shows the first significant rise in elevation out of a river valley, usually around 200 to 300 feet above sea level, thus indicating the full scope of a valley. The contour line also marks the beginning of the upland areas. Hawkins's descriptions of the environment around the towns are predominantly of vegetation types and soil conditions. Both are placed on the figures according to Hawkins's description. If Hawkins did not mention any environmental features, these areas are left blank on the figures, as I only wanted to plot documented environmental features. Hawkins also noted topographical features such as river bends, uplands, "flats," and so on. These conform remarkably well with modern-day features, so much so that I did not have to alter the modern maps to designate eighteenth-century topographic features. As a historical environmental source, Hawkins is unsurpassed. His descriptions are so detailed that towns can be located with precision and environmental features can be plotted with fine resolution.

Figure 6 also shows Coweta Tallahassee (or Coweta Old Town), which was also located on the western side of the river, south of Coweta about two and one-half miles as the crow flies. Cusseta was located about one and one-half miles south of Coweta Tallahassee, but on the eastern side of the river.[17] The fields for both of these towns were located between the two towns, in the points of three tight bends in the river. The Cusseta fields took the two most northern points, and those of Coweta Tallahassee filled the third point. The people of Coweta Tallahassee had to travel only about a half-mile to their fields, which were also on the same side of the river. According to Hawkins this point was very rich and had been "long under cultivation."[18]

Hawkins listed 69 gun men in Coweta Tallahassee and 180 gun men for Cusseta. The term "gun men" was a common way to reckon Indian population sizes during the eighteenth century. A 1789 report to the secretary of war suggests multiplying the number of gun men by four to arrive at a total population.[19] This would mean that Coweta Tallahassee had about 264 people and Cusseta had about 720. Hawkins does not give population figures for all the towns, but in general the large towns had about 500 to 1,000 people, and the villages had about 150 to 200.[20]

The Cusseta fields were about three miles north of the town and on both sides of the river. Because of the distance, Cusseta farmers used horses or canoes to reach the fields and to carry the produce back to their town. Three fords connected the Cusseta fields, which comprised about 1,000 acres total. As mentioned in Chapter 3, the people of Cusseta had recently moved off the high flat on the eastern side of the river, where their fields once extended as far as one could see. The town was now located at the base of the bluff, on a terrace "just above flood mark" (see fig. 7). Hawkins described the land around

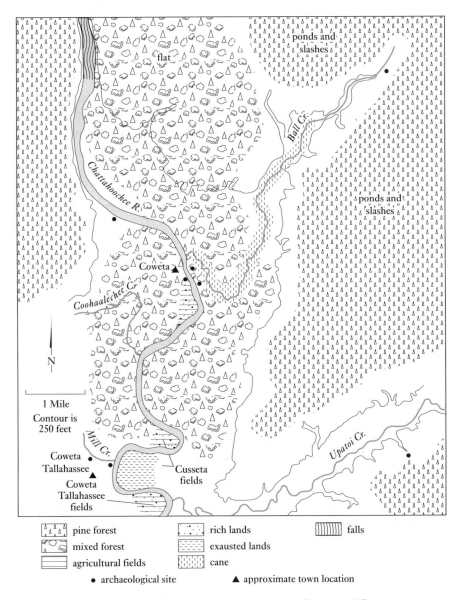

ponds and slashes

flat

Ball Cr.

Chattahoochee R.

ponds and slashes

Coweta

Coohaalechee Cr

N

1 Mile
Contour is
250 feet

Mill Cr.

Coweta
Tallahassee

Coweta
Tallahassee
fields

Cusseta
fields

Upatoi Cr.

	pine forest		rich lands		falls
	mixed forest		exausted lands	
	agricultural fields		cane	

• archaeological site   ▲ approximate town location

FIGURE 6. A section of the Chattahoochee River, showing Coweta and Coweta Tallahassee

the town as "poor, and much exhausted." Although they grew a little corn here, the inhabitants mostly depended on the fields to the north. According to Hawkins, the fertility of these fields also was questionable, since in his words, "to call them rich must be understood in a limited sense; they have been so, but being cultivated beyond the memory of the oldest man in Cusseta, they are almost exhausted." Still, the people of Cusseta continued to farm them into the nineteenth century, although they apparently grew "barely a sufficiency of corn for their support." The fields on the eastern bank were in the active floodplain. Here the first terrace, which was about twenty feet higher than the active floodplain, extended back from the river for a mile, where it met the upland longleaf pine forest. In the floodplain, between the fields and the first terrace, was a large, forty-acre beaver pond. Hawkins called the pond "old" and believed it could be successfully drained. He, of course, saw this as potential agricultural land. Hawkins also described some prehistoric mounds as bordering these fields; from its top the platform mound in particular afforded an excellent view of the river and the Cusseta fields.[21]

Hawkins described the Chattahoochee River valley and the towns in it in great detail. The entire river valley was bordered by upland pine forest, probably longleaf, but there may have been some scrub and shortleaf pines as well, since he often described these upland pines as "small." The terraces contained numerous "slashes" and ponds ("slashes" probably referred to the small, curvilinear bodies of water formed out of old meanders). The river through here ran wide and deep and was interspersed with small islands, which afforded good crossing places, and some of these were under cultivation.[22]

The areas of the floodplain not cleared for cultivation were in a typical southern mixed forest of oak, hickory, and pine, although as mentioned above, most of the trees were relatively small.[23] However, between Cusseta and Coweta Tallahassee, the people of Coweta Tallahassee maintained a 2,000-acre stand of hickory and oak trees just west of the town.[24] Creek women collected quantities of hickory nuts and acorns in the hinterlands, but the large stands of hickory and oak trees near the towns were undoubtedly maintained for this purpose.[25] Additional evidence is provided by Bartram, who, passing through the Chattahoochee towns, repeatedly described alternating prairies and groves of hickory and oak trees.[26] When Hawkins wanted to build a blacksmith shop near Tuckabatchee on the Tallapoosa River, the townspeople became upset when the smith and his assistants cut trees when clearing land on the site.[27] The practice of maintaining groves of nut-bearing trees, in fact, may have been quite old. Bartram, while exploring an abandoned Mississippian mound center on the upper Little River, in present-day Georgia, observed a large grove of shell-bark hickory and black walnut in the vicinity. Although he does not indicate where he got this information, Bartram understood that the "ancients" had cultivated these trees for their nut masts.[28]

According to the archaeological and documentary evidence, acorns and hickory nuts were by far the most important wild food for the southern Indi-

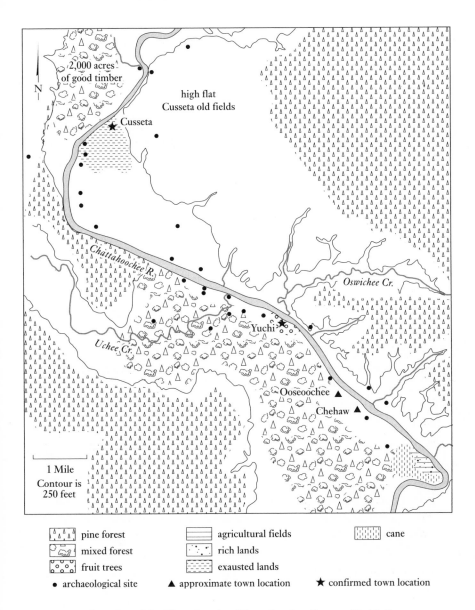

pine forest   agricultural fields   cane

mixed forest   rich lands

fruit trees   exausted lands

• archaeological site   ▲ approximate town location   ★ confirmed town location

FIGURE 7. A section of the Chattahoochee River, showing Cusseta, Yuchi, Ooseoo-chee, and Chehaw

ans, and they also used them as fuel.[29] Women gathered enough nuts in the early fall to last the year; the nuts were easily stored in the hull and could be used year-round. The archaeological record of floral remains at historic Creek sites shows that both acorn and hickory nuts were consumed, with hickory being the more predominant.[30] Bartram observed one Creek family with 100 bushels of hickory nuts.[31] On one occasion, when Hawkins visited a Creek hunting camp, the women told him that during the hunting season the whole camp often lived on hickory nuts.[32] Hickory nuts were easily made into an oil or "milk" by boiling the cracked nuts, hull and all. The oil rises to the surface and can be skimmed off.[33] Hickory oil was used extensively in cooking, for frying, as a seasoning, and as broth in stews. Bartram claimed this oil to be as sweet and rich as fresh cream.[34] Sweet potatoes in hickory milk were commonly served to white visitors. Bear oil was a popular substitute for hickory oil, but it would not have been so readily available.[35]

About ten miles below the Coweta Tallahassee hardwood stand, on the western side of the Chattahoochee, was the town of Yuchi. With about 1,000 people, Yuchi was one of the largest Lower Creek towns (see fig. 7). Hawkins believed this town to be situated in the best stretch of land on the river. The river valley here opens from a 50- to 100-yard-wide strip just south of the hardwood stand to a 2- to 3-mile-wide "flat." Hawkins listed the tree types around the town of Yuchi as hickory, oak, blackjack oak, and longleaf pine, but just south of there he also listed the specific species of southern red oak, post oak, and white oak. A pine forest spread over the uplands.[36] Two other towns in this section of river valley were Ooseoochee and Chehaw. These two towns had a close relationship, as evidenced by their combining both their households and their fields. Bartram was quite surprised at this relationship because the towns spoke languages "as radically different perhaps as the Mulcogulge's and Chinese." The Chehaws were Hitchiti speakers; the Ooseoochees (Ussetas in Bartram) were more than likely Muskogee speakers.[37] Their combined fields were located in a bend about a mile south of Chehaw. This point was the 1,000-acre canebrake mentioned earlier.[38] On the eastern side of the river the landscape was "a very delightful territory, exhibiting a charming rural scenery of primitive nature, gently descending and passing alternately easy declivities or magnificent terraces supporting sublime forests, almost endless grassy fields, detached groves and green lawns for the distance of nine or ten miles."[39]

The expanse of Chattahoochee River valley from Coweta to Chehaw is in a geological belt known as the Fall Line Hills. This belt conforms closely to the Fall Line ecotone, that ecologically rich region between the Piedmont and the Coastal Plain. Hence, it makes sense that the largest towns of the Lower Creeks would be located here. South of the Fall Line Hills, one enters the Coastal Plain and the geological belts known as the Red Hills and the Dougherty Plain.[40] In the Red Hills and Dougherty Plain belts, the floodplains along the river are wide and subject to much flooding. Only a few small towns were located south of the Fall Lines Hills (see fig. 2). About four miles south of Chehaw on the eastern side of the river, on "a narrow strip of good land" at the confluence of present-day Hitchiti Creek, was the small town of Hitchiti (the residents of which were Hitchiti speakers). Behind Hitchiti, to the east, were high hills and ridges covered in pine forests. Across the river the river valley was substantially wider, about two miles. But Hawkins evaluated this land as being of "thin quality," by which he meant the soils were not adequate for cultivation. He adjudged this by the small post oaks, hickories, and pines in the area. Hawkins concluded that the town of Hitchiti was poor and the people indolent. He also thought them friendly to whites and reported that "no charge of horse stealing from the frontiers has been substantiated against them."[41] For white officials, this statement would have been an important endorsement of the character of the people of Hitchiti.

Continuing downriver, the next town was Cheauhooche, which was actually not on the Chattahoochee but one and a half miles upstream of present-day Ihagee Creek. After passing Cheauhooche, one reached Patachoche. The people of Apalachicola, after they had abandoned their old town site, had built Patachoche. This town retained little if any of its former glory as the center of a Mississippian chiefdom. Patachoche was on the west side of the river in a "poor, pine barren flat," and only ninety people lived there. Their fields were likewise in poor land across the river. All in all, Hawkins commented that the town was "not now much in estimation."[42] Continuing south, the small Hitchiti-speaking villages of Oconee, Sauwoogelo, and Sauwoogelooche were strung within a few miles of one another downriver. The southernmost Lower Creek towns on the Chattahoochee were Eufaula, which was about fifteen miles south of Sauwoogelooche, and Okteyoconnee, which was about eight miles downstream of Eufaula. (There was also a town called Eufaula among the Upper Creeks.) All of these towns were small and located in low-lying terraces, but the active floodplains here were still arable. In a few cases, the towns were located on sections of high ground in mixed hardwood and pine forests; in others the towns were right in the longleaf forests.[43]

Unlike the people of Cusseta, whom Hawkins declared to "prefer roving idly through the woods and down on the frontiers to attending to farming or stock raising," he understood the people of these more southerly towns to conform to his ideas of good yeoman living. Apparently the people of Eufaula, in particular, had a new attitude. Forty years earlier, the English trader Thomas Bosomworth had described the Lower Creek Eufaula: "Chiefly composed of Runagados from all other Towns of the Nation, it is reckoned one of the most unruly, as they all Command and none obey."[44] In 1761 some of the people of Eufaula moved to present-day Florida, and by the time Hawkins visited them, according to him, they were quite industrious.[45]

All of these towns were located on only moderately rich lands, and Hawkins usually described them as "poor." But he was confident that they were inclined toward the plan for civilization, and he pointed to their fences and livestock as evidence. The people of Okteyoconnee especially fared well in Hawkins's eyes, since they had been given several black slaves from the British in payment for their services during the Revolutionary War. They called their slaves "King's gifts."[46]

Sometime in the late eighteenth century, many towns on the Chattahoochee River splintered, and most of the splinter groups settled towns on the Flint River, forming the easternmost Creek towns and the towns closest to the state of Georgia. One such town was the Yuchi satellite town of Padjeeligau, which translates as "pigeon roost" but was known by whites as "Buzzard's roost." Padjeeligau was about ten miles south of the intersection of the Lower Trading Path and the Flint River (see fig. 8). A few years before Hawkins's arrival in Creek country, renowned Indian hater, the one-eyed Benjamin Harrison, and his gang had attacked this outlying town, killed sixteen of the men, and left their decapitated bodies floating in the Flint. Afterward many people had moved closer to the central towns, and Padjeeligau now contained fifty families. It was situated on a small hill overlooking the northern section of a three-mile-wide and twenty-five-mile-long cypress swamp on the Flint River.[47]

The lower Flint is within the Dougherty Plain, which is a large limestone plain upon which swamps and ponds form; Hawkins called the whole "limestone land."[48] Padjeeligau sat in an oak and hickory forest, on Carr's Bluff, 150 feet above the swamp, where the land was rich and good for agriculture. Hawkins understood the river here to be a good fishery, and he thought the swamp might be useful for rice cultivation, in which the Creeks were already engaged and which Hawkins hoped to raise to a commercial scale.[49] But it was really the river cane and reed, which grew in the swamp along with large sassafras and sumac, that made the area valuable, and then as rangeland for livestock.[50]

On the southern edge of this swamp, the Indian countryman Timothy Barnard lived on his large ranch with his Yuchi wife and his eleven grown sons and daughters, all of whom had homes on the large expanse of property.[51] Other than the small Yuchi town of Intuchculgau, about fifteen miles west of Barnard's, only five small Lower Creek towns were on the Flint or its tributaries (see fig. 2). Another small Yuchi town, Toccogulegau, had been recently settled on present-day Kinchefoonee Creek, a tributary of the Flint.

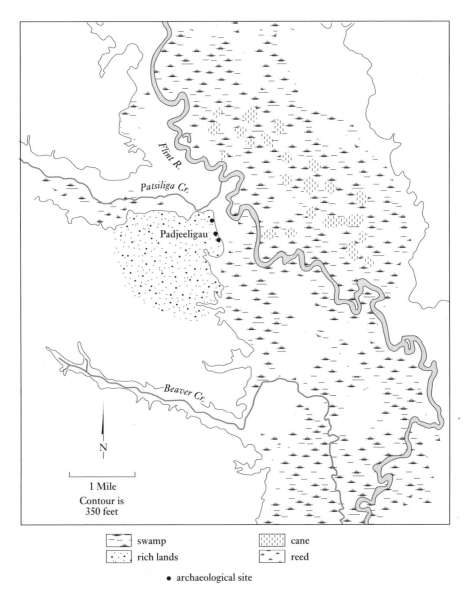

swamp

rich lands

cane

reed

• archaeological site

FIGURE 8. A section of the Flint River, showing the Lower Creek town of Padjeeligau

There were also the small Hitchiti towns of Hitchetoochee, or "little Hit-chiti," and Tuttallosee, or "Fowl Town," and the Chehaw towns of Aumu-cullee, or "pour on me," and Otellewhoyaunau, or "Hurricane Town." All of these towns except Tuttallosee were on the lower Flint or its tributaries and surrounded by swamps, ponds, and longleaf pine forest. They were not well situated for agriculture, since all only had access to small pieces of arable land.

However, the cane and reed in the surrounding lowlands and the grasses of the longleaf forest made the whole a good place for ranching, and Hawkins noted, with some satisfaction, that most of the people of these towns had herds of cows, pigs, and horses and good fences.[52]

Tuttallosee, however, was located on the headwaters of a stream the Creeks called Tuttaloseehatchee and which is known today as Fowltown Creek. The length of Tuttaloseehatchee's floodplain was covered in a hardwood/pine forest of post oak, black oak, hickory, dogwood, and longleaf pine. Hawkins described these floodplains as "level, rich and fine for cultivation." He also related that the people of Tuttalosee, who numbered only around fifty, were "decent and orderly and are desirous of preserving a friendly intercourse with their neighbors."[53] By neighbors, Hawkins undoubtedly meant the Georgians. Given Padjeeligau's experience, these border towns certainly had cause to desire friendly relations with Americans. Finally, the southernmost Creek household on the Flint was another sprawling ranch, that of the notorious métis Jack Kinnard.[54]

About ten miles north of Padjeeligau was the office and plantation of Benjamin Hawkins, known as the Creek Agency, located near the Lower Trading Path at the Flint River in present-day Crawford County, Georgia. One visitor to the Creek Agency described it as "handsome and romantic." Still it was a working plantation, though subsidized.[55] The Creeks had assigned, rent free, the land for Hawkins's Creek Agency to him in the 1802 Treaty of Fort Wilkinson. However, Hawkins did not own the property. He reported to Georgia governor John Milledge that he did not personally own the land, and that if the Creeks ever ceded it to Georgia, any title he held would be extinguished.[56] Hawkins did not elaborate on from whom he had received his land grant; he only said the land was assigned to him by "the Chiefs."[57]

The Creek Agency consisted of the home of Hawkins and his family, houses for the dozens of slaves they owned, and a cotton gin, saw- and gristmills, a blacksmith shop, and a tannery (see fig. 9).[58] Hawkins, his wife, and his children lived at the agency, although the children sometimes attended school in Milledgeville, Georgia. About seventy black slaves worked there as well as two Moravian missionaries and other white assistants hired to run the mills, blacksmith shop, and tannery or to perform other duties.[59] Hawkins's wife, Lavina Downs, managed many of the day-to-day activities, as Hawkins was usually engaged in public duties.

Whites on official business typically stopped at the Creek Agency before entering Creek country. If he were at home, Hawkins would introduce the guests to the plan for civilization, issue passports, and otherwise accommo-

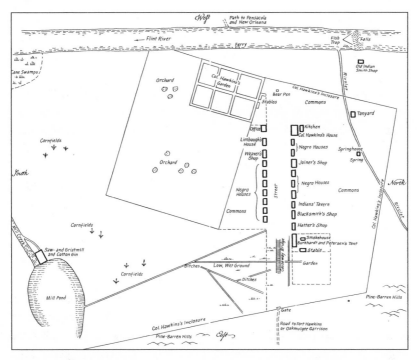

FIGURE 9. Hawkins's Creek Agency on the Flint River. From a plan drawn by F. H. Shuhman, 1810. (Moravian Archives, Winston-Salem, North Carolina. Redrawn for publication in Henri, *Southern Indians*. Copyright © 1986 by the University of Oklahoma Press.)

date the party. In fact, any non-Creeks venturing into Creek territory were required to present themselves to Hawkins or one of his assistants for a passport. So the agency served as a clearinghouse for whites and blacks and other Indians in Creek country, at least for those on legitimate business.

Hawkins also induced Creek men and women to visit the agency, in part so that they could see firsthand the methods that the plan for civilization proscribed for a well-organized farm. Hawkins's goal was to make the agency a self-sufficient working model of the plan for civilization. As he put it, "At the agency, we tan and dress our leather, make our saddles, shoes, boots, and clothing, do our blacksmiths, coopers and carpenter work and shall soon make our tinware and hats. We begin to enjoy real independence by depending on ourselves."[60] Hawkins hoped that by viewing his plantation, the Creeks would be swayed to the plan for civilization. At the agency, Creek visitors could view the new scientific farming techniques he wished them to adopt; they could inspect his orchards and cornfields and the drainage ditches his slaves dug to control the waters of a nearby swamp; they could sample his strawberries, radishes, or other subsistence crops with which he was experimenting; they could inspect the commercial crops such as wheat, rye, oats, and cotton that Hawkins hoped would do well; or they could tour the small school where cloth weaving was taught to teenage girls. To solicit Creek visitors, Hawkins insisted that Creek men and women wishing to speak with him make the journey to the agency.[61] He also dispensed medicine at the agency, free of charge, further prompting some Creeks to make the visit.[62] He even built an Indian tavern for their accommodation when they were there on business.[63] Hawkins also declared the agency a "public establishment" in that the mills, gins, and blacksmith shops were at the disposal of any Creeks participating in the plan for civilization and in need of such facilities, and he was pleased when Creek visitors began showing an interest in them.[64]

The Creek Agency, although on the easternmost boundary of Creek country and closest to the Lower towns, was still connected to the Upper towns via the Lower Trading Path, which crossed into the center of the Upper towns on the Tallapoosa River. Most of the large Upper Creek towns were located here, at the Fall Line of the Tallapoosa River valley. Like the Chattahoochee River valley, the Tallapoosa River valley was also within the ecotone of the Fall Line Hills. Hawkins described this thirty-mile stretch of river valley, especially the southern side, as "good flat land."[65] Here the Fall Line curves northward, forming a crescent shape as it begins its loop around the Missouri boot hill. The Fall Line Hills follow this line. The easternmost reach of the crescent-shaped prairie of the Black Prairie, the *hiyucpulgee*, hugs the southern edge of the Fall Line Hills.[66]

By 1796 Tuckabatchee only had about 460 people living in the town proper, but it was still the principle Upper Creek town (see fig. 10). Tuckabatchee, whose ancient name was once Ispocogee, was one of the head towns during the formation of the confederacy. But by 1800 both Tuckabatchee and Coweta could only claim some vague social precedence in Creek oral traditions, in the case of Tuckabatchee, through their ownership of some famous brass plates said to be of ancient origin (and, in fact, resembling some artifacts and symbols of the Mississippian Period Southeastern Ceremonial Complex).[67]

Tuckabatchee was located in one of the most beautiful areas of the river valley, about two miles below the Tallapoosa falls. The Tallapoosa falls must have been spectacular in the Historic Period; they were more than fifty feet wide and almost a mile long. The falls were actually divided into two steep channels: the eastern channel fell forty feet in fifty yards, and the western channel fell twenty feet in ten feet. Above the falls, for four miles the river was a one-half-mile-wide shoal. Cattle, horses, and deer congregated here in the

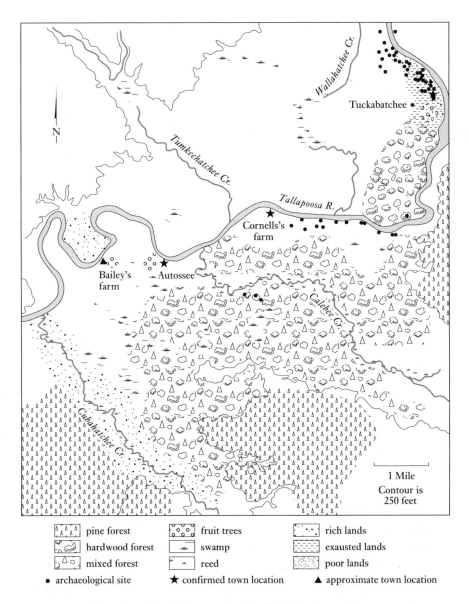

Legend:

- pine forest
- hardwood forest
- mixed forest
- • archaeological site
- fruit trees
- swamp
- reed
- ★ confirmed town location
- rich lands
- exausted lands
- poor lands
- ▲ approximate town location

FIGURE 10. A section of the Tallapoosa, showing Tuckabatchee and Autossee and Alexander Cornells's and Richard Bailey's farms

summer to eat the moss on the rocks, which was a source of salt. Swans, geese, and ducks wintered here. Four islands covered in old fields and cane were situated within these four miles. At the falls, the Tallapoosa cuts into Paleozoic rock, "light gray, very much divided in square blocks."[68] Hawkins was impressed with these rocks, which were "so nicely fitted and so regular as to im-

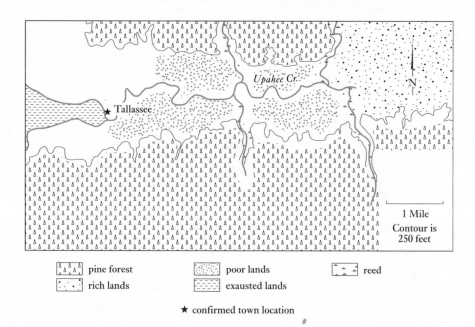

pine forest		poor lands		reed	
rich lands		exausted lands			

★ confirmed town location

FIGURE 11. The confluence of Upahee Creek and the Tallapoosa River, showing Tallassee

itate the side of an antient [*sic*] building where the stone had passed through the hands of a mason."[69] But he assessed the surrounding areas as poor for agriculture, noting the stony and gravelly land and the small post oaks, hickories, and pines. In fact, most of the river valley below the falls had small trees, like those of the Chattahoochee River valley, which probably reflected past agricultural activities.[70]

Upland longleaf pine forest formed the northern boundary of the valley. The uplands of the southernmost finger of the Ridge and Valley meet the Piedmont province here, and therefore the uplands can be quite steep and abrupt, sometimes forming high bluffs overlooking the river valley.[71] For instance, Hawkins mentioned two bluffs just south of the sharp bend to the west that the Tallapoosa makes at present-day Upahee Creek and where the town of Tallassee was located (see fig. 11).[72] These bluffs were high enough to give one an "extensive view of the town, the river, the flat lands of the opposite shore and a range of hills to the NW."[73] As mentioned earlier, Hawkins thought that Upahee Creek (which was known as Eufaula or Euphabee creek in the late eighteenth century) to be "the most valuable creek known here for fish," specifically sturgeon, trout, perch, rockfish, and red horse.[74] The Upahee floodplains were also fine agricultural lands, with plenty of cane and reed for livestock ranging. The people of Tallassee, numbering approximately 200, had begun to settle individual farmsteads along this stream to take advantage of these features.[75]

Hawkins, who always saw things with his developer's eye, found the lowlands of the Tallapoosa River valley to be somewhat uneven in economic usefulness. Put another way, he saw a great amount of ecological diversity in this area. Mostly the river valley was covered by the Southeastern Mixed Forest of oak, hickory, and pine. Hawkins noted specifically southern red oak, post oak, hard-shelled hickory (shagbark or shell-bark hickory), longleaf pine, and shortleaf pine. Swamps and secondary streams were interspersed throughout (see figs. 12 and 13). This expanse of river valley had some very rich agricultural lands, especially along the floodplain of Cubahatchee Creek. According to Hawkins, the slightly higher lands of the secondary stream floodplains were the better lands. He recorded tree types such as sassafras, red bay, willow, white oak, cypress, tulip poplar, cherry, ash, magnolia, persimmon, eastern white pine, and American beech in the secondary stream floodplains and around and in the swamps. He also noticed that the trees got much larger as one moved away from the river in these secondary floodplains. All of these streams had cane and reed growing in abundance along the edges of their entire length.[76]

The soils, likewise, were not uniform in their fertility. Hawkins understood Tuckabatchee to have been "on the decline" by the turn of the nineteenth century. He cited a recent war with the Chickasaws in which the town lost thirty-five men as one cause. But after speaking with the residents, he found that soil exhaustion and a lack of fuelwood were serious problems for the town as well. Plus, the river cane around the area was almost gone because of free-range ranching. Because of these problems, the people of Tuckabatchee had begun to move out of the town center and to spread themselves over the entire river valley.[77]

Figures 10, 12, and 13 show a number of Historic Period archaeological sites in a portion of the Tallapoosa River valley. Most of these sites probably represent households, not towns, and although they are not contemporaneous and represent only areas known through archaeological survey and excavation, they reflect a trend among both Upper and Lower Creeks by the late eighteenth century to scatter their households throughout a river valley. Before this time, Creek households were clustered around the town center in a tightly nucleated town plan.[78] In contrast, Caleb Swan, writing in 1791, described Creek households as "irregularly distributed up and down the banks of rivers and streams."[79] Hawkins also noted the dispersal of households throughout a river

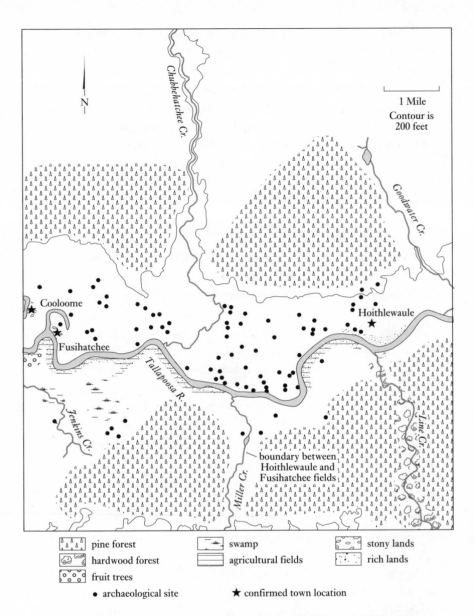

FIGURE 12. A section of the Tallapoosa River, showing Hoithlewaule, Fusihatchee, and Cooloome

valley. Since little archaeological work on Creek towns has been done to date, the evidence is inconclusive, but the pattern that is emerging, shows that Historic Creek towns maintained a concentration of households near the town centers while also dispersing throughout the river valleys. The archaeological evidence from Tuckabatchee, for instance, shows that the households of a

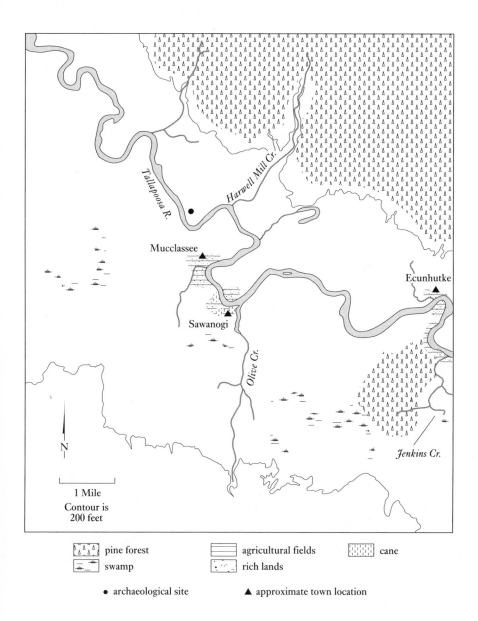

FIGURE 13. A section of the Tallapoosa River, showing Mucclassee, Sawanogi, and Ecunhutke

town center were relatively close together, only about 50 to 100 meters apart.[80] But the Creeks also had as many households widely spaced throughout the adjacent river valley. In short, a large percentage of Creek households were near the town center, but many Creek families lived up and down the river valley, within a day's walk or less of the town center.[81]

The typical Creek house was actually a compound wherein two to four structures surrounded an open courtyard.[82] A single nuclear family lived at the compound, but the basic domestic unit was an extended kingroup that the Creeks called the *huti*.[83] The Creeks were matrilineal, reckoning their kinship through the female line, and they were matrilocal, which meant that upon marriage the husband moved into his wife's *huti*. Thus the *huti* consisted of a cluster of nearby house compounds occupied by the members of a residential matrilineage—a woman and her husband and children and some of her female relatives, such as her mother, her mother's husband, her unmarried brothers and sisters and married sisters and their husbands and children, and perhaps even aunts and their families. Each *huti* varied in makeup, but most contained some extended family members. Members of the the *huti* shared and depended on one another for labor, land, and resources.[84]

The *huti* as a collective body owned the domestic structures. The town-owned agricultural fields were divvied among the town *hutis*, and each portion was worked by the women of a *huti*. The women of a *huti* shared most of the daily domestic tasks. Males in a *huti* fell into two categories: those connected by blood and those connected by marriage. Both had significant economic and social roles. Male economic contributions were predominantly meats and trade items. A man connected by marriage had little sanctioned voice in the decisions of his wife's *huti* (his clout rested with his own matriline). Only the adult males of the matriline participated in domestic decision making. Matrilineal blood ties also formed the strongest emotional, social, and obligational ties between men as well.[85] Like the women of a *huti*, the blood-related males of a *huti* shared tasks and pooled their labor.

In a matrilineal society, the children are considered to be "blood" descendants of only their mother. They know who their fathers are and usually live with their fathers, but the father is not a blood relation. Therefore, a father has little authority over his own child and little responsibility for his or her upbringing. In Creek society, a man was more instrumental in rearing his sister's children. In the case of divorce or the death of a parent, the children always belonged to their matrilineage.[86]

Creek women had the right to divorce, as did Creek men. Divorce was a simple affair. One partner declared a separation. In the case of the woman, she then deposited her ex-husband's belongings outside the compound. In the case of the man, he collected his things and departed.[87] No litigation was necessary, and many adult Creeks went through two, three, or more marriages in a lifetime and had two or three children per marriage. Women also had reproductive rights; abortion and infanticide, while not an everyday occurrence, were options.[88] The property of a *huti* was divided along kinship and gender lines. Creek men owned and were responsible for the manufacture or acquisition of the implements necessary in their activities, such as guns, ammunition, horses, saddles, bows and arrows, tobacco pipes, and war bundles. Women likewise owned and were responsible for the manufacture or acquisition of the implements necessary for their work, including baskets, seeds, hoes, ceramic containers, sifters, and horses.

Figure 14 shows a typical Creek household compound as drawn by William Bartram. Bartram drew four structures in the Creek household, but the number of structures actually varied depending on the number of people living there. Generally, one side of the compound had a pavilion, or summer house, which could be little more than an open-air shade house. On one side of the compound was a cooking area, which may or may not have been enclosed. Across from the cooking area was a storage building. These were sometimes two-story structures divided down the middle. One half of the structure was open on three sides; on the bottom story Creek men stored their deerskins, saddles, and other gear. The upper loft on this half was a "spacious airy pleasant Pavilion" where men lounged and received their guests. On the other half of the storage building, the upper loft was used as a corncrib, and the bottom room was used for storing corn, potatoes, and other produce.[89] Some families also had a separate "skin house," which was an enclosed storage shed for storing deerskins. The lodging house was an enclosed wattle-and-daub structure roofed with bark, with rounded corners and a central fireplace.[90] These were used as sleeping quarters and had small storage areas for personal belongings.

By the turn of the nineteenth century, some Creeks were building log cabins modeled after the American frontier style. These were basically horizontal, notched-log constructions made of unhewn logs with roofs of bark and gable-end chimneys. These houses became more and more popular throughout the first decades of the nineteenth century, and by the time of Removal, most Creeks lived in these kinds of log cabins.[91] Basil Hall sketched a Creek log cabin (see fig. 15). In this sketch, Hall clearly depicted a storage crib and an open space on one side of the house. Although the Creeks adopted the log cabin, they continued to arrange their structures around a central compound.

Enclosed places such as log cabins or lodging houses were the only truly private spaces for a Creek family; most activities took place out-of-doors in the yard compound or in the open summer house. Archaeology provides some clues as to what went on inside their houses. The excavations at Tuckabatchee uncovered artifact distributions that suggest a division of labor within the household. Ceramics and glass bead artifacts, things with which women would

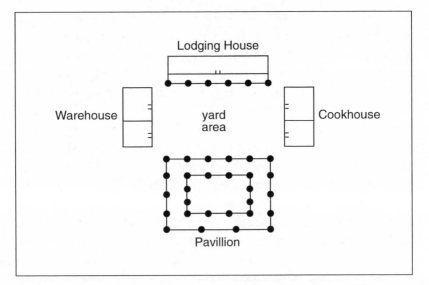

FIGURE 14. A Creek household, based on a drawing by William Bartram (Bartram, *Bartram on the Southeastern Indians*, 154)

have worked, are typically concentrated in the southwest and southeast corners of a Creek household compound. Lithic debris, the detritus of men's activities, are usually located on the side of the house opposite the ceramic concentrations. Archaeologists found concentrations of bottle fragments, mostly from liquor bottles, adjacent to the lithic debris and on the eastern side of the compound. Although it is premature to draw conclusions from such a small sample, the patterns suggest gender-specific activity areas and perhaps a symbolic opposition of summer and winter activities.[92] One well-documented activity that took place within a Creek household was the burying of the dead in the house floors.[93] When a family member died, the survivors dug an oval pit in the floor of the household, flexed the body into the fetal position, and buried him or her in the pit. Grave goods were common in eighteenth-century burials, including ceramic bowls, guns or gun parts, beaded necklaces and bracelets, the occasional silver gorget, a headpiece, or an armband.

Some people abandoned their house when an important family member died because they believed that the ghost of the deceased would haunt the house. People abandoned a household not only to escape ghosts but in the event of a fire or when the structures became old and not worth the increasing investment of time required by repairs. A family would abandon their whole compound and simply rebuild in an adjacent location.[94] Again, the archaeology at Tuckabatchee verifies these accounts; some of the houses at Tucka-

FIGURE 15. Basil Hall's sketch of a Creek log cabin, ca. 1830 (courtesy of the Lilly Library, Indiana University, Bloomington)

batchee appear to have been periodically abandoned.[95] Other than what archaeology can tell us, we know little of what went on inside the lodging houses and log cabins because accounts of Creek household activities are sparse. Creek families rarely invited white people inside their homes. Rather, they conducted their business in the public spaces, and if they desired private consultations, they conversed under the shade of the storage house. Hawkins was surprised on hearing of this, considering that some white people had been living in Creek territory for decades and had established close friendships and family ties with many Creeks.[96]

The men to whom Hawkins referred were traders who had married into Indian families, established farmsteads and ranches, owned slaves, and lived out their lives among their wives' people. They were known as "Indian countrymen."[97] Many of these men served as interpreters and assistants to Hawkins. Despite his harangues against the general lot of traders, some of these men, such as Timothy Barnard, became Hawkins's friends and confidants.

Although many had started as traders, most of the Indian countrymen had become ranchers by the late eighteenth century, but some, like Barnard, maintained their trading networks as well. Indian countrymen usually lived on individual farmsteads and ranches with their wives and their unmarried and married children.[98] These ranches and farms had a distinctively American flavor, with log cabins, outbuildings, and fenced fields.[99] Creek towns had granted these men large and small tracts of land, and they were considered citizens of those towns.[100]

Indian countrymen did not own the land on which their farms and ranches were located; rather, they were granted usufruct, or use rights, to it. A case involving the Indian countryman Richard Bailey exemplifies this land policy. In the 1798 National Council meeting at Tuckabatchee, Autossee headmen complained that Bailey treated the Indians with contempt, had "repeatedly declared his determination to live on their lands without their consent," and had declared that his farm was his private property. The National Council voted to have Bailey removed from Creek territory. Bailey denied the charges, and an altercation ensued. When the other white traders present entered the argument, Hawkins stepped in and calmed the situation.[101]

Richard Bailey passed away soon after this meeting, and his Creek wife then maintained his ranch. The Bailey farmstead was just west of Autossee, on the Tallapoosa River (see fig. 10). Her ranch consisted of their house, a stable, gardens, fenced yards for their stock, fenced fields, a small peach tree nursery, beehives, and peach trees.[102] Bailey owned 200 head of cattle, 120 horses, 150 hogs, and 7 slaves.[103] Other than some of the experimental fields, Bailey's fields, and those of other mixed households, may have more resembled the multicropping of Creek fields, since the Creek wives were responsible for the agricultural duties.

Because his letters have been collected, the most well-known Indian countryman in Creek country was Timothy Barnard. His ranch, as already mentioned, was located on the Flint River, about twenty-five miles south of the Creek Agency. Barnard and his family lived in an American-style house. His adult children and their families settled "with and around" Barnard's household, and the whole group attended to the ranch. Barnard, who was a rancher, not a farmer, did not put his land into commercial agricultural production. Rather, he maintained "a garden well stored with vegetables" as well as peach and nectarine trees. He also had a vineyard, begun with some vines that Hawkins gave him. His herds were large and comprised of not only cattle and hogs but sheep, goats, and "stock of every description."[104]

By the end of the eighteenth century, the métis children of Indian countrymen and Creek women were establishing large American-style plantations. Alexander McGillivray, for instance, had a plantation near Tensaw on the Little River, just above Mobile. He also built another plantation in Creek country called "Old Tallassee" (also referred to as "Little Tallassee"), on the Coosa River, just north of its confluence with the Tallapoosa. McGillivray's Creek plantation resembled that of prosperous American planters. Here McGillivray kept about sixty slaves, all of whom lived in slave quarters. He hired a white overseer to supervise his slaves. McGillivray's house was a log house with dormer windows and a stone chimney. He had two small orchards of apple trees. He kept a large stock of horses, hogs, and cattle and hired some white drovers to maintain them.[105] The plantation was abandoned after McGillivray's death, and by 1796 some dilapidated buildings and peach trees were the only things left of this once prosperous plantation.[106]

The farm of Hawkins's métis assistant Oche Haujo, or Alexander Cornells, was on the Tallapoosa, just downriver from Tuckabatchee, the town of which he was a headman. Cornells's farm consisted of a house, stables, fenced fields, and outbuildings (see fig. 10). Cornells owned nine slaves. He had a plum and peach orchard. He raised a considerable number of cattle and hogs and, as a favor to Hawkins, 150 sheep to see how these animals would fare in the southern climate. Devoted to the plan for civilization, Cornells experimented with various cash crops, and he had fields planted in rye, oats, and cotton.[107]

Alexander Cornells had agreed that Hawkins could place one of his "public establishments" near his farmstead, in this case principally a blacksmith shop.[108] Hawkins set a second public establishment among the Upper Creeks at Tuckabatchee and a third among the Lower Creeks at Coweta.[109] Like the one at Cornells's, these public establishments initially were merely blacksmith shops, but Hawkins hoped they would be the future sites of saw- and gristmills and cotton gins. Hawkins once suggested that the Creeks build an American-style school, but they were adamantly against the idea because they felt that American-educated Indians were "troublesome and mischievous."[110]

The evidence is unclear as to whether or not the public establishments ever achieved the stature for which Hawkins had hoped. There are some hints that cotton gins and saw- and gristmills other than those at the Creek Agency may have been built. In 1809 Hawkins reported, "The erection of a grist mill was murmured at by the Indians and the addition of a saw mill opposed by those in opposition."[111] Alexander Cornells may have had a cotton gin on his farmstead.[112] In 1801 a miller at Tuckabatchee complained that the Indians treated him so badly that if they did not change, he would close the shop.[113] This, of course, implies that a miller operated a shop at Tuckabatchee. No traces of these mills and shops have yet been uncovered by archaeologists, and Hawkins only directly mentioned saw- and grist-mills and cotton gins as being at the Creek Agency.[114]

Blacksmith shops definitely were established; the Creeks had requested such as part of the Treaty of Colerain and the Convention of Washington.[115] In 1808 the Upper Creeks hired a blacksmith and paid him out of their federal stipend, the money paid to the Creeks by the United States for land purchases.[116] In 1812 the Upper and Lower Creeks requested an additional blacksmith each, placing two in each division. Hawkins also listed two gunsmiths in the Creek territory in 1809.[117] The blacksmiths made spinning wheels and looms, and they engaged in other kinds of metalwork for the Creeks and whites residing among them.[118] Hawkins insisted that the smiths limit their metalwork to repairs and to making implements necessary to the plan for civilization.[119] However, in 1811, as partial payment for allowing the Federal Road to run through their territory, the Upper Creeks requested that one and a half tons of iron per year for three years be transported to their towns.[120] Why the Upper Creeks desired such a large quantity of iron is not known, but undoubtedly blacksmiths were involved if the iron were used for making metal implements.

The small town of Autossee was just west of Cornells's plantation, on the south side of the river, just across from Bailey's ranch (see fig. 10). When Hawkins wrote his *Sketch of the Creek Country* in 1799, an unnamed disease had recently struck Autossee, and almost half of the population had been lost. Typically, when disease struck a southeastern Indian town, most of the townspeople would fall ill, and therefore no one could attend to daily tasks. Perhaps this is why Hawkins believed the town to be a "poor, miserable looking place."[121]

Traveling along the "river path" from Bailey's ranch, Hawkins next came to Hoithlewaule, or "to share or divide out war," so named because in the past this town had the right to declare war (see fig. 12). Hoithlewaule was situated on the northern side of the Tallapoosa and within the shadow of a high red bluff.[122] There was a narrow strip of arable land around the town; the rest was cypress swamp. Their fields were in the floodplains on the opposite side of the river, which is also where they grazed their livestock. Hawkins, who saw this as the height of mismanagement, conferred with the townspeople about this arrangement and encouraged them to move across the river, to spread out on individual farms down Ofuckshe Creek (present-day Line Creek), and to fence their fields. The latter two suggestions, of course, were part of the plan for civilization. Apparently the town could not agree, as he later reported that the "town divided against itself." Hawkins, in his unapologetic ethnocentric way, was convinced that any reasonable, hardworking person would see the benefit of his suggestions. He wrote that only the "idlers and ill-disposed remained in town."[123] A better interpretation (and one that Hawkins would have done well to understand) is that perhaps those who chose not to follow the plan for civilization are the ones who stayed in town. Hoithlewaule later was one of the towns to divide against itself during the Red Stick War.

Two miles downstream was the town of Fusihatchee, from *foosowau*, "a bird," and *hatche*, "tail."[124] Like Hoithlewaule, Fusihatchee was located on the northern bank of the river, and its fields were in the narrow floodplain on the opposite side (see fig. 12). The fields of Fusihatchee met those of Hoithlewaule at Noocoosechepo Creek (present-day Miller Creek), which formed the boundary between the two. At their western boundary, the Fusihatchee fields were joined by those of Cooloome, a small town about a mile west of Fusihatchee, as the crow flies. Although once located on the opposite side of the river where old fields and some remnants of the town now stood, when Hawkins visited Cooloome, it was on the northern side of the river, on a terrace that was flooded about every fifteen years. According to Hawkins, people had begun to move farther from the river because of this. A high, rocky bluff abutted this portion of the river valley.[125] Rocks regularly sheared off the cliffs, "splitting and bursting to pieces, scattering their thin exfoliations over the tops of the grassy knolls beneath."[126]

The soil around Cooloome was "broken," which meant it was not well suited for agriculture. Hence their fields were also across the river, which was at this point about 300 yards wide and 20 feet deep. The fields of Cooloome and Fusihatchee, which were about 100 to 200 yards wide, stretched for four miles along the river's edge. (Hawkins does not specify if all of this was in cultivation or if some of these fields were fallow.) A large swamp abutted the backside of the fields. Hawkins deduced that the swamp could be drained and opened to corn and rice cultivation. A thirty-foot diameter, ten-foot tall, conical mound was in or near the Cooloome fields, along with several large peach trees. The size of the peach trees and the presence of the mound may indicate that both were relics of some antiquity. Fruits did well here. The people of Cooloome and Fusihatchee were renown for their melons. They took such pride in them that the people would hail travelers from the path just to give them the best melons from their fields, when in season.[127]

The next three towns, before the confluence of the Tallapoosa, Coosa, and

Alabama Rivers, were small and not well situated. These were Ecunhutke, or "white ground"; Sawanogi, a Shawnee town; and Mucclassee (see fig. 13). All three towns were located on small rises in low-lying areas subject to flooding. A cypress swamp that was especially prone to destructive flooding was just west of Mucclassee. Ecunhutke and Sawanogi had their fields on both sides of the river to take advantage of the small patches of arable lands. Those of Mucclassee were just below the town, but Hawkins noted that these people had some fenced potato fields within the town.[128]

About ten miles downstream from Mucclassee, in a convoluted juncture, the Tallapoosa River joins the Coosa River to form the Alabama River (see fig. 16). Indians had lived at this confluence perhaps since the Early Archaic Indian Period, and Hawkins noted five mounds on the bluff formed in the point where the Coosa and Tallapoosa meet. Archaeologists now understand these mounds to be the remains of a palisaded Mississippian town that dates to the Middle Mississippian Period, ca. A.D. 1200. This Mississippian town had been abandoned long before De Soto came through the South in the 1540s. But sometime in the seventeenth century some Alabama Indians migrated to this area as the Creek Confederacy began to form. In 1717 an Alabama Indian headman, known only as the grand chief of the Alabamas, invited the French to build a fort near them. They built Fort Toulouse on the forty-six-foot-high bluff where the Indian mounds were. Fort Toulouse was abandoned in 1763, but during the period of the fort's occupation, several Alabama towns were located in the vicinity.[129] By the late eighteenth century the Upper Creek town of Tuskegee (an Alabama town) was located near the site of the fort.[130] By this time, all that remained of the fort were "brick bats" scattered on the bluff and five iron cannons (with the trunnions broken off), which the people of Tuskegee displayed in the square ground.[131]

This confluence is large and complex. River activity accounts for much of the topography, vegetation, and soils around this confluence. The bluff where Tuskegee was located was and still is subject to serious scouring by the Coosa in times of high water, so much so that in 1751 the original Fort Toulouse had found itself dangerously close to the edge. The old fort was abandoned and a new one was built.[132] As the Coosa meets the Tallapoosa, it curves westward, forming a 1.5-by-2-mile-wide, low-lying cove. This was the area of the 3,000-acre canebrake mentioned earlier, a clear indication of river and probably agricultural disturbances as well as of fertile soils. The Creeks informed Hawkins that a third of this floodplain had been under cultivation "in times past," but when Hawkins visited the area in 1799, it was fallow, with small oak and hickory trees and giant river cane growing thickly along the edges of the

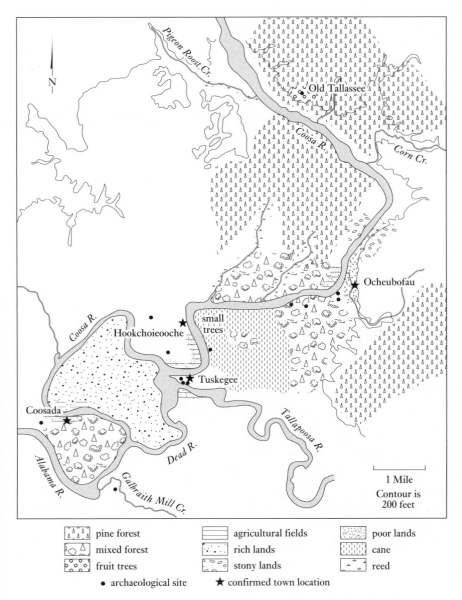

FIGURE 16. The juncture of the Coosa and Tallapoosa Rivers, showing Coosada, Tuskegee, Hookchoieoooche, and Ocheubofau

rivers. On the southern edge of this floodplain, formed by the Tallapoosa River, the soils were a distinct white clay. The longleaf pine forest, as usual, characterized the uplands.[133]

The people of Tuskegee, however, did not take advantage of this rich cove. They had their fields in the floodplain on the other side of the Tallapoosa

River and in the rich land below the bluff. Tuskegee was a small town of about thirty-five families. Hawkins viewed the town as quite progressive, since the people were ranching in earnest. He noted that they had perhaps the most livestock of any town in Creek country—some cattle "and a fine parcel of hogs." Hawkins singled out Sam Macnac, an uncle to Alexander McGillivray's children (probably McGillivray's wife's brother), a Tuskegee métis who had 180 cows. In an unusual statement, Hawkins also mentioned a single apple tree claimed by Tuskegee but "now in the possession of one of the Chiefs of Hookchoie."[134]

Hawkins's statement bears investigating. According to the early-twentieth-century Creek informants who worked with the anthropologist John R. Swanton, sometime in the Historic Period a group of Alabama Indians asked to join the square ground of the Muskogee town of Okchai (Hawkins refers to this town as Hookchoie). "The Okchai said, 'All right; you can seat yourself on the other side of my four backsticks and I will protect you. They did so, and for some time afterwards the two tribes busked together and played on the same side in ball games."[135] The Alabama left at some point because of a dispute about a ball game. They moved to the confluence of the Coosa and Tallapoosa and named their new town Okchaiutci (which Hawkins spells Hookchoie-ooche), or "Little Okchai."[136] Hawkins described Hookchoieooche as a "pretty little compact town," but he reported that it had recently relocated because of some Chickasaw raiding. The inhabitants still ranged their livestock around their former location but had their fields in some "rich low grounds" just south of the new location, an area they called Sambelloh (see fig. 16). This oral tradition helps account for the intermingling of households between Tuskegee and Hookchoieooche that Hawkins also observed. Both were Alabama towns. It could also help explain Hawkins's observation about the Tuskegee apple tree. Since Hookchoieooche and Hookchoie more than likely would have maintained social ties, it would not be unusual for a Hookchoie man to claim an apple tree in Hookchoieooche or, by association, Tuskegee.

Hawkins reported that Sophia Durant, the sister of Alexander McGillivray, had fenced some of the fields in Sambelloh. This is somewhat puzzling, since the McGillivrays, who once all lived in and around Alexander McGillivray's plantation, Old Tallassee, left the plantation after his death and settled Ocheubofau, also known as Hickory Ground. Sambelloh may have been common property, in which case Durant would have had free access to the rich fields. It is just as likely that since the soils around Ocheubofau were stony and gravelly, Durant applied to the people of Hookchoieooche and Tuskegee to lease some portion of Sambelloh. Hawkins had a bad impression of Durant. He found her "poor, and dirty in a small hut, less clean and comfortable than any hut I have seen belonging to any Indian however poor."[137] He also thought she mismanaged her eighty slaves, but he simply did not understand how many Creeks conceived of and used slaves.[138]

Across the river from Tuskegee was the most prominent feature formed by the merging of these rivers: a large island known today as Parker Island (see fig. 16). This island is really a product of the hydrological process that takes place when a meander gets too large. When this happens, a new stream forms at the path of least resistance at the neck of the meander, forming an island, at least temporarily, until the meander is cut off altogether from the river, at which point it forms an oxbow lake. With Parker Island, a meander in the Coosa River forms three of its sides; the meander is connected at its neck by present-day Dead River. Hawkins did not have much to say about this island, except that the people of Coosada planted most of their crops on this "high, rich island."[139] His descriptions reveal the area of this confluence to have contained the mixed pine, hickory, and oak typical of the Southeastern Mixed Forest in the Fall Line Hills. The uplands that bordered the north were dominated by a longleaf and shortleaf pine forest, although these upland pines tended to be smaller than those in the longleaf ecosystem of the Coastal Plain. The southern edge led into the Black Prairie.[140]

Coosada was another Alabama town, located on the Coosa River across from the southern shore of Parker Island. The land around Coosada was likewise bordered by a wide meander where the Coosa and Dead Rivers converge to form the Alabama. This cove, like all the land in this area, was rich, although Hawkins failed to mention the vegetation types here. He did, however, notice more mounds in this area. The people of Coosada had also recently begun to raise hogs and some cattle.[141] Below here, on the Alabama River, were the remaining four Alabama towns, each with about 200 people. These were Ecunchate (from *ecunna*, "earth," and *chate*, "red"), Toowoossau, Pauwocte, and Attaugee. Ecunchate and Toowoossau faced each other across a mile-wide peninsula formed by a great meander of the river (see fig. 17). Toowoossau was more favorably located on a high bluff with some rich soils around it. Ecunchate sat in a low-lying area, which Hawkins described as "of a thin quality" and with a lot of ponds. The whole was in oak, hickory, and pine. Pauwocte, like Toowoossau, was also on a bluff overlooking the river, with level and rich lands all around. All three towns cultivated the floodplain in the peninsula across the river. The floodplain of this peninsula, on the inside curve of the meander, was covered with giant river cane, which undoubtedly reflects former agricultural activities. The towns still cultivated these lands.[142]

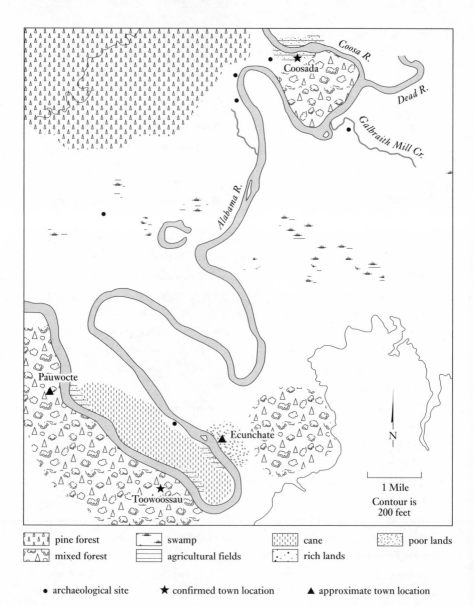

[pine forest symbol]	pine forest	[swamp symbol]	swamp	[cane symbol] cane	[poor lands symbol] poor lands

| [mixed forest symbol] | mixed forest | [agricultural fields symbol] | agricultural fields | [rich lands symbol] rich lands |

● archaeological site   ★ confirmed town location   ▲ approximate town location

FIGURE 17. A section of the Alabama River, showing Coosada and three Alabama towns

Attaugee was four miles south of Pauwocte, near the confluence of present-day Autauga Creek. Unlike the other Alabama towns, which Hawkins uniformly described as "compact," Attaugee spread out for two miles along the river. This is in the Black Prairie of the Coastal Plain. Hawkins paid particular attention to this area, perhaps because it was so sparsely populated and, in his opinion, under utilized. Despite the numerous swamps and wet areas, he thought the area could be productive, especially for ranching, probably because of the many canebrakes and the abundant grasses. Also, peavine, a particularly good forage for cattle, grew in the floodplains that ran through this section of the Coastal Plain.[143] The people of Attaugee had already taken advantage of the good ranging possibilities; they had horses, cows, and hogs. This probably also accounts for the dispersed pattern of their town. Hawkins always looked for good agricultural lands, and he assessed the stream floodplains in this area as such. These floodplains obviously had not been cleared for agriculture in the past, since the tulip poplars, southern red oaks, hickories, and walnuts were large.[144]

The people of Attaugee had a custom that Hawkins found curious. Although they preferred not to have much to do with whites, they were friendly and hospitable to any who passed through their towns. But when the white person finished eating, any remains were thrown away. Plus, as soon as the whites left, the Attaugee washed whatever they had touched.[145] Considering Creek ideas on purity and impurity, the Attaugee probably understood whites to be impure and thus felt it would be dangerous to keep anything from which they ate or to not purify anything they touched.[146]

Other Upper Creek towns were located above the Fall Line on the upper reaches of the Coosa and Tallapoosa Rivers, in the areas of the Abihka and Oakfuskee provinces, respectively. These are too numerous to discuss individually, but I can characterize some of them. Above the Fall Line, the Tallapoosa moves through the Piedmont while in Alabama, then it enters the Blue Ridge province, where its headwaters are located. The Coosa, above the Fall Line, demarcates the eastern line between the Ridge and Valley province and the Piedmont.[147] The Ridge and Valley province, which extends from New England into central Alabama, was once an ancient coastal plain onto which sediments from the Appalachian Highlands were deposited. At the end of the Paleozoic (270–600 million years ago), a geologic event occurred in which the crust now represented by the Piedmont and the Blue Ridge Mountains was thrust to the earth's surface, squeezing the ancient coastal plain between them and the hard metamorphic rocks of the Appalachian Highlands. The resulting topography was the famous folded mountains of the Ridge and Valley. From a bird's-eye view, the province looks like an accordion, with alternating ridges and valleys. As an ancient coastal plain, the province had many swamps filled with treelike ferns and much organic material. These ancient swamps and organic materials now form the coal and iron ore deposits for which this region is famous. In the Alabama portion of the Ridge and Valley, iron ore and coal are relatively close to the earth's surface, which Hawkins noticed. These deposits later made northern Alabama and Birmingham a booming mining district.[148]

During the late eighteenth century, however, the area was thinly populated. As one moves up the Coosa past Old Tallassee and enters the Ridge and Valley, the topography abruptly becomes steep and rocky, and the vegetation is mostly small pines, oaks, and hickories. In his *Sketch*, Hawkins noted only a few small towns in the sixty miles from Tuskegee to the town of Coosa. Except for Wewocau, these were all located a fair distance up secondary streams, and hence they were closer to the upper Tallapoosa towns than to the Coosa River. These were Woccoccoie, Opilthlucco, Pochusehatche, and Pucantallahassee, all of which had about forty to fifty families and were located on small creeks, with fertile but small floodplains (see fig. 2).[149]

Certainly one of the most beautiful areas of the upper Coosa River in the eighteenth century was between the confluences of Nauchee Creek (present-day Tallaseehatchee Creek) and Eufaula Creek (present-day Talledega Creek), just north of present-day Childersburg, Alabama. The Abihka provincial towns of Coosa, Aubecooche, Eufaulauhatchee, and Nauchee were located in this vicinity (see fig. 18). Coosa, which bore the name of the protohistoric Mississippian chiefdom centered in northwest Georgia, was settled by the descendants of some of the Coosas sometime in the eighteenth century as the Creek Confederacy began to coalesce. Aubecooche was the eighteenth-century name of Abihka. Nauchee was the Muskogean pronunciation for the Natchez, some of whom had sought asylum here in the mid-eighteenth century after their defeat by the French in present-day Mississippi.[150] Hawkins described this area simply as a "high and beautiful hill," the land "waving and rich," with "fine springs."[151] The people also reported that in the spring the creeks were full of fish, especially rock trout, buffalo, red horse, and perch. There is much limestone in this particular ridge and valley, and Hawkins saw some "fine large limestone springs." He also reported a large cave nearby, most certainly the one known today as DeSoto Cavern.[152]

Hawkins was impressed with the upper Coosa and its environs. Surveying it for its usefulness to the plan for civilization, he noted the reed along the creeks, the peavine in the hollows and hillsides, and the moss in the stream beds. Although the ridges could be high and rocky, the stream floodplains were very fertile and lovely, and the valley floors were covered in oak, hickory, poplar, and mulberry. Pines grew in especially craggy areas. Giant river cane was somewhat limited here, but reed was common along these upland streams. Hawkins was careful to note that once one moved into the uplands, one could

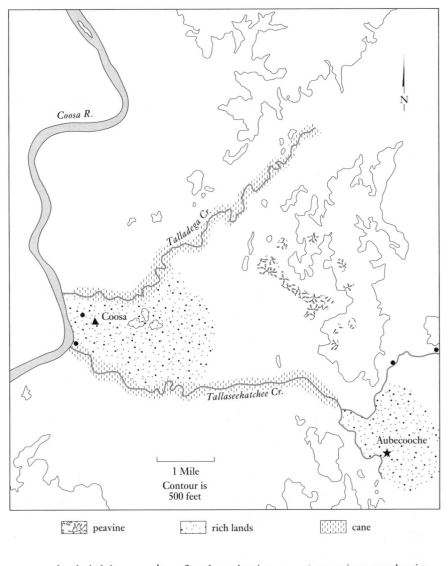

Coosa R.

Talladega Cr.

Coosa

Tallaseehatchee Cr.

Aubecooche

1 Mile
Contour is
500 feet

N

▨ peavine ⬚ rich lands ⬚ cane

● archaeological site ★ confirmed town location ▲ approximate town location

FIGURE 18. A section of the upper Coosa River, showing Coosa and Aubecooche

find a certain moss that grew on the rocks of the stream shoals and that wild animals and cattle ate for its salt. This was probably meadow spikemoss, *Selaginella apoda*.[153] The townspeople further informed Hawkins that there were also some salt licks in the uplands.[154]

On the Tallapoosa, the uplands were in the Piedmont physiographic province. The Piedmont extends from the Hudson River in southeastern New York state into central Alabama. Although formed by an altogether different geologic event, the Piedmont is thought of as the foothills of the Appalachian Highlands. It is underlain by a variety of metamorphic and igneous rocks and hence has a varied topography. The elevations are not so high, but the topography varies from rolling hills to some steep ridges to relatively wide river valleys.[155] The Southeastern Mixed Forest ecoregion roughly corresponds to this province.

Sixteen Upper Creek towns stretched along the upper Tallapoosa, with the most northern, Auchenauualgau, or "cedar grove" (discussed in Chapter 3), located in the transition between the Piedmont and the Ridge and Valley (see fig. 2). Below this, in the Piedmont proper, the Upper Creek towns were well situated in fertile alluvial river valleys. Certainly these valleys are not so extensive as those in and below the Fall Line, but they were the sites of some populous towns, in particular those of the Oakfuskee province. "Oakfuskee" translates as "in a point," and the name describes its eighteenth-century location in a curve of the Tallapoosa River about thirty-five miles northeast of Tuckabatchee. Oakfuskee, taken with all of its numerous satellite towns, was the largest township in the Creek Confederacy. Oakfuskee had about 180 families, and there were approximately 270 more families in the satellite towns.[156]

Oakfuskee and its satellite towns were located in typical Piedmont settings. The river valleys of the Piedmont range from about a half-mile wide to a few hundred feet wide, and every town was situated near a section of fertile floodplains that contained the agricultural fields. Peach trees did especially well in the Piedmont, and Hawkins noted many towns had thriving groves of them. Hawkins generally characterized the surrounding uplands of the Oakfuskee towns as "stoney hills" and gravelly, and he noticed extensive rock outcrops in a few stream valleys as well. The hills and stream valleys were in oak, hickory, and pine. Hawkins specifically named southern red oak, black oak, and post oak. He also occasionally remarked on the pine forests of the higher elevations, which also contained American chestnut. Cane and reed stood along the stream edges, and the salty moss grew on the rocky shoals throughout the Piedmont. In some cases, giant river cane covered large portions of the river floodplains. Hawkins usually remarked that the floodplain trees were small, which would indicate that the areas had once been cleared for cultivation.[157]

Some Piedmont towns were better situated than others. For instance, by Hawkins's standards, the town of Kialijee had "nothing to recommend it."[158] It was located at the juncture of the Tallapoosa River and Kialijee Creek, and the poor and gravelly land around it was unfit for cultivation and bore only small oak, hickory, and pine. Hawkins also reckoned it as the poorest range-land in the nation.[159] In contrast he considered the Hillaubee towns, which included Hillaubee, Thenooche aubaulau, Aunette chapco, Echuseisligau, and Ooktauhauzausee, to be located in one of the best areas of the upper Talla-poosa. The Hillaubee towns were small; most had about twenty families each, although by 1799 only one headman, Enchauthlucco Haujo, and his family remained in the main town, Hillaubee. Everyone else had moved out, along present-day Hillabee Creek and its tributaries. Although surrounded by gravelly and stony uplands, the floodplains of these streams were especially rich, as evidenced by the amount of reed in them. The hickory and oak masts, which occurred every other year, were abundant, and the creek beds all had rocky bottoms covered in meadow spikemoss. The people of Hillaubee, living in the best rangeland in the Piedmont, had been involved in ranching for some time. This is probably why most people had moved out of Hillaubee. In fact, most of the Oakfuskee towns were heavily engaged in ranching, and people were moving their households along secondary streams for access to good rangelands.[160]

The heart of Creek country was in its river valleys, but the whole historic landscape constituted Creek country. I have endeavored to show that the landscape, the animals, the plants, and even the insects did not form a mere back-drop to Creek country—they were Creek country, as much as were the towns and people who also constituted it. The people of Creek country mostly resided in the heart of this landscape, but they were instrumental in forming the whole of this landscape; they gave it meaning, and their lives were intertwined with it. This relationship between the people and their landscape was one of the most important in Creek country; indeed, at the turn of the nineteenth century, it defined Creek country.

CHAPTER FIVE

THE PEOPLE OF CREEK COUNTRY

The people of Creek country at the turn of the nineteenth century were quite diverse and included not only descendants of the original provinces that coalesced to form the Creek Confederacy but other Indians who had sought refuge in Creek country throughout the Historic Period, foreign Indians who had married or were related to citizens of Creek country, individuals from various European countries, Americans, and African slaves or descendants of African slaves who had either run away from slavery or who were freedpeople that thought that life would be easier among the Indians. The progeny from the genetic mixing of these people were also part of the citizenry of Creek country. There were other social enclaves as well. Because it was originally composed of several disparate groups, the Creek Confederacy, as other southeastern coalescent societies, was cross-cut by several divisions. There were township affiliations that ran strong, there were multiple clan divisions, there were divisions based on gender and age, there were linguistic divisions, and there were civic divisions of war (red) and peace (white) towns.[1] In addition, divisions existed between those who favored Euro-American reforms and those who did not, and by the late eighteenth century there was a corresponding widening gap between the wealthy and the poor. Stitching these factions together into a workable collective were kin relations and township structures. Through the structures of kinship and township, long-term social institutions such as town councils, blood revenge, reciprocity, and matrilineality governed behavior and directed most individual and collective decisions.[2]

Of these, one of the deepest and most abiding affiliations and loyalties for a Creek lay with one's township. Unless there were a crisis of international proportions, members of the Creek Confederacy rarely referred to themselves as Muskogee. People usually considered themselves Yuchis, Alabamas, Coosas, Cowetas, Cussetas, Chehaws, Hitchitis, Tuckabatchees, Oakfuskees, and so on.[3] For these reasons, whites often described Creek towns as distinct "tribes." Hawkins uses the terms "tribe" and "town" interchangeably. Other whites did the same, often causing much confusion. Thomas Woodward, an American who lived with the Creeks as a young man, was critical of one account of Creek life, saying that the author never could distinguish between a tribe, a town, or a clan.[4] But even modern scholars have not yet explored the full nature of the political, social, mythical, and religious ties binding national, provincial, town, and clan identities and affiliations for the Creeks and other southeastern coalescent societies.

During its formation, the provinces of the Creek coalescence admitted immigrants as townships. In a province, the townships were divided along red and white moieties, or war and peace towns. The townships of a province may also have been ranked into a hierarchy.[5] War and peace towns, or red and white towns, were long-term civic institutions among the southeastern Indians.[6] The war towns provided leadership in matters of war; the peace towns provided leadership in matters of peace. Exactly what constituted matters of war and peace among the historic southern Indians and how these may have changed during the colonial years, however, has not been fully sorted out. For instance, among the Chickasaws, during the early years of the Indian and European trade in the late seventeenth century, when trade was largely a matter of capturing slaves, trade was associated with warfare, and hence the war (red) leadership made most decisions regarding trade with Europeans. However, the Chickasaw peace (white) leadership challenged this monopoly within the first four decades of the European trade, and they eventually gained some say in it as well.[7]

The dual organization of the Creeks into red and white towns is still cloudy. There is evidence that the early-eighteenth-century provinces had their own red and white town divisions. In other words, the Abihka province had both red and white towns; the Tallapoosa province had both red and white towns, and so on.[8] When refugee towns sought admittance to a province, they may have entered as citizens of the peace towns. Among the Chickasaws, the peace towns were responsible for the *fanimingo*, or office of the Squirrel King, which was the institution that solidified relations between the Chickasaws and outside groups through a symbolic adoption of the group. During the first century of colonization, when refugees sought admittance to the Chickasaws, they were admitted through the *fanimingo* and hence entered as citizens of the peace towns.[9] There is evidence that the Creeks had a similar institution, although the *fanimingo* among the Creeks has received only a small amount of scholarly attention.[10] In some cases, several affiliated towns sought admittance to the Creek Confederacy as a group, such as the Alabama towns. In the latter cases, it may be that the towns seeking admittance did not enter entirely as peace towns but merely transplanted their own divisions of red or white towns. In other words, the Alabama province would then have its own internal division of red and white towns.

As the Creeks had to deal with Europeans and territorial rights throughout the eighteenth century, the Creek Confederacy began to take political and territorial form.[11] It appears that the provincial polity organization and the war/peace dual organization were gradually eclipsed by the Upper and Lower divisional organizations and the more inclusive national umbrella of the Creek Confederacy.[12] The red and white divisions within a province, in fact, may have been replaced by a single red and white division within the Upper Creeks and within the Lower Creeks.[13] There is also evidence that the duties associated with the red and white towns were truncated by the turn of the nineteenth century as well. For instance, white towns usually served as sanctuaries. One could escape revenge and retaliation if one could make his or her way to a white town, because blood was not to be spilled in a white town. In 1812 Hawkins reported that an Upper Creek warrior who had killed some Americans and was being pursued by the warrior police took refuge in Tallassee, a white town. The warrior police entered the square where the man sat, and they shot him "through the head and body."[14] In former times, such actions would have been unthinkable.

As these organizational principles began to fade, Tuckabatchee and Coweta, the "mother towns," claimed status as divisional capitals. The townships, although still united by this hierarchy of organization, acted independently. Each township made its own decisions and formed its own alliances with whomever it could make common cause. The townships could sometimes act together as red or white towns, as a province, division, or nation, but the structural rules dictating how, which towns, and when this should happen are ambiguous.[15] The people of a township understood themselves as belonging in a distinct category, separate from other townships and with some differing patterns of life. For example, each town practiced a slight variation of the

Green Corn Ceremony, or Busk, a harvesttime festival and ceremony of re-newal.[16] Townships also had their own or variations on common legends and myths.[17] In his *Sketch of the Creek Country*, Hawkins often remarked on the differences between townships. For instance, Hawkins understood Aube-cooche (Abihka) and Tuckabatchee to have been of ancient origin, and he at-tributed Abihka with the origin of some of the most ancient customs among the Creeks. In contrast, he wrote that the Alabama villages on the Alabama River did not "conform to the customs of the Creeks." In particular they did not have the Creek law of adultery, which among the Creeks was punishable by thrashing, cutting a piece out of the adulterer's ears or nose, and cutting his or her hair. Alabama men also helped the women in their agricultural duties, even forgoing hunting if need be.[18] This was unheard of among most Creeks. In another case, Hawkins adjudged the Tuskegees, who were originally in the Alabama province but who probably were descendants of the Koasati subset, to be more Creek than Alabama. By 1799 the Tuskegees had "adopted the customs and manners of the Creeks," and they had lost their original lan-guage, which was probably in the Alabama-Koasati language group. They now spoke Creek.[19]

Hawkins reported that the Yuchis also "retain all their original customs and laws and have adopted none of the Creeks." In particular he noted that Yuchi men, like Alabama men, helped the women in their agricultural tasks and that divorce was less common than among other Creeks. Apparently Hawkins thought highly of the Yuchis. He claimed that their women were more chaste, that their men were better hunters, and that they were generally more indus-trious than their neighbors. As evidence, he noted their peach trees and the worm fences "in and about their town," which, in Hawkins's eyes, were indi-cators of economic development and proper land use.[20]

The basic political unit of the Creek Confederacy was the township, or *talwa*. Townships consisted of a square-ground town (also known as the *talwa*), associated non-square-ground towns or *talofas*, and affiliated individ-ual farmsteads.[21] (For ease of reference I will henceforth refer to townships as such and to square-ground towns as *talwas*). The *talwa* was the central town of a township. It was the largest and contained the public buildings for the town councils and ball games. The *talofas* were smaller towns that had been settled by a splinter group from the *talwa*, but they remained closely affiliated with their *talwa* and participated, as much as possible, in the town councils, ceremonies, and other events.[22] *Talofas* sometimes were located near *talwas*, in some cases in the next stream valley or just across the river. The *talofas* of Oakfuskee, for example, were just upstream from the *talwa* (the town of Oakfuskee); those of Hillaubee were likewise on nearby tributary streams. In other cases, *talofas* were several miles away. As we have seen, the Yuchi, Chehaw, and Hitchiti satellite towns were on the Flint River, but their *talwas* were on the Chattahoochee, about sixty miles, or two days' travel, away. Individual farmsteads retained an affiliation with their *talwa*, although these, too, could be many miles away. No doubt such distances prevented regular intercourse with the *talwa*, but the fact that each *talofa* and farmstead claimed an identity with its *talwa* indicates that each participated, to some extent, in the affairs of the central town.

The number of satellite villages per *talwa* varied over time. In the late eighteenth century, Tuckabatchee had none. Cusseta had only one, Upatoi. Oakfuskee had at least seven. Yet the small town of Hitchiti had three: Cheauhoochee, Hitchetoochee, and Tuttallosee. The reasons for such disparities are unclear.[23] According to the Creeks, *talwas* split when their fields became exhausted, when the population became too large, or when firewood ran short.[24] *Talwas* also split because of internal factionalism. As in any small community, the people in Creek towns did not always get along. In Creek society, consensus and balance in life were highly valued, and when a party could not reach a consensus or could not maintain decent and civil comportment, for whatever reason, toward fellow townspeople, one mechanism for mediating these tensions was withdrawal. In large disputes, a whole family or group would withdraw from the community and establish a *talofa*. Even so, the *talofa* maintained close relations and affiliations with its *talwa*, and over time, tensions would subside.[25]

Hawkins lists some *talofas*—for example, Tuttallosee (Hitchiti) and Intuchculgau (Yuchi)—as having recently established their own square ground, and archaeologists believe there may have been a council house at Upatoi, the Cusseta *talofa*.[26] What this meant in Creek eyes is uncertain, and Hawkins does not elaborate. One supposes that a *talofa*, by building its own square ground, could separate entirely from its *talwa* and become a real township. Since not all disagreements fade with time, perhaps some withdrawing factions sought such a separation. The towns Hawkins mentioned in this context were located several miles from their *talwas*. Perhaps the people simply grew tired of traveling to their *talwa*, had concerns of their own, reached a suitable size, or became more distant socially, politically, and economically from their *talwa*. They decided to handle their own affairs and symbolically communicated this to others by building their own square ground.

Talwas were instantly recognizable because of the public buildings and the town plaza (see fig. 19). The public buildings included the square-ground cabins and the rotunda. A rotunda was a large, circular, wattle-and-daub construction with a central fireplace. The Creeks called it *tcokofa*, or "hot house," probably because it resembled the domestic "hot houses" that were a part of Creek households in earlier years.[27] Before commercial hunting became integral to Creek life, household compounds also contained a semisubterranean, closed, circular house known as a hot house. The hot houses were used in winter as a family's lodging. However, Creek families quit building hot houses with the ascension of the deerskin trade, probably because whole families spent the winter months in the woods, and the communal rotundas could serve as winter sleeping quarters for the old and young who stayed in town.[28] Only a few Historic Period rotundas are known archaeologically. At Fusihatchee, archaeologists located the remains of three rotundas. These rotundas were built at different times, so only one stood at a time.[29] At Okfuskenena, or Burnt Village (a town burned in 1793 by the Georgia militia and subsequently abandoned), archaeologists likewise discovered the remains of three rotundas; again, all of them were built at different times.[30]

The rotundas at Fusihatchee and Okfuskenena indicate that the Creeks built these edifices by constructing outer walls of wooden posts in a circular pattern and then placing four to five larger support posts in the center of the building. They then built a hearth in the middle of these support posts. The roof was conical and covered with bark or thatch. Additionally, cane was woven through the wall posts, and the whole structure was plastered with mud. The rotundas at Fusihatchee averaged about fifteen to twenty meters in diameter; those at Okfuskenena were about fifty meters in diameter.[31] Raised seats or benches covered with woven mats circled the inner wall.[32] The rotunda served as a meeting place during the winter and in inclement weather, much like the town plaza, and as sleeping quarters for people who did not go hunting during the winter.[33]

The people of Sawanogi (on the Tallapoosa River; see fig. 13), however, had a different kind of townhouse, which reflected their distant origins. Sawanogi was a Shawnee town. We know very little about the Shawnees except that their history is one of extraordinarily complex movements from Pennsylvania to the Savannah River to the Great Lakes to Maryland. Archaeologists propose that the Shawnees may have originated in the upper Ohio River valley, which would also account for their different townhouse at Sawanogi.[34] Hawkins described the Sawanogi townhouse as an eight-foot, oblong, square structure with the roof and sides covered in pine bark. The residents spoke Shawnee and retained "the manners of their countrymen to the N.W."[35]

Adjacent to the rotunda was the town plaza, a large rectangular area swept

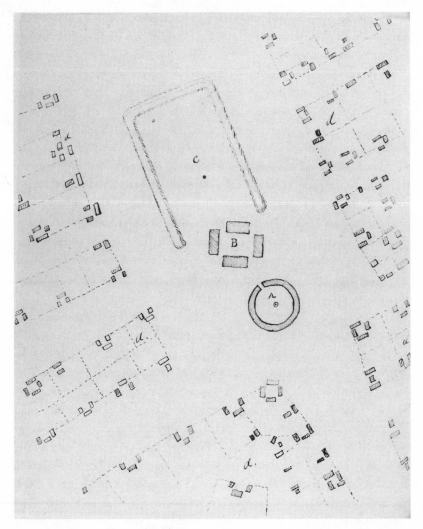

FIGURE 19. William Bartram's sketch of a Creek town, ca. 1770. (Courtesy of the National Anthropological Archives, Smithsonian Institution. This drawing is in Edwin H. Davis's copy of William Bartram's "Observations of the Creek and Cherokee Indians, December 15, 1799.")

clean and sometimes enclosed by a raised earthen embankment. During the day the plaza was a place to meet, socialize, and do business. In the late eighteenth century, Creek men especially spent most of their day at the town plaza playing games, socializing, haggling with resident traders, and tending to town and personal affairs. Because of this, many whites visiting Creek towns witnessed the women hard at work and the men hanging around the plaza.

Observers depicted Creek men as lazy and addicted to gambling and rum, while the women kept the bodies and souls of their families together.[36] Creek men did spend much of their day at the plaza when they were in town, so these white people saw what Creek men did when they were at home. They were seldom at home, however, since their occupations of hunting, trading, war, and with the increase in stock raising, livestock herding required prolonged absences from their towns.

During the hunting season, women also were usually absent from the towns. Women prepared the hides on hunting expeditions, and they usually accompanied their husbands or male kin on prolonged trips. However, a woman could opt to stay at home. So during certain times of the year when the men and some women were away, usually the fall and winter, there was a disproportionate number of adolescent and adult females and elderly people in Creek towns. On Hawkins's first travels through Creek territory, he happened into the towns during the winter. He was received by females, many of whom were teenage girls and unmarried, young adult women. These girls and women were delighted to have a visitor; they prepared meals and lodging for Hawkins, gave him a tour of their towns and fields, and consulted extensively with him on the plan for civilization and the place of Creek women in it.[37]

Everyone returned to the towns during the spring and summer agricultural season. The men, as mentioned, spent much of their time together in the plaza, but they also used this time to repair or rebuild the public buildings or work on their own homes or those of their kinspeople. The women also spent most of their day together. The women of a *huti* tended their fields in the morning, taking advantage of the cooler part of the day. In the afternoon they would gather at one of their compounds to sew, cook, and make pottery, baskets, and other implements used in the household or in farming.[38] As needed, groups of women would also make forays to gather firewood, to collect water, or to gather nuts and other wild foods, in part for one another's company but also because it was safer to go in numbers. They shared child-rearing tasks, sought comfort with one another, and consulted with each other on almost everything. During this season the men helped clean and burn the fields but left the planting and tending to the women and children.

In the agricultural season the late afternoons and evenings were a time to socialize. Townspeople gathered in the plaza to visit, play games, gamble, drink, and perform their various dances. By nightfall the plaza was filled with great and raucous activity. Creek men and women loved to dance adorned with turtle-shell rattles and accompanied by musicians on drums, flutes, and gourd rattles. Their dances took place in the plaza (or the rotunda if the weather were bad) and continued into the night.[39] The plaza also served as a field where people played various games such as chunky, which involved rolling a stone disc and throwing poles, as well as a game called *thlechallitchcau* or "roll the bullet."[40] The plaza was sometimes called a "chunky yard." Drinking rum, another favorite pastime of the Creeks, was not a solitary affair. Evening gatherings in the plaza often included much drinking of alcohol and often resulted in arguments and disorderly behavior.

Visitors were expected to participate in the evening gatherings. While visiting Tuskegee, William Bartram joined in one evening and "had a grand entertainment at the public square, with music and dancing."[41] Some white visitors were not so amused, and they complained about being kept awake into the morning hours by the uproar around the plaza. For instance, in 1812 John Innerarity, the testy agent of the John Forbes Company (formerly Panton, Leslie, and Company of Pensacola) visited Tuckabatchee for several days to discuss the Creek trading debt to the company. After facing a deadlock in council, Innerarity retired to his visitor's house. This was obviously unacceptable to the Creeks, and Innerarity was besieged all night by drunk men beckoning him to the plaza. This happened every night of his stay and aggravated him beyond words.[42] Hawkins mentioned that his days in Creek towns were extra long because after speaking and meeting with various men and women all day, he was expected to participate in the evening festivities, excusing himself only after midnight.[43] Hawkins strongly disapproved of drinking and was a teetotaler, something the Creeks thought strange. Even so, Hawkins's choice to participate in the plaza activities must have set things right, as he never described enduring an evening like that of Innerarity.[44]

Most Creek *talwas* also had a ball field in an area cleared for that purpose on the outskirts of town. Basil Hall described an early-nineteenth-century Lower Creek ball field as "in the bosom of the forest" in a grassy area cleared of trees covering a 20-by-200-yard area. At either end stood two poles about six feet apart. The game was similar to modern lacrosse, and using ball sticks, the object of the game was to get a small leather ball through the poles.[45] The Creeks, as well as most of the southeastern Indians, had been great ball players and spectators of ball games probably since the Mississippian Period, and they still play the game today.

The ball games pitted teams of men from opposing towns against each other in a turbulent contest with few rules.[46] Women apparently had their own version of the ball game, but ordinarily the two sexes did not play together.[47] Ball games were big affairs with large teams and many spectators from competing towns crowding around the field. The Creeks gambled heavily at the games; piles of goods bet on the outcome were displayed around the field. In the ball game, known as the "little brother of war," men honed some of the skills needed in warfare: agility, swiftness, and considering the roughness of the game, bravery and a tolerance of pain from personal injury.[48]

Hall described the ball game he witnessed here. Hall and his Creek friends went to the ball field at the appointed time one morning, but no one was in sight. Over the next three hours women and children gathered at the field, but the players still had not shown. Hall reported that one could hear them in the woods performing their songs and rituals and preparing for the game. Hall eventually went to inspect their preparations. He found forty or fifty players "lying flat on the grass, seemingly in a state of listlessness, or fatigue," apparently from the previous night's dances and rituals. Further on, he came upon some players painting themselves for the game. They painted one eye black and one yellow, and several others were placing long black feathers in their turbans; yet others were "fitting their naked bodies with tails, to resemble tigers and lions, having already daubed and streaked themselves over from head to foot with a variety of colours . . . in making them look as much like wild beasts as possible."[49]

The opposing team suddenly advanced from the woods onto the field, with a loud cry and "in a most tumultuous manner, shrieking, yelling, hallooing, brandishing their sticks, performing somersets [sic], and exhibiting all conceivable antics." They, too, were dressed only in their paint, tails, turbans, and slight breechclouts, and Hall remarked that all of the players were athletic and fit. The opposing players, once on the field, danced around the poles at their end of the field and then proceeded to the middle of the field, where they squatted in a cluster, waiting for their opponents. The opposing team appeared, performed a similar dance, and also squatted in the center of the field. "The two groups remained eyeing one another for a long time occasionally uttering yells of defiance." Then, "at a signal from one of the chiefs, the two parties suddenly sprung to their feet, brandishing their sticks over their heads."[50] But the game still did not begin.

The teams settled down and stood facing each other in silence while a deputation of men counted and inspected the players to ensure even play. An elderly man stepped forward and talked about fair play and the importance of the game. As soon as he finished, the players took their positions over the field, with two of the most expert stationed near the goalposts as guards. Finally, a referee moved to the center of the field and threw the ball into the air. Hall described the action in some detail. Basically the players, each with two sticks, attempted to grab, pass, or run the small ball through the goalposts. The other team attempted to stop the opposing players by any means. The game was assuredly rough and accompanied by yells that, according to Hall, made his blood run cold. Hall was almost seriously injured as a spectator when the players, oblivious to boundaries, plowed through the crowd gathered at the margins of the field. As Hall recounted, "The ball pitched within a yard or two of the spot where I was standing. In the next instant a dozen or twenty Indians whizzed past me as if they had been projected from cannons. I sprung to the nearest tree, as I had been instructed, and putting my hands and legs round, embraced it with all my might."[51] After the game, the teams joined for celebrations that usually included drinking and fighting.[52]

The most important public space in a Creek *talwa* was the square ground. The Creeks called the square ground the *tcoko-thlako*, or big house, probably because it resembled the layout of a Creek house.[53] The square ground was an open plaza surrounded by four "cabins" and with a place for a fire in the middle.[54] Archaeologists have identified one of these at Fusihatchee.[55] The square ground was the focus of all formal public events, and this is where the town councils met unless the deliberations required privacy, in which case the council would retire to the rotunda.[56]

The town council was the body politic responsible for all town decisions. It was also a male affair. The council consisted of all ranked and unranked warriors. Each rank had an associated public office, but the ranks and offices differed slightly from town to town. Generally, each town had its headmen, or *micos*.[57] The *micos* were sometimes divided into *mico apotkas*, or vice *micos*, and *micalgis*, or collective vice *micos*, although all men of this rank probably used the appellation of *mico*.[58] There were also the *isti atcagagi*, or beloved men, who were elderly men who had gained prominence through their prowess in war, as makers and keepers of peace, through their savvy in trade, or perhaps as the spokespersons of their clans.[59] This was the term the Creeks gave to Hawkins.

There was no electoral process in designating a headmen. The town council made the decision. Once the council decided that a man deserved this rank, they approached him in council; called to him "in a loud, long, and shrill tone by a name that he is thereafter to go by"; and then smeared his face with white clay.[60] Almost all towns claimed to have several *micos*. In 1802, for instance, Creek headmen submitted a list to Hawkins for dividing up the federal stipend. The list included the number of *micos* and distinguished warriors. Only two towns, Wewocau and Tooseehatchee, listed one headman. Many towns listed two headmen, but the majority of towns listed anywhere from four to eighteen.[61] This list should not be considered definitive, since it may represent only those people entitled to a portion of the federal stipend, and we do not know how the towns decided this. Still, it indicates that almost all of the towns had several headmen or that vice headmen were considered *micos* in some capacity.

Town headmen were probably warriors of a certain rank who had demonstrated abilities in council or war. There are hints that headmen may have been chosen from certain clans or were clan representatives, but this is by no means certain.[62] George Stiggins stated that in "former times," Creek headmen were more despotic, rude, and "more frequent in their mandate of tyranny" toward their townspeople.[63] By the late eighteenth century, Creek headmen in no way had despotic power. The power of Creek headmen seems to have come from excelling in masculine enterprises such as warfare, oratory, council, trade, spiritual pursuits, and as the eighteenth century wore on, wealth and influence with Euro-Americans.[64] For instance, many headmen were medal chiefs, or men who had received medals from the United States for their friendly attitude toward and willingness to cooperate with federal and state officials.[65] In other words, some men may have been headmen simply because the U.S. government designated them as such. Thomas Woodward was explicit about this. He wrote, "The Indians soon learn who the whites look upon as being their leader, and not being as ambitious of distinctions as the whites generally are, when any talking or compromising is to be done those persons are put forward."[66] Hawkins likewise showed favor to men who were well disposed to his office, the United States, and the plan for civilization.

Adult Creek men were ranked according to their exploits in war. A Creek warrior could attain the rank of *tastanagi*, or warrior; *imala*, a rank below *tastanagi* that was an advisory or assistant position; or *tastanagi tako*, or great warrior. The *tasikyalgi* were unranked warriors.[67] According to Hawkins, the highest rank a warrior could achieve was that of *isti puccanchau thlucco*, or great leader, but few ever achieved this title because it required many successes in war over many years.[68] Other offices include the *hiniha*, or dance leaders, and the *hobaya*, or prophets, who accompanied war parties and knew all the rituals and taboos of war. In addition to the rank titles, warriors received descriptive appellations such as *hadjo*, or mad, which signified not insanity or lack of control but that a man could be reckless and not mindful of his own safety in war. Another was *fikisiko*, which translates as "no heart" or "heartless," meaning that a warrior showed no mercy toward his enemies.[69]

The Creeks took warfare very seriously, and every man in a town avidly sought war titles and to be ranked. A warrior's rank depended on his accomplishments in warfare, usually signified by the number of scalps he had taken but also by talents such as swiftness, bravery, stealth, and a certain recklessness. By the end of the eighteenth century, however, any frontier hostilities by the Creeks and other Indians could have calamitous results if the federal or state governments became involved. This curbed some acts of warfare, but the cult of the warrior was so deeply rooted among the southeastern Indians that Indian men continued to pursue war titles through acts of warfare as well as through more unconventional means such as theft and raiding white frontier farmsteads.[70]

When gathering for council, the officers and warriors, "with a grave, sedate, consequential deportment," gathered at the square ground and took their assigned seats.[71] The cabins, known as the warriors' and *micos*' cabins, were built of wattle and daub and were roofed, but the sides facing the plaza were open. Inside, rows of benches divided into compartments faced the plaza. One cabin was reserved for the headmen, or *micos*; their assistants; any white officials (Hawkins usually took a seat in this cabin); and any visiting *micos* from other towns or Indian groups. The ranked warriors sat in one cabin, and the unranked warriors took places in the remaining two cabins.[72] The warriors' cabins were decorated with the emblems of war. Scalplocks, painted red, hung around the open side. The wooden posts were carved with figures of snakes, raptorial birds, panthers, and other creatures, some of which may have represented clan totems. The walls were painted with various animals as well as some mythical characters with mixed human and animal traits, such as a man with horns. Some figures had human bodies and heads of animals such as ducks, turkeys, bears, foxes, wolves, or deer. These creatures were depicted in various poses, some of which were sexually explicit. The rotunda and some domestic structures were painted in a similar fashion.[73]

Town councils were formal affairs where sobriety and proper conduct were strictly enforced. Women could not enter the rotunda or square ground when deliberations were in process. They prepared food for the men in attendance and discreetly left it at one of the four entrances to the plaza.[74] Council meetings took place every day, and the men discussed town issues, listened to grievances, and appointed work units when necessary. Depending on the issues brought up, council meetings could last a few hours or several days.[75] The day's deliberations were timed by the burning of a spiral of cane splints in the center of the yard. The end of the spiral was lit when the council began, and deliberations continued until the spiral was completely burned. This could sometimes take hours.[76]

Council meetings opened with passing the pipe or calumet, a symbolic gesture of goodwill, and the black drink ceremony. In the black drink ceremony, a young warrior, suitably purified and trained, prepared and served *Acee*, the black drink, which was a decoction of *Ilex vomitoria* (commonly known as yaupon or cassena), a plant high in caffeine. The men would drink the black drink, and then some minutes later some might regurgitate. This ritual ensured purity and, according to Louis LeClerc Milfort, Alexander McGillivray's brother-in-law, sobriety.[77] All attendees could smoke throughout the deliberations, and the men circulated pipes continuously. The council began with a speech by one of the leading orators in the town. All ranked warriors had the right to speak during council; unranked warriors attended as helpers and to run errands, but they could not give their opinions.[78]

In council, oration was the primary method of manipulating public opinion. Oratory was highly valued among Creek men, and many gave lengthy speeches during council.[79] White officials recorded Creek speeches during treaty negotiations and other big affairs. Hawkins recorded several lesser talks with Creek leaders. Creek talks, couched in the language of diplomacy, were moving and full of allegories and were often intended to soothe hurt feelings and defuse tempers.[80] However, when circumstances demanded it, Creek men in council could be demanding and to the point. Although they had no official voice, southeastern Indian women influenced public opinion and councils by influencing their male kin through informal channels. According to Hawkins, southeastern Indian women could be quite stubborn, persistent, and protective of their rights.[81] In sending his regards to a friend's wife, Hawkins once commented that he "must send her a chapter on the rights of my Cherokee daughters, to the end that if she has any contest with the commandant, she may easily prove at all times that she is in the right."[82]

The Creeks attempted to establish some cohesion of the separate township polities through the National Council, which met once a year, usually in late spring. We do not know how long the National Council had been in existence when Hawkins arrived. Some believe Alexander McGillivray instituted it; Hawkins bragged that he created it, but there is some evidence that it began much earlier.[83] At any rate, the National Council was a meeting of all the Creek towns, Upper and Lower. National Councils were modeled on the town council and were usually held at Tuckabatchee or Coweta. Both towns had a special square ground for the National Council. These have not been found archaeologically, and they may not have been permanent buildings but temporary structures built for a National Council meeting. At the National Council square ground, twelve cabins were arranged around an open plaza, in groups of three cabins on each side. These cabins were similar to the cabins at a town's square ground, except they were larger and painted white. About sixty people could be comfortably seated in one cabin.[84] A Speaker of the Nation was elected to preside over the National Council.

The Speaker of the Nation was actually two men—one Upper Creek and one Lower Creek—who took on the role as Speaker depending on where the National Council was held that year.[85] The speakership was an elected office wherein all warriors of rank voted for their preferred candidate. The Speaker's duty was to "deliver the voice of the Nation."[86] He conducted himself like other headmen and had no symbolic accoutrements or special privileges associated with his office. The office held some power because it was the Speaker with whom U.S. officials wanted to conduct business. However, these men led only so far as public approval and support allowed. They were elected because they had proven diplomatic skills, especially with regard to Americans. If they promoted policies not in line with general public opinion, they were turned out of office and, in some cases, killed.[87]

National Council meetings were grand occasions. Not only did Creek headmen and warriors attend, but most of their families, Indian countrymen, Hawkins, and any other person with business for the Creek Confederacy. Each town contributed beef, pork, corn, tobacco, cassena, or other foodstuffs for the meetings.[88] Hawkins, as the U.S. representative, supplied flour, sugar, coffee, and other foods not so readily available in Creek territory.[89] As at the town councils, liquor was not permitted, and attendees were expected to conduct themselves properly. Although Hawkins was present, he did not attend the meetings unless he was asked to do so. Other white men, most commonly those associated with the trade but also any white man who had an issue to present to the Creek Confederacy, convened at Tuckabatchee or Coweta during the National Council, but they also were not permitted to enter the square unless they were summoned.[90]

The National Council opened with the same ceremonies as the town councils, namely the calumet and black drink rituals. After ensuring purity and goodwill, the Speaker of the Nation delivered a speech on the history and traditions of the people, exhorting them to courage and bravery and "to sacrifice everything for the love of nation and liberty."[91] Afterward, every man of rank spoke his piece. Participants listened attentively, with no chatting, indecent remarks, untimely applause, or immoderate laughter.[92] The council deliberated on all matters until they were resolved or postponed for a later meeting.[93]

The purpose of the National Council was to attend to national affairs. Affairs between townships, provinces, and divisions were discussed at the National Council, although white men were usually not privy to these talks, and the discussions about these issues, therefore, are mostly unrecorded.[94] Land cessions and boundary lines were usual topics of debate with the white attendees and, therefore, were recorded. The collective debt of the Creek Confederacy came up in these discussions as well, since the debt and land payments, as we shall see, were intimately connected. The National Council was also the forum for resolving disputes with and evicting some of the white traders living among the Creeks. The Creeks viewed the National Council as the appropriate place to address international affairs, not only with the United States but also with other Indians.[95] Although the alliance ultimately failed, some members of the Creek Confederacy, Big Warrior in particular, endeavored through the National Council to form a Council of the Four Nations, wherein the Cherokees, Chickasaws, Creeks, and Choctaws would present a united front to the United States.[96] When Tecumseh made his appearance before the Creeks, he did so at the National Council meeting in Tuckabatchee.[97]

Often the National Council deliberations revolved around Hawkins's agenda. This, in part, reflects the documentary evidence, since Hawkins recorded only those meetings he was allowed to attend; but it is also a measure of his influence and his office. The U.S. government insisted on dealing with the Creek Confederacy as a nation, with a representative government, and Hawkins, in turn, used the National Council as such. Hawkins needed to have some sort of accountability on the part of the Creeks. He continually reminded the National Council that the United States would consider any infraction against any white as a hostile act of the Creek Confederacy as a whole.

The leaders of the National Council took Hawkins's words to heart. By the first decade of the nineteenth century, the leadership of the National Council was dominated by the wealthy, market-oriented Creek men who had a vested interest in paying attention to the confederacy's relationship with America. After all, they were gaining economic, social, and political prominence by so doing. Led by these men, the National Council passed decrees introduced by Hawkins such as revoking blood revenge, instituting punishments for horse thieves and murderers, and appointing "warrior police" wherein each town appointed a warrior to act as a chief magistrate.[98] In a few cases, they made decisions to punish wrongdoers and appointed men to carry this out.[99]

Still, despite all the pomp and circumstance of the National Council and no matter how much Hawkins tried to make it the central governing body, these and any other decrees made by the National Council were binding only insofar as each town or individual was willing to comply.[100] All council agreements, whether town or national, were by consensus. There were no coercive police forces among the Creeks, despite Hawkins's statement to the contrary, and compliance with town and national decrees was an individual decision.

Because consensus was a valued social trait, everyone was under intense pressure to comply with majority opinions. In other words, a person of good sense would agree rather than risk confrontation in a disagreement. In a serious dispute where accord could not be reached, one party would eventually withdraw. In many cases, conflicts at council were avoided when one party simply would not attend. For instance, during Hawkins's tenure, anyone opposed to a land sale would not attend the council meeting.[101] Plus, in these kinds of disagreements, one was not obligated to comply with majority opinion. If one could not bring him- or herself to assent, he or she was free to do as he or she saw fit.[102]

Although Creek men and women eschewed confrontation in public life, this is not to say the Creeks never argued. They were famously argumentative. In enmity they were terrible foes, and by all accounts Creek men (and probably women) were easily insulted and quick to quarrel, especially when drinking, and they harbored grudges until they could even the score.[103] Arguments usually took a ritualized form in which the two parties stood closely face-to-face, grabbed each other's ears, and traded insults.[104] Punishments, such as scratching and whipping, were meted out for bad behavior and as correctives to the young.[105] For a particularly recalcitrant person, the ultimate threat was that the people of the town and clan would disown the individual and his or her death would go unavenged—a horrifying thought to a Creek.[106] If a quarrel ended in injury or insult, the injured party sought revenge. This was one reason why it was so important that a quarrel not get out of hand. If a Creek man, woman, or child believed him- or herself to be wronged or injured, physically or otherwise, he or she did not always confront the injuring party immediately. Aggrieved parties would bide their time until they could inflict a similar injury in revenge.

Creeks were equally interested in maintaining friendships as well as in seeking revenge. In friendship they were unsurpassed. During the eighteenth and nineteenth centuries, the Creeks were renowned for their hospitality. Creek men and women openly welcomed visitors into their towns. When visitors approached, people gathered at the path's entrance and hailed them into town. If need be, they sent canoes to bring them across the river.[107] Unrelated visitors stayed in the rotunda or the square ground; those with clan ties stayed with a family of that clan. All were invited to the town plaza at night. There were ritualized greetings wherein the host inquired of the visitor his or her residence, destination, and business. The questions were mere formality, and no one expected detailed answers.[108] But the Creeks were by no means reticent. They were inquisitive of their visitors, and they spent much time talking with them about their travels, gathering frontier news, and more often than not, trading and bartering goods, rum, and favors.[109] According to the Indian countryman Timothy Barnard, Creek men could carry on for hours like this. Once, perhaps more irritable than usual since he was not feeling well, Barnard wrote, "I have two or three Indians now sitting round me, pestering me with their discourse, which has been the case ever since I have been up."[110] Creek hosts also fed their visitors well, and in fact, visitors could expect meals from any house in front of which they paused. Stiggins believed this custom contributed to the "loafing idleness" of some visitors.[111] Visitors were also allowed to participate in some rituals and to observe some dances, and male visitors could attend the town council if invited. Basil Hall, for instance, attended the dance and ritual performed the night before the ball game described above. Hawkins clearly attended the Busk, since his descriptions are so detailed. But the Creeks expected proper behavior from their guests. They were especially hospitable to people who conformed to Creek custom. They disdained anyone who carried themselves with too much self-import or who asked "too many impertinent questions." According to Stiggins, such behavior could end in "bad consequence," although he does not explain what this would be.[112]

However hospitable to visitors, in day-to-day affairs, Creek men and women felt most comfortable with the members of their matriline, the members of their town, and their clan. The term "clan" is an anthropological one used to designate an extended unilineal kinship group, which in the case of the Creeks, united several matrilineal lineages. People in a clan believe themselves to be blood related, but they cannot actually trace their line through known ancestral links. Rather, they are linked because each lineage believes itself to derive from a mythical ancestor. For instance, the Wind clan consisted of all those lineages in Creek country who believed themselves descended from the mythical Wind lineage.

Such extended kinship organizations are typical in what anthropologists call "kinship-based societies," or societies whose basic social, economic, and political relations are determined by who is or is not of one's kin group. One of the most rude remarks a Creek could use against someone was *esté dogo*, or "you are nobody," implying that you have no kin. This was considered so offensive that one used it with caution.[113] To exist outside kinship was abhorrent. In fact, in kinship-based societies, foreigners are commonly adopted into a kin group because people do not know how to act or do not understand their obligations toward people who exist outside kinship. This is also one reason why kinship terms appeared so frequently in Indian "talks" with Euro-

Americans. In diplomacy, as in all social affairs, relationships were determined according to kinship designations and obligations. This led to much confusion and many cultural clashes because Euro-Americans came from a patriarchal bilateral system wherein a term like "father" had the connotations of a descent relationship characterized by control and authority. For a matrilineal southeastern Indian, however, one's father was only a relative by marriage, not descent, and the relationship was usually one of indulgence and kindness but carried few obligations, little responsibility, and certainly no authority.[114]

Among the Creeks, the clan was exogamous: a person was required to marry outside his or her clan. The clan, however, did not form an economic unit; that lay with the *huti* matriline. A person would probably know and could name all the people of one's matrilineage, but he or she would not necessarily know everyone in his or her clan. Clans also crosscut township lines, and in fact, the clan system was one of the glues binding the various townships together to form the Creek Confederacy. The American spy Caleb Swan, although he obviously did not understand much about the Creek clan system, recognized that pervasive kinship ties united Creek country. As he reported, "By a confused intermixture of blood, a whole tribe becomes uncles, aunts, brothers, sisters and cousins to each other; and as some member of each clan commonly wander abroad, and intermarry in distant towns, and others from those towns come in and supply their places, the whole body of the people have become connected by the ties of blood and hospitality, and are really but one great family of relations."[115]

If the town was a person's most important civil entity, the clan was the most important social one. People of the same clan had strong, proscribed relations and obligations to one another — even to members one did not know personally.[116] Clan members could depend on one another as allies in certain endeavors, which also meant that some of the larger clans may have had more influence in public affairs than others.[117] Of course, one of the deepest obligations among clan members was to avenge deaths, which will be discussed later. There is also some hint that Creek headmen may have been chosen from particular clans; for example, George Stiggins names the Wind clan as particularly prominent.[118] Alexander McGillivray was of the Wind clan.

The Creek clan system at the end of the eighteenth century is only poorly understood, and much of the information comes from scattered historical sources and early-twentieth-century anthropological reports. Hawkins never listed the Creek clans, and he rarely discussed them. Stiggins, the Creek *métis* who wrote between 1835 and 1843 in Alabama, listed the Wind, Bear, Panther, Bird, Polecat, Fox, Potato, Red Paint, and Isfauna, "which is composed of many small ones."[119] In the early nineteenth century, the anthropologist John R. Swanton compiled a list of Creek clans. Using the ethnographic present, Swanton collapsed historic sources with contemporary sources, and therefore all of the clans on his list may not have existed in the eighteenth century. Swanton's list of clans includes the Alligator, Arrow, Bear, Beaver, Bird, Bison, Cane, Corn, Deer, Eagle, Earth, Fish, Fox, Hair, Hickory Nut, Long Dew, Lye Drip, Medicine, Mole, Muskrat, Otter, Panther, Potato, Rabbit, Raccoon, Raven, Paint, Salt, Skunk, Spanish, Spanish Moss, Toad, Turkey, Turtle, Water Moccasin, Weevil, Wildcat, Wind, and Wolf.[120] The plethora of Creek clans undoubtedly reflects the Creek Confederacy policy of taking in refugee groups, and it also reflects something of the origin of the Creeks as a coalescent society.[121] In addition, the clans were divided into two groups, or moieties, between Creek and non-Creek speakers, although the functions of such a dual division may have been somewhat muted by the late eighteenth century.[122] This, too, may reflect something of Creek origins.

Creek towns actually had quite a variety of people associated with them. In addition to those immigrant townships admitted to the confederacy, many other people of foreign origins had been living in Creek country for many decades. Hawkins once wrote Thomas Jefferson that "at the moment I am writing I hear the language of Scotch, French, Spanish, English, Africans, Creeks, and Uchees."[123] He does not mention the language of any foreign Indians in this passage, but by the late eighteenth century and probably before, people from different Indian groups were living in Creek towns and marrying Creek men and women. One would undoubtedly have heard Cherokee, Choctaw, Chickasaw, Shawnee and northern Indian languages as well.[124] Some of these people were long-term visitors; some had married into Creek families and were permanent residents.[125]

As mentioned previously, Indian countrymen had been living among the Creeks for several decades, and although they often lived on individual farms and ranches, these families still took residential associations with the woman's township. There were other whites in Creek towns as well. One estimate put the number of whites in Creek country at approximately 300, but who these people were is still sketchy.[126] At the turn of the nineteenth century, some of these whites were Hawkins's assistants, whom he posted in Creek towns to aid in implementing the plan for civilization. Some were associated with the Indian trade. Most towns had a trading store and a resident trader, most of whom were white; but some *métis* sons who had inherited the business from their fathers were resident traders, and in some cases the town insisted on having an Indian "factor," as the storekeepers were known, rather than a white one.[127] The trading firm of Panton, Leslie, and Company stationed men in Creek towns, and in a few cases, the U.S. government posted civil servants to these stores. One count for 1796 put the number of resident traders for the Lower Creeks at twelve and for the Upper Creeks at thirty-five.[128] The trading stores were near the town center, and both men and women congregated here during the day, bartering, visiting, and drinking.[129] Although some of the larger trading stores that existed during the deerskin trade era have been documented through archaeology, we know little about the architecture of the small trading stores in Creek country.[130] Bartram described the one at Mucclassee; it was a compound modeled after Creek architecture, with four structures situated around a yard.[131] We also know little about the white men stationed here. Some married into Creek society and were long-term residents, and some remained unmarried and only spent a few years in Creek country.

Hawkins's assistants and the white storekeepers had an uneasy position among the Creeks. They were permitted to stay in town only so long as they did not cause any trouble. The Creeks did not always make this easy, and Hawkins had a high turnover of assistants. The men would quit because, according to them, the Creeks treated them rudely and were overly demanding. Richard Thomas, who resigned from his office in 1806, complained about Creek men and women harassing him, calling him a liar, and generally testing his authority and patience. Apparently Thomas had a short fuse, and the Creeks knew it. The name they had for him translates as the "cross white man."[132]

Hawkins instructed his assistants to be on their best behavior, as their future and their tasks depended on it.[133] He knew that the Creeks scrutinized the deportment of his assistants and the traders. The Creeks had evicted several traders from Creek territory because they thought them unscrupulous troublemakers, rumor mongers, liars, or just obnoxious.[134] Hawkins occasionally ordered out of Creek territory unlicensed traders and any traders the Creeks distrusted or disliked as "unworthy characters and unfit to be in their land."[135] Hawkins castigated all traders as exploitative, there to amass fortunes from the Indian trade while having no regard for the betterment of Indian conditions.[136] The Indian countrymen could also be expelled; but their behavior apparently was better, and the Creeks (and Hawkins) had a little more tolerance toward them.

In addition to traders, many disreputable Euro-American men were on the frontier for no apparent reason except to cause trouble. Hawkins characterized their type as "with few exceptions a lazy, cunning, thievish animal."[137] Some of these men were the agents of land speculators, sent into Indian territory to make secret deals with corrupt Indians. Others were smugglers, horse thieves, criminals eluding the authorities, freebooters, and anyone else seeking personal gain on the frontier. They often formed alliances with Creek men and women through a black market in rum, guns, ammunition, and land deals. Some joined young Indian men to form the banditti. They even organized a large horse-stealing ring that tested Hawkins's patience at every turn.[138]

Those who settled in Creek country, however, found themselves under pressure to take a Creek wife. Since the Creeks were polygamous, white traders could take more than one wife. In fact, Swan reported that more traders than Creek men had multiple wives, since they could more easily support them.[139] The Creeks certainly preferred to have these white men married. Since they reckoned all social relations through kinship and marriage, unmarried whites and unmarried free blacks had an ambiguous role in Creek society, and no one knew how to relate properly to them. Plus, for Creek women there was sometimes status in marrying a white.

Even Hawkins found himself under pressure to marry. When Hawkins first came among the Creeks, he was single. The mother of Timothy Barnard's wife approached him one day about marrying one of her daughters, a young widow with several children. Hawkins, lecturing her on the merits of patriarchy, replied that he would do so if his wife obeyed only him and if any children from the marriage and all the property belonged to him. The woman, at first attentive, grew silent and "could not be prevailed on to acquiesce in the conditions proposed. She would not consent that the women and children should be under the direction of the father, and the negotiation ended there."[140] Lavina Downs, an American woman, eventually came to live with Hawkins at the Creek Agency. They lived most of their lives together unmarried, and they had several children together. They married when Hawkins was gravely ill and not expected to live, so that she could inherit his property at his death. Hawkins survived this bout.[141]

Many of Hawkins's assistants took Creek wives. But Hawkins could not abide a matrilineal society wherein the children and much of the property of a family belonged exclusively to the wife and her kin. As Hawkins once explained, the blacksmiths at the agency had Creek wives, and the women's relatives were constantly hanging around the agency. According to Hawkins, they "took direction of the provisions, then the house and pay, and finally the absolute government of everything at the agency whether connected with the smith or not." At this point Hawkins issued a proclamation ordering the separation of his assistants and their Creek wives, and he sent the women and their relations back to their towns.[142]

The Creeks understood sex to be a healthy activity, and unmarried men and women were under few constraints. Once a couple married, however, fidelity was expected and adultery was punishable.[143] Whites were under the same rules. Unmarried whites in Creek country, however, were not required to abstain from sexual encounters. In fact, the Creeks could be suspicious of celibacy. When the French agent Louis LeClerc Milfort was among the Creeks from 1776 to 1796, he at first thought it prudent not to get involved in any romantic or sexual entanglements. He did not take a Creek lover or wife. The women in the town were curious about this strange behavior. One evening they conspired to have a young woman seduce him. The young woman, dressed in "a beautiful printed calico skirt, a nice chemise, silver pins, two pairs of bracelets also of silver, an enormous quantity of ribbons of all colors fastened to her hair, and five pairs of earrings which hung in graduated sizes like chains," approached Milfort and made her interest known. They later rendezvoused at her home, and when he moved into her sleeping quarters, four women seized him, chided him for his modesty, "and told me that they had not yet seen a capon-warrior" (a capon is a castrated rooster). Milfort related that he had to prove to them "that a French warrior is well worth a Creek warrior" and that he came out of the incident "with honor." Milfort married McGillivray's sister soon after this.[144]

White women were also present in Indian territory. The story of these women has not yet been told, and they remain obscure. Some were captives of the Indians, waiting to be released, which came about after their captors bargained with their relatives or friends.[145] Some were former captives who had married Creek men.[146] In at least one case a woman, Jenny Stephenson, was given to Passcote Emautlau in "payment for a brother of his who was killed accidently by a gun while on the corn house." Stephenson had four children while in Creek country, but she is known to us through her petition to Hawkins to return to America.[147] Many women, however, chose to stay. Considering that Euro-American white women had few prerogatives regarding property and divorce in their own society, it should come as no surprise that many stayed in Creek territory. When the relatives of these "captive" women attempted to "rescue" them, the rescuers were embarrassed when the women refused to leave.

The enterprising Hannah Hale typifies the successful white woman in Creek country. Hale became a rancher and slave owner, and now living in a matrilineal society, she did not have to worry about her husband's relatives leaving her destitute if he died. After spending almost twenty years with her Creek husband, a headman of Thlotlogulgau, and raising five children, Hale decided to visit her mother in Georgia. Once there, her relatives refused to let her return to Creek country. Her husband asked Hawkins to intercede. Hale returned to Creek territory, perhaps even more convinced that life with the Creeks was superior to life with her Georgia relations. She later became devoted to Hawkins's plan for civilization and ran a successful cloth-making industry.[148]

A white woman married to a Creek man, according to Hawkins, possessed all the rights of a Creek woman, including the right to "throw away her husband whenever she chooses."[149] White women also were not usually subjects of eviction. The reasons behind this are elusive. The townspeople of Abihka were known for their acceptance of whites but especially for their good treatment and acceptance of the white women among them.[150] Some Cherokees once explained to Hawkins when they were negotiating the removal of some white intruders that the white women married to Cherokee men could remain "as men love women and women love men." The white men married to Cherokee women, however, could stay only so long as they behaved themselves.[151]

Matrilineality and the southeastern Indian practice of adopting war captives into a family may help explain this. War captives had one of many fates. They could be killed outright; they could be tortured to death; they could be made into slaves; they could escape; they could be adopted by a family; or by the late eighteenth century, they could be held for ransom. Many of the white women in Creek country were held for ransom, and Jenny Stephenson may have been a slave, since she was traded as a payment. Although the practice is not documented, Creek families might have adopted some white women who had entered Creek country as war captives. Once adopted, these women would have become full-fledged members of a matriline and clan, with all the associated rights, duties, and privileges. Once a woman became a member of a matriline, her children would be children of the matriline. White men, on the other hand, usually came into Creek country as traders and trader assistants. Therefore they would not necessarily have been eligible for adoption. If they married Creek women, although affinal kin, they would have been considered foreign relations, and they still would not have a matriline affiliation. The difference in kinship status between white men and white women, then, may help account for the differences in Creek attitudes.

Blacks also played a role in Creek town life. Blacks had been a part of southeastern Indian life since Africans began arriving in North America. The history of their role in Creek affairs cannot be summarized here, but suffice it to say that at the end of the eighteenth century their place in Creek society was considerable.[152] Some blacks were slaves under Creek or white ownership. However, their status was considerably different from that of slaves in American society. In Creek territory, slaves were property, but the slave owners gained little from them in terms of labor. Consequently, the position of slaves among the Creeks was more like that of tenant farmers. They lived with their owners and tended agricultural fields, but the crops were theirs except for a small payment to their owners.[153] Slaves also took care of ranching and other tasks; but all of the work was divided between them and the matrilineage, so they were never the main laborers. But they were property, and they were bought and sold as such.

There were also many runaway slaves and free blacks in Creek country, many of whom married into Creek society. These men were probably considered like the white males in Creek territory; they were granted leave to stay so long as they behaved themselves. The women probably fared well, like the white women in Creek country. Given the many languages in which African slaves needed to be proficient, many had considerable linguistic skills. In Creek country they often acted as interpreters and even tutored some Creeks in English.[154]

The number of black slaves in Creek territory at the turn of the nineteenth century has not been thoroughly studied. The largest concentration of black slaves, estimated to be around 300, was on the *métis* and Indian countryman plantations on the Coosa and Tallapoosa Rivers.[155] For instance, Sophia Durant and Elizabeth, sisters of Alexander McGillivray, who lived in Ocheubofau, owned 80 and 30 slaves, respectively. Richard Bailey of Autossee owned 8. The Upper Creek headman Efau Haujo owned 8, and Alexander Cornells owned 9.[156] But there were also many black slaves in other parts of Creek country. The Indian countryman Richard Grierson, who lived along the upper Tallapoosa, owned 40. The letters of Timothy Barnard, who lived on the Flint River, do not give precise numbers but indicate that he, too, owned several slaves.[157] Once Hawkins moved to the Creek Agency, he acquired about 70 slaves.[158]

After the American Revolution, the place of blacks in Creek society took a menacing turn. Whites had always offered rewards for runaway blacks, and before this time, the Creeks and other southeastern Indians were averse to turning over runaways, largely because they did not conceive of them as property. After the Revolution, more and more Creeks acquired slaves, so the danger that runaway slaves and free blacks would be returned or sold to white owners increased because many Creeks began to advocate chattel slavery and the plantation economy and to think of slaves as property.[159] In fact, historian Claudio Saunt documents an emerging division among blacks in Creek country around the turn of the nineteenth century. A nucleus of Indian slave owners on the Coosa and Tallapoosa Rivers promoted chattel slavery, and a nucleus of independent blacks with strong African leaders formed on the lower Flint and Chattahoochee Rivers. As tensions heightened for blacks among the Creeks, more and more slaves and free blacks joined the independent blacks, and they eventually joined the Seminoles, with whom they would later fight for their lives in the bitter, brutal, and protracted Seminole Wars of the early nineteenth century.[160]

The Creeks apparently made some distinctions between the progeny of Indian/white couples, Creek Indian/other Indian couples, and Indian/black couples, but one's father's lineage was probably unimportant. A child was of his or her mother's lineage. "Mixing," in terms of descent, probably made little sense to an eighteenth-century Creek. Cultural mixing, however, was an important indicator to Creeks.[161] A great amount of cultural blending took place in these mixed households. The ranches of Indian countrymen, for example, may have resembled American ranches, but much about life still revolved around Creek rules. The division of labor in these households fell along Creek lines, which, except for the men refusing to farm, resembled that of frontier whites. The wife and her children took care of the agricultural tasks, and her husband saw to the commercial hunting interests and ranching. If a Creek woman owned stock (and many did), her husband usually included her animals in his ranching activities, although the proceeds from her livestock went to her. She, during his absences, took care of his business interests. Indian countrymen hunted for meat, but they participated in commercial hunting as middlemen, supplying trade goods for skins or acting as liaisons with the large trading houses.[162] The Creek wives of these men usually adopted white standards of cleanliness, manners, and clothing. Hawkins lauded such Creek women; he commented that Richard Bailey's wife, who was of the Otalla clan but is known only as Mrs. Bailey, was "neat, cleanly, prudent and economical, as careful of her family concerns as a white woman."[163] According to Hawkins, Mrs. Bailey could become quite vexed about neatness, and she regularly scolded unkempt Creek men to see that their wives washed their clothes.[164]

Despite adopting some American habits, the wives of white men held rigidly to their Creek matrilineal rights regarding property, children, and divorce. In fact, Mr. and Mrs. Bailey used this to their advantage when they began acquiring livestock. The Creeks of Autossee, the town with which Richard Bailey was affiliated, were wary of the Baileys' venture because the cattle, hogs, and horses caused much damage in the agricultural fields. The usual solution to such intrusions was to just shoot the trespassing animals. Bailey deeded the livestock to his wife because he believed that they were safe only if they were considered the property of his wife and children.[165] Since the cattle were now his wife's, any complaints about the livestock or any damage to her property would be taken up by her clan. Another indication of the cultural blending typical of these households is that every morning, winter or summer, Mrs. Bailey and her children went to water. Hawkins believed this custom was the reason the whole family was "remarkable for being healthy and cleanly."[166]

Cultural blending cuts both ways, and in many cases blacks and whites adopted Creek lifeways. Hawkins once described one white man as being so much like an Indian that he was indistinguishable from any Creek.[167] Timothy Barnard commented that many of the traders in Creek country were more like Indians than whites.[168] As a testament to this, when Bartram visited Mucclassee, the white trader there greeted him wearing only a breechclout, as did his fellow townsmen who had come out as well.[169] Many blacks adopted Creek lifeways whole cloth, and some black men became successful traders and prominent headmen.[170] There is some indication, however, that the Creeks pressured free blacks to conform to Creek customs. The Creeks may have thought blacks who retained some of their African customs strange. For example, a black man from Tuckabatchee was executed on the grounds that he was a sorcerer.[171]

Many Indian/white métis successfully combined the social and cultural patterns of both their parents and succeeded in a blended world. These are the men and women who rose to prominence during the late eighteenth and early nineteenth centuries and who have received much attention from Indian scholars. Other métis, however, turned away from their Creek side and chose American lifestyles. These families tended to live in the Tensaw and Bigbe areas, on the lower Alabama and Mobile Rivers, close to Mobile. They distanced themselves from their Creek relations and never participated in Creek life. These people were some of those who suffered the wrath of the Red Sticks during the Red Stick War of 1813. Afterward, when Andrew Jackson took their lands in the Treaty of Fort Jackson, Hawkins pleaded amnesty on their behalf, since it was doubtful they would be readmitted to the Creek Confederacy, and they were, therefore, in danger of becoming a dispossessed people.[172] Some métis found themselves torn between two worlds. For instance,

Richard Bailey's son, also named Richard, after being educated in Philadelphia, returned to his home "with so much contempt for the Indian mode of life that he has got himself into discredit with them."[173] Apparently the younger Richard suffered an identity crisis, as Hawkins described him as "neither an Indian nor a white man."[174]

CHAPTER SIX

THE HINTERLANDS

B ackcountry" was the term applied to Indian territory in the eighteenth and early nineteenth centuries by literate whites. The term carried with it commonly held perceptions of Indian territory as a vacant place of remoteness, isolation, wilderness, and danger. Of course, this was a considerable exaggeration. As we have seen in some detail, the so-called southern backcountry was the home of many people and the locus of many towns and habitations. Even though most Creeks lived in the towns along the Flint, Chattahoochee, Tallapoosa, and Coosa Rivers, the Creeks of the late eighteenth century believed themselves to be the sole owners of large parcels of what is now Georgia, Alabama, Florida, and Tennessee. Surrounding Indian groups—the Cherokees, Chickasaws, Choctaws, and Seminoles—also claimed territorial rights over large areas, although their population centers were located on only a small portion of their national land claims. After the American Revolution, the southern states acquired the territory that the British had earlier acquired from the Indians, which amounted to relatively narrow strips along the coast, and Americans soon began working to increase these holdings by purchasing Indian lands through either fraud or legal means. Most southern American population centers, such as New Orleans, Mobile, Pensacola, Savannah, Charleston, and Jamestown, hugged the coastline. A few small frontier towns popped up whenever a land purchase occurred, and American frontier farmers were always crowding the new borders. But by and large the hinterlands, those areas between the various Indian and American population centers, were sparsely inhabited. This should not be construed to mean that only a few people were in the hinterlands. People of every sort were constantly moving through these areas.

By the late eighteenth century, overland trails and paths crisscrossed the Southeast, connecting all the Indian towns with one another and with major American frontier towns and port cities. At this time, most Creeks did not use water routes for much long distance travel.[1] Most of the rivers in Creek country ran north-south, and the shoals at the Fall Line were tricky to navigate. Above the Fall Line, the river corridors were narrow and the current could be swift, with many shoaly areas. Below the Fall Line, the rivers were more easily navigated. The Indians used canoes; American-made barges and bateaux (large, flat-bottomed boats) could be used below the Fall Line, but they could not navigate the Fall Line shoals. During the Red Stick War, Hawkins suggested bringing munitions from Pensacola to Cusseta on the Chattahoochee by bateaux.[2] But he only had a single mention of people regularly using the river as a transportation route. These were the people of Coosada, whom Hawkins called "good oarsmen" and noted that they often traveled to Mobile by water, obviously via the Alabama River, which runs to Mobile Bay.[3] Hawkins did not specify what kind of watercraft the Coosadas used, but it was probably canoes. Canoes were certainly the preferred method of river travel, since larger craft were cumbersome on these waters. For instance, when the French naval officer Jean-Bernard Bossu attempted to travel from Mobile to Fort Toulouse on a bateau on the Alabama River, it took him almost two months to cover about 170 miles. Taking a bateau upriver was difficult because oarsmen had to use poles to pull the boat along. Bossu traveled during the rainy season, and the current was so swift that the oarsmen could only pole the bateau one league (about three miles) a day, and his boat was constantly being snagged by submerged trees.[4]

The Tennessee and Cumberland Rivers, because they run east-west across the Interior Plateaus physiographic province, are wide and relatively slow, with few shoals; hence they were more navigable by both canoes and American-made boats. Most river traffic of the American South at this time took place on these rivers. Once Tennessee became a state in 1796, frontier whites hoped to use the Coosa as passage to Mobile. The Coosa fell within the territory of the Creek Confederacy, and the Creeks refused to grant these rights. The goods of any trespassers were subject to confiscation, and since the United States had no treaties issuing water rights, the federal government would not protect any Americans trespassing down Creek rivers.

One incident occurred while Hawkins was in office. In 1809 James McIntosh (no relation to the Lower Creek headman William McIntosh) loaded 120 bateaux with goods, mostly liquor and ammunition, and starting in Cherokee territory, headed down the Coosa River. When the barges entered Upper Creek territory, more than 100 Upper Creek warriors stopped them and took all the goods, finding, in the process, a passport to travel through Creek territory issued to McIntosh with Hawkins's forged signature.[5] McIntosh, who stood to lose a great deal of money, notified the War Department, the agency under which Indian affairs fell, of what had happened. According to McIntosh, the Cherokee headman Pathmaker had given him permission to float down the Coosa.[6] The Upper Creeks responded that such might have been the case, but that the Cherokees had no right to grant him free passage through Upper Creek territory, especially with contraband goods such as liquor. McIntosh was known far and wide as a scoundrel, and officials at the War Department did not uphold his plea. The confiscated goods were eventually distributed among several Upper Creek towns.[7]

Such incidents regarding water travel in Creek country were rare at this time, since most long-distance travel was overland. Without a doubt, the major thoroughfares in Creek country, were (1) the Lower Trading Path, which ran along the Fall Line from Augusta, Georgia, through Coweta to Tuckabatchee and then into Choctaw country in present-day south-central Mississippi and down to New Orleans, and (2) the Upper Trading Path, which ran through the Piedmont, also starting at Augusta, but north of the Lower Trading Path and west to Oakfuskee and then into Chickasaw country in present-day northeast Mississippi. The Federal Road, which was opened in 1806 as a postal route and later carried general traffic, roughly followed the Lower Trading Path through Creek country.[8] From Augusta, these trails connected the Lower and Upper Creek towns to the Atlantic port towns of Savannah and Charleston. A major north-south artery, known as the Great Warrior Path, connected the southern Indians with the Indians of the Northeast.[9] There were other well-known paths moving north-south down the Alabama River to Mobile and down the Chattahoochee and Flint Rivers to connecting paths to St. Augustine and Pensacola.[10]

The most frequently traveled trails within Creek country were the ones connecting the towns. These trails typically ran on both banks of a stream and connected with one another at the fords. In addition, narrow, obscure trails, largely known only by local Indians, ran through the countryside.[11] For whatever reasons, whites passing through Indian territory began using these paths and hiring Indians or traders "of bad or doubtful character" as guides.[12] The

Creeks, already nervous about whites traveling through their territory, were not pleased when whites strayed off the regular routes.[13]

Most travel was on foot or horseback and occasionally by wagon or coach. Supplies were usually transported on packhorses or in wagons, but loaded wagons were difficult to move on the primitive roads. The Upper and Lower Trading Paths, which had served as packhorse routes for more than 100 years, were well mapped and well known and could easily accommodate large traveling parties. The lesser paths were footpaths that could accommodate a small party with horses and perhaps a wagon. There is some indication that the Creeks distinguished trails by the traffic they could accommodate. They had a term for packhorse trails, *chelako nini*, or "horse trail."[14] The Creeks also understood the trails to be owned by certain towns and groups. In fact, different towns had their own paths for reaching the same destinations, and these paths were named after the people who used them. For instance, there was the Yuchi Path, the Cusseta Path, and the Chickasaw Path, all of which lead to Augusta. Smaller towns and/or groups of the Creek Confederacy also had their own paths, such as the Chehaw Path, which was used by the Chehaws, and *sulenojuhnene* or "buzzard roost trail," which was a trail formerly used by the people of Sulenojee ("buzzard roost"; this was not Padjeeligau, but another town that had been abandoned by the early nineteenth century).[15]

Citizens of Creek country knew these paths well, and men often hired themselves out as guides to foreign travelers. For the foreign traveler, these paths were difficult to follow, since they intersected with many other paths; they were also narrow and not well worn. Indians blazed trees while traveling to indicate their passing. Depending on how high a mark was placed on a tree or the angle of the cut, Indians could identify the nation to which an Indian traveler belonged by these blazes.[16] Although whites usually had Indian guides, white travelers also commonly blazed trees as markers for fellow travelers and quite likely for themselves in case they had to retrace their steps. They sometimes posted makeshift signs at intersections, with arrows indicating the way to, say, Pensacola.[17]

East-west trails typically crossed waterways at the Fall Line because here the streams were shallow and shoaly, thus affording a good place to cross. The current on the Chattahoochee River, however, was too swift at the falls, and the Chattahoochee fords were about three miles below the falls.[18] When crossing streams at the Fall Line, travelers usually just waded across. Creek place-names indicate that the fords were named, and they give some clue as to their nature or use. Some examples are *tcahki lako*, or "big ford," and *holi taiga*, or "war ford."[19] The Creeks differentiated these fords from other kinds of crossings. In some cases, a log or two lay across the water, forming a kind of bridge. Creek place-names noted such features: for instance, a crossing point of a creek in present-day Cleburne County, Alabama, was called *chulafinee*, or "pine log crossing"; another creek in present-day Coosa County, Alabama, took its name from its bridge, which was called *finikochilka*, or "broken foot log"; a swamp in present-day Wayne County, Georgia, was crossed by a *fin-halui*, or "high foot log."[20] Bartram relayed that a single sapling laid across a stream was called a "raccoon bridge." He also said that his Indian guide could cross such bridges "quick and light as that quadruped, with one hundred weight of leather on his back, when I was scarcely able to shuffle myself along over it astride."[21] At some streams a small, two-person canoe could be found concealed among the foliage at a crossing spot. Experienced travelers knew their locations and could retrieve them for a crossing. Hawkins described one of these as being made of a red oak log about ten feet long with the bark still on it. His Creek companion explained that the small canoe was easier to conceal if left unfinished; indeed, Hawkins observed that it resembled an old log when turned over.[22]

Bartram once described a raft his Indian guide made to cross the swollen waters of a creek. The Indian man cut some small trees about eight to nine inches in diameter and used vine to lash them together into a scaffolding about twelve feet long. He then bundled cane into bunches "as thick as a man's body" and laid several of these over the scaffold. Bartram and his guide piled their goods on top of it. Next, his guide cut a piece of vine long enough to traverse the stream, gave one end to Bartram, and plunged into the water holding the other end in his mouth. With a man now on either bank, together they ferried several loads across, guiding the raft along the vine. Bartram drove the horses into the water, and then he stripped down, except for his pants, which he kept on because he did not want to expose himself "naked to the alligators and serpents," and swam across.[23]

Basil Hall, while still in Georgia, described a footbridge and ford across a stream he called Yam Grandy. The ford was simply several logs laid sideways across the bottom of a shallow point in the water. Over the ford someone had constructed a footbridge that also consisted of "felled trees, laid two and two, sidewise [*sic*], over the greater part of the width" and held up by a few posts about six to eight feet above the water. In this case, the middle logs had been washed away, leaving only a single pole on which to walk across "the worst part of the passage." Hall, who was traveling via stagecoach with his baby daughter, his wife, her maid, and an experienced driver, described the passage as particularly difficult because the water was extremely swift and high from recent rains. According to Hall, his driver, a man named Middleton, did not like the looks of this stream and advised against a crossing. After investigating the footbridge, Hall decided to try driving the carriage across the ford, with the party following on the footbridge. Middleton "muttered something about being washed away, drowned, or bedeviled in the creek." Still, Middleton "mounted the vehicle like a Roman charioteer, and dashed forward into the ugly-looking tide." Middleton, the horses, and the carriage made it across, undoubtedly due to Middleton's expertise, the strength of two horses, and the sturdiness of the ford, of which every log held. Hall and the others nervously crossed on the slippery footbridge. Eventually all made it across safely.[24]

Hall's experience was typical. Travel, in general, was difficult during the rainy winter months, and sometimes it was impossible. Needless to say, the dirt roadways were impassable for loaded wagons, and they became a mire for horses and foot travelers, especially if they carried much baggage.[25] If the waters were high, the fords and bridges, as we have seen, were dangerous. Late-eighteenth-century travelers were advised to check the water level of high streams before crossing. This could be easily done because travelers etched water-level marks on trees on the banks at dangerous crossings.[26] If waters were high, travelers often attempted to swim themselves, their horses, and goods across. This was hazardous, and sometimes equipment, horses, and even traveling companions were swept away.[27] Thus, rainy-season crossings required much care, and they could be difficult and long, taking a full day or even two. The hazards of crossing southern creeks and rivers were legendary. Adam Hodgson, an American who passed through the southern frontier on his way to New Orleans, was stopped at the Ogeechee River in Georgia by three "hearty, resolute and experienced foresters" with a wretched account of bridges being washed out and the swamps being impassable. They advised Hodgson not to attempt his expedition.[28]

In some cases, Creek men ran ferries across rivers and large creeks, wherein they would carry travelers and their baggage while the horses swam alongside the craft. In the late eighteenth century, before the massive migration of Euro-Americans to the Mississippi Territory, these ferries were simple operations usually of one man and his makeshift boat built from a frame of saplings and a cowhide covering in which he ferried goods across for a price. In some cases, Indian guides carried leather for this purpose and made cane frames at a crossing point.[29] By the second decade of the nineteenth century, with the ever increasing number of foreign travelers through Creek country, ferries became well-run Creek businesses with substantial watercraft and prices ostensibly regulated by treaty.

Travel through Creek country at the turn of the nineteenth century should not be imagined as remote and isolated. Residents of Creek country used these routes on a daily basis for visiting, hunting, trading, livestock roundups, and so on. When white immigration escalated after the acquisition of the Mississippi Territory, and once the Federal Road was completed in 1813, traveling parties of all kinds encountered one another all day. Even before this, travelers met others on the paths or at river crossings at least once a day. Little interrupted the flow of traffic, and even during the Red Stick War people trekked to and fro through Creek country.

Crossing the hinterlands of the American territory, white and Indian travelers commonly took room and board with frontier white farmsteaders; once in Indian territory, they took room and board in Indian towns and households. In between, however—once they were outside the boundary of white settlements and before they reached the Indian towns—travelers pitched camp in the woods. In some cases they simply reoccupied former Indian camps. The remains of an Indian camp varied, depending on if it were a hunting, war, or traveling camp. War parties left no traces, but hunting and traveling camps generally consisted of scaffolding for lean-tos, a fire circle, and a small cleared area. At one such camp Hawkins carved his initials and the date on a nearby tree.[30]

Creek men (and probably women) were not concerned with comfort while traveling. This clearly impressed Hawkins, as he once commented on the fortitude of two Creek male guides, one of whom was elderly. These men ate little while on the trail. They carried only a small pouch of parched cornmeal, or *wissoeta*, a handful of which they mixed with a pint of water and drank when they were hungry. Hawkins remarked that he preferred it mixed with a little sugar. Furthermore, these men, dressed in breechclouts, leggings, and a shirt, only spread their shirts under them when sleeping and covered themselves with a "small half worn blanket." One evening when it rained, Hawkins managed to prepare a lean-to covered with a blanket, bearskins, and an oilcloth cloak. The Indian men, however, slept as usual in the open, laying only on their shirts, and according to Hawkins, "They both slept soundly the whole time it rained. . . . They never stirred until daybreak."[31] Rain may not have perturbed most Indian travelers, but ghosts were worrisome. The Creeks believed the woods were haunted. According to an Indian companion traveling with the Alabama historian John Pope, Indian always camped on the right-hand (east) side of the trail because the left-hand side (west) was reserved for the spirits of the unavenged dead, who wailed and moaned throughout the night.[32]

If the environs at the site of a river crossing were especially pleasant, had a good stock of fodder for horses, were not haunted, or had good, flat rocks for camping, permanent campgrounds were established on the banks. Some of these were former packhorse camps. Packhorse trains, at least in earlier times, sometimes had up to 100 horses and men. Packhorse men camped at regular intervals on the major tails at favorite flat spots at water crossings. Although these camps are not well described, one can imagine a scene of cooking debris such as old campfires, lean-tos, scattered animal bones, and the occasional lost tool. Packhorse men also liked to amuse themselves at the end of the day by drinking and holding boxing matches, which may have left some detritus as well.[33] Where the Lower Trading Path crossed present-day Ochille Creek in Chattahoochee County, Georgia, was apparently a well-known camping spot. The Creeks called the campsite *nochilleehatchee*, or "dead asleep creek," apparently indicating that one slept particularly well here.[34]

Indians traveled these trails with great confidence, fearing only ghosts, banditti, and war parties. City dwellers, on the other hand, feared the hinterlands for many reasons. Southern thunderstorms are still fearsome and terrible events, and eighteenth-century newcomers were advised to not make light of them. The curious remains of lightning-struck trees, which peppered the countryside and which Indian guides were careful to point out to their white companions, served as reminders of a southern storm's ferocity. The Creeks believed that terrapins (turtles) and wizards could direct lightning strikes, *atoyahåti*, and that lightning-struck trees were especially good medicinals.[35] Foreign travelers also took as truths the tales of aggressive wolves, alligators, bears, and snakes, or "vipers," so poisonous as to a kill a man with one strike. The Coastal Plain swamps had such a reputation for poisonous snakes that white travelers were afraid to get off their horses or out of their wagons when traveling through such areas for fear of stepping on one.[36] The wolves, as related to Bartram, assembled "in companies in the night time, howl and bark altogether, especially in cold winter nights," which terrified and bewildered travelers.[37] Inexperienced travelers mistook the cacophony of frog and insect night calls for the noises of scary forest monsters or mysterious wild animals. Of course, the great swarms of gnats and flies were a constant torment to humans and horses.

The fear of losing one's way in the forest worried Euro-American travelers to distraction. More often than not, even with experienced and knowledgeable guides, Euro-American travelers took the wrong fork. There also was the ever present danger of being mistaken as enemy Indians by warring parties. In fact, whites were advised to keep their hats on when traveling and to hang them on poles in clear sight when camping. That way a war party would not mistake them for Indians. Southeastern Indian men preferred turbans to Euro-American style hats, and they often went bareheaded.[38] In addition, the banditti marauded the roadways, robbing and molesting travelers, hats or not. Passage was never safe or guaranteed. Highway robbery was so prevalent that most people took it for granted. Even Hawkins, the one person in charge of quelling such lawlessness, could only advise Timothy Barnard to travel light on a trip so that "in case you are dismounted by a thieving party, you will not be inconvenienced with baggage."[39]

Adam Hodgson described one incident when his party, forced to make camp one evening, luckily happened upon five other traveling parties camping together. They felt lucky because they believed there was safety in numbers. After everyone had retired and their campfires were burning low, two Indian men entered the campground. Hodgson, sleeping lightly, was immediately alert to their presence, but he feigned sleep out of fear. The Indian men silently threaded their way around the sleeping campers, sometimes bending to inspect an article. Then, just as stealthily as they entered, they disappeared. Needless to say, the occurrence unnerved Hodgson and robbed him of his night's sleep if nothing else.[40]

Communication, like travel, was slow and not always reliable. Since the Creeks had no writing system and since most frontier blacks and whites also were illiterate, the main form of communication was verbal, face-to-face messages. However, in most Creek towns there lived someone who could read and write English, Spanish, or French. For a fee, these people sometimes would pen a written correspondence or read one that had been sent. Long-distance messages, written as well as verbal, usually were passed along to a traveler who could be trusted to deliver the message to a person on their route. For twenty-five cents a day, one could hire Indian runners to carry verbal and written messages long distances. These young men reportedly could jog up to twenty-five miles a day; so barring a banditti ambush, runners were the quickest means of long-distance communication.[41] Once the Creeks agreed to a U.S. postal path, the federal government employed mail carriers on horseback, although Indian runners were still used, especially for places off the mail routes. The mail carriers were subject to robbery and ambush by the banditti, and many postal riders reportedly had a tendency toward excessive drinking, all of which stopped the mail delivery in its tracks.[42]

For national news, people in Creek country relied on others passing through and the occasional newspaper. Hawkins was also a source of national news, since his correspondences with the War Department and with his friends and associates in Washington, Savannah, and other major cities kept him fairly well informed of national events. As one can imagine, information about happenings on the frontier was generally haphazard and prone to exaggeration. In his writings Hawkins occasionally mentioned rumors, usually of a horrifying nature, such as reports of large Indian or white armies on the march. Such rumors usually sent the white border settlers running to the nearest fort. For the Creeks, there was a real nervousness about U.S. and Georgia military reprisals for frontier offenses, and such rumors usually put an Indian town in immediate preparation for war.

American military forts and trading houses were well-known fixtures in the hinterlands of Creek country. After the American Revolution, in an effort to regulate the Indian trade, the U.S. government initiated the Factory System wherein the federal government controlled the trade and established trading houses or factories on the borders of Indian territories. For the Creeks, under the 1790 Treaty of New York, one factory was to serve the entire population. Initially the Creek Factory was at Colerain, Georgia, on the St. Mary's River. With the 1796 Treaty of Colerain, the factory was moved farther inland, to Fort Wilkinson on the Oconee River. In 1803 it was once again moved westward to Fort Hawkins on the Ocmulgee River in present-day Macon, Georgia, when the Creeks ceded a portion of land between the Oconee and Ocmulgee Rivers. Finally, in 1817, after the Treaty of Fort Jackson, the factory was moved to Fort Mitchell on the Chattahoochee River near present-day Columbus, Georgia.[43] Even before the Fort Mitchell Factory was built, the U.S. government was contemplating abolishing the system, and in 1819 the Fort Mitchell Factory was dismantled.[44]

The Factory System in the Southeast was never profitable and was always struggling.[45] At first the government subsidized the factories, but in 1801 Congress decided not to allocate any money to the Indian trade. Henceforth the factories were to be supported by their own proceeds.[46] In other words, all federal subsidies were stopped, and for the Creek Factory, this made a difficult financial situation even worse. The Creek Factory was regulated through Washington officials who set prices, requisitioned goods, and dictated the rules of commerce and local behavior. For instance, the factory bought deerskins for twenty-five cents a pound, and the Creeks found this price agreeable; but the factor found the fixed price a hindrance to business. When the price of deerskins on the European market declined, the factor could not lower the amount he paid the Creeks for their skins.[47] The result was an overall loss. At one point the quarterly income from the factory was so dismal that the factor, Jonathan Halstead, suggested to the Treasury Department that he be allowed to raise the price of trade goods to compensate for the loss. He was not allowed to do this, and the Creek Factory continued to operate in the red.[48]

Because of such top-down management tactics, the Creek Factory could never effectively compete with Panton, Leslie, and Company, the British trading house that had held a near-monopoly on Creek trade since the end of the American Revolution. Panton, Leslie, and Company was located at Pensacola in Spanish-held Florida under a mutually beneficial agreement between Spain and Britain. The Creek Factory was never a serious competitor to Panton, Leslie, and Company for the Indian trade. For example, the company shipped 203,000 pounds of skins in 1803, compared with the 50,000 pounds shipped yearly from the factory.[49]

Panton, Leslie, and Company had several business advantages. For one, although the home store was in Pensacola, the company stationed traders to Creek towns, as we have seen, which made access to the trade much easier for the Creeks.[50] The Creek Factory, on the other hand, was located on the eastern border of Creek country, at a considerable distance from the towns. Independent traders who served a town sometimes purchased goods from the factory, and the War Department, which oversaw the traders, allowed them to mark up the prices on goods they took back to their towns to sell. But the traders were to post a list of both the factory's and the trader's prices in each town so that the Indians would know the markup.[51] The War Department and Treasury Department involvements also reflect the complicated jurisdictions the federal and state governments constructed in regard to Indian affairs, and especially the Indian trade.

Prices at the Creek Factory were regulated from Washington and had little bearing on frontier economics. Panton, Leslie, and Company could lower and raise prices according to the market. The Creeks sometimes grumbled at the difference in prices, but they still preferred Panton, Leslie, and Company over the U.S. Factory. For one thing, the quantity and quality of supplies offered by Panton, Leslie, and Company were superior to those at the Creek Factory. Also, the company was free to trade in any goods. Panton was an astute businessman and recognized and reacted to the changing economy. The company was a primary buyer of hogs and cattle on the hoof, as meats, or as skins. It readily purchased agricultural goods, chickens, snakeroot and other herbs, hickory oil, and all the other commodities the Creeks now began to sell in larger quantities. Panton, Leslie, and Company also responded to changes in Creek demands by increasing their stores of salt, sugar, and coffee.[52]

The factory, on the other hand, was barred from purchasing anything other than conventional Indian trade goods, and only with special dispensation could the factor trade in anything else.[53] In addition, despite the fact that livestock and agricultural produce were becoming the predominant trade items, the Treasury Department prohibited the factory from buying cows and hogs from the Creeks.[54] Hawkins recognized the need to diversify the trade at the factory. He petitioned the War Department several times to intervene with the Treasury Department to allow the Creek Factory to buy and sell cattle, hogs, corn, tobacco, butter, cheese, and other products that the Creeks were producing for sale.[55] Because there was actually little oversight, the factor traded in these and other illegal goods, but always at a meager level, and Hawkins's requests to make this trade legitimate were never granted.

The factory had few permanent employees, and the factor had to wait for federal money before he could hire assistants. Therefore the Creek Factory was extremely inefficient. It had innumerable problems in just getting the skins out of the storehouse. In one case, more than 8,000 pounds of skins sat in the storehouse, and some of these skins had been there for twelve years. When they were finally brought out for shipping, the factor was not surprised to find that most of them had rotted.[56] Finally, the Creek Factory never had a sufficient quantity of manufactured goods, especially cloth, salt, guns, and ammunition, the top four trade items.[57] The factor was instructed to keep only a meager eight-month supply of goods on hand.[58] Hawkins upbraided the factors for letting the supplies dwindle, and he occasionally took matters into his own hands by writing requisitions directly to the Savannah merchants with whom the factors had to deal.[59] He sometimes paid for factory supplies out of his own funds.

Hawkins's office was under the War Department, whereas the factory was under the Treasury Department, and therefore the factory officially did not come under his jurisdiction.[60] In practice, however, the two had a close relationship. Hawkins kept a close eye on the factory and the factor, and he made sure the Creeks were given a fair deal at the factory. He also initiated a system whereby Creek traders would be given supplies for the journey home. He even agreed to allow a little rum for the return trip with strict instructions that it was not to be drunk at the factory.[61] Much of the economic activity of Hawkins's office centered on the Creek Factory. Creek stipend money and goods were requisitioned through the factory, and the factory held the stipend accounts. When a Creek man, for instance, wanted his portion of the stipend payment in guns and ammunition, Hawkins sent him to the factory for the payment.[62] The U.S. government would reimburse the factory; however, these funds were chronically delayed and sometimes not paid at all.

Hawkins also relied on the factory for the food and supplies needed at treaty negotiations and for his contribution to National Council meetings, both of which could be substantial because, as the representative of the United States, he was supposed to host many of these affairs. He also requisitioned goods from the factory to compensate Indians and whites who had lost personal property through theft. For example, if a white person stole a bag of shot or a gun from a Creek hunter, and if this could be proven, Hawkins sent the Creek man to the factory with a voucher for payment for the thefts. If a Creek stole a horse from a white farmer, and this could be proven, Hawkins paid the white farmer for his loss with goods from the factory. Theft was so common on the frontier that much in the factory correspondences and ledgers is devoted to it.[63] Ostensibly, the factory would be compensated for these outlays by the U.S. government or from the Creek stipend, but again the compensation either lagged by a few years or was never paid. All of this only added to the factory's chronic financial problems.

The Creek Factory also served as the commissary for military and government personnel. The factory, wherever it was located, was always defended by a military fort, which the Creeks had agreed to because the military was supposed to provide protection against white "intruders," which is what early-nineteenth-century illegal settlers were called. Military personnel received their rations from the factory, and they were to purchase goods only at the factory.[64] They, too, were disgruntled at the lack of supplies. The U.S. government was to reimburse the factory for the expenditures, but the money and replacement goods were invariably late or not paid, as usual.[65]

In addition to the military fort associated with the Creek Factory, several other forts were stationed at Indian boundary lines. The Indians agreed to these forts because they ostensibly were there to protect Indian lands from American squatters and border jumpers.[66] The exact number of forts on the southern frontier at any one time is difficult to pinpoint, since most were short lived or moved. In addition to those associated with the Creek Factory mentioned above, others near Creek country included Fort Fidius on the Oconee River in present-day Georgia, Fort St. Stephens and Fort Stoddart on the lower Tombigbee River in present-day Alabama, Fort San Marcos in Florida, and numerous forts built when the Red Stick War broke out, most notably Fort Jackson on the site of the old Fort Toulouse near Tuskegee town.[67] Probably the most famous frontier fort from this time period is Fort Mims, the site of a bloody Red Stick victory.[68] The forts usually were walled enclosures with corner bastions, a kitchen, a blockhouse, some houses for officers' families, a drill yard, and in the case of those associated with the Creek Factory, an Indian trade store. The buildings were ramshackle affairs, leaky, cold, and generally uncomfortable. We do not yet have a full reckoning of frontier military life except to say the conditions were deplorable.[69] In fact, soldiers thought being stationed to a southern garrison was the worst possible assignment. Rations were always meager, and the pay was low.[70] Soldiers at these posts actually saw little military action. They occasionally marched out to intimidate white intruders. They also accompanied the U.S. and Creek commissioners when running boundary lines. However, they were not to enter Creek territory, nor could Hawkins use them as a police force, although he did occasionally request their aid in apprehending white criminals.

The soldiers were simply bored. The commanders, in an effort to keep morale up and to prevent desertions, relaxed the rules.[71] Therefore, although it was forbidden by regulation, the soldiers welcomed the visits of Creek men and women coming to the trading houses to barter and socialize. These visits occurred year-round, but they were especially frequent during the hunting season, when so many Creek hunting parties were in the hinterlands. The soldiers usually wanted fresh fruits, vegetables, and fresh meats. From the soldiers the Creeks could get rum and other goods that were either not available at the trade house or that the traders were prohibited from selling.[72] Creek women also sold sexual favors to the soldiers. Soldiers and Creeks competed in horse and foot races with heavy betting. They had wrestling matches, drinking parties, and any number of other diversions.

Conversely, relations were uneasy between the military personnel and the factor. Because there were only a factor and one or two assistants at the factory, whenever the building or storehouses needed repairs, the factor, as instructed by the Treasury Department, asked soldiers to do the job.[73] Soldiers also performed other factory tasks, such as beating worms out of the skins, packing them, loading and unloading goods, and guarding the storehouse. The soldiers resented having to do this work. They argued with the factors over goods, prices, work orders, and any number of things. In fact, in one case at Fort Wilkinson, some soldiers murdered the factor, Edward Price, because of a disagreement.[74]

The military garrisons attracted independent Georgia storekeepers to the vicinity. These were small operations run by private owners, but because they were not under government regulations, they attracted both Creek and military trade away from the factory.[75] These stores sold rum to the Creeks, something strictly forbidden at the factory. They also took in substandard skins and other goods, such as hogs and cattle, that the factory was not allowed to buy.[76] It was illegal for these stores to engage in the Indian trade, so they served as trading posts for frontier whites. Of course, they actively and openly traded with Indians as well as with military personnel and frontier whites. The U.S. factor was powerless to stop them.

Given all of these obstacles, it is a wonder the Factory System in the Southeast stumbled along as long as it did. This minor success can be directly attributed to Benjamin Hawkins.[77] The factories served more as supply depots for Hawkins and the military than as viable trading outlets for the Creeks. Officials in the War and Treasury Departments were well aware that the Indian trade needed revamping if it were to continue. However, the Factory System was not designed to guide the Indian trade along a new path. It was a political tool intended to cement relations between the United States and various Indian nations. By the nineteenth century in the South, the deerskin trade was in a serious decline, and the importance of maintaining Indian allies was rapidly disintegrating. Political tools to maintain Indian alliances, such as the Factory System, were simply obsolete.

The fall and winter hunting season marked the time of intense activity in the hinterlands. As mentioned earlier, hunting was a male occupation, but with commercial hunting, women had begun to participate. The number of people "in the woods" during the hunting season is difficult to assess. Towns were almost empty, and Hawkins once estimated that more than a thousand hunters were near the Georgia border alone.[78] This number only referred to the men, and if one included women and adolescents, the number would increase three- to fourfold. One archaeological study for the Coastal Plain estimates that 300 camps could be made in a single hunting season.[79]

The hunting season was a dangerous time. Hunters took advantage of their proximity to white settlers to raid a few farmsteads. White farmers were often in the woods ostensibly to pursue a thieving party, but generally they were a menace themselves. Also, enemy warriors preferred the hunting season for striking a blow.[80] Because of these dangers and because commercial hunting required a shared labor pool, it was unusual for a Creek hunting party to consist of only a husband, his wife, and their children. This was the basic unit; but the party joined other parties, probably *huti* and other lineage members, and they camped together for mutual protection and to share tasks.[81] We know little about these camps. Philip Georg Friedrich von Reck, a German immigrant in Georgia, drew an early-eighteenth-century Indian hunting camp. It is reasonable to suppose that hunting camps of the late eighteenth century would have been similar.[82] Von Reck's drawing depicts a makeshift structure like a large lean-to. Several poles lean against a central pole (probably a tree). Across the tops of the poles, cypress barks and skins have been laid. The drawing shows various metal pots as well as gourd containers and some skins hanging from the rafters and over the fire. Two small dogs are curled next to the fire. Two figures (probably women) are sitting under the lean-to, engaged in what appears to be hide skinning, and one figure (probably a man), dressed in a long shirt and leggings, stands outside the shelter. Although not shown in von Reck's drawing, riding horses and packhorses would have also been around the camp. When hunting became a full-time seasonal occupation during the deerskin trade era, hunting parties built corncribs stocked with corn in the hinterlands for hunting parties; these were called *toohtocaugee*, which glosses as *toohto*, "a corn house," and *caugee*, "fixed or standing."[83]

When hunting, however, men proceeded on foot. They could wander up to thirty miles a day, stalking deer. Men hunted with guns and with bows and arrows, and they may also have set fire circles to entrap the deer or to run the animals out of hiding.[84] This would also help account for the widespread firing of the hinterlands. Meanwhile back at the camp, women tanned and treated the hides to protect them against worm infestation. They also smoke-dried any meat they were to take home, cooked for the hunters, and generally maintained the camp. Women also gathered seasonally available foods while encamped, especially hickory nuts, which fell during the late fall, and honey, which was a rare treat.[85]

The hunting season usually lasted into February. People often made short trips back to their towns during this time, but for the most part this season was characterized by long stays in the hinterlands.[86] The mischief that occurred during the hunting season presented a problem to Hawkins. He endeavored to regulate the movement of hunting parties by issuing them "tickets" or passports designating their destinations. He assigned each a leader who was to oversee the party's activities and to report any misdeeds to Hawkins.[87] Although it is difficult to assess, it appears that the Creeks never or only rarely adhered uniformly to Hawkins's edicts.

Hunting parties did not just wander through the hinterlands. Hunting grounds had a complex but obscure hierarchical allocation between townships, provinces, Upper and Lower divisions, and national levels. Historian Kathryn Braund documents some of the provincial hunting grounds. According to Braund, Coweta and Cusseta hunters (who would have been of the Apalachicola province) had access to the east and north of their town, all the way to the Ogeechee and Oconee Rivers. The southernmost Lower Creek towns, probably the Hitchiti towns, hunted to the south, near the border of present-day Florida. The people of the Tallapoosa and Abihka provinces had access to northern Alabama and central Tennessee. The Alabama towns could hunt to the south and west of their towns.[88]

Hawkins also recorded some tracts as being the hunting grounds of particular towns.[89] Hawkins's statement is corroborated by the documentary evidence, although the exact boundaries of township hunting grounds cannot be determined from these sources. For instance, in 1802, when the United States wanted to buy the land from the Oconee to the Ocmulgee Rivers, Creek headmen explained to the commissioners that they could not sell the lands because they were the hunting grounds of some disaffected towns on the Flint and Chattahoochee Rivers whose representatives had boycotted the meeting in protest of the sale.[90] U.S. commissioner General James Wilkinson, believing that the British adventurer William Bowles, who was among the Seminoles at this time, was behind this and being angry over the delay, retorted, "Who are these people? Mischief makers? Are you not masters of your land and are you going to let a few mischief makers rule you?"[91]

A month later, in a quieter moment, the headmen explained to Hawkins that they were afraid to sell these lands without the permission of the towns to whom they belonged because "those tribes might attack our frontier and spill blood."[92] The representatives of the two towns (Chehaw and Tuttallosee) refused to attend the meeting because they opposed the cession. The headmen in attendance told Hawkins, "We cannot cede any lands belonging to people who are not here."[93] They then delineated the exact tract in question as running from below Rock Landing and south of the Altamaha River. The headmen contended that the lands south of Rock Landing were not worth a general war, since the Georgians did not highly value this tract anyway.[94]

In a later case in 1811, the Creeks contested a Choctaw land cession, and the War Department investigated the contradicting claims. The deposition of headman Hopithle Micco to the president included a description of some of the Alabama towns' hunting grounds. The Alabama hunting grounds began at the creek above Cedar Creek, a tributary of the Alabama River. The western edge was marked by "a large path running from the edge of the swamp on the Tombigbee and crosses two creeks to the path from Sam Connels that crosses the Alabama River about two miles below Cedar Creek."[95]

As both of these examples demonstrate, townships and/or provinces had clearly defined hunting grounds that were recognized by other towns in the Creek Confederacy. People of a township probably had exclusive hunting and grazing rights within their specified hunting grounds, although this is unclear. Given that hunting parties traveled far and wide and that free-ranging livestock could not be controlled in their wanderings, townships must have relaxed these rules as a matter of goodwill. Any arguments ensuing from such trespassing were strictly Indian affairs and went unrecorded by whites. It is also unlikely that every acre of Creek territory was divvied among the townships. Each township probably claimed specific tracts as hunting grounds, and any unclaimed lands fell under the proprietorship of the Upper or Lower divisions. Anyone belonging to the Creek Confederacy had hunting and use rights to these vacant lands.[96] This is one reason why "hunting lands" figured so prominently in treaty negotiations; hunting legitimated far-flung land claims.

By all accounts, Creek hunters had to broaden their hunting ranges as the deerskin trade era continued. The Creeks often protested land sales because they needed every inch of hunting territory, and they claimed that many people were naked and poor because their hunters could no longer get enough skins. Literate travelers through Creek hinterlands during the late eighteenth century also often commented on the scarcity of white-tailed deer. Hawkins wrote, "It is difficult for a good hunter in passing through it [Creek territory] in any direction to obtain enough for his support."[97] Bartram observed that the southeastern Indians "waged eternal war against deer and bear, to procure food and other necessaries and conveniences; which is indeed carried to an unreasonable and perhaps criminal excess."[98] The deer were not entirely gone. The trade records show that deerskins continued to be traded, but they also show an increasing number of other pelts from beavers, otters, muskrats, wolves, bears, foxes, raccoons, wildcats, and even opossums.[99] Hawkins and Bartram, as well as other white travelers and Creeks, ate much venison as well as pork, beef, and chicken.

The decreasing number of deer certainly was a contributing factor to the decline of the deerskin trade.[100] Before commercial trading, Creek men had hunted selectively. They understood that they could not kill mature females and young deer without affecting the reproductive rates of the deer population. Faunal remains of deer from precontact archaeological sites are mostly mature males. With commercial trading, however, Creek hunting strategies changed, and Creek hunters were no longer concerned with selective hunting. They killed deer of all ages and sexes for their skins.[101]

By the end of the eighteenth century, another factor contributed to the diminishing number of deer in Creek territory. Cows and hogs increased substantially during this time. Because cows and hogs compete with deer for forage, their presence may have forced deer out of the range of free-range and feral cattle and hogs. The ecological impact of ranching will be discussed later, but the increasing number of livestock among both the Creeks and the white settlers led to serious imbalances in deer and perhaps bear habitats. The Creeks had been complaining about the presence of hogs and cattle in their territory for this very reason since the animals were first introduced into the Southeast. Ironically, as deer became scarce, Creeks themselves turned to ranching, placing further pressure on the deer population.

Hawkins hoped to work the decline of the deerskin trade in his favor. One important aspect of the new economic diversification, especially in the plan for civilization, was a proposal to curb men's hunting activities. This was crucial to the success of the plan for civilization, since the motivation behind the plan was to turn Indian families into yeoman farmers. The plan for civilization called for men and women to work together in the fields and to raise livestock like frontier whites. Whenever he had the chance, Hawkins lectured Creek men on the benefits of stock raising, and he tried to convince them to aid the women in the fields.

Creek men were already engaged in ranching. However, they could not reconcile themselves to laboring in the fields. Hunting had been a commercial enterprise for almost 100 years, and although the deerskin trade was in serious trouble, Creek men were still reluctant to give up the hunt. According to the Quakers, women ridiculed men who worked in the fields, and men were simply embarrassed to be doing this type of work.[102] There is probably some truth to this, since ridicule would have been a common response to men doing women's work, and vice versa. For Creek men, to be a man was to be a hunter and warrior. Even though Hawkins knew much about Creek life and was an astute observer, he may never have realized the extent to which a Creek man's definition of himself rested on this premise. To deprive a Creek man of the hunt was, in effect, to deprive him of his manhood and his conception of himself as a social being. Even if Hawkins did understand what it meant to a Creek man to be a hunter, he must have had to underplay or ignore such considerations because it was antithetical to the civilization plan.

Herein one arrives at the political significance of hunting and the Indian trade and its implications for ownership of the hinterlands. Simply put, hunting was tied to land. In treaty negotiations, Creek chiefs invariably refused to cede more land on the grounds that they needed it for hunting. By insisting on hunting, the Creeks held a legitimate and mutually recognized claim to the hinterlands. To Creek men, then, to give up the hunt also meant relinquishing their land. Creek men knew only too well that hunting was no longer economically viable. They were aware of the economic problems they and their families now faced. Many of them had already turned to livestock raising and other opportunities. Assuredly, Creek men continued to hunt and were averse to agricultural labor, but their insistence on hunting, although clothed in social value, rested on its political implications about their land rights, national sovereignty, and access to commercial goods.[103]

CHAPTER SEVEN

CREEK FARMERS

The backbone of the new Creek economy of the late eighteenth and early nineteenth centuries was not farming and the deerskin trade but farming and ranching. Farming was nothing new to the Creeks, as they were the descendants of farmers from as far back as the Woodland Period (1000 B.C.–A.D. 1000). Interestingly, other than the use of metal tools and types of crops, southeastern Indian agricultural techniques probably did not change much from the Woodland Period through the Mississippian and Historic Periods.[1] Like their prehistoric counterparts, Historic Period Creek agricultural techniques were simple and did not require a large investment of labor. The Creeks practiced basically swidden and hoe agriculture, and the indigenous staples were corn, beans, and squash, although by the nineteenth century, Creek farmers had added many introduced products.

Because of their long association with agriculture and rural life, southern soils are generally thought of as rich and fertile, but they are in aggregate, as one environmental historian reflects, "really only mediocre."[2] The soils in Creek country, like most southern soils, are varieties of podzols, which are loamy soils formed in part by decaying forest debris and a warm, moist climate. A notable exception in Creek country are the soils of the Black Prairie. These are rendzina soils associated with grasslands.[3] Of course, soils vary tremendously at the local level, and some southern soils are better than others. In the late eighteenth and early nineteenth centuries, American farmers and developers generally assessed soils at the local level according to the trees that grew on them. In parts of the South, land was categorized as either river land or uplands, and each category was subdivided into qualitative grades of first, second, third, fourth, and so on.

Like the Creeks, Euro-American farmers understood the alluvial soils of the river valleys to be the best for agriculture. Unlike the Creeks, however, Euro-Americans reckoned the first-quality river lands to be the former alluvial deposits of the terraces, denoted by oak, hickory, and pine. Because of the yearly flooding, Euro-American farmers considered the active floodplains second-quality river lands. These were denoted by river cane, walnut, American beech, maple, sassafras, and persimmon. Upland soils were likewise graded. First-quality upland soils had a good growth of white oak, hickory, and dogwood. Second-quality upland soils contained a mixed oak, hickory, and pine forest. Third-quality upland soils were mostly pine forests with a smattering of oak and hickory and were sandy. Fourth-quality upland soils, characterized by pine forests, were the least desirable farmlands to southern white farmers. Using this assessment, the worst lands were in the Coastal Plain, which could support agricultural activity only on the hammocks.[4]

Not surprisingly, Creek settlement patterns correlated with these Euro-American soil assessments. As we have seen, almost all of the Creek towns were located in first- and second-quality river lands and first- and second-quality uplands. However, one should keep in mind that the locations of Creek towns were not solely dictated by where good arable lands were located. Security, trade routes, hunting ranges, and livestock forage also figured into late-eighteenth-century Creek decisions regarding town locations.[5]

In addition to hunting ranges, towns also owned portions of the river bottom, usually on both sides of the river up- and downstream of where their towns were located. These areas could be large. The towns on the Tallapoosa, for example, owned eight- to ten-mile stretches of land along the river.[6] A town had exclusive rights to the active floodplains within its property lines as well as to other resources. The Chattahoochee fisheries, as discussed earlier, were divided between Coweta and Cusseta.[7] The 2,000-acre hardwood preserve on the western side of the Chattahoochee River valley belonged to Coweta Tallahassee.[8]

As we have seen, agricultural fields were either in meander coves or followed long, linear patterns conforming to the active floodplains, and they covered several acres. As discussed in Chapter 3, Hawkins recorded the agricultural lands owned by some of the Creek towns.[9] Sometimes towns agreed to share agricultural lands, as in the cases of Chehaw and Ooseoochee, Fusihatchee and Cooloome, and Tuskegee and Hookchoieooche. In other cases, field boundaries were marked by natural divides, usually creeks or river bends, as in the case of Fusihatchee and Hoithlewaule, discussed earlier.[10]

In addition to the communal fields, Creek women also maintained small gardens, located adjacent to their households on the terraces.[11] The average size of these household gardens is not known, but they are described as small.[12] Household gardens were privately owned by the households and worked by the women of the households, with perhaps occasional help from other female relations. Hawkins noticed that the people of the Alabama town of Pauwocte did not have household gardens, but this was unusual.[13] Bartram states that Creek women planted these gardens early; therefore the corn and beans from the gardens probably provided an early harvest that the household relied on before the crops in the communal fields ripened.[14] The redundancy of garden and communal crops, especially corn and beans, was probably a risk strategy in case the larger field crops failed, and it may also have ensured that at least a seed crop was produced each year.[15]

Within a town's communal agricultural lands, each matrilineage had the use of a portion of the communal field, and the divisions between these portions were marked by rows of small trees or shrubs.[16] Bartram described these family lots as adjacent to one another and "divided or bounded by a strip of grass ground, poles set up, or any other natural or artificial boundary—thus the whole plantation is a collection of lots joining each other, comprised in one enclosure, or general boundary."[17] Milfort described the whole communal field as being enclosed "with old pieces of wood and stakes set in the ground."[18] How these lots were assigned goes unrecorded. Bartram, who gave the lengthiest description of Creek land tenure, only stated, "Every town, or community, assigns a piece, or parcel, of land."[19] Milfort, equally terse, wrote only that "they then divide the lands in this enclosure among the families."[20] Romans wrote that the Creeks "have a strict notion of distinction in property, and even divide their lands, [and] we never hear them quarrel about boundaries."[21] Hawkins did not explain intra-Creek land divisions and rights.

Knowing town politics, however, one can surmise that each family perhaps petitioned for certain lots through the head of their lineage, and the requests were granted through consensus after discussion and debate at a town council. Since women were the farmers, they knew about soils and other agricultural requirements. They, therefore, would have been the ones to survey the lands and choose the plots. Their advice and decisions would have been relayed to the town councils through the male head of their lineage. The size of these allotments goes unrecorded by white observers. One recent estimate based on average historic Creek corn production and consumption put the acreage at two per family (five people) per season.[22]

From an 1881–82 manuscript on the Creeks, who were now living in Oklahoma, H. N. B. Hewitt related that whenever a child was born, "the town got an additional allotment."[23] According to this manuscript, the town took a census during the Green Corn Festival, and if there was any increase in the population, more land was put under cultivation. Hewitt's manuscript indicates that land was assigned according to need, and therefore only the amount of land that could be cultivated was assigned. However, Hawkins noted that at Coweta Tallahassee, "they have enclosed more land then they can use."[24]

However land lots were assigned, a matrilineage did not have exclusive rights but, rather, use rights to its lot. When a field was abandoned, it returned to town ownership. Also, a town could dictate certain rules about the use of agricultural fields. For instance, at Upatoi, a Cusseta satellite village where Tussekia Micco acted as headman, the whole village had built worm fences around their fields. Tussekia Micco told Hawkins that there was a village rule that no one was allowed to live there unless they fenced their fields.[25] Town councils sometimes allotted garden plots to white men living in town, with instructions that they could only grow a small amount of food for themselves. The expectation was that these men would buy produce from local farmers.[26]

Furthermore, in his campaign for the plan for civilization, Hawkins often had to deal with a whole town's acceptance or rejection of the plan. For instance, in 1808 he reported to Secretary of War Henry Dearborn that "an entire town, Chehaw, has come over." The year before, Hawkins found the Chehaw so "obstinately opposed" to his new farming methods that the women planted five times as many seeds in a corn hill than Hawkins suggested. He attributed the town's change in attitude to the subsequent poor harvest.[27] As mentioned earlier, the town of Hoithlewaule could not come to a consensus on whether or not to conform to Hawkins's farming instructions, which created internal divisiveness.[28] In most instances, however, the women in a matrilineage were given much latitude about use of their agricultural lots, as evidenced by individual women's choices to experiment with wheat, cotton, and other crops that Hawkins was advocating.

The loose, friable floodplain soils were necessary for Creek agriculture because of the simple technology of swidden cultivation. Other than the axes needed for clearing a new field, the only agricultural tools used in swidden agriculture are hoes and digging sticks. In the Historic Period, the Creeks preferred European-manufactured iron hoes, although some people could and did make and use stone hoes, which were broad, flat pieces of worked stone hafted onto a hefty but short handle. The European hoes looked very similar to modern hoes—wooden handles with attached iron heads—except that the hoes were broader and the handles shorter. Women made their own digging sticks. A digging stick is a long, straight stick with a point on the end used to poke holes in the ground for seeds.[29]

As part of the plan for civilization, Hawkins launched a campaign to win the Creeks over to plow farming. Except for about 100 families, everyone stayed with hoes.[30] The Creeks once explained that Creek farmers who used the plow had an advantage over others because they could produce more. With good plows, farmers could turn soil much deeper and till more ground than with hoes, thus increasing both production and output of an agricultural field. This unevenness in output meant that those with the plow could sell more food to visitors, whites, and others, to the particular disadvantage of the older men and women who depended on the sale of foodstuffs for part of their livelihoods.[31] In reality, southern plows were notoriously bad and "killing to horse flesh," and despite any increases in productivity, even white farmers refused to use them until the mid-nineteenth century, when plows were substantially improved.[32] The Creeks called the plow "nothing but a horse trap."[33] Besides, Creek agricultural fields were in active alluvial floodplains, where the soil was easily worked with hoes and digging sticks. These soils also tend to be clayey, and hence plowing them is somewhat difficult. Also, hoe farming does not impact the soil like plowing, which digs deep into the soil and increases runoff and erosion. In fact, neither runoff nor erosion were problems for Creek farmers.

The only other tools needed were axes for clearing the fields. As with the hoes, most Creeks by this time preferred European-made steel axes, although they could and did continue making stone axes throughout the Historic Period.[34] In swidden agriculture, fields are in various stages of fallow; therefore, the tasks involved in clearing agricultural fields depend on how long an area has been fallow. Swidden agriculture is characterized by relatively frequent field rotations. A field is used until it shows signs of decreased output, at which time the farmer abandons it and leaves it fallow for a number of years until the soils have regenerated.[35] In early-nineteenth-century southern swidden agriculture, signs of soil fatigue appeared after about fifteen to twenty years.[36] After abandoning a field, the farmer moved on to a fallow field that had recovered enough to be farmed. Creek farmers recultivated fallow fields before they had time to revert to old-growth forest, and they were characterized by younger, smaller trees. As we have seen, the floodplains in the heart of Creek country had mostly small trees in them, indicating previous agricultural clearing. So for about fifteen years at a stretch, Creek women simply rotated their allotted fields.[37]

Clearing these fields was not so onerous a task as clearing a field of historic old-growth forest. In these cases, field clearing simply required burning of recent agricultural debris and weeds. The task fell to women and children, who began clearing and preparing the fields as early as January.[38] Since many women accompanied their male kin on winter hunting excursions, they either returned home before the men to prepare their fields, or else they left the task to the women, girls, and boys who stayed in town for the winter. After a harvest, Creek women did not clear the crop debris. They left corn husks, leafy matter, and stems for deer and livestock browse.[39] Upon returning to a field, they simply burned the remaining debris.[40] In swidden agriculture, the ash from yearly burning usually acts as a fertilizer, and nitrogen especially is replenished in this way.[41]

When these fields showed signs of strain, Creek men cleared new fields in areas that had been fallow long enough for small trees to appear on them (again, probably about fifteen to twenty years). Hawkins lived among the Creeks for twenty years, yet he only mentioned Creek men clearing "new fields" once, in 1809 at Cusseta.[42] The Creek hunting season usually ended in late February or March, although it sometimes lingered into April and even May. The agricultural season began a few months earlier, which meant that sometimes men would have to return to town early to clear fields. In these cases, the men of a town, or at least those designated for the job, returned home in January to "make new fields."[43]

In clearing such a field, Creek men did not actually cut down the trees and remove the stumps. Rather, they girdled the trees a few years before the final clearing to kill them.[44] In this process, they would ring a tree with a deep incision near its base. This ring would eventually kill the tree, and within a few years rotted limbs would fall off and sometimes the trunks would topple to the ground. The ground debris was then burned. The stumps would be left in place to rot.[45] Girdling was also practiced by plantation owners and some frontier farmers. Frontier whites moving onto recently ceded lands always preferred "old fields," or land with small trees, because clearing a historic old-growth forest was so difficult. These white farmers even opted for land of secondary quality when primary quality land posed such problems in clearing.[46]

Plantation owners had their slaves clear large tracts of historic old-growth forest by girdling. Philip Henry Gosse described a girdled field near Mobile in the 1850s: "After the twigs and smaller boughs have dropped off and the bark has dried and shrunk, and been stripped away, and the naked branches have become blanched by the summer's sun and winter's rain, these tall dead trunks, so thickly spread over the land, look like an army of skeletons stretching their great white arms."[47] These trees were hazardous to field workers and to crops because of the falling limbs. Still, to cut them would have been backbreaking work, and they usually fell over in the winter storms when no one was in the field.[48]

After the fields had been cleared, women and children began the planting. In planting corn, Creek women turned the soil and then built up small hills of earth in which they placed their seeds. These hills were in rows about five feet apart. Each hill contained between five and ten corn seeds. Between the rows they planted certain supplemental crops such as squashes and gourds, pumpkins, and beans, the vines of which would grow up the cornstalks or on cane stalks placed in the field.[49] Intercropping in this way helped break the rain as it fell and decreased rainfall runoff. It also acted as a kind of mulch, leaving little of the soil exposed to direct sunlight, which would leach and dry out the soil.[50] Intercropping also helped control pests such as insects, birds, rodents, raccoons, deer, and other animals. Intercropping makes a grown field almost impenetrable. Small animals, raccoons in particular, can wreak havoc on an agricultural field. But the animals need room to maneuver, and they prefer more open foraging areas. The dense Creek agricultural fields, again while not completely stopping small animals, made the fields uninviting and, therefore, decreased the number of small animals searching for daily meals among crops.[51] Some animals, such as deer and birds, required human vigilance. The Creeks built small lookout stands within and adjacent to their fields. Women, girls, and boys took turns manning the stands and scaring off birds and deer by shouting, waving pieces of cloth, or firing their guns.[52]

Hawkins promoted fencing one's fields against pests. Fences figured much in Hawkins's understanding of good agrarian practices. Following Euro-American ideas of proper stewardship, to Hawkins, fences represented good land and livestock management.[53] Late-eighteenth-century fences were worm or snakerail fences, which were made of saplings and small trees stacked in panels six to eleven rails high and meeting at an angle. The fences zigzagged around a field and required little cutting and no planing or nails.[54] They could also be easily disassembled to allow livestock to graze in the fields after harvest or for moving when and if a family relocated its fields. When worn out, the fences could be used as firewood.

These low fences would have posed little problem for a deer, but they would have functioned to keep livestock out. The Creeks were uneven in their acceptance of fences. Although they used fences for garden and specialized plots, for the most part, Creek farmers refused to fence the communal fields.[55] Hawkins always attributed this to ingrained habits of poor management, but historian Claudio Saunt argues that fences symbolized a person's commercial interest and that building or not building fences indicated whether or not one was oriented to the market. As we will see, there were also some practical considerations involved in fencing. However, there can be no doubt that the Creeks, as Hawkins, viewed fences as a symbol of America. In the Red Stick War, the Red Sticks made deliberate efforts to destroy fences because they represented the acceptance of American ways.[56]

Although the Creeks had a diversity of wild and domesticated foods by the turn of the nineteenth century, corn, supplemented with beans and squash, was still the staple food crop and, by all accounts, constituted their primary field crop. The southeastern Indians had been cultivating corn since the Mississippian Period, and it has figured prominently in their lives and ideology since then. The *poskita* or Busk, also called the Green Corn Ceremony, was the principal ritual of renewal and purification of most southeastern Indian groups, and it is still practiced today by many groups. Although each group and even town had variations of it, the ceremony typically was several days long and consisted of a series of solemn rituals wherein the world was swept clean, purified, and hence renewed. It took place in the fall, with the ripening of the new corn.[57]

Corn is a highly variable cultigen. Several different species were grown by Native Americans, prehistorically and historically. Many of these species were crossed, producing an additional variety of hybrids. Creek women undoubtedly grew flint corns (*Zea mays*), and mostly they grew varieties of the northern flints.[58] Gosse described *Zea mays* as growing "to the height of ten feet; the stem strong and thick, surrounded and partially enveloped in its large flag-like leaves, here and there the swelling ears projecting from the stalk, each enclosed in its membranous sheath, from the extremity of which the pendulous shining filaments hang out, called the silk, and which are the pistils of the female flower; and the tall elegant spike of male flowers, called the tassel, crowns the whole."[59]

We also do not know precisely how much corn the Creeks of the late eighteenth century produced in their floodplains. Bernard Romans estimated that in the soils of the Tombigbee and Mississippi Rivers, one could grow as many as 80 bushels of corn per acre, and even in the "sandy lands" one could harvest 15 to 25 bushels per acre.[60] Romans mentioned that in the Upper Creek town of Coosada, Creek women produced 60 to 80 bushels per acre.[61] But he put the average riverine soil production at 50 to 60 bushels per acre.[62] Hawkins noted that the Indian countryman Richard Bailey, who lived on the Tallapoosa River, produced 50 bushels of corn per acre.[63] Archaeologists have demonstrated that Indian corn production was variable, depending on local soil conditions and how long parcels of land had been cultivated, among other factors. For southeastern alluvial soils, corn production probably ranged from approximately 15 to 30 bushels, with an average of about 30 bushels per acre.[64] A statement by Hawkins's assistant Richard Thomas may hint that some women decided to decrease their corn production. Thomas said that some Creeks saw little use in planting corn, since they could buy all they needed from Georgians.[65]

Hawkins and other white elites who were in Creek country believed Indian farming techniques wasteful and indolent. These men were certainly ethnocentric, but one must keep in mind that this was the beginning of the era of scientific farming and agrarian reform. Hawkins kept a close correspondence with Thomas Jefferson, the leading proponent of scientific farming, on agrarian experiments and advanced methods. Therefore it is not surprising that Hawkins viewed Creek agricultural methods as below par and in need of reform. Even so, the civilization plan, although not explicitly designed to do so, squared well with the new frontier economy and Creek women's proscribed roles in it. Because of the plan's agricultural base, Hawkins understood that Creek women would be instrumental to its success. Thus in addition to soliciting support from the Indian countrymen and métis Creeks, he also targeted Creek women from the beginning. Much to his surprise, they became his strongest advocates for the plan.

Hawkins's success with Creek women was partly due to the genuine affection with which Creek women regarded him. They were pleased that Hawkins inquired into their situation. He included them in his councils, and he even invited them to dine with him and the men, which was unprecedented in Creek society. His solicitations greatly impressed the women and surprised the men. As a measure of their regard, one can point to the incident when Hawkins's life was threatened at Coweta Tallahassee. The women came to him, asked for guns, and swore they would protect him. Hawkins, likewise, held a high opinion of Creek women. He recognized them for the hard workers they were; he appreciated their progressive attitude toward farming; and he understood that, with the decline of the deerskin trade, the welfare of the Creek family rested to a large extent on their shoulders.[66] This is not to say that Creek men did not have input into these matters, and Hawkins sought the compliance of Creek men to the reforms in farming and cloth making.[67]

As envisioned by Hawkins, in the plan for civilization Creek women would continue their subsistence agricultural roles, but they would also raise cash crops. Women would engage in cottage industries, especially cloth making, and ranching. They would grow their own cotton, some of which would be used in manufacturing their own cloth and some of which would be sold on the market. Until they became self-sufficient, Hawkins would supply each family that wanted to participate with spinning wheels, cotton cards, hoes, plows, and other manufactured items necessary to the plan.

Creek women were already engaged in ranching, and they had already adopted some Old World cultigens before Hawkins's arrival. The southeastern Indians actually were slow to adopt Old World cultigens. The archaeological evidence suggests that until the late eighteenth century, the Indians selected only those introduced cultigens that fit within their conventional farming techniques and that had high yields and low risks, particularly cowpeas (today commonly known as black-eyed peas), peaches, and African watermelons, all of which probably were introduced via the Spaniards of La Florida in the late sixteenth century.[68] By the time Hawkins arrived, the Creeks were expert cultivators of these plants. Hawkins admired Creek peach orchards and encouraged the Creeks to grow more by giving them free access to the peach tree nursery at the Creek Agency.[69] The Upper Creek towns of Fusihatchee and Cooloome, as mentioned earlier, were famous for their melons, and Hawkins also noted that the Alabama town of Ecunchate grew "fine melons in great abundance." The Creeks especially liked cowpeas, which also originated in Africa.[70] A few Euro-Americans observed cowpeas being grown in the communal fields, and cowpeas have been recovered from historic Creek sites; but the botanical samples are too small to indicate the amount being grown.[71]

By the late eighteenth century two other Old World domesticates had become important additions to Creek agriculture: rice and sweet potatoes. According to Bartram, the Creeks grew a variety of rice that North Carolinians planted in river bottoms and swamps. Presumably this is the Old World domesticated rice *Oryza sativa*, which would have been introduced through the English rice plantations on the Atlantic coast.[72] Four or five seeds were placed in "hills on high dry ground in their Gardens."[73] Bartram states that when this variety of rice was planted in dry ground, the plants were more prolific and the grains were "larger, firmer, or more farinaceous, much sweeter and more nourishing."[74] Bartram is obviously describing a method of dry-rice cultivation.

Although Bartram saw rice growing only in the household gardens, the bottoms of the Tallapoosa, Alabama, lower Chattahoochee, and Flint Rivers had ample swampy areas for wet-rice cultivation. As we have seen, the Flint and

Alabama Rivers ran through the Coastal Plain, which has much wetlands. The lower Chattahoochee bottoms had numerous ponds, "slashes," and swamps. On the south side of the Tallapoosa, swamps abutted Autossee, Hoithlewaule, Cooloome, Fusihatchee, Mucclassee, Sawanogi, and Ecunhutke (see figs. 10, 12, and 13). Some of the towns on the Flint River already were engaging in rice production when Hawkins arrived. The people at Aumucullee, at the confluence of the Flint River and Muckalee Creek, grew plenty of rice.[75] Pad- jeeligau was situated by a "valuable" swamp (see fig. 8).[76] Hawkins encour- aged wet-rice cultivation, but he did not envisage rice as a good cash crop ex- cept in the swampy margins of the Flint River. He believed wheat, cotton, and corn would fare better as cash crops in most of Creek country.[77]

How much rice the Creeks grew is uncertain. Rice, to date, has not been re- covered in the botanical samples from Historic Creek archaeological sites.[78] Bartram listed rice as one of their main vegetable foods along with corn and sweet potatoes, and literate travelers mentioned large fields of rice "in the flat low-Grounds" of the rivers.[79] Romans, on the other hand, stated that they bought most of their rice.[80] No matter whether they were buying or growing rice, the Creeks were definitely consuming quantities of the grain. Whites in- variably mentioned rice when describing their own repasts at Creek towns.

Sweet potatoes were another important introduced cultigen and a favorite food of the Creeks. By the late eighteenth century, sweet potatoes had begun to compete with corn as a staple crop. Although the southeastern Indians col- lected a wild potato, sweet potatoes as a cultigen were probably introduced into the Southeast early in the colonial years, and probably by African slaves.[81] Africans were experts in sweet potato cultivation, and their knowledge spread to white farmers and to Indians. Sweet potatoes produce high yields, yet other than "banking" they require little attention throughout the growing season.[82] Because sweet potatoes only seed in especially warm climates, farmers en- sured a crop for the next year by storing a number of sweet potatoes through the winter to use as "seed" potatoes. This was known as banking. These sweet potatoes were allowed to sprout, and the slips were transplanted to the fields at planting time.[83] The slips were placed in a dirt hill, and as the plant grew, dirt was occasionally mounded around the base of the plant.[84]

Growing sweet potatoes posed one serious problem for Creek farmers. Hogs love sweet potatoes and will root them out if given half a chance. Most Creeks owned hogs, so planting sweet potatoes in the garden or communal fields required extra vigilance to keep the hogs out. The danger of damage from hogs may have prompted Creek women to keep their potato fields sep- arate from their other fields. Plus, sweet potatoes could be grown in lesser-quality soils, even on hillsides, which would have made separate potato fields a good option as well.[85] Creek women built low worm fences to protect their sweet potato fields.[86] Hawkins often mentioned separate, fenced "potato hills." But these fences would not have kept deer out, and as most southern gardeners know, deer love sweet potatoes. It may be that the deer population was so low by this time that they were not a problem in and around Creek household gardens.

The amount of sweet potatoes grown by the Creeks is not known. Because they are tubers, sweet potatoes are not likely to leave any archaeological traces in botanical samples, and no traces have been recovered to date.[87] The accounts from people traveling through Creek towns show that sweet potatoes were eaten at most meals and may have been used for winter fodder. Bartram described Creek storage houses as having the ground floor devoted to sweet potato storage, implying that each family grew enough to necessitate ample storage space.[88] The environmental historian Thomas Hatley claims that the sweet potato practically revolutionized Cherokee agriculture, although he does not elaborate.[89] Sweet potatoes were certainly an important new cultigen, and by the late eighteenth century they were a mainstay of the Creek diet along with corn.

Hawkins also encouraged Creek women to experiment with a great variety of introduced food crops. Most of this experimentation appears to have taken place in the household gardens. Here Creek women planted some native domesticates such as corn, beans, squash, and gourds as well as tobacco and some introduced cultigens such as watermelons, cantaloupes, grapes, raspberries, apples, cabbages, cucumbers, radishes, beets, shallots, varieties of peas, turnips, celery, onions, and lettuce.[90]

Stimulated by the plan for civilization, many Creek farmers were beginning to experiment in cotton and wheat agriculture. Creek farmers kept these crops in separate fields, since they learned the techniques of growing cotton and wheat from Hawkins and Indian countrymen, all of whom planted these in separate fields. In 1807 Hawkins estimated that he needed 100 bushels of wheat seed to supply the demand for that year. In 1812 he reported that forty-three more families were requesting wheat seed so they could begin to grow the grain.[91] Women brought their wheat daily to his gristmill, and the cotton gin was in use two to three days a week.[92] Despite Hawkins's optimism, wheat agriculture did not appeal much to the Creeks, probably because the grain requires more labor than corn, as well as specialized harvesting tools. More seriously, it produces less.[93] In fact, neither wheat, barley, oats, nor rye did well in the South because of the climate. Although Hawkins continued to promote their use and despite his bragging, it is unlikely that Creek women invested much time in these grains.

Cotton production, however, appears to have been on the increase. In 1801 two canoes with 1,500 pounds of "Tallapoosa cotton" arrived from Creek territory at Mobile. Judging from the regular use of Hawkins's cotton gin and a request by Lower Creek women for another one, cotton was becoming a popular and profitable crop. People could be protective of their seeds. During one season a Creek woman named Sookahoey had two gallons of cotton seed. When Hawkins's assistant Richard Thomas asked her to share the seed with others interested in growing cotton, she refused, saying she needed all she had. Of course, it is also possible that Sookahoey did not feel obligated to share with people with whom she did not have any relationships of reciprocity.[94]

Despite such agricultural activities, Creek women did not lose their expertise with wild plants. Creek women added variety and nutritional supplements to their families' diets through gathering wild plant foods. Most wild plant foods were consumed when they were seasonally available, but some, such as grapes and persimmons, were dried and stored for later use.[95] The Creeks also transplanted a wild plant far from its original habitat. Black drink, the ceremonial tea made from the leaves of the cassena plant (yaupon, or *Ilex vomitoria*), originally grew only along the coast.[96] Hawkins noted the Creeks tending the plant in the towns of Oakfuskee, Tuckabatchee, Yuchi, and a Hillaubee town (where it grew up to eight feet high).[97] *Ilex vomitoria* was never domesticated in the true sense of changing its genetic composition; it was probably a semidomesticate.[98]

Hawkins wrote that in the whole of Creek territory there was little fruit of any kind.[99] Surely Hawkins's claim can be interpreted to mean that he did not see any domesticated berries, since elsewhere he described several varieties of wild fruits. Fox grapes and muscadines grew in the floodplains; blackberries and persimmons grew in abandoned agricultural fields; and wild strawberries grew on the "sand hills."[100] Hawkins also observed that many Creek hunters subsisted on china briar (greenbriar) roots while hunting. They were undoubtedly making *coonti*, a flour made from the roots, which when mixed with water, formed a paste that could be fried into a fritter or eaten uncooked as a jelly.[101] Encountering a hunting camp, Hawkins observed Creek women gathering hickory nuts and wild potatoes, and Romans reported that the Creeks ate the wild potato "in abundance."[102] In addition to foraging, Creek women also probably modified the environment around their towns and households to increase the amount of useful wild plants. Wild fruits such as persimmons, wild grapes, hackberries, and maypops grow in disturbed, sunny areas. The amount of such wild fruits in the archaeological record of Historic Period sites has led archaeologists to conclude that the Indians were modifying their surrounding landscape in order to increase the habitats of these plants.[103]

Bartram made perhaps the most extensive observations on Creek plant use. He listed the following as wild foods: acorns, hickory nuts, mulberries, grapes, persimmons, honey locust, mayapples, blue palmetto fruits, and Chickasaw plums. Some wild plants, such as the spider flower and arrow arum, or Indian turnip, were used as herbal seasonings.[104] Creek women gathered some wild grains such as wild rice and barnyard grass.[105]

In the mid-twentieth century, anthropologist John Swanton compiled an extensive list of wild plant foods used by the Creeks, many of which the archaeological evidence shows to have been used during the Historic Period as well.[106] The small botanical samples from the Late Tallapoosa Phase (A.D. 1770–1837) at Tuckabatchee include hickory nuts and maypops as wild edibles. At Fusihatchee, flotation samples recovered evidence for grapes, persimmons, maypops, sumac, hackberry, and varieties of chenopodium. Chenopodium is a leafy green wild vegetable that can be cooked as a food similar to turnip greens, and it also produces an edible seed. Southern Indians had included chenopodium in their foodstuffs for many centuries.[107]

They also made dyes from wild plants. The Creeks, as all southeastern Indians, practiced various forms of body and hair adornment, tattooing being the favorite. They also used vegetable dyes for coloring cloth, skins, and other items. Hawkins once saw some Creek women near Nauchee collecting the roots of a plant they called *talewau*, which they mixed with bear oil and used as a dye for reddening their hair.[108] In addition to using wild plants as food, the Creeks understood them to have many medicinal qualities and used them as such.[109] Creek medicine men and women, or *heni hijas*, collected wild plants, but they also maintained special gardens for their medicinal herbs. Creek women would occasionally aid in tending the herb gardens in payment for the services of medicine men and women.[110]

Anthropologists understand the gathering of wild foods among subsistence agriculturalists to be a risk strategy, a method of dealing with the uncertainties of agriculture. By retaining the knowledge of what wild plant resources are available and where they can be found, people minimize the risk of famine if a prolonged crop failure should occur. They can subsist on wild foods, if need be.[111] In 1807 the Creeks suffered a major crop failure because of an excessive drought. That year, "the hungry year," people subsisted mostly on wild foods, but Hawkins made it clear that this dependence on wild vegetable foods was unusual.[112] Such strategies were necessary for southern swidden agriculturalists because the successful growing of crops depended on natural elements such as soil fertility, rain, and sunlight, none of which are consistently uniform across an area and most of which are not always reliable.

Generally, Creek country was in that part of the American South that receives about forty inches of rain a year, which is about perfect for corn cultivation.[113] Creek agricultural practices depended on rainfall as they did not irrigate their fields, although they occasionally brought water from the river between rains.[114] Too much rain could turn their fields into a quagmire—so much so that the women could not even get into them.[115] Annual flooding usually occurred in the spring, which could mean disaster if the floods came after the planting and if the waters did not recede quickly. One reason that Creek farmers in the towns on the Alabama gave to Hawkins for not fencing their fields was that the flooding would wreck any fences.[116]

Larger flooding episodes also occurred intermittently. The people of Cusseta told Hawkins about what must have been a large twenty-year flood that inundated much of the Creek farmlands along the Chattahoochee River.[117] The confluence of the Coosa and Tallapoosa Rivers was especially prone to large floods. The Coosa and Tallapoosa together drain a massive portion of former Creek country, and in times of flooding much of this water converges at their confluence. The Creeks told Hawkins that every fifteen to twenty years the Coosa, in particular, had a flood "which overflows the banks, and spreads itself for five and six miles in width in many part of Alabama. The rise is sudden, and so rapid as to drive a current up the Tallapoosa for eight miles." In 1795 the water rose forty-seven feet and flooded the western side of the Alabama for three miles.[118] The elderly Creeks informed Hawkins that the mounds, which they called *ecunligee*, or "earth placed," were built as refuges against such flooding. In fact, free-ranging livestock congregated atop some of these mounds in extreme floods, such as the one in 1795. Still Hawkins wondered why most were built on the terraces, above flood level, if this were indeed the case.[119] We know now, of course, that the mounds were built for quite different purposes.

The Creeks were not overly concerned with too much rain, but drought was a continual specter for them. The infamous "hungry year," which occurred in 1807, was one particularly dire year of an eight-year-long drought (1804–12) that resulted in some serious crop failures throughout Creek country.[120] Towns were prepared for occasional crop failures. Not only were Creek women knowledgeable foragers, but everyone was expected to contribute a portion of their harvest to a public granary. This food was then used to feed any family who could not farm that year, any family whose crops did not do well, visitors and travelers, any family who ran short on food that year, and the whole town in case of a general crop failure.[121] The public granary held only enough surplus for a year or so, so repeated crop failures could pose serious problems. During this eight-year drought, Creek families relied on wild plant and animal foods and the milk and meats from their cows and hogs. They also sought aid from Hawkins, who provided bread, corn, watermelons, pumpkins, and anything else he could spare for those who came to the agency, until his own crops failed in 1811. People could also buy foodstuffs from Creek farmers who had a surplus and from frontier white farmers, but Hawkins noted that the price of corn inflated to three dollars a bushel during the years of crisis.[122] These years accented the growing disparities in wealth and property, as people of means weathered the hardships while others starved and suffered. Not helping those in need was a new attitude, something many Creeks considered immoral. The new attitude also reflected a growing rift in Creek society between those who endorsed accommodation to America and adoption of new ways of making a living and those who rejected the new order.[123]

Hawkins understood the differences differently. He believed that those who adopted his scientific farming got through the drought, and those who insisted on Creek techniques suffered because of it. He thought Creek agricultural methods poor, and he lectured both men and women on the benefits of scientific farming every chance he got, and he had an open invitation to anyone interested to come to the Creek Agency to see his demonstration gardens. Time and again he instructed women to lay out their cornfields in the "proper manner," which according to his calculations was a five-and-a-half-square-foot plot with straight rows. He also had particular ways to plant each kind of crop and detailed instructions on hoeing, topping, thinning, and general tending. Needless to say, he always advocated the plow, and he even sent instructors into Creek towns to teach people how to use it.[124] Although he advocated planting beans and corn together, intercropping generally was out of the question. He never reflected on it in his extant writings, but I assume that Hawkins would have thought the Creeks plain superstitious in their use of rainmakers and other magical means to control the climate and other agricultural factors.[125]

Rather, Hawkins believed Creek farming methods to be responsible for many of the agricultural problems, such as soil exhaustion and poor production, about which the Creeks were complaining.[126] The Creeks told Hawkins about exhausted soils around Tuckabatchee and Oakfuskee. At Cusseta, Hawkins noted that the fields around the town were so exhausted that only small corn could be produced.[127] When Hawkins inquired about the conditions of the soils around Cusseta, you will recall that the Creeks replied that the fields had been in cultivation "beyond the memory of the oldest man" in the town.[128] One Lower Creek man told Bartram that a town moved because of soil exhaustion, but he gave no indication of how often this occurred.[129]

Archaeologists are beginning to understand that soil exhaustion, while not widespread, could have occurred in catchments where swidden corn agriculture had been conducted for anywhere from 50 to 150 years.[130] A recent archaeological evaluation of ten Lower Creek towns shows that decreasing productivity of soils was a factor in the movement of towns during the Historic Period. This same study also reveals that the soils around Cusseta and Coweta probably had low production yields, as the people of these towns had informed Hawkins, but that the people probably preferred to stay in these towns because they were located on the Lower Trading Path.[131]

It does not seem likely that alluvial floodplain soils, replenished yearly by fresh and nutrient-rich sediments, would be exhausted by swidden, subsistence-level corn agriculture. But corn is hard on soil. It requires thirteen nutrients, the most important being nitrogen.[132] Other than the ash from clearing fires, the Creeks did not fertilize their fields. Intercropping with beans supposedly replenished nitrogen by fixing it in the soil. But this commonly held idea has recently been challenged. According to this argument, nitrogen in legumes is fixed in root nodules during the growing stages.[133] As the plant matures, the root nitrogen is taken up by the leaves and stem of the maturing plant. Hence, nitrogen that would be fixed in the soil at the root nodules is, in fact, diminished as the plant grows. The only way legume nitrogen could be returned to the soil is if, after harvesting and when the leaves and stems wither, the debris is turned back into the soil.[134] There is no evidence that the southeastern Indians did this. Plus, a recent archaeological study of Mississippian Period agriculture suggests that friability of soils, and not nitrogen, was the more important factor for Mississippian farmers.[135]

A more serious problem may have been weed infestation. Weeds compete with cultigens for water and especially nutrients, since they serve as nitrogen and phosphorous sinks.[136] In the South, weeds grow rapidly and can become large very quickly. On the floodplains, floodwaters spread light weed seeds, and the moist, fertile soils ensure that weeds can tower over a person within a few weeks. They can become so thick that a person must hack his or her way through them.[137] Pollen analysis from archaeological investigations at Fusihatchee and Tuckabatchee indicate a healthy population of invasive weeds typically associated with southern agricultural fields. At Fusihatchee, the analysis shows knotweed, American pokeweed, morning glory, ragweed, carpet weed, little barley, and goose grass (this is an introduced species). At Tuckabatchee there were wild weedy plants such as sedges, spider flower, carpetweed, and pigweed. Archaeologists believe that the pollens from these plants were chance inclusions in the pollen and flotation samples from the surrounding environment and probably reflect agricultural activities.[138] Furthermore, giant river cane was an invading grass that would also have been difficult to control.[139]

Controlling weed (and probably cane) infestations would have required laborious and frequent hoeing and picking. But after a crop was planted, other than the labor needed to run off birds and deer, Creek women did not devote much time to their fields. They hoed only two or three times: once when the corn reached about one foot, again when it reached knee height, and perhaps again after the tassels appeared.[140] Even then, the hoeing was done only to pile up dirt at the base of the cornstalks and not necessarily to control for weeds or cane. Consequently, the weeds sometimes "towered over their Corn."[141] White farmers, who likewise hoed irregularly, reported that after about three or four years the weeds became so thick that they had to abandon their fields.[142] The Creeks often pointed out canebrakes that had once been agricultural fields.[143]

Even with these limitations, at first glance Creek agricultural production seems to have been sufficiently low so as not to overtax the floodplains, especially those of the Tallapoosa and Chattahoochee Rivers. By the turn of the nineteenth century, however, many Creek families were moving out of the major river valleys and into the smaller floodplains of the tributary streams. But another factor was now at work. Some Creeks had become ranchers.[144]

CHAPTER EIGHT

CREEK RANCHERS

B y the turn of the nineteenth century, the Creeks faced an uncertain
economic future. Certainly their
subsistence farming guaranteed daily meals, but the deerskin trade, their link
to the commercial market, was failing. Thus they became ranchers, and by so
doing they continued their participation in the market economy.[1] At the time
of European contact, the southeastern Indians possessed only a single domesticated animal: the dog. Dogs were undoubtedly useful sentinels for a town,
guarding against surprise enemy attacks and notifying townspeople of ap-
proaching visitors. Bartram wrote that the Creeks never ate dog meat, but later
anthropologists believe that the southeastern Indians occasionally ate dog in
ceremonial feasts.[2] Dogs may also have been used in hunting, if not for tracking animals then certainly as camp watchdogs.[3] Native American and European dogs interbred, and most Indian dogs were mongrels. Bartram saw a Seminole dog, "which seemed to differ in no respect from the wolf of Florida,"
herding horses. Bartram's observation is the only evidence that Indian dogs
were used in herding, and even Bartram considered the sight of a herding Indian dog as remarkable.[4] Dogs, however, were constant companions of both
Indians and whites, whether on the trail or at home.

The Creeks, as most southeastern Indians, adopted the horse soon after it
was introduced into the South. With the deerskin trade of the eighteenth century, horses became indispensable for transportation, trade, hunting, and war-

fare. There were some renowned Indian horses of Spanish stock. Eighteenth-century white opinion varied on which of the Indian stock was better; Bartram believed the Seminole horses were "the most beautiful and sprightly species."[5] The Indian trader James Adair attributed sublime characteristics to Chickasaw horses.[6] By the early nineteenth century, however, the southern Indians owned every sort of horse, and writers made little mention of any single outstanding stock.

After their introduction, horses quickly became a part of daily life. Every household had a least one horse, and usually more. Creek men and women, by all accounts, were good at handling and managing horses. They bought saddles, bridles, and horse tack on the market, although by the late eighteenth century, Hawkins noted that many Creeks were making saddles and bridles for themselves as well as to sell.[7] A few Creeks raised herds of horses and became horse dealers, selling to both Indians and frontier whites and blacks. As we will see, the stealing and selling of horses was an important element of the frontier exchange economy.

Whites had also brought with them cattle, hogs, sheep, goats, and chickens, all of which the Creeks eventually acquired. When domesticated cows and hogs first appeared on the frontier, the Creeks were initially wary of them. They believed that consuming the flesh of these cumbersome, slow-moving animals would impart to one these same qualities. They also believed that cattle were polluted animals and hence unfit for human consumption. According to the Creeks, if one ate beef, one would be susceptible to the "cattle's distemper," a nonfatal disease in which one's face, throat, and (for men) testicles swelled "in a very extraordinary manner."[8]

Some Creeks began to acquire cows and hogs in the early years of colonization, but not until after the American Revolution did they own them in any number.[9] The zoological samples from Historic Period southeastern Indian archaeological sites suggest that the southern Indians only gradually added Old World domesticated meats to their diet, and that wild meats such as deer, turkey, and fish comprised the bulk of their meats until the turn of the nineteenth century. When southern Indians did add Old World domesticates, these meats did not replace the wild meats; they were additions to the diet.[10]

The full number and kinds of domesticated animals in Creek territory by the end of the eighteenth century is not known. Chickens were certainly common sights at Creek household compounds, and eggs and poultry were regular food and trade items. Yard fowl were relatively easy to maintain. Indians and frontier settlers preferred chickens because they roosted high off the ground and, therefore, were not as vulnerable as geese and domesticated ducks to predators.[11] Chickens scratched around house yards for food scraps, which must have been plentiful in Creek compounds, where most of the cooking and food preparation took place outdoors. A few handfuls of corn strewn about the yard would suffice if the scraps were not sufficient.

Sheep and goats, on the other hand, were not popular. Goats were not profitable, as neither goat milk nor goat skins sold well.[12] Even so, Hawkins persuaded some people in the Creek Confederacy to try sheep and goat herding. Hawkins himself kept sheep at the Creek Agency.[13] Timothy Barnard raised forty sheep at his ranch on the Flint River, after Hawkins supplied him with the animals. Hawkins's experiment with sheep herding among the Creeks never blossomed because sheep raised in the South grew coats of poorer quality than those from the North.[14] The Creeks did not devote a lot of labor to the upkeep of their domestic animals, and sheep, which require constant herding, were burdensome in that way. Plus, sheep are sensitive to heat and humidity, and they are especially vulnerable to predators and require much human vigilance against wolves, bears, and wildcats.[15] The Creeks, already disinclined to constant herding, did not wish to invest labor in an unprofitable enterprise.[16]

However, the Creeks avidly took to raising hogs and cattle. Although the records are incomplete, the Creeks probably bought most livestock from local ranchers and traders, and they worked diligently at increasing their herds through breeding. The women of Coosada, for instance, within three years had significantly increased their number of hogs from a few given to them by their local white trader, Robert Walton.[17] Theft was also a predominant way to acquire livestock. Both whites and Indians allowed their stock to range freely. Under free-range conditions, strays were common, and Creek men and women simply appropriated any strays that came their way.

Most white and Indian farmers had only a few cattle, hogs, and horses, but some were big ranchers. The Creeks did not raise cattle and hogs for their own consumption but for sale. In fact, during the eight-year drought, even though corn was in short supply, Hawkins was still surprised to see the Creeks slaughter many of their livestock for home consumption.[18] On another occasion he also considered unusual, Hawkins saw some Cusseta men slaughter their cattle for the hides, with which they bought liquor.[19] Other white observers confirm that most stock were driven to markets in Savannah, Darien, Macon, and Pensacola, where they were sold on the hoof.[20] They also began trading cow skins to Panton, Leslie, and Company. Some animals were slaughtered in town, and the meats were sold to travelers, white farmers, soldiers, and other Creeks. The increase in Euro-American travelers through Creek territory during the late eighteenth and early nineteenth centuries provided a ready market for fresh beef and bacon, although some of the meat was probably salted and preserved for transport to more distant markets in the frontier towns.

Ranching gave the Creeks a much-needed new link to the commercial market and manufactured goods. Since most livestock were used as a trade commodity, ranching was a relatively easy alternative to the deerskin trade.[21] It functioned to keep the Indian trade afloat and operated within the well-established confines of the trade system. Livestock raising was profitable. Because the livestock were free ranging, raising them required little labor and only small outlays of money for salt. Cows and calves cost about $10.00 each. Beef steers were sold by age at $2.50 per year. Hawkins does not record the price for hogs, but bacon sold for about 30 cents a pound.[22]

The number of cattle and hogs in Creek territory by the turn of the nineteenth century is not known, but most Creeks, men and women, in almost every town owned some kind of livestock—if nothing more than a horse.[23] However, there is every indication that most Creeks owned cattle and hogs as well. Hawkins listed almost every town as having herds of livestock, and some individual herds ranged from 30 to 150 head and were "spread over the whole nation."[24] In addition, the emerging strata of métis elite displayed their wealth through the size of their livestock herds, although these men and women were more planter than rancher, as they were usually engaged in various commercial agrarian pursuits.[25] Indian countrymen, on the other hand, were now ranchers more than they were traders or farmers, and these men undoubtedly had large herds. Jack Kinnard, who lived on the lower Flint, reportedly owned a herd of cattle numbering in the thousands. Timothy Barnard owned hundreds of cattle and hogs. Barnard and Kinnard lived in especially good rangelands.[26] Other Indian countrymen probably did not own such impressive numbers of livestock, but their livelihoods depended on both ranching and trading. Hawkins wrote that all the Indian countrymen, "without exception," were like Barnard in that they were "not much acquainted with farming."[27]

As women became ranchers, they were able to participate in the Indian trade in a capacity heretofore unknown. Some of the women's ranching activities were within well-defined economic roles. Women were responsible for feeding guests, and many women realized profits from ranching by selling meats to foreign visitors and travelers. But women also became engaged in the trade system by selling their hogs and cattle on the hoof to traders. Sophia Durant, Alexander McGillivray's sister, for example, had been a trader "for some time" with Panton, Leslie, and Company when Hawkins came to Creek country.

She had since had a falling out with Panton over credit. Her stock of cattle and hogs was also depleted by then.[28] Durant was a métis of some status because of her relation to Alexander McGillivray, who had a close relationship with Panton, Leslie, and Company. This, in part, can account for her access to the trade house. Still, her participation also indicates that significant changes in Creek gender roles were under way by the turn of the nineteenth century. Much has been written about the conservative attitude of southeastern Indian women and their contribution to the stability of long-term cultural traits. But scholars also acknowledge that within their defined roles, southeastern Indian women actively experimented with new ideas and economic activities to which they were exposed.[29] Ranching, however, was opening a new door for Creek women.

Documentary evidence reveals a commercial aggressiveness in late-eighteenth-century Creek women and a dogged pursuit of their own economic interest. With ranching money Creek women garnered a purchasing power that the old gender roles had denied them. Hawkins noted that many women had begun to buy slaves with the profits from their ranching activities, and others had increased the number of animals in their herds.[30] Women lodged as many complaints as men about horse stealing and cattle rustling. They sought compensation for losses to their herds through legal petitions to Hawkins. In some cases of the wealthy, they contested the inheritance of cattle and hogs, demanding their legal rights to the livestock of deceased relatives.[31] As Hawkins noted, many Creek women were profiting through ranching, and as the Creek men complained, they were becoming quite independent.[32]

Both men and women could be involved because ranching did not appreciably alter the hunting and agricultural cycle of labor requirements. Although the full range of Creek ranching techniques is not documented, it does not appear to have required a large labor force or any special technology. Free-ranging livestock required little maintenance for most of the year. Most roundups and drives to market probably occurred in the late fall and early winter, when the stock was fattest from the spring and summer foraging, but people encountered drovers on the trails year-round. Both men and women participated in driving the animals to market. En route to Creek country, Hawkins once encountered two women on horseback driving "ten very fat cattle" to market.[33] The roundups and drives required a few wranglers on horseback, probably with cow whips, which good wranglers wielded with "power and skill."[34] Roundups were simple routines. Creek ranchers went to places where cattle and hogs congregated, such as salt licks, mossy shoals, grassy fields, or abandoned agricultural fields, and selected those best fit for sale or butchering. Those selected for sale were herded along the trading paths to the trading houses in Mobile, Pensacola, and other places. Some traders stationed in Creek towns bought and sold livestock, but their prices were not as good as those of the trade houses. In fact, in 1807 the Lower Creek headmen asked Hawkins to forbid the town traders from trading in livestock because of the lower prices.[35] Livestock selected for butchering were shot, skinned, and butchered.[36] A Creek place-name indicates that instead of driving animals selected for butchering back to the towns, some ranchers may have butchered them on the spot. An Oafuskee *talofa* was called Soocheah, which is derived from *suka-ispoka*, or "hog-killing place" or "place for getting hogs."[37]

Frontier ranchers, whether Creeks, white or black frontier settlers, or Indian countrymen, allowed their stock to range freely. Creek livestock were generally healthy, or at least not seriously unhealthy. Reports of healthy hogs and cattle being driven to market were common.[38] This is not to say that livestock in Creek country had no afflictions or pests. Fleas, ticks, and flies could be deadly. The Creeks called one particular pesky tick to cattle *ikfancho*, or "cattle tick."[39] Hawkins reported that in the Coastal Plain region, flies were so bad as to be fatal to horses.[40] Hawkins noted that Creek cattle rarely suffered from distemper.[41] But he reported a disease called "yellow water," to which horses were especially susceptible and which almost depleted the stock of Creek horses in 1801.[42] About ten years earlier, another horse distemper had struck, killing many animals. Timothy Barnard, who owned a few dozen, lost all but six packhorses, including his three favorite riding horses.[43]

Compared with northern herds, however, the health of southern livestock overall was poor. A southern cow rarely weighed more than 700 pounds.[44] The southern razorback hog "was almost universally maligned as being more like a greyhound than a pig."[45] Gosse described those he saw in Alabama in the early eighteenth century as "a queer breed; very singular creatures indeed; one does not often laugh when alone; but, really, when I have looked on these animals, with their sharp thin backs, long heads, and tall legs, looking so little like hogs, and so much like greyhounds and have observed the shrewd look, half alarm, half defiance, with which they regard one, I have laughed till the water has run out of my eyes."[46]

The average meat yield of a hog was only 130 to 150 pounds.[47] The difference in weight and quality between northern and southern cattle and hogs is partially attributed to free ranging, which produced smaller hogs and cattle than pasture-fed stock.[48] Under free-range conditions, a cow, for example, could gain up to 200 pounds in the spring and summer but then lose that gain during the leaner winter months when pasturage was not so readily available.[49] Moreover, the differences between northern and southern livestock were primarily a result of the lack of selective breeding among southern herders, including the Creeks.[50] Again, under free-range conditions, ranchers could not regulate breeding between animals. Because many free-range animals became feral, a rancher could not ensure that a sow or cow did not mate with a feral male, which always tended to be lean and energy efficient. As Hawkins put it, Creek stock was "fine, but wild."[51]

Creek country was excellent rangeland, but not uniformly so. In the southern mixed forest such as that which covered much of Creek country, free-ranging cows and hogs would require about fifteen to twenty acres per animal to stay healthy and not overgraze.[52] Free-ranging livestock avoided the swamps and lowlands and instead preferred the browse of the southern mixed forest of the Piedmont and especially of the river valley hardwood forests. They would venture into the Coastal Plain longleaf pine forests only during the winter months. Free-ranging southern hogs could stay healthy by eating roots, tubers, fruits, insects, eggs, and nuts, especially acorns.[53] They preferred the southern mixed forest and the mixed mesophytic forest of the uplands because the nuts and fruits were plentiful. They also rooted the young saplings. They would venture into the longleaf pine forests in the spring and summer. Hogs liked to dig up and eat the roots of the smaller longleaf trees, hence the name "piney rooters."[54]

Cattle selectively grazed on the wild grasses and flowers that carpeted the floor of the mixed mesophytic and southern mixed forests. So Indian burning of the forests benefited ranching as well as hunting. Peavine, a wild legume, grew in some places in Creek territory, most notably in the Ridge and Valley province along the upper Coosa and Tallapoosa Rivers and in the floodplains of the longleaf forest of the Coastal Plain.[55] Cattle liked to graze on peavine, and in later years, American farmers attempted to grow peavine for pasturage, with little success.[56] Instead, the plant became extinct in the South by the mid-nineteenth century through overgrazing.[57] In the longleaf forest, cattle would eat palmettos and the young shoots of wiregrass.[58] Recently abandoned old fields with secondary growths of shrubs, weeds, and gasses were inviting pasturage as well. Both cattle and hogs loved river cane. Giant river cane, especially reed, was essential winter fodder for free-ranging livestock because it does not become dry and brittle in the colder months.[59]

The ranging habits of livestock affected the forest and wildlife. The primary ecological problem with free-range hogs and cattle is their destructive patterns of foraging. In their search for roots and tubers, free-range hogs dig out and expose plant roots, eat the roots or tubers, and leave the plant to die.

Free-ranging cattle do not do as much damage as free-ranging swine, but they habitually deplete preferred forage because although they can subsist on a variety of vegetation, cattle are selective grazers and move on to less desirable foods only after the more desirable fare is gone.[60]

One measure of the impact of free-range livestock can be seen in the depletion of giant river cane and reed during the forty or so years of intensive livestock raising among the Creeks. Modern studies of cattle show that cane is one of the most valuable wild forages in the South, providing crude protein, calcium, and phosphorus well above the requirements for maturing cattle. Plus, cane is a resilient plant and usually rebounds quickly from any disturbance. However, cattle tend to "patch graze," or congregate and feed as a group. When cattle graze on cane, their weight and numbers compacted the soil around a canebrake and inhibit renewed growth. Also, cattle can defoliate an entire canebrake in one grazing season because they eat the leaves first. The rooting of swine, of course, kills the plant, and hogs also prefer the young cane shoots.[61]

By the turn of the nineteenth century, cane was already disappearing in the Southeast. Cane can withstand flooding, drought, and intense fires, but it is very sensitive to overgrazing.[62] American farmers and herders noted that cane grew scarce after only eleven years of continuous grazing.[63] The canebrakes around Tuckabatchee were depleted by 1797.[64] With the increasing number of livestock grazing and rooting on cane, the Creeks and American settlers regularly set fire to canebrakes in an effort to regenerate the cane.[65] But even this deliberate measure did not stem the depletion of cane. The Creeks bitterly resented the presence of white-owned livestock in Creek territory for this very reason.[66]

Creek livestock strayed up to fifty miles in their yearly foraging, which meant that Creek ranchers needed every inch of available grazing land for their own herds. In 1805, for instance, the Creeks were faced with ceding lands between the Oconee and Ocmulgee Rivers. Their main objection to the cession was that American-owned stock that had strayed over the Oconee line had already destroyed the cane and grass for ten to fifteen miles across the boundary from Fort Wilkinson to the High Shoals of the Appalachee.[67] The Creek negotiators argued that because the Ocmulgee River had many shoals that were easy crossing points for livestock, if the river were made the new boundary, they feared that white-owned stock would cross into Creek territory and overgraze the area along the Ocmulgee. This area, they asserted, was used as grazing land for the people who lived on the Flint, whose cattle and hogs wandered as far as the Ocmulgee in their winter ranging.[68] Despite such arguments, the cession went through. As the Creeks predicted, the number of American-owned livestock in Creek territory subsequently increased, placing even more pressure on an area already obviously overpopulated by free-ranging animals. In fact, overgrazing was a continual problem throughout the ranching era, and stock intrusions remained a source of contention between the Creeks and U.S. officials until Removal.[69]

The Creeks also understood that free-ranging livestock competed with deer, bear, and turkeys, the three main wild meats used by the Creeks, as well as other wild animals for forage. Although they certainly ate beef and pork, the Creeks mostly relied on wild animals for their meat. Wild turkeys subsist on seeds, grains, and especially acorns, which can make up to 60 percent of their diet.[70] Southeastern bears subsist on nuts, fruits, berries, and grasses.[71] Deer eat the young shoots of cane, grasses, and saplings and acorns and chestnuts, along with agricultural debris left in old fields.[72] Acorn mast in the historic forest was so abundant that both hogs and wild animals, such as turkey and deer, could subsist on it with little competition. Even after Removal, when white settlers inundated the former Creek territory, hogs did not appreciably diminish the acorn mast.[73] Other wild forage, however, did not regenerate after free-ranging livestock fed on it; the number of livestock subsisting in Creek country and the destructiveness of their foraging was the most serious factor in the decreasing amount of most wild forage.

As discussed earlier, the declining number of deer was due to several factors, overhunting being perhaps the primary reason. However, the competition with hogs and cattle for food cannot be overlooked.[74] At land cession negotiations, Creek headmen admittedly had their own agendas, but they invariably mentioned the loss of deer browse to the increasing number of livestock in Creek territory. Sensitive to ecological indicators of stress, Creek negotiators asserted, quite correctly, that the territory could not support Creek livestock, American-owned livestock, and the number of deer they needed.[75] Bear, likewise, were becoming more difficult to find. Black bear forage up to a fifteen-mile radius in a mixed pine and hardwood forest searching for nuts, fruits, berries, and grasses.[76] Unlike deer, however, bear have a low reproductive potential and are especially vulnerable to habitat disturbance.[77] Bear will move to less-disrupted regions rather than return to a disturbed area. The Creeks noticed the diminishing number of bear. In one case, when white settlers laid the blame for the loss of Creek-owned cattle on bear, the Creek owners protested that the bear were almost gone because of white-owned livestock, and therefore it was unlikely that there were still enough bears in Creek country to be a threat to their livestock. They believed, with some reason, that the whites had killed their cattle.[78]

The Creeks used the bear for its oil and hides, and perhaps more importantly the bear held mythical significance for the Creeks.[79] In response to the diminishing number of bears, the Creeks may have established bear reserves along certain stream corridors. Hawkins referred to one such "beloved bear ground" on Ofuckshe (Line) Creek, associated with the town of Hoithlewaule on the Tallapoosa River. Hawkins commented that each town had its own bear reserve where the residents hunted bear.[80] Whites, on the other hand, understood the bear as only a predator of livestock and a raider of cornfields. Like wolves, bears were animals whites hoped to eliminate.[81]

Free-range hogs and cattle were quick and ferocious and could protect themselves relatively well against wolves, wildcats, and bears, but not always. Hence both Creeks and white settlers saw livestock predators as pests and sought to eliminate them. Wolves were the predominant menace to livestock, and Indian and white livestock owners showed no compunction in ridding the forest of what they considered a threat to their livelihoods.[82] People shot wolves on sight or set traps in the forest at favorite livestock grazing areas.[83] The Creeks began buying wolf traps for the first time in the late eighteenth century.[84] White farmers feared wolves more than any other predator. Reports circulated early that southern wolves had grown so accustomed to humans and livestock that they circled cow pens without fear and were so daring that neither fire, dogs, nor humans could run them off.[85] White farmers had begun a campaign to rid the forest of wolves in the early years of colonization, offering bounties for every wolf killed. By the nineteenth century the wolves in the coastal regions were almost gone. When ranching became integral to Creek livelihoods, the Creeks unofficially joined the campaign. With the increasing number of white settlers in the interior also purposefully hunting wolves, southern wolves came close to extinction.[86]

Philip Henry Gosse described the efforts of his planter friend to kill a bear that had been raiding his cornfields. Gosse's friend was "in a state of feverish vexation" over the bear's visits night after night to the same place in the cornfield. One evening a young slave boy alerted the planter to the bear, and the planter and his overseer grabbed their rifles while slaves cast bullets, "a job that has always to be done at the moment they are wanted." Led by the young boy, the men crept out to the field but found only the bear's paw prints, a badly scratched fence railing, and downtrodden corn rows. The planter later rigged a contraption wherein a rifle would fire in the direction of the bear the next time the animal climbed the fence. Gosse did not report on the outcome of this experiment.[87]

Livestock need salt. The Southeast had some mineral salt outcrops, or salt licks, but they were few and far between. Hawkins only mentioned some on Calabee Creek in Upper Creek territory.[88] Livestock and deer also ate the moss that grew on the rocks in the shoals of streams for its salt. In fact, the Creeks called such mossy shoals *itchocunnah* or "deer trap," because deer were drawn there and hence were easy to find and kill.[89] The Creeks themselves used river moss as one of their sources of salt. They made a sauce from the moss into which they dipped their meats.[90] Mossy shoals were common enough in Creek territory. Hawkins observed moss growing in most rivers and creeks. It is unlikely that livestock overgrazed the river moss. The Creeks, not reluctant to lodge other complaints about overgrazing, do not mention anything about a diminishing supply of salt moss. Still, after most Creeks began ranching, salt became a major trade item. Trade lists from the eighteenth century show a gradual increase in salt as a trade item, and by the turn of the nineteenth century it was a principal item.[91] By supplementing naturally occurring salts with purchased salt, Creek ranchers, wittingly or not, diminished the competition between livestock and deer for river moss.

A favorite feeding area for livestock was active or recently abandoned agricultural fields. Both cattle and hogs would browse on crop debris after a harvest. But they also liked to browse during the growing season. Cows liked the young, fresh shoots, and hogs liked the corn, cowpeas, and sweet potatoes, once they appeared. Creek farmers naturally did not allow their livestock to forage in their agricultural fields. As mentioned earlier, Hawkins continually encouraged the Creeks to fence their fields, and he noted with pride when some did. Still, most Creek farmers did not fence their fields. The deliberations behind fencing or not fencing assuredly rested in part on the symbolic significance of doing so and on related political attitudes, but Creek farmers had alternative methods of keeping livestock out of their fields.

Young men and boys patrolled the fields to scare off or kill pests. The burden of keeping livestock out of an agricultural field fell to the livestock owners and not the farmers, since the accepted method of control was to shoot a pest on sight. It behooved livestock owners, then, to see that their animals did not stray into the fields. Hence livestock wandering around the towns and fields were regularly hobbled, which inhibited their range.[92] In some cases, however, fences were required. Sweet potato fields, located outside the guarded communal fields, required fencing, and many Creeks did fence their sweet potato fields. Of course to Hawkins the fences were not good enough; he commented that they were barely substantial enough to keep out hogs.[93]

After a harvest, Creek women opened the communal fields to hogs, cattle, and horses, who would feed on the plant debris. The fences around the sweet potato fields were dismantled so that hogs could root out the smaller sweet potatoes left after the harvest. Livestock were also free to wander into old fields or fields that had been left fallow.[94] Fields abandoned for only two to three years had a dense growth of wild grasses and weeds, such as horseweed, white aster, and bunch grass.[95] These weedy meadows provided a preferred forage for cattle. In fields abandoned for more than three years, pioneer pine trees began replacing the grasses and weeds. The small pines would have attracted the piney rooters. Old fields were also favorite browsing areas for deer, and the incursions of livestock into these areas once again edged out deer.[96]

However, livestock grazing in old fields interrupted the natural succession and regeneration of old field soils. Livestock removed the ground cover of old fields, and patch grazing and rooting churned and exposed the soil. All of this led to increased soil erosion and sun leaching in the old fields.[97] Creek farmers preferred to return to old fields in their rotations, but the increasing erosion after livestock foraging would have rendered these fields unsuitable for future cultivation. The magnitude of such adverse impacts on old fields for Creek agricultural land-use requirements cannot be fully assessed, but such disturbances of old field soils would have had dire consequences over the long term.

It looks as though the Creeks were already adjusting to this and other livestock ranging problems by the turn of the nineteenth century by separating from their *talwas* and dispersing their settlements over the countryside.[98] As we have seen, Creek towns had a tradition of fissioning and establishing satellite towns, so migrations from larger towns were not unusual. We have only the barest outline of the structure of Creek satellite towns, and most seem to have been small, outlying villages of about twenty to fifty families.[99] When the movement out of towns became a response to the demands of ranching, however, the patterns were different and could be dramatic. For instance, at the town of Tallassee on the Tallapoosa River, almost all of the families had moved out of the town and up Upahee Creek for twenty-five miles. Formerly one of the largest Upper Creek towns, Oakfuskee, on the Tallapoosa River, was in 1797, in Hawkins's words, "quickly becoming an old field" as people established farmsteads along tributary streams to the north. The people of the Lower Creek town of Eufaula had spread down the Chattahoochee River to its confluence with the Flint, leaving only a few families in the town proper. At Hillaubee, only one man and his family remained in town; everyone else had moved onto individual farmsteads on other streams.[100] Hawkins noted many cases where people of a town had "spread out" along creeks that flowed into the Tallapoosa, Coosa, Flint, and Chattahoochee Rivers: Coweta, Cusseta, Yuchi, Tuckabatchee, Kialijee, Hitchitee, Hoithlewaule, Hookchoi, Oakfuskee, Tallassee, and Eufaula, among others.[101] Archaeologists believe that towns along the Flint River were settled in the late eighteenth century and, therefore, were established as a response to the demands for free-range ranching.[102] The Flint River valley, as we have seen, had plenty of wild grasses, especially cane and reed, and supported the large ranches of Kinnard and Barnard. Even more importantly, by moving there, Creek ranchers had access to more eastern lands, as indicated in the dispute with the Georgians.

Many Creek families were moving onto the narrow floodplains of secondary streams, away from the major towns and river valleys, so that, as they explained it, their livestock could have access to undisturbed grazing lands and because of soil exhaustion around the larger towns.[103] Such a dispersed settlement pattern would have eased the pressure for grazing lands in the major river valleys. In most cases, families or matrilines from a town established independent farmsteads along the entire length of a minor stream, and they had no town center.[104] The archaeological record shows Historic Creek farmsteads as typically dispersed up and down river corridors and the uplands abutting tributary streams.[105] Generally, the houses were located away from the stream, usually on the more elevated lands. This was necessary because the floodplains of the tributary streams were narrow and limited, and a Creek family settled on an individual farmstead would have had to use the whole floodplain for agriculture and grazing lands.

For the late-eighteenth-century Creeks, Upatoi is the best known of these types of settlement. Upatoi was a satellite town of Cusseta apparently established by the mid-eighteenth century. Hawkins listed 43 gun men, or about 172 people, as living at Upatoi in the 1790s. Archaeologists located approximately thirty-one sites in Upatoi, most of which appear to be Creek households. These sites are on the uplands above the Upatoi floodplain in two clusters separated by a stream that feeds into Upatoi Creek (see fig. 20).[106] Hawkins was impressed with the people of Upatoi, whom he called "the best characters of any among the Lower Creeks." Part of his opinion was due to the fact that the *mico* of Upatoi, Tussekia Micco, fully endorsed the plan for civilization. This was the town where fenced fields were required if one wanted to live there.

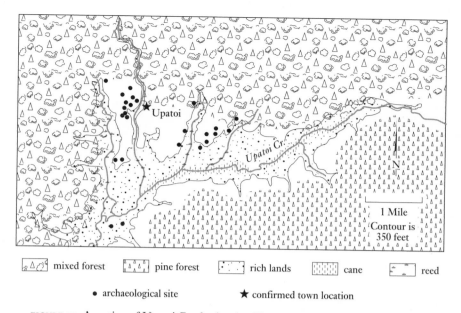

mixed forest   pine forest   rich lands   cane   reed

• archaeological site   ★ confirmed town location

FIGURE 20. A section of Upatoi Creek, showing Upatoi. The location of Upatoi and the archaeological sites are taken from Elliott et al., "Up on the Upatoi."

Hawkins called the site of Upatoi "well chosen."[107] It was situated in the Piedmont, right on the Fall Line. In fact Hawkins, standing in Upatoi, reported that he could view both the longleaf pine forest to the south and the "waving oak, pine, and hickory" (the southern mixed forest) to the north. The town was adjacent to the best and widest alluvial plain of Upatoi Creek, which was covered with large poplar, white oak, sycamore, hickory, and beech trees, as well as with an abundance of cane and reed. The rangelands were good, and the families of Upatoi had "fine cattle and hogs." The only problem was a lack of naturally occurring salt in the area. Clearly Upatoi was well chosen, as Hawkins said, and the people had access to both good agricultural lands and good rangelands.[108]

Other outlying settlements were not so well chosen. Figure 21, showing Newyaucau, Tookaubatchee Tallahassee, and Ocfuscooche, illustrates the landscape of the smaller floodplain areas on the Tallapoosa River uplands. Newyaucau, named after New York City, was settled by some Lower Creeks in 1777. According to Hawkins, these folks decided not to get embroiled in the American Revolution and retreated to this area to get away from any American reprisals that might have ensued because of their neutrality. In looking at where they chose to relocate, rangeland, not farmland, seems to have been the major factor. The floodplains were narrow and had poor soils. Hawkins noted

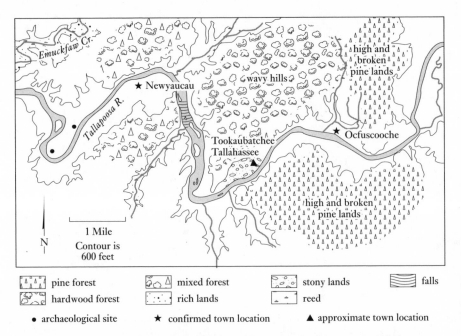

FIGURE 21. A section of the upper Tallapoosa River, showing Newyaucau, Tookaubatchee Tallahassee, and Ocfuscoochee

that people from these and nearby towns had begun to settle up Immookfau
Creek on individual farmsteads for access to other farmlands. Rangeland,
however, was good and fairly abundant, although not so much as in the Piedmont proper. These towns were located in the transition zone between the
upland mixed mesophytic forest and the southern mixed forest and hence had
especially good nut masts. Hawkins listed the whole area as covered with oak,
hickory, and pine, with small pines and chestnuts on the high ridges.[109] The
streams, as usual, had plenty of cane and reed.

Because it conformed to the plan for civilization, Hawkins encouraged the
settling of individual farmsteads. As relocating out of town began to be more
and more popular, Creek elders became concerned that if everyone lived on
individual farms, the town structure would fall apart. Hawkins reassured the
elders that settling on farms did not necessarily mean the towns would be
abandoned altogether, although he never investigated the implications of such
resettlement for the towns.[110] There also is every indication that the Creeks
held fast to their township identities and political structures into the twentieth century.[111] If the archaeology is correct, settling on individual farmsteads
was nothing new to the Creeks, and they may have been doing so for many
years prior to 1800, and with the towns still intact.

However, according to the plan for civilization, living on individual farm-steads required abandoning communal farming, which, in turn, called for a restructuring of Indian gender relations and ideas about land ownership. These reforms were not Hawkins's ideas, although he eagerly promoted them. Rather, they came from the architects of the plan for civilization for the American Indians, the Quakers. The Quakers had long been proponents of the plan for civilization. They had petitioned the U.S. government for aid, and they had supported the plan for civilization among the Creeks by sending looms, spinning wheels, and plows.[112] Hawkins knew of both the Quaker reforms in America and those being initiated in Europe.[113] Although he never discussed in print the origin of his ideas for the plan for civilization, it is rea-sonable to suppose that he drew heavily on such reform plans as these.

In 1801 the Quakers wrote to Secretary of War Henry Dearborn that one reason for wanting the Indians to settle on individual farms was to get the men to work in the fields. If each family worked its own fields, the men would be shielded from ridicule. Also, if Indian men who lived in dispersed farm-steads worked in the fields, they would not "meet daily like men in the villages to dance, have shooting matches, and other amusements."[114] Hawkins was well aware of the habits and passions of Creek men, and he probably understood individual farmsteads as a way to overcome Creek men's unwillingness to labor in the fields alongside the females. According to Hawkins, by 1808 many of the Lower Creeks were settling on individual farmsteads and fencing their fields, and they "were determined to try the hoe or plow for food and the wheel and loom for clothing. It is the general theme of conversation and the men seem determined to share in the labor of the fields with the women."[115] Hawkins was overestimating the extent to which Creek men were willing to farm.

Certainly, the Creeks who chose to live on individual farmsteads had to ad-just to new patterns. Some scholars have proposed that when Creeks lived on individual farmsteads, the matriline was broken up, and these families instead adopted white patterns of life such as the patriarchal, nuclear family.[116] How-ever, no detailed written descriptions of these farms have surfaced, and only recently have archaeologists examined these kinds of sites. There is a smatter-ing of evidence to support the idea that matrilineality, in fact, could be adapted to this new settlement pattern.[117] At Upatoi, for instance, archaeologists found evidence for both conventional Creek wattle-and-daub constructions and log cabins.[118] Furthermore, although they did not excavate the sites, ar-chaeologists examining Upatoi were still able to determine that people lived in both single-family and multiple-family farmsteads.[119] When Hawkins visited

Dog Warrior, who lived at Upatoi, he mentioned that five families lived in close proximity on the same hill. They had household gardens and sweet potato fields on the hillside, and "their corn [was] made on the flat land." In other cases when Hawkins visited Creek farmsteads, although he failed to describe the farms, he mentioned the presence of several females of varying ages and married children and their offspring. All of this would indicate that in some outlying farmsteads, members of the matrilineage lived in close proximity and still practiced communal farming of the floodplains.[120]

One result of this movement away from the major towns and river valleys is that it effectively dispersed livestock throughout Creek territory, which put a high premium on the smaller alluvial floodplains. In effect, by the nineteenth century, Creek settlement patterns had begun to resemble those of whites. As one archaeologist put it, one could expect to find an early-nineteenth-century Creek farmstead wherever one could expect to find an early-nineteenth-century white farmstead.[121] Whereas during the deerskin trade era the Creeks held a job peculiar to the southeastern Indians, during the ranching era their modes of gaining their livelihoods were virtually the same as those of frontier Americans.

CHAPTER NINE

ENTREPRENEURS, WAGE LABORERS, THIEVES, AND THE CREEK FRONTIER EXCHANGE ECONOMY

With the decline of the deerskin trade, people in Creek country began to diversify their economy, primarily through ranching but also by increasing the exchange of other goods and services. Although farming and gathering remained largely subsistence activities, the goods produced through these entered a larger exchange network. European goods flowed into Creek country primarily through the Indian trade system, although many came as gifts from the U.S. government. Once in Creek country, these goods continued to circulate through private exchanges among the regular folk on the frontier.[1] Indian men and women also offered new kinds of services, such as guides, translators, cowboys and cowgirls, innkeepers, and ferry operators. By the turn of the nineteenth century, a great variety of goods, services, and labor moved through Creek country as people attempted to balance their commercial interests with their daily needs. Everyone—Creeks, blacks, and frontier whites—relied on one another for minor wage-labor jobs, foodstuffs, household goods, and cooperation in illegal activities, among other things. These exchanges gave Creek country much of its color as people's lives became intermingled not only economically but socially as well. This kind of economy, called a "frontier exchange economy," was largely made of daily, face-to-face, and taken-for-granted exchanges between people and was rooted largely in interpersonal relationships, private needs and ambitions, and local conditions. These exchanges helped tie all of the people and regions of Creek country together.[2]

Creek women had entered the frontier exchange economy early by trading goods such as baskets, sashes, buckskin clothing, and sexual favors for manufactured goods.[3] Creek women, because they owned the agricultural produce, also sold their surplus corn, melons, pumpkins, fowls, breads, bacon, beans, peas, and other foods to frontier whites. After the Mississippi Territory and the Federal Road were opened at the turn of the nineteenth century, there was ample opportunity for Creek women to sell food to frontier whites and blacks as white settlers with their slaves and free blacks passed regularly through Creek territory.[4] Creek women easily expanded their economic niche by providing food and lodging to Euro-American and African travelers for a price. Creek women were largely responsible for the Creek reputation for hospitality, as they went to great lengths to make sure their visitors were well fed and comfortable.

All kinds of traveling parties were trekking through Creek country: packhorse trains, Indian warriors, Indian hunting parties, white immigrants, banditti, Indian countrymen, free blacks, black slaves, government officials, military personnel, renegades, and herders with their animal flocks. Some of these people traveled in large parties of twenty-five to fifty, some as single families, and some as solitary sojourners. In later years, Creeks and Americans established taverns and inns on the Federal Road to accommodate travelers. But at the turn of the nineteenth century, virtually all traveling parties took bread and board at Creek households when crossing Creek country. In fact, when the U.S. government was trying to persuade the Creeks to allow the building of the Federal Road through Creek country, the Creeks insisted that they alone had the right to operate the ferries and "houses of entertainment" for travelers, for which they would receive "ready cash."[5] The lodging industry was important enough that the United States could use the promise of profits from such transactions as one of the enticements to persuade the Creeks to agree to the Federal Road in the first place.[6]

Travelers paid, with goods or cash, for their meals and accommodations, and the payments went primarily to Creek women. Travelers also frequently replenished their supplies at Creek towns by buying provisions from Creek women. With invited guests such as foreign Indian delegates, federal or state government officials (including Hawkins), or military personnel touring Creek towns, meals and lodgings were given free of charge. However, Indian etiquette required something in return. Hawkins always carried extra items such as mirrors, trinkets, blankets, and cloth to give in return for Creek hospitality. He also tutored other official visitors on Creek etiquette so that they, too, would bring a supply of goods to give to their hostesses.[7]

Creek men and women also frequented the small settlements and farmsteads that sprang up along the U.S. and Creek boundary lines. These visits usually occurred in the hunting season, just after harvesttime, and Creek visitors brought produce, wild meats, baskets, and other items to trade. Frontier white women often made homespun cloth for sale or trade to supplement their income, and the Creeks bartered for cloth or clothing as well as any extra metal pots and pans, trinkets, ammunition, and other items that a frontier family could spare. But most frontier homesteaders were not wealthy and did not have large quantities of goods to exchange. Rum, however, was freely bartered. Its preponderance in the records suggests that it was a major exchange item. Given the increase in stock raising among the Creeks at the end of the eighteenth century, hogs, cattle, and horses were undoubtedly major exchange items.[8]

Yard fowl were a popular trade item between neighbors. Creek families with chickens and geese to spare traded them to whites. In one case, a Creek man traveled to Pensacola with several chickens to trade for rum, which he owed to someone else.[9] We do not know how these chickens were transported such a distance, but given the temperament of yard fowl, cages were more than likely built and packed on horses for the journey. The usual mode for selling chickens, however, was as a meal. Many white travelers' accounts have descriptions of the meals they were served in Indian towns. In these descriptions, chicken and eggs were usually mentioned as part of the fare that also included venison, hominy, potatoes, and rice, as well as a variety of corn breads.

The Creeks also procured some food from frontier Americans. The kinds and quantities of foods bought by the Creeks from Americans are not clear. Corn, as we have seen, was such a popular and easily available item on the frontier exchange market that Creek farmers may have even decreased their production of it.[10] Cornmeal was also popular, and buying it would have saved Creek women the task of grinding their own in their corn mortars.[11] The Creeks also bought rice, although from whom and in what quantities was not recorded.[12] The Creeks had acquired a taste for coffee and sugar, which were available from frontier Americans in small quantities. Wheat never did well in the southern climate; flour, therefore, generally had to be bought. Salt, of course, was increasingly important since ranching was spreading rapidly. When Hawkins bartered with the Creeks or compensated them for certain services, he paid them predominantly in salt, cornmeal, flour, and corn.[13]

Many of these goods moved through the frontier exchange economy as commodities, bought not for personal consumption but for resale. Rum, salt, corn, cornmeal, and some meats served almost as currency, flowing though many economic exchanges. These items could be bought with lesser goods such as fowl, various garden produce, and baskets and then resold at higher prices and for more substantial commodities such as cloth, guns, and livestock. The Creek Factory account books record several such transactions, although many details of who was involved in the exchanges go unrecorded. For instance, in 1797 Big Feared traded some skins to Timothy Barnard for six kegs of rum with which he intended to pay an unnamed person for "two horses and some other property." In 1798 an unnamed white man exchanged a rifle with an unnamed Creek person for an older rifle and a horse. Hawkins recorded this exchange because the white man complained about the transaction. He wanted to get his own gun back because the "rifle of the Indian's is no good."[14]

Hawkins always figured such complaints to breed ill will. He never had a high opinion of frontier Americans, and he wanted to minimize interactions between them and the Creeks because he believed, with some reason, that this visiting and bartering led to trouble. Hawkins believed that trouble brewed when settlers swindled the Creeks in these transactions. He introduced weights and measures to Creek women so that they could get a fair price for their produce.[15] Unscrupulous settlers and Creeks undoubtedly attempted and succeeded in cheating some of their bartering partners, but most of the informal bartering seems to have been conducted fairly. Both frontier settlers and Creeks knew enough to recognize a swindle when they saw it. The Creeks, when sober, were "seldom over matched in trade."[16] Frontier settlers, in general, may not have had much formal education, but they, too, knew how to look out for their own interests. Besides, a swindle was dangerous because both Indians and whites, when cheated, would seek redress through violence.

Hawkins, his assistants, and the factory personnel provided another market for Creek goods. As we have seen, Hawkins intended the Creek Agency to be a model for the plan for civilization. Hawkins always endeavored to make his office self-sufficient. But with a wife, seventy slaves, two Moravian missionaries, seven children, and a constant stream of Indian and white visitors, the Creek Agency had a large number of people to support. After Hawkins died, his property was inventoried. Other than household goods, farming implements, and slaves, Hawkins left relatively little to his wife and children.[17] In other words, the Creek Agency did not turn much of a profit, and neither did it make Hawkins wealthy. Any surplus produced at the Creek Agency went to the National Council and town council meetings, to feeding visitors, to provisioning Indian visitors for their journey home as was the custom, or to paying Indians for various types of labor. The agency was fairly self-sufficient, but Hawkins's trade ledgers show that he periodically bought foodstuffs from the Creeks to supplement what was produced at the agency.[18]

Hawkins also established the Creek Agency as a market for surplus cloth, hickory oil, and livestock. Hawkins bought any surpluses and acted as middleman, sending these goods to Mobile to be sold on the open market.[19] For instance, in 1801, after encouraging Creek women to make hickory oil to sell, he shipped 300 gallons of the oil, priced at $2.00 a gallon, to Mobile.[20] Hawkins only intended his middleman function to be temporary. He urged the War Department to allow the factory to hold a spring and fall fair "for the sale or exchange of horses, cattle, hogs, sheep, homespun and such things as are useful to the Indians, to concentrate the trade of the Creeks at and near the U.S. factory, there the government can superintend it and make arrangements for having it conducted with the requisite fairness and there people of good character may be licensed to trade."[21] The fairs never came to pass, and instead he issued permits to some local traders to buy and sell hogs and cattle.[22]

Hawkins's assistants, posted in various Creek towns, also bought supplies from their Creek neighbors. In fact, the Creeks frowned on whites who lived in Creek towns growing their own food and only allotted them small plots of gardening space, probably to ensure that they would have to buy food from the townspeople.[23] The Creeks had allotted Richard Thomas, who was stationed at Coweta, a small piece of land on which to cultivate a vegetable garden, and Thomas frequently purchased corn, flour, bacon, chickens, beans, and other foods from Coweta women.[24] The other white assistants certainly must have had similar arrangements, although they are not recorded.

Medicinal plants, such as some varieties of snakeroot and sassafras, took on new importance in the Creek economy.[25] Women and men collected medicinal herbs to sell to the traders or to barter with their white neighbors. The factor at the Creek Agency could also purchase these, as one storekeeper recorded paying $1.50 for twelve pounds of snakeroot in 1809.[26] Ginseng was especially popular, but it could only be found in the uplands of Creek country. The curative benefits of ginseng were well known also by European and American merchants, and they had been buying the roots of the plant from the Cherokees for years. As early as 1789 Henry Knox had appointed a group of U.S. commissioners to explore the possibility of a Creek ginseng market. They reported the prospect dim, since ginseng grew in the uplands and hence there was not much to be found in most of Creek territory.[27]

Creek men and women also had a taste for exotic items, which denoted prestige. In fact, archaeologists believe that prestige items had been important in attaining social status for the southern Indians since at least the Mississippian Period, and perhaps earlier.[28] In prehistoric times, prestige items (things such as copper, seashells, and fine stone) were controlled by an elite, who used them to buttress their high positions, as gifts to solidify alliances and create social obligations, and as items in political strategy. When European-made objects became available, the Creeks began to use many of these as prestige items for garnering social position. However, European-made prestige items were readily available to any man who could hunt—which meant virtually any adult Creek male had access to them. The elite could not control the items. Hence, prestige items were found throughout Historic Period Creek households, but the elite still attempted to distinguish themselves symbolically by acquiring more of them.[29]

Creek men and women displayed their status markers during ceremonial and public occasions, especially in their dress. Creeks, when turned out in their finery, had an ornate sense of fashion. They decorated their fancy wear with a number of European items, especially ribbons, sashes, mirrors, and beads. Creek women loved silk ribbons, which they attached to the silver barrettes in their hair in an "incredible quantity . . . of various colors" and let them "stream down on every side, almost to the ground."[30] Belt buckles were a favorite adornment for clothing, as were bells and other noisemaking trinkets. Mirrors were also very popular. Creek men and women painted themselves on special occasions. Vermilion and indigo, natural red and blue dyes, were big trade items, as were rings, bracelets, and earrings.[31]

Other strands of old patterns persisted throughout the Historic Period.[32] For instance, although by the late eighteenth century all Creek families were engaged in the trade through hunting or ranching, and although a strata of wealthy Creeks was taking form (mostly métis, but not only so), the rank-and-file Creeks owned few possessions, and they were not interested in accumulating property.[33] They did consider what they owned to be private, not communal property, though. Goods were taken as needed, and such was considered "borrowing."[34] What Euro-Americans understood as borrowing was really codified in a system of reciprocity, where sharing relationships were firmly established and where sharing was habitual and expected. Private property was never simply taken without asking, but requests for sharing were rarely declined. And sharing was always reciprocated.[35]

People who practice reciprocity have little regard for property as wealth; they understand it mostly as social capital, something with which to solidify social relations. Stiggins stated as much when he said, "Many years may intervene before you see two sober Indians quarrel about property. In their sober moments they seem to be totally disinterested in their own concerns; all the avenues to lucrative or other passions in them are absorbed in their wish to be social and civil to each other."[36] Stiggins, a wealthy métis, understood this disregard as a measure of improvidence, as did Hawkins and others. According to this interpretation, Creek men and women squandered their goods for superfluous items when they should have been saving for a rainy day. According to Hawkins, "If a man wants a keg of taffia, he will give a horse for it. If he wants a whore he clothes her in fine Calicoes with rich silverware. If he wants a beef he give 10 Chalks a year for it, and he wants fowls or corn he gives Chalks for them, 30, 40, 50, 100, 200, 400 Chalks are nothing for a horse, he must have his hireling and they must all have coffee & sugar every day."[37] Hawkins and other whites failed to understand that, in Creek eyes, saving against future, potential misfortunes did not make sense. To a Creek, risk was a part of life, and sharing and reciprocity were proven devices for attending to hard times.

As the eighteenth century wore on, though, some elite Creeks came to understand property as private wealth. Adopting a capitalist mind-set, these Creeks were becoming wealthy, and they became interested not just in displaying fancy status items but in accumulating property in Euro-American terms, such as land, livestock, commercial crops, and cash. With this new mind-set, a faction of wealthy Creeks began to redefine "borrowing" as "stealing." The redefinition placed more stress on the tensions between rich and poor that were now running through Creek country because the common Creeks—those who owned little and were not interested in accumulating stuff—still "borrowed" items that they needed.[38]

It is difficult to know who understood the "borrowing" of items as reciprocity and who considered it stealing. Except for Hawkins, who was an honest man, and perhaps his assistants, who were not always so virtuous but whose conduct was closely supervised by Hawkins and the Creeks, it almost seems as if everyone else in Creek country was borrowing, or, to some, stealing. This, of course, cannot be true. But the multitude of complaints about theft shows that stealing was integral to the livelihood of many Creeks and frontier whites and blacks. The multitude of complaints about theft also indicates that the rank and file were adopting this way of thinking about property. In other words, for the rank and file as well as for the elite, borrowing was becoming stealing.[39] The Creeks recognized this at the time. They explained that before whites came among them, theft was unknown because they did not want more than they had.[40] The amount and kinds of borrowing/stealing that occurred in Creek country also make it unlikely that most of these incidents were simply acts of reciprocity.

Stealing had no political, national, or ethnic bounds. Everyone stole from everyone else: Creeks from Creeks, Creeks from whites, whites from Creeks, whites from blacks, blacks from Creeks, whites from whites, blacks from whites, and so on. The Creeks also raided the Chickasaws, Choctaws, and Cherokees. People stole every sort of goods available on the frontier: corn, cloth, shot, powder, guns, saddles, bridles, horses, hogs, cattle, cash, deerskins, dishes, silverware, shirts, belts, buckles, pouches, and tobacco, among other things. Even Hawkins was not immune from thefts. The Creek Agency was robbed on several occasions, once by some elderly women accompanied by two elderly men who acted as lookouts. The old men and women entered Hawkins's fields in broad daylight and took eighty heads of cabbage.[41] Hawkins's horses were stolen on several occasions. Hawkins usually was magnanimous about the thefts. After one series of thefts at the Creek Agency, Hawkins told the Creeks in council that he knew these things were going on but that he preferred to ignore them in order not to increase ill feelings. However, he sought to catch and punish the horse thieves.[42]

The Creek Factory was besieged by thieves, and the factor dutifully reported quarterly the amounts lost to theft. According to the factor Jonathan Halstead, American soldiers were stealing him blind, taking deerskins so regularly that he could not keep an unbroken padlock on the warehouse.[43] Timothy Barnard, whose corncribs were regularly assaulted, complained that he could not buy a padlock strong enough to thwart thieves.[44] Travelers were regularly accosted by banditti and had their goods ransacked and their horses stolen. White frontier farmsteads were targets of traveling Creeks as well as banditti. And Creeks were the victims of frontier whites and blacks who crossed into Creek territory under various pretenses and waylaid hunting parties. One of the reasons Creek headmen gave for not wanting roads through their territory was that Creek cattle would stray farther once a wide road was available, and whites could more easily steal the strays.[45]

The most prevalent form of theft was horse stealing. Horses were absolutely necessary on the frontier. They were the major form of transportation, and they were the primary method of freighting goods. Accoutrements were also necessary, and riding saddles, pack saddles, and horse tack were important elements of the trade for most of the eighteenth century as well.[46] By Hawkins's era, however, some Creek men were beginning to make their own saddles and bridles for themselves and for sale.[47] That such valuable items as horses and horse tack should find an illegal market is not surprising, and the frontier provided ample opportunities for stealing horses. Like other livestock, horses were free ranging, and many strays were stolen by opportunistic thieves. Indian, white, and black hunters and travelers commonly took strays they happened upon or stole outright from one another. At nightly encampments while traveling or hunting, people let their horses loose to graze. Horse thieves shadowing such parties could make off with a dozen or more horses while remaining outside the firing range of rifles. Not all horse thefts were by stealth; some occurred in broad daylight. In one case at Milledgeville, Georgia, a white man insisted on testing the strength of two horses owned by a Creek male acquaintance. They decided to race the two horses. The Creek man rode one horse; the white rode the other. The two galloped headlong through the main street of Milledgeville. But when they reached the finish line, the white man kept riding and disappeared.[48]

The Creeks were not the only ones involved. The Choctaws, the Cherokees, the Seminoles, the Chickasaws, frontier whites, and free blacks were all stealing horses. According to the British surveyor Bernard Romans, the Chickasaws were the most notorious. Romans, who never liked Indians, related one incident with the Chickasaws in which his "razors and a case of instruments and other trifles of no real use to them, besides every horse I had with me, vanished in one day among these deceitful people."[49] In Creek country, some individuals were well-known horse thieves who had been stealing horses for several years when Hawkins arrived.[50] There also were infamous mixed gangs of horse thieves made up of whites, blacks, and Indians. These gangs roamed far and wide raiding frontier settlers, traders, and Indian camps and taking several horses at a time along with other goods such as clothing, rifles, metal tools, and anything else that struck their fancy.[51] The victims of these raids, often surprised and usually outnumbered, defended their property at the risk of losing their lives.

The range of horse stealing is apparent in Hawkins's plan for branding. He suggested a different letter for horses from Tennessee, South Carolina, North Carolina, and Georgia as far east as the St. Mary's River, and from the territories bordering the Mississippi River.[52] Hawkins hoped to initiate this branding system so that horses from these areas could be identified at least by state of origin, if not owner, when they showed up in Creek country. Obviously, branding the animals would have gone a long way in preventing thefts, settling disputes, and returning stolen livestock. But both Creeks and frontier Americans were stubborn in this regard, and although some people branded their animals, most did not. Stealing strays was commonplace and perhaps the major mode of acquiring livestock. No one wanted to begin branding, since almost everyone participated heavily in cattle, hog, and horse stealing. Everyone knew that livestock thefts contributed to the general disorderliness of the frontier and often provoked violence, but the benefits of blurred ownership outweighed the costs of refusing to brand.

A ready market for stolen horses provided a quick and profitable way to dispose of the stolen goods. Proving legal title to a horse was difficult, if not impossible, on the frontier. Horse swapping and trading were common, and people did not bother to keep their paperwork in good order. Obtaining proof of identity and legal purchase was difficult because horses were so rarely branded, and many of those that had been branded had changed hands so many times that they had several different brands.

Indian countryman John Galphin's claim to a stolen horse exemplifies the confusion in establishing legal ownership of horses. Galphin filed a claim with Hawkins for a horse that was in the possession of David Walker, who claimed to have bought it from Emautly Haujo of Coweta. Emautly Haujo told Hawkins that the horse had been stolen from Peyton T. Smith of Greene County, Georgia. But Galphin swore that he (Galphin) had sold the horse to John Mulegan of Savannah, and that Mulegan sold the horse to John Randolph of the Tensaw settlement on the Mississippi, and that Randolph sold the same horse to his father, Benjamin Durrants. Somehow Galphin assumed that Walker had stolen the horse.[53]

There is no direct evidence for what price a horse fetched on the black market; however, one can assume it was comparable to the amount legally paid for horses or reimbursed for stolen horses. The price of a horse ranged from $25 to $130, but most were bought or sold for around $40 to $50. The higher prices appear to have gone for good saddle horses; the lower prices, for horses of poor quality. Horses also were used in bartering and were usually exchanged for a rifle, which sold for about $40 or $50 as well, or perhaps for a keg of liquor.[54]

To assess the relative value of a horse worth $40 or $50, one can convert this amount into a comparable quantity of dressed deerskins. The factory price for dressed deerskins was 25 cents a pound.[55] A dressed deerskin weighed between one and two pounds, with a pound equaling eighteen ounces in the eighteenth century.[56] Therefore, $40 to $50 was the equivalent of 100 to 200 deerskins, depending on the weight of the skins. In short, horse stealing could be quite lucrative.

Upon his arrival in Creek territory, Hawkins took immediate steps toward halting horse stealing. He issued a decree requiring all buyers and sellers of horses to obtain licenses that gave clear title to the horses.[57] Because Hawkins believed that frontier settlers constituted the bulk of buyers, he asked the states to enforce his licensing plan, but the state governments gave little support to Hawkins's program of licensing.[58] His scheme for and insistence on branding, as we have seen, also went unheeded by most Creeks and frontier settlers.

Hawkins reported that he convinced the Creek National Council to pass a decree against horse stealing and to sanction punishments for thieves.[59] The punishment for horse stealing was severe: disfigurement and confiscation of all property for the first offense and death for a second offense.[60] Hawkins regularly made cash rewards to persons searching for or returning stolen horses, and he hired Sackfield Maclin, a white man, to travel though Creek territory rounding up stolen horses.[61] At one point, frustrated that horse stealing continued unabated, Hawkins threatened to reimburse stolen property with Creek land and warned the National Council that unless it could effectively curb the activity, "every theft of a horse might be considered as the stealing [of] a plantation from the Creeks."[62]

But horse stealing continued throughout his tenure. The best Hawkins could do was to offer reparations to the victims. As mentioned earlier, when a case of theft could be proven and the thieves were identified to Hawkins's satisfaction, he repaid the victim out of the Creek stipend or from the Creek Factory funds. In some cases, he had the thief pay reparations out of his or her own personal property or return the stolen goods.[63] To his credit, Hawkins fulfilled his judicial role fairly. Contrary to all other U.S. and state courts and judicial proceedings, Hawkins allowed Indians and blacks to testify against whites, and he applied the same standards of evidence to white testimony as he did to Indian and black depositions.[64]

Another illegal exchange involved selling freedpeople into slavery. Both Creeks and whites participated in the common practice of proclaiming a freedperson to be a slave, taking the person into custody, and then reselling him or her back into slavery or presenting the person as a runaway or stolen slave and claiming the reward money. Hawkins particularly abhorred the capture and selling of freedpeople. He even advised his nephew against migrating to the Mississippi Territory because this practice was so widespread there.[65] As a man of his time, Hawkins was not an abolitionist; but he did believe in certain rights for slaves, and he insisted that freedpeople were, in fact, free. He carefully studied all claims presented to him, and he wanted proof that the person in question was stolen or a runaway and not free.[66] If the proof was not forthcoming, Hawkins dismissed the case. When this happened, the whites who were buying the slaves or offering the reward usually took the matter to their state governments, which were always willing to intercede and annul Hawkins's decisions.[67] Hawkins had no choice but to comply, sometimes under protest, and turn over the person to his or her supposed owners.

Returning runaway slaves was profitable. Hawkins, following state and federal laws, offered a $12.50 reward for returning runaway slaves, a substantial amount of money in Creek country.[68] Many Creeks took advantage of the situation by turning in blacks who had been living among them for several years. It is also likely that with the decline of the deerskin trade, many Creeks viewed the collection of runaway rewards as a means of acquiring cash and trade goods. In time, many blacks in Creek territory would flee to the Seminoles.

Returning runaway slaves was one way for Creek men and women to obtain cash. Cash was in short supply in Creek country, but at the turn of the nineteenth century, a nascent cash economy was emerging. Currency itself was not so readily available, and most cash transactions were done with chalks. A chalk was simply some diagonal marks on a piece of paper signed by the person issuing the chalks. Chalks were redeemable at the Creek Factory or through the resident town trader. One chalk was worth about thirty to forty cents.[69] The factor or resident trader would accept chalks and then either receive payment for the chalk from the person who initially issued them or add the amount to that person's credit bill. Chalks, then, served as legal tender on the frontier. However, their distribution was somewhat limited. People were reluctant to accept chalks from just anyone. They wanted some sort of proof that the person was good for the money. In many cases, people participating in such an exchange knew the parties involved and could evaluate the trustworthiness of the chalks on personal grounds. Often Hawkins or some other trusted white, such as Timothy Barnard, wrote vouchers for a person trading in chalks attesting to that individual's character and reliability.[70]

From the records of Hawkins and the Creek Factory it is difficult to determine whether U.S. currency changed hands. Amounts paid out are indicated as cash and at a cash value, but many of these may have been issued as chalks. Some currency undoubtedly made its way onto the frontier; but it was the exchange of goods that kept the economy flowing, and cash, for the most part, was only beneficial if it could be used to purchase goods for barter. Even Timothy Barnard dealt mostly in goods and only infrequently in cash.

However, cash was beginning to be more valued by the turn of the nineteenth century, and rendering services was another way a person could get cash. Ferrying was one such service that was highly valued and for which there was ample opportunity in Creek country. The Creek factor once paid some Cusseta men fifteen dollars to ferry goods across the Ocmulgee.[71] Foreign travelers frequently employed Creek guides while traversing Creek territory, and these guides were paid extra to ferry goods. These men, as Bartram's experienced guide demonstrated, crafted rafts and small boats on the spot. They were strong swimmers and knowledgeable hydrologists. Sometimes a Creek man would station himself at a creek or river and ferry people, livestock, and goods across for payment. In these cases, rafts were ready and waiting. The Creeks knew that ferrying would be very profitable once the Federal Road was opened. They would not agree to any bridges being built, and some Tuckabatchee warriors once arrested a U.S. military guard and survey crew attempting to construct a bridge.[72] On the eve of the Red Stick War, an Upper Creek faction led by Big Warrior began a heated argument with a Lower Creek faction led by William McIntosh for control over the ferry at the Chattahoochee River. The crux of this argument was that the ferry would be profitable and bring in cash to its operators.[73]

Renting horses was by far the service most in demand.[74] Although horses were numerous on the frontier, the demand outstripped the supply, and many people had to rent horses for various purposes. A person could rent his or her horse for $13 to $15 a day.[75] A good horse cost about $50 to $100, so by renting a horse, a person could get a full return on his or her purchase in a half-dozen rentals. Renting one's horses, however, had some degree of risk. Theft, as we have seen, was always a high risk. Plus, the rental horses were sometimes worked so hard as to be unfit when they were returned.[76]

Various part-time jobs were also available in Creek country by the late eighteenth century. In the early eighteenth century, according to reports, the Creeks considered it a disgrace to work for wages.[77] A hundred years later, they attached no such stigma to laboring for wages. Creeks, whites, and blacks were paid in cash and chalks to perform a variety of labors and services. Hawkins's office and the Creek Factory offered many forms of wage labor, but settlers and travelers often employed people for some types of work as well. This work was irregular and, therefore, did not provide a permanent occupation.

One job on the frontier was that of pony express rider. As the fabled riders of the American West, these men carried the mail on horseback across long distances. One of Hawkins's responsibilities was to see that the U.S. postal riders got though Creek territory safely. The Creeks had only reluctantly agreed to allow postal riders through their territory, and the job, therefore, was extremely dangerous because so many Creeks resented the agreement. In addition, the banditti regularly assaulted the riders in hope of finding something worth a ransom. Postal riders were continually harassed and sometimes killed while en route. Hoping to offset the hostility, Hawkins hired Creek riders because he believed that they were less likely to be threatened than American carriers. He usually preferred métis because he believed that they had less of a propensity to heavy drinking than "full bloods."[78] The riders were paid $1.50 a day, during which time they were expected to cover about forty miles.[79] Hawkins also had to rent horses for the riders, but since this was such a hazardous job and because it taxed a horse's limits, many people did not want to rent their horses for postal rides. He once seriously contemplated using mules instead, since postal horses wore out so regularly.[80]

Indian men also earned wages as runners. Using Indian runners to convey messages was a mode of communication that had been employed among the Indians for perhaps centuries, and certainly through all of the eighteenth century. Runners were Indian men who could travel at a trot twenty-five or more miles in a day. Hawkins regularly employed Creek runners at twenty-five cents a day.[81] Creek headmen, Euro-American traders, and others also employed Indians runners, presumably at rates similar to those paid by Hawkins. Hawkins and other Euro-Americans also enlisted Creek couriers on horseback to deliver written messages, usually to other Euro-Americans at some distance. According to Hawkins, Indian couriers were more reliable than the postal service. When the factor Jonathan Halstead mentioned his uncertainty over sending mail with Indian couriers, Hawkins reassured him that he had "never lost a paper in the care of an Indian."[82]

The amount paid for a courier was probably calculated according to distance and danger. In 1815, for instance, as the Seminole resistance was taking hold, Timothy Barnard hired a Chehaw courier to deliver a letter to General Blackshear, an American military officer stationed among the Lower Creeks during and after the Red Stick War. Barnard asked Blackshear to pay the Chehaw courier $4.00 upon delivery. According to Barnard, the service was worth it because the Yuchis, whom he usually hired for odd jobs (his wife was a Yuchi), would not take the job for even $10.00. Apparently the Yuchis had been "acting as spies here and at the Agency," and many Creeks were upset with them. Yuchi men, therefore, were wary about traveling long distances alone. The Chehaw courier said that he would take his payment in homespun if Blackshear did not have the cash.[83]

Barnard's comment about Yuchi spying points to another job, albeit a dangerous one, that was available in Creek country. During the Red Stick War and Seminole resistance, Hawkins hired Creek informants and spies, or rangers, under an American commander. He chose his informants carefully for their trustworthiness and their access to information. The spies were apparently a different class. He gave no information on the nature of this spying, except to report that these spies could penetrate into hostile areas and retrieve detailed information.[84] Hawkins paid the spies $1.00 a day; the captain of the spy company received $1.50 a day. All of the company received provisions, ammunition, and even horses. Given the expense of outfitting such a company, the activities of the spies, whatever they may have been, were obviously deemed necessary and worth the expenditures.[85]

In addition to these jobs, Creek men could perform a variety of other services for cash. White and black travelers, when crossing Creek territory, usually employed Creek guides, not only because they knew the trails but also because they were effective mediators with other Indians in the woods, and especially the banditti. Hawkins also hired Creek men as guides and hunters during treaty negotiations, which could sometimes last weeks.[86] Interpreters were always in demand, and since many Indians, particularly métis, as well as blacks and whites in Creek country spoke several languages, there were many available. Hawkins often employed literate Indian countrymen not only to interpret at official meetings but also to translate and write out Creek "talks," which he then forwarded to the War Department. Timothy Barnard often acted in this capacity, as did James Durouzeaux, the Coweta trader who worked for Panton, Leslie, and Company and the Spanish governor of West Florida. Hawkins's métis friend Alexander Cornells, who was probably illiterate, earned cash through interpreting. Cornells earned $131 for three months of interpreting in 1797.[87] Many people passing through Creek country as well as the factors and military personnel occasionally hired interpreters, and they did not necessarily need one who was literate.

With the increase in livestock raising, wranglers found seasonal work offered by both Indians and Indian countrymen. Packhorse men were always in demand, and Indian, black, and white packhorse men received 37 cents a day.[88] Big Warrior, an Upper Creek headman, charged $12 for overseeing the transport of some iron to the Upper Creek towns.[89] Hawkins's efforts to institute Euro-American urban standards of law and order also generated some jobs. Hawkins offered $2.50 and a blanket for any Creek who could return stolen property.[90] He hired Creek warriors to pursue Creeks accused of murder and also to catch Creek and American thieves. These men received 25 cents a day plus provisions, and they were paid even if they did not apprehend the accused.

The Creek Factory also provided some irregular work for folks on the frontier. The factors recorded many of these transactions in the ledgers. For instance, while the warehouses were being built at the Ocmulgee Factory, two Creek men received $1.50 each for peeling off sheets of bark that were used as temporary roofs for the goods.[91] Hewing logs for the factory brought $5.00 a day.[92] Airing out the cloth and blankets stored at the factory earned $2.00 a day.[93] Casks and boxes for transporting goods were built on site, and the factor paid by the box or cask.[94] When goods had to be moved from one store to another, the factor paid men $2.00 apiece to do so.[95]

Hawkins convinced some Indian countrymen and wealthy métis to set up blacksmith shops for making spinning wheels and looms. In some cases, these men allowed their black slaves to be taught blacksmithing skills. In other cases, their métis sons learned the craft.[96] For instance, in 1801 Timothy Barnard reported that his oldest son had made ten spinning wheels, three of which he kept for the Barnard family and seven of which he sent to Cusseta.[97] Hawkins supplied the materials for Barnard's and others' efforts, but the products were to be given free of charge to any Creeks requesting them.

Blacksmithing was one of the few secure jobs on the frontier. According to treaty, the United States was to provide blacksmith shops for the Creeks and pay the wages of the smith and his assistants. Blacksmiths received $26 a month, and their assistants, the "strikers," received $10 a month plus the value of one ration per day.[98] Hawkins initially hired experienced white or métis blacksmiths; part of their job, however, was to teach any Creeks interested in learning the trade. By 1808 many young Creek men were becoming interested in blacksmithing and other manufacturing and mechanical skills as an alternative to deer hunting for an income.[99] Hawkins hoped that eventually all of these operations would be self-sufficient and provide good employment for Creek men. Whites in Creek country paid for the smithing, but the service was free to Creeks as stipulated in previous treaty agreements, although they had to supply their own charcoal.[100]

Most of the wage labor available went to men; however, Creek women could also find irregular employment. The most prevalent form of employment for women was prostitution, for which a woman would receive cloth and food items. Prostitution was not stigmatized among the Creeks and, in fact, seems to have been considered good business. As his Creek hosts once explained to Jean-Bernard Bossu, a woman's "body is hers to do with as she wishes."[101] Hawkins was fairly complacent about Creek women's blatant sexuality. He lamented prostitution not because he necessarily viewed it as morally wrong but because he believed it hindered his efforts to turn Creek women to the plan for civilization.[102]

Other than prostitution, wage labor for Creek women was an extension of their domestic roles and centered on agricultural and domestic tasks. When he provided a portion of the fare at National Council meetings, Hawkins hired Creeks (presumably women) to butcher the beef and to prepare the breads.[103] At his first post at Coweta Tallahassee, Hawkins paid Creek women to fence and farm 250 acres according to the methods he hoped to introduce.[104] The Indian countryman Robert Grierson hired Creek women to separate cotton fibers from the seed. He paid each woman a half-pint of salt or three strands of "mock wampum" per bushel, or else one half-pint of rum for two baskets. Grierson told Hawkins that when the cotton was fully opened, a woman could pick between two and three baskets a day.[105]

Once introduced by Hawkins as part of the plan for civilization, cloth making, especially, appears to have caught on among many of the women in Creek country. Cloth was also a prime trade commodity. Cloth was not a necessity, since Creek women were quite capable of fashioning buckskin clothing and of making cloth from mulberry and other native fibers. But making cloth from natural fibers and buckskins was laborious and time-consuming work. Naturally, Creek women preferred buying European-made cloth, and a variety of cotton, linen, and wool cloth is found on eighteenth-century trade lists. Broadcloth, calico, cambric, chintz, denim, flannel, muslin, linen, stroud, and duffel, to name a few, were sold by the yard.[106] Creek women made shirts, skirts, leggings, and breechclouts from these cloths. (Creek men did not like trousers because they found them too constraining.) Needles, thread, and scissors, necessary for sewing manufactured cloth, also sold well.

Blankets, which replaced the buckskin and feathered matchcoats, were premade of stroud or duffel. The Creeks were particular about their blankets. They wanted five-point stroud blankets with three- to four-inch blue borders, two inches from the edge. The wool had to be dressed downward with the points so as to shed rain better.[107] The Creeks also occasionally bought some manufactured articles of clothing. Waistcoats were popular among Creek men. Some men bought ready-made cloth breechclouts. Gloves, petticoats, the famous ruffled hunting shirts, and handkerchiefs were all popular.[108] However, these clothing items constituted a sideline of the cloth trade, and most cloth was sold by the yard.

As part of the plan for civilization, Hawkins envisioned Creek women growing their own cotton and making their own homespun cloth. To get them started, he asked some of the Indian countrymen to allow white women he had hired as instructors onto their farms, where they were to conduct schools in spinning and weaving for Creek girls and women.[109] In some cases Indian countrymen, with an eye toward profit, hired and paid the salaries of American women spinners and weavers, and they had their black slave women working with them making homespun. Robert Grierson, for instance, hired Rachel

Spilliard, who had until then been working as one of Hawkins's assistants among the Cherokees. In 1802 Timothy Barnard hired her sister in the same capacity.[110] Rachel Spilliard not only tutored Creek girls in spinning and weaving, but with the help of four slave girls, she apparently made enough homespun to sell to Indians.[111] Hawkins also enlisted the aid of white women in Creek country. He subsidized Hannah Hale, the Georgia woman who married into Creek society, with the necessary tools for textile manufacturing—spinning wheels, cards, and shuttle—and he ordered her a loom made at his expense.[112] Hawkins made particular mention of one such school run solely by Indian women at Patachoche as early as 1799.[113]

Hawkins beseeched Creek mothers and grandmothers to allow their daughters and granddaughters to live at the schools and be tutored in cloth making. Five Creek girls lived at the Creek Agency, where Hawkins's daughters served as instructors.[114] Comparable numbers of girls were placed in other schools. These schools did not always work out as planned. In 1802 Lavina Turner, probably the weaver at Alexander Cornells's farm, reported to Hawkins that the girls "had of themselves or from their Grandmothers's advice, conceived their learning to spin was conferring a singular favor on the agent," and they demanded a suit of fine clothes in payment. Turner reported that she declined whipping the girls as their parents had suggested and instead sent them back to live with their mothers. She then began tutoring the girls in their own towns instead of bringing them to the school.[115]

Hawkins subsidized cloth making by using some of the stipend money to buy cottonseed and all the cotton cards, spinning wheels, looms, and other necessary items for the establishments. Hawkins hoped that the cloth manufacturing stations and schools eventually would become self-sufficient and not dependent on federal subsidies.[116] The idea was to have Creek men and women growing cotton, to have enough blacksmith shops and blacksmiths making spinning wheels and looms, and to have Creek women and girls carding, spinning, and weaving the cloth. As a measure of his commitment to the plan and to setting an example, Hawkins's family wore clothing made of homespun cloth, which considering his position, was especially notable.[117]

Four years after Hawkins arrived, Creek women and girls were making enough cloth to clothe 300 people and enough surplus to barter for livestock.[118] In 1811 Hawkins reported that there were nine imported looms and an unspecified number of looms made by slaves and whites in the Upper towns and twenty imported looms and thirty Creek-made looms in the Lower towns.[119] In 1812, 500 spinning wheels were delivered to Creek women.[120] Creek women became good cloth makers; their cotton threads were "even and well spun."[121] When available, they used sheep's wool for making blankets "comparable to the Yorkshire Duffel," except Hawkins found wool cards difficult to obtain.[122] Anyway, sheep raised in the South did not produce good enough wool. In 1811 seven Upper Creek towns sent a special request to Hawkins for spinning wheels and cards. The headmen of the Coosa, Ocheubofau, and Nauchee towns (the Abihka province) told Hawkins that the women of the towns had instructed the men to use their share of the stipend money to purchase these things. Hunting no longer provided enough cloth for their families, and the women, seeing other Creek women and Cherokee women clothing themselves, wanted to do the same.[123] In at least one case, an elderly man participated in cloth making. Micco Auchulee, the Old King of Coweta, was especially proud of forty yards of 5/4-point cloth his female relations had made and for which he had carded most of the cotton himself. As he explained to Hawkins, "I am old . . . and as such according to our old ways useless but according to the new way more useful than ever."[124]

Creek women's interest in cloth making is revealing. Cloth was one of the most important trade items in the eighteenth and early nineteenth centuries, second only to guns and ammunition. Women bartered for cloth themselves, but most cloth, by far, was purchased with deerskins that the men procured. Therefore, women became dependent on men for cloth. Hawkins designated the cloth manufactured at the schools to be the property of the girls and their families, which accorded with Creek ideas about ownership anyway. Although it is by no means clear, Creek women may have perceived cloth making as a way to gain economic independence. One of the main complaints lodged by Creek men against the plan for civilization was that the women, by growing cotton and making cloth, would become independent, "proud and not obedient to their husbands."[125]

The new opportunities for women and men in cottage industries, small businesses, thieving, and wage labor jobs, among other things point to the increasing economic diversification in which most Creek men and women were involved. Farming and subsistence hunting were successful long-term practices for keeping one's family fed. However, the Creeks, as all southern Indians, were now fully linked to the global market. Guns, ammunition, cloth, horses, cows, metal tools, strike-a-lights, trinkets, Jews's harps—these things, too, made up part of life in Creek country in the early nineteenth century, and they had done so for at least 100 years. When deerskins no longer provided ready access to these goods, Creeks found other things that would. But wage labor, business ventures, and cloth making could only provide irregular and temporary access to cash and goods. Ranching looked promising at first, but it, too, was already hitting an ecological wall. By the first decade of the nineteenth century, Creek men and women began to cast about for another commodity. The one their own gaze landed on was Creek country itself.

CHAPTER TEN

THE SELLING OF CREEK COUNTRY

From the moment Europeans set ashore in the New World, they had cast an appraising eye over the landscape. Creek country had come under this eye as well, and especially after the American Revolution, when America's economic aim was unabashedly one of commercialism and western expansion. America wanted Indian lands, and the state and federal governments supported and sometimes sponsored the naturalists, surveyors, government officials, agents of land companies, and others who journeyed to Creek country to appraise its potential for Euro-American development. The reports were unanimously good. Creek country was beautiful—"a noble and fruitful country."[1] Of course, the Creeks had known this for centuries. They assuredly looked on their land as "their blood and their life," and they were supremely reluctant to part with it.[2] As with any people who depend on hunting, gathering, agriculture, and ranching for their livelihood, land had always been central to Creek life. It was also central to their political independence, and they understood this.[3] However, as the nineteenth century got under way, land itself entered the new Creek economy as a commodity, something to be bought and sold.

After the American Revolution, the U.S. government's first order of business was the so-called Indian problem. At the heart of the "problem" was the question of westward expansion and land acquisitions, which, in turn, dictated American Indian policy. American Indian policy was first formulated in the Articles of Confederation, ratified in 1781.[4] Following British policy set in the Proclamation of 1763, the Articles of Confederation demarcated a clear boundary line between Indians and Americans, which, in effect, sealed international recognition of Indian national land claims.[5] According to the Articles of Confederation, Indian lands could only be acquired through the federal government and only through consultation and agreement with representatives of an Indian group empowered to make land cessions.[6] This policy has come to be known as the Treaty System.

In the South, state governments challenged federal authority almost immediately after independence. In these early years the question of states' rights mainly pertained to the acquisition of Indian lands.[7] Who had the right to acquire Indian lands? Which treaties were binding, state or federal? The uproar led to an ambiguous clause in Article 9 of the Articles of Confederation that reads, "The United States in Congress assembled have the sole and exclusive right and power of regulating the trade, and managing all affairs with the Indians, not members of any of the states, *provided the legislative right of any State, within its own limits, be not infringed or violated.*"[8]

The southern states, all of which made outrageous territorial claims as their "own limits," took advantage of this clause, setting in motion an immense land grab that left Indian policy under the Articles of Confederation in shambles by 1786. Land companies formed to take advantage of the ambiguous loopholes in American Indian policy, and the entire South became a hotbed of land speculation.[9] The shareholders of these companies included, as one historian notes, "almost every man of the area important enough to be recorded by historians."[10] The schemes instigated by the land companies and the audacity of the men in charge are truly astonishing and, in at least one case, seditious. The Yazoo land companies, the nucleus of which formed as early as 1785, for instance, claimed holdings from present-day Vicksburg, Mississippi, to Muscle Shoals on the Tennessee River in Tennessee, all of which were Indian lands.[11] In 1788 prominent men such as James Robertson, John Sevier, James Wilkinson, and Andrew Jackson began plotting to secede from the Union in order to ally themselves with Spain and to grab a large portion of the territory around the Mississippi River.[12] The Tennessee Land Company, formed in 1789 (William Blount, the governor of the Southwest Territory was a prominent shareholder), claimed title to 4 million acres of Indian land along the Tennessee River.[13] The tactics of speculators appalled not only the Creeks and Hawkins but a wide range of people in American society. When high state officials were revealed to be involved in many of these nefarious schemes, the national reputation of America degenerated. As Louis

LeClerc Milfort put it at the time, "Americans are very dishonest."[14] Still, speculators operated freely throughout southeastern Indian territory. The Creeks had a name for land speculators: *ecunnaunuxulgee*, or "those greedily grasping after our lands."[15]

Wanton land speculation spread throughout not only the South but the entire eastern seaboard, causing serious problems with the northern Indians. In the South the Cherokees and Creeks carried on a seven-year series of raids against Americans. When land frauds began to gain public notoriety, the U.S. government responded in 1790 with the Trade and Intercourse Act as a measure to stop land speculation and to put Indian relations with the federal government on a more agreeable footing, so that land acquisitions could proceed peacefully. This is the act that also introduced the plan for civilization. Section 4 of the act stated clearly that only the federal government could acquire Indian lands.[16]

Needless to say, Section 4 outraged the proponents of states' rights, and it did not stop the land speculators. Since many of these men held political offices or had friends and close associates in political office, they formulated subsequent state and federal legislation to undermine Section 4 and to suit their own interests.[17] Speculators also became noticeable players in federal land cession negotiations. The Creek treaties of Shoulderbone, Galphinton, and Augusta, all signed in the 1780s and all nullified several years later, had been pushed through by Georgia land speculators.[18] William Blount, whom Washington appointed governor of the Territory of the United States South of the River Ohio and whom the Creeks called "the dirt king" because of his avariciousness in acquiring Indian lands, was heavily involved in land speculations for most of his career. He was instrumental in the 1791 Treaty of Holston, much to the disadvantage of the Cherokees.[19] The 1802 Treaty of Fort Wilkinson was overseen by the notorious speculator Gen. James Wilkinson (also a self-proclaimed double agent for Spain, code name Agent 13). Georgia land speculators were present at treaty negotiations in an unofficial capacity as "observers," but they spent much of the time behind the scenes pushing for the tracts of land they wanted.[20] Southern land speculators maintained an incessant clamor for Indian land. By 1805 even Secretary of War Henry Dearborn was weary of dealing with the southern states, Georgia in particular. He wrote Hawkins, "If the Ocmulgee can once be established as the boundary, I trust I shall not live long enough to hear any contention for any other boundary line between Georgia and the Creek Nation."[21] Despite the pique expressed by Dearborn and other high federal officials with land speculators, most of them became noteworthy public figures, and one became president of the United States. Federal policies never formed a coherent system, had ambiguous clauses and loopholes, and were never fully formulated, legislated, or enforced. Such shoddy policies could in no way control the late-eighteenth- to early-nineteenth-century land frenzy. Since the federal government's true agenda was expansion, it did not attempt to regulate Indian land purchases. Land speculators, then, had free reign.

The influence of land speculators in Indian policy not only carved away Creek country, but it also resulted in a restructuring of the Treaty System wherein annuities, or cash payments, were granted in exchange for land. On the surface, the annuity system appears to have been in the best interest of the Indians, since they were to receive a price for any land ceded. In reality, the system undermined Indian sovereignty and land holdings because through the annuity system, land became a commodity.[22]

During the colonial period, land was a primary issue between Europeans and Indians. However, when Europeans treated with American Indians for land, in most cases the land was not actually bought and sold. When Europeans acquired land from the southeastern Indians, the treaties ceding the lands were usually treaties of peace, trade, or alliance, and land cessions were made as part of a larger agreement. In these cases, gifts were certainly exchanged, and they were often quite lavish on the part of the Europeans, especially the British. But the gifts were not considered payment for land. In southeastern Indian life, exchanging gifts was part of the system of reciprocity, whereby social, economic, and political partnerships were established. This idea carried over to Indian trading partnerships with Europeans, and the gifts exchanged symbolized the new alliances. The kinds and amounts of gifts exchanged changed throughout the Historic Period, and in the process the nature of Indian leadership also changed. *Micos* who could negotiate with Europeans for many gifts received respect, admiration, and support from their fellow townspeople; these *micos* also had plenty of gifts with which to form additional social partnerships among the group, widening their spheres of influence.[23] Land cessions almost always accompanied these early treaties; however, land was part of the gift-giving system, and it was exchanged for gifts, favors, trade agreements, military assistance, and so on. The closest thing to purchase occurred when the British began to offer cancellation of trade debts in return for parcels of land.[24]

In the early years of American Indian policy as well, no monetary compensations were offered to the Indians. Modeled after the British system, these early treaties were ostensibly peace treaties, although they were inevitably accompanied by requests for land, and the Indians were guaranteed U.S. protection against white squatters, recognition of their land claims, and "gifts."[25] After instituting the Treaty System, federal and state officials understood treaties as a way of acquiring land and not as a way of making trade alliances. Hence, gift giving, although still a part of diplomacy, diminished and was replaced by purchase through the annuities. The 1785 Treaty of Hopewell with the Cherokees, for example, offered no compensation for the 6,000 square miles ceded, although Hawkins and the other commissioners broached the subject. In comparison, the 1791 Treaty of Holston with the Cherokees was designed by the dirt king, William Blount, and the Cherokees were to receive $1,000 annually for the cession.[26] Hawkins, who never appreciated reciprocity much less the symbolic code of gift giving, applauded the change; he thought the custom of gift giving bred laziness and dependency among the southern Indians.[27]

In the Treaty System, monetary compensation was dispensed through annuities, wherein the United States guaranteed a yearly stipend to be paid to the Indian group. Initially, the annual payments were guaranteed "in perpetuity," but later the U.S. Senate insisted that the number of years be fixed and with a lump sum to be paid upon signing. For the Creeks, the 1790 Treaty of New York initiated the annuity system. In this treaty, negotiated by a contingent of Creek *micos* led by Alexander McGillivray, the Creeks were to receive $1,500 a year in perpetuity in return for land.[28] In addition, McGillivray added a secret article whereby certain medal chiefs were to receive $100 a year for life, and McGillivray was to receive a commission in the U.S. military and $1,200 a year for life.[29]

The Treaty of New York was the model for the next three land cession treaties between the Creeks and the United States. The 1796 Treaty of Colerain affirmed the Treaty of New York and added $6,000 in goods with provisions for two blacksmiths, with strikers, for the Creeks.[30] In the 1802 Treaty of Fort Wilkinson, the Creeks ceded an additional portion of land between the upper Oconee and Ocmulgee Rivers in return for $3,000 annually and $1,000 every year for ten years "to the chiefs who administer the government," $10,000 in goods and merchandise, $10,000 to satisfy debts to the Creek Factory, and $5,000 to satisfy claims of U.S. citizens against property taken by individuals in the Creek Confederacy.[31] By 1805, the United States had capped the number of years for annuity payments. The Treaty of 1805 (or the Treaty of Washington) reiterated the Treaty of Fort Wilkinson and clarified the boundary lines. In addition to agreeing to a postal route through their territory, the Creeks were to receive $12,000 in money or goods annually for eight years and then $11,000 for ten years, "making, in the whole, eighteen payments in the course of eighteen years, without interest."[32] The next treaty with the Creeks, the Treaty of Fort Jackson, was between the victors and the defeated.[33]

Although U.S. commissioners were instructed to evaluate the monetary value of Creek lands in terms of hunting grounds, Creek negotiators clearly understood the expanding resource value of their land and the value of currency, and they expected the annuities to reflect the market value of their land. In the talks for the 1796 Treaty of Colerain, Creek headmen discussed Creek country in Euro-American terms of value. They explained to the American delegation that they knew the tract in question had valuable pines and oaks and that foreign countries paid top dollar for such timber. They continued that there was abundant range for cattle and hogs and good streams for mills, and that the soils grew good tobacco. Plus, there were a lot of pine trees, which could be tapped for tar, even the dead ones. The Creek headmen pointed out that all of these resources were "lasting profit" for the State of Georgia and that the payment in no way reflected this value.[34]

Another example of the Creeks' understanding of the monetary value of their lands comes from the negotiations for the Treaty of 1805. This treaty not only included the lands between the Oconee and Ocmulgee Rivers, but it also requested that the Creeks give permission for the postal route that would become the Federal Road to be built through Creek country. As was the usual procedure, Hawkins broached the subject well before any official negotiations took place. In 1804 Hawkins found the Creeks, the Lower Creeks especially, opposed to the U.S. requests. The Federal Road was a particularly troublesome point. Members of the opposition party among the Lower Creeks were so adamant about the road and not selling any more land that they proposed to remove Hawkins's agency to the Upper towns or to Georgia and thereafter not allow any more whites among them. They also swore to kill any headman that did sign such an agreement. After much talk, some diplomacy, and a threat of war issued by Hawkins on behalf of the secretary of war, the Creeks agreed to the cession, provided that the question of roads not be mentioned and that the price they set be paid.[35] Hawkins agreed to submit the proposed draft treaty to the U.S. Senate. Hawkins wrote to Secretary of War Henry Dearborn that he thought the price reasonable, since the United States was getting 2 million acres of "unquestionably the best land in this country," but that he did not think the Senate would ratify the treaty because it might believe the price was too steep.[36] Hawkins was correct; the Senate did not ratify the treaty on the grounds that the price was too high and that the method of payment was unacceptable.[37] Despite much opposition that resurfaced, a

Creek delegation went to Washington, accompanied by Hawkins, to talk with Jefferson about the cession.[38]

The price and the method of payment the Creeks requested in this land cession demonstrate that the Creeks not only understood the commercial value of their land but were knowledgeable financiers in general. For the 2 million acres between the Ocmulgee and Oconee Rivers, the Creek delegates requested $200,000 in stock bearing 6 percent interest payable twice a year, with the stock to be held in trust for the Creeks.[39] Disregarding the interest, this comes out to about ten cents an acre, which, as the Creeks stated to Jefferson, was well below what Americans paid for land among themselves and was therefore a bargain.[40] Jefferson upheld the Senate's decision, telling the Creeks that the price was too high and that the United States had never paid that much for Indian lands.[41] Jefferson was correct; U.S. land purchases from Indians averaged about two cents per acre.[42]

The Creek delegates patiently explained to Jefferson that they "begin to know the value of land," that some young métis had learned how to evaluate land in white terms and had taught this to the headmen and others. They knew that the land in question had good streams for sawmills, valuable swamps, and good stands of cypress and white oak for timber. Furthermore, the delegates told Jefferson that they themselves had inquired independently into the value of the land and they knew the price they asked was really only half of its true value.[43] The Senate finally agreed to pay $196,000 for the land, without interest, as an annuity for eighteen years.[44]

Annuities were allocated as yearly stipends through the Creek Factory and were paid in goods or cash to towns, headmen, and others. After the 1805 treaty, Hawkins dutifully sent a yearly invoice for Creek annuities to the War Department, specifying the amount and kind to be paid in goods and the amount to be paid in cash.[45] In practice the annuity system never operated smoothly, despite Hawkins's and the factors' attempts to keep the records straight. The U.S. government perpetually delayed payments or only gave partial payments. From the beginning, with the Treaty of New York, the United States paid only a portion of the 1796, 1797, and 1798 stipends.[46] Not until December 1799 did the factor Edward Wright receive the back payments for these years.[47] As of 1802, the medal chiefs who were to receive $100 yearly according to the secret article of the Treaty of New York had not been paid.[48] The Treaty of Fort Wilkinson payments came in slowly and partially. In 1816 Hawkins complained to the War Department that the Creeks were still due back annuities for 1812, 1813, 1814, 1815, and 1816, in total about $64,000.[49] The War Department never informed Hawkins why payments were not forthcoming, and Hawkins was left to explain to the Creeks why they were not receiving their money. Hawkins, as was his bent, honestly told them that he did not know, that he had not been informed by the War Department on the subject.[50] One can surmise that even the least cynical Creek suspected some underhanded stratagem or motive on the part of the War Department, since as Hawkins stated, they already believed "there was a deliberate plan in operation on the part of the U.S. to get possession of their country."[51]

This is not to say that the federal government was never forthcoming with the money owed the Creeks. The annuities were entangled with the Creek Factory finances; Panton, Leslie, and Company affairs; the plan for civilization, and a strange system for reparation to Euro-Americans for damages and thefts by Creeks. Moreover, the money was used to manipulate the Creeks. Thus all these factors made what appeared on paper to be a straightforward payment plan into a morass of credits, debits, and balances owed and due to a variety of people. To make matters even more confounding, the Creeks had a confusing method of allotting among themselves money and goods from annuity payments.[52]

These treaties agreed to provide some things necessary to the plan for civilization. In Article 12 of the 1790 Treaty of New York, which inaugurated the plan for civilization among the Creeks, the federal government agreed to "furnish gratuitously the said nation with useful domestic animals and implements of husbandry."[53] The Treaty of Colerain promised $6,000 in goods and blacksmith shops with the men to run them.[54] The Treaty of Fort Wilkinson guaranteed two additional blacksmiths and tools, but for only three years.[55] Finally, in the Treaty of 1805, all previous arrangements for blacksmiths were nullified and replaced with a single agreement stipulating two blacksmiths, strikers, and tools for eight years.[56]

The United States kept its promise of blacksmiths because Hawkins reported in 1812 that four resided in Creek territory and that the Creeks hired two more with their stipend money.[57] However, part of the cost of the domestic animals and tools of husbandry for the plan for civilization were deducted from the Creek stipend. Hawkins's office was allotted approximately $2,000 annually, and most of this went to pay Hawkins's assistants and the cost for Indians commissioned to run boundary lines and for hosting treaty negotiations and National Council meetings, among various other contingent expenses.[58] When Hawkins bought plows, spinning wheels, looms, seed, and cotton cards, he usually did so with Creek stipend money.[59]

The United States also deducted any money or goods due American citizens from thefts or damages done by Creeks. Robbery, as we have seen, was rife on the southern frontier. Frontier settlers submitted claims on the Creek stipend to Hawkins, who investigated the claims and, if they proved valid, paid the complainants out of the factory funds, which were to be reimbursed once the stipend money arrived.[60] The Treaty of Fort Wilkinson alleviated some of this debt by paying $5,000 against claims made by Georgians who had, by that time, remitted their grievances to the state, which in turn demanded theft reparations at the treaty negotiations.[61] Claims on stolen horses especially drained the yearly stipend. For example, Thomas Carr received $50 from the Creek annuity in payment for a horse stolen by a Lower Creek and $35 for one stolen by a Tallassee.[62] When a Creek man or woman had a horse stolen, he or she likewise was granted a claim on the annuity as compensation. In these cases, town headmen decided the case, as when Cusseta headmen allowed Holiji Tustunnuggee his claim for a horse stolen when he aided U.S. commander Major Adams in an unspecified raid on some Indians near Fort Fidius.[63]

Victims of other kinds of thefts petitioned for compensation from the stipend money. In 1797 Mrs. Brown, an American woman whose farm was raided by Creeks and whose husband was killed in the fray, petitioned for damages to her property. Hawkins agreed to pay her an unspecified sum from the Creek stipend.[64] When some Coweta and Cusseta men stole furs out of the "skin house" at the Creek Factory, the headmen of the towns agreed that the factor could deduct the value of the skins, $216.22, from the stipend.[65] The account books from the Creek Factory and Hawkins's letters are replete with such examples as these, and the amount claimed by American and Creek complainants took a sizable amount out of the yearly stipend.

The annuity was also entangled in the Creek trade debt to Panton, Leslie, and Company. Despite the competition, Panton, Leslie, and Company cooperated with the United States in many ways. William Panton and Hawkins kept a friendly correspondence, and each relied on the other for various favors. After Panton's death, John Forbes concentrated the company's resources, energy, and political connections on resolving the company's Indian debt and on establishing trade relations with the growing number of American settlers.[66] Forbes and Company continued to trade with the southern Indians, but the company's relations with the Indians grew brittle as Forbes began insisting on land to settle Indian debts.[67] Around this time the U.S. government made a deal with the company whereby in exchange for Forbes and Company (as Panton, Leslie, and Company was now called) putting pressure on the Creeks for their debt payments, the company could have their debts paid either in cash, through the annuities, or in land.[68] Company agent John Innerarity's meeting with Upper Creek headmen in 1812 reveals much about how this worked. Innerarity journeyed to Tuckabatchee in 1812, by which time Creek headmen had about fifteen years of experience with the annuity system, currency, and the use of land as a commodity.

Forbes sent Innerarity to Tuckabatchee to discuss formulating a payment plan for Creek debts to the company. Forbes knew that the Creeks received about $17,000 a year in annuities, and he hoped Innerarity could persuade the Creeks to use some of their money to pay their debts to the company. Upon meeting with Innerarity, the Upper Creek headmen asked for a breakdown of the debts. Innerarity promptly presented them with a prepared list of traders and Indians, the amount each owed, and the interest on the total debt. The Creeks then retired to study the list and to look into "those who were traders and those who were not, those who were dead and those who were living, those who had property and those who had none, that they would see if they could do anything, but they told me that would not hear of interest."[69]

The Creeks' scrutiny of Innerarity's list of debtors indicates something about how the Creeks perceived individual and collective debts. The Creeks accepted collective debt, but they placed some limitations on it. For instance, any debtors with property were to pay as much as possible, if not all, with their personal property.[70] The Creek Confederacy would take on any remainder of the debt. Furthermore, some Indian countrymen and town traders had separate accounts that the Creeks did not recognize as part of the Creek Confederacy account. Some such names had already been struck from the list at an earlier meeting with Forbes, and Innerarity deleted three more.[71] Finally, debts were dissolved upon death, or so the Creek headmen tried to persuade Innerarity, who, in turn, refused to make a distinction between dead and living debtors. The Creeks negotiated the issue; the headmen agreed with Innerarity, but only if the interest were waived.[72]

On the issue of interest, the Creek headmen were unwavering. This is understandable, since out of a debt of approximately $40,000, $21,916 was the principal and the remainder was the interest. The Creek headmen refused to pay the interest, and Innerarity, not an especially skilled negotiator, grew more and more irritated and only repeated his favorite phrase, that the "interest was as sacred as the principal."[73] Everyone grew impatient and angry. Innerarity believed the headmen to be feigning ignorance, and he told them to ask Timothy Barnard, who was at the council, about interest. He told them that Forbes and Company was simply passing on the interest costs of the company to the Creeks, as was standard business procedure. The headmen told Innerarity that they knew nothing about interest, that they did not understand it, that there was no word for it in their language, and that Forbes and Company were the first to mention it.[74] This, of course, was a blatant lie, since the draft treaty of 1805 clearly included interest on the annuity; also, Hawkins regularly added the amount due from interest when compiling Creek debts, apparently without any complaint from the Creeks.[75]

In all fairness to Innerarity, he unwittingly stepped into an extremely hostile and divided situation. Tecumseh had been among the Creeks a few months earlier, and some Creek warriors had journeyed to Ohio to participate in Tecumseh's Red River raids. They had murdered some American settlers on the Duck River as they returned. Hawkins's assistant Christian Limbaugh had earlier delivered a harsh and bitter talk from Hawkins to the Creek council demanding that these warriors be immediately apprehended or else the United States would consider the Duck River slayings an act of war.[76] The situation at Tuckabatchee was tense; it was not a propitious time to bring up the subject of trade debts, and especially not a good time to argue over interest.

Even the usually cool-headed Alexander Cornells was irritated by Innerarity's obstinate insistence on the interest payments; Timothy Barnard, normally in the thick of things, kept a low profile. Big Warrior of Tuckabatchee, under intense pressure to execute the men responsible for the Duck River killings, was livid. When Innerarity, believing himself to be capitulating, agreed to cut the interest to $10,000, "the cry of pay no such thing as interest, Pay only the debt was reechoed from every quarter."[77] Innerarity dropped the issue, although his journal does not record how or why he did so. The final agreement signed by the Creeks stipulated only that $21,916 would be paid out of the yearly stipend over three years.[78]

The Creek Factory likewise deducted Creek debts due the factory from the stipends, although there were no negotiations like Innerarity's involved in this. Individual Creeks purchased goods on credit and paid the debt out of their stipends when they could not do so through hunting. As the hunting economy continued to falter, purchasing goods with stipend money became the norm.[79] The factor kept an account of goods purchased with stipend money, and since the stipends were delivered through the factory, he merely kept a balance sheet of debts due and stipends allocated.[80] Using annuities as individual income and for manufactured goods made sense at first because the annuities were granted "in perpetuity," and as General Wilkinson once explained to the Creeks, they offered a reliable and dependable source of support.[81] Hawkins, too, promoted the system because, in his reasoning, if the Creeks sold tracts of land, present and future generations of Creeks could expect to have access to manufactured goods through yearly annuities.[82]

Since many Creek men and women bought on credit from the factory, the amount due the factor after a year was substantial. The exact numbers are difficult to gauge, but a few invoices give an idea of the balance between what the Creeks owed and what they were due. In 1797 Creek purchases at the factory totaled $585.21 for blankets and rugs, $462.99 for blue stroud and rugs, $254.89 for 704 yards of Irish linen, $187.37 for 578.25 yards of calico, and $9.65 for rope, wrappers, and a trunk. The total was $1,500.11.[83] At this time the Creeks were receiving $1,500 a year in accordance with the Treaty of Colerain. After the Treaty of 1805, the total Creek annuity rose to $17,800, a substantial amount of money for that time. In 1806 Hawkins tabulated the Creek Factory debt to be deducted from the stipend as $10,380.[84] Land had indeed replaced deerskins as the unit of trade.

The allocation of stipend money by the Creeks among themselves only contributed to this commodification of land and whittling away at national monies. The annuities were divided between the Upper and Lower Creeks. The towns of each division would hold a council meeting to decide how much of the stipend would be spent on goods, what goods were to be bought, and how much was to be given in cash. The Lower Creeks had agreed on a system whereby a portion of the stipend was set aside for tools, seed, and other things necessary for the plan for civilization. The rest went to certain towns one year, to other towns the next year, and so on. A town receiving a portion of the stipend for a particular year divided its payment among the townspeople.[85] Although it is not clear, all of the Lower towns were probably on this rotation schedule.

Upper Creek stipend money was divided at Upper Creek divisional meetings. A certain amount was earmarked for specific goods, and the cash portion was divided among only the towns represented at the meeting. If a town representative did not attend the meeting, that town forfeited its right to a share of that year's annuity.[86] Apparently some towns were regularly excluded or did not attend these meetings, although why this was so goes unexplained. In 1811 the headmen from the Abihka province complained to Hawkins that their towns (seven in all) had never received any of the stipend because "certain Great Chiefs" controlled its division and excluded them from the payments. In this case the women were asking for spinning wheels and looms.[87] The headmen asked Hawkins to intervene so that the stipend would be more equitably distributed. Hawkins declined to intervene and only suggested that they convince other Upper Creek towns to use some of the stipend to buy looms, plows, and other items needed in the plan for civilization.[88]

There is other evidence that the Abihkas' charge that some headmen were hoarding a larger part of the stipend than was their due was warranted. Hawkins had heard rumors as early as 1807 that some Upper Creek headmen had been "doing all they can to get possession of the stipend," and Big Warrior of Tuckabatchee, whom Hawkins described as "a discontented, ambitious man," especially was implicated.[89] The opportunities for embezzlement of these funds were certainly obvious and abundant. Under the annuity system, land cessions became the common mode of debt payments, and many influential Creeks supported such a system because the liquidation of collective debts meant that individual debts would also be exonerated. Hence, those Creeks most in debt and most engaged in the trade were the primary beneficiaries, as their personal debts comprised the bulk of the national debt.[90]

Even so, many Creek men and women believed they were entitled to a portion of the stipend, and they trailed into the Creek Factory to spend it. Tustunnuggee Thlucco's $1.00 debt for salt came out of the annuity, as did the $28.09 Thlohfidju borrowed to buy a horse.[91] When Tuskegee Tustunnuggee bought $3.75 worth of medicine for his ailing wife, the amount went as an annuity debit in the factory's account book.[92] The $12.00 Big Warrior charged to transport some iron to Tuckabatchee came out of the Creek stipend.[93] Efau Tustunnuggee requested $42.00 of his portion of the stipend in cash.[94] Big Warrior deducted the $9.50 he paid for a shotgun out of his annuity.[95] The $10.00 Tobler was paid for going to Milledgeville for Little Prince and Mico Thlucco came out of the stipend. Sofloffeogee received $105.00 for "sundry claims of Yuchis."[96] On one occasion, Hawkins was met in the woods by a large group of Creeks on their way to the factory to receive their stipend. The group had come on their own initiative, and the money was not at the factory. So Hawkins and Jonathan Halstead issued pay slips redeemable at the trading houses in amounts that were to be deducted from the stipend once it came in.[97]

The factor did not have a record of who was due what from the stipend. When someone came into the store and directed the factor to deduct his or her purchase from the annuity or requested a cash advance on his or her portion, in most cases the factor accepted the individual's word. Individuals occasionally brought letters from Timothy Barnard, Oche Haujo (Alexander Cornells), a local headman, or even Hawkins vouching for their good character and honesty and explaining how they came to be due a certain amount of the annuity. In 1797, for instance, Opoeehaujo of Cusseta gave Edward Price a letter from Timothy Barnard in which Barnard explained that Opoeehaujo was due a larger share of his town's annuity because he had been "a firm friend of the U.S.," specifically, he had been finding and returning stolen horses.[98]

Sometimes warriors with well-known anti-American reputations appeared at the factory to purchase goods using the stipend money. In one such case, Hawkins's predecessor, James Seagrove, instructed the factor to accommodate "Methlogee and his gang" because of their reputation for being troublemakers.[99] With innumerable charges such as these, factory debts mounted, stipends were spent, and Creek country was turned into a commodity.

That most Creeks understood themselves to be due a portion of the stipend was a result, in part, of their system of land tenure. A common stereotype of Indians is that they did not have a conception of the ownership of land, and that they never understood Euro-American conceptions of national and private ownership of land.[100] This is simply not true. When De Soto ventured through the Southeast in the mid-sixteenth century, the native peoples let him know, in no uncertain terms, when he passed from one polity to the next. The Mississippian chiefdoms had well-defined territories, and some were engaged in wars of conquest to acquire more.[101] But we do not know precisely how the precontact Indians defined territorial rights and land tenure among themselves. Once Europeans entered the picture and after the decline of the Mississippian chiefdoms, the time of purely indigenous rules of land tenure was over.

As far as we know, the question of disposing of or selling land did not come up within or between Mississippian chiefdoms before European contact. Once Europeans introduced the idea of alienation and pushed for land cessions, the unavoidable question of who had the rights of alienation was posed. As we have seen, within the Creek Confederacy, land tenure was based on communal, not private, ownership. But Creek communal ownership existed within a complex yet obscure matrix of land tenure including usufruct and alienable rights between townships, provinces, Upper and Lower divisions, and national levels. The Creeks had an abstract sense of geography, and many could draw accurate maps to scale.[102] The average Creek man or woman certainly knew well the agricultural, river valley, and hunting regions and boundaries of his or her township, and he or she probably knew the territories of neighboring townships and perhaps even of more distant townships. The intricacies of the full sweep of Creek land tenure, however, may have been more specialized knowledge, known only to clan or town representatives.

The most inclusive level was national, wherein all Creek lands belonged to the Creek Confederacy. This will be discussed below. At the next level, Creek lands were divided between the Upper and Lower towns, but the exact boundaries of each are not certain. The Upper and Lower divisions each owned the river lands on which their towns were situated and the watersheds that each river drained. Thus, the Upper Creeks laid claim to the Coosa, Tallapoosa, and Alabama drainages, and the Lower Creeks claimed the Chattahoochee, Flint, and Ocmulgee drainage (until it was ceded to the United States in 1802). Each division also claimed adjacent hinterlands as their hunting territory. In addition, each division claimed any lands attained through conquest by their warriors. Throughout the seventeenth and eighteenth centuries, the Creeks were involved in wars of conquest, the winners of which laid claim to some of the lands of the losers. In fact, in Creek eyes, they and not the Spaniards were the eighteenth-century colonizers of La Florida, which many Lower Creeks had settled after they had defeated the Apalachees in 1704.[103] These Creek colonists would later form the core of the Seminoles, who would break away from the Creeks by the turn of the nineteenth century.

Within the Upper and Lower divisions, lands were further divided by province, as discussed earlier. These were the hunting lands, and they appear to have been large areas of hinterland. The men of the towns in a province had access to these hunting ranges. Provincial hinterlands were enlarged when refugee groups joined, because this gave the province (and probably the division) rights to former lands of the refugee groups. In the 300-year diaspora of southeastern Indians, larger groups often splintered into many refugee groups, who then sought asylum with different Indian groups. This often led to intra-Indian territorial disputes as different groups claimed the former lands of their refugees.[104]

As discussed earlier, agricultural lands were allocated by town, and each town had access to certain portions of the active floodplain and river valley. How these river valley lands were allocated among the original groups that made up the Creek Confederacy is not known. Refugee groups who entered during the mid- to late eighteenth century, however, appear to have applied to the divisional or provincial councils for admittance and to have received an allotment of land suitable for the number of people who wished to settle there. This is what William Bartram stated, although he admitted that he was uncertain.[105] But, as in the League of Iroquois, the refugee groups were not given the land outright.[106] Like all township lands, they remained ultimately the communal property of the Creek Confederacy.

There is also a recorded case of a foreign group who did not actually join the Creek Confederacy but applied for a land grant within it. The Lower towns of the Cherokees suffered horribly during the American Revolution. Afterward, a town of the Lower Cherokees applied to the Creeks to rebuild in Upper Creek lands. The Upper Creek headmen Chinnabee and Old Lieutenant were appointed to "lay off the bounds of said lands," which ran from the confluence of the Oostaunaula River and Hightower Creek, down the Coosa, to the mouth of Wills Creek.[107] The town became known as Turkey Town. In time, a sizable number of Creeks moved to Turkey Town as well.[108] Some years later, in the 1814 Treaty of Fort Jackson, the ownership of Turkey Town became a point of contention between the Cherokees and the Creeks, because it was included as part of the tract being ceded in the treaty.[109] The Cherokees admitted that the land where Turkey Town was located was not theirs, but that they had "borrowed" it from the Creeks and were only "tenants-at-will."[110] The Cherokees claimed, however, that it now belonged to them because of their long-term occupancy. Conversely, the Creeks claimed the land through conquest. The Creeks explained that the controversy was generated because they did not wish to draw absolute lines between themselves and the Cherokees and instead allowed both Cherokee and Creek hunters to hunt in this zone.[111] The U.S. government eventually settled the dispute by agreeing that the Creeks had the strongest claim to the land.[112]

At the most inclusive level, Creek country belonged to the Creek Confederacy as a whole. Early in their colonial experience, the towns of the Creek Confederacy recognized that they had to work together when dealing with Europeans over land issues, and the towns agreed that any territory claimed by the Creeks (Upper or Lower) could only be ceded with unanimous agreement made with a full representation of towns. Exactly when the Creeks passed this decree is not known. When James Oglethorpe made the Treaty of Coweta with the Creeks in 1739, in which the Creeks granted the British colony the right to settle in coastal Georgia, the treaty read that "all the said lands are held by the Creek Nation as Tenants in Common."[113] Over the next four decades, the British led several "congresses," as treaty negotiations were called, with the Creeks. During this time, British pressure for land cessions and the constant menace of land speculators forced the Creeks to formalize their land policies, to invest their township institutions with some sort of negotiating power, to clarify their boundaries, and to consolidate their land holdings under national ownership. One of the consequences was the forging of a national consciousness.[114] The land belonged to the nation and could only be ceded by its representatives.

Given the hierarchal nature of Creek land tenure, however, the decree was difficult to put into practice. The Upper and Lower divisions had the final word on land cessions within their domains, and townships had the final word on land cessions regarding their hunting ranges. This undoubtedly helps account for the confusing allocation of stipend money—money paid for certain lands was divvied according to a poorly recorded reckoning of ownership. It was also an ambiguity exploited by land speculators. Agents of land companies penetrated Creek country in order to negotiate land and resource-use deals with anyone they could sway with promises of gifts, money, and shares in the company, and by the turn of the nineteenth century there were many Creeks who could be easily swayed.[115] They also sponsored the illegal settlement of white towns on Indian lands, including places such as Muscle Shoals in Tennessee and Wofford's settlement in Georgia. They promoted border jumping and squatting on Indian lands by financing the migration of white settlers and by using their influence with state governments to protect the fraudulent land claims of these settlers. These squatters became known as "intruders."

Land speculators, involved in formulating American Indian policy at every level, insisted that part of the plan for civilization must entail that the Indians should become "individual possessors of land."[116] These men made no pretense about improving Indian life; they frankly made their request so they could rent or buy lands from individual Indians and therefore be freed from having to wait for lengthy treaty negotiations before they were able to buy newly ceded lands from purchases made by the federal government.[117] The Creeks opposed private and exclusive ownership altogether because they recognized that if land speculators were given the opportunity to deal with individuals instead of the Creeks as a whole, there was a ready supply of Creek men and women who would put their own interests above that of the nation, and little by little, territory would be given over to land speculators. Even market-oriented métis and others who had settled individual "plantations" may have had exclusive access to their lands, but they did not have rights of alienation over their farms.[118]

Hawkins, likewise, knew of the designs of land speculators, and he understood that Creek national ownership was an effective deterrent to land speculation.[119] He stated, "It is questionable with me whether the division of lands among the individuals would tend to their advantage or not. In such an event, the long and well tried skill of land speculators might soon oust a whole tribe, whereas the whole country being a common, each of the community having exclusive property in his own farm only, the combined intelligence of the whole might be sufficient to resist such an evil and secure at all times land for the cultivation of the indijent [sic] and improvident."[120] In the new economy, however, even the "combined intelligence of the whole" was not enough to thwart the designs of land speculators or the intentions of many Creek men and women to profit from the land in ways such as selling timber or mineral rights, renting land, and exacting fees for grazing and farming.

The Creek Confederacy, as a whole, granted Americans some rights to resource extraction. As we have seen, both Indian countrymen and Hawkins were given land grants, provided the Americans did not make private claims on such. The Creeks likewise expected payment for any livestock belonging to the military forts and the Creek Factory that grazed on Indian lands, and Hawkins apparently also paid for grazing privileges when his personal stock wandered off the Creek Agency.[121] By treaty, any Americans who wished to cut timber on Creek lands had to pay for the privilege.[122] In one case, Creek headmen were upset with Panton for cutting cedar that was on Creek lands. Apparently Panton had made a deal with John Randon, whom he was paying to cut the timber. The headmen sent a message via Hawkins that if Panton wanted timber, he should apply directly to them and not buy it illegally from men such as Randon.[123] One unnamed Creek man discovered some lead deposits along the headwaters of the Ocmulgee River, and he requested that Hawkins look into the matter to see if he "could turn it to account for the Indians."[124]

In some cases, a divisional council allotted a piece of borderland to white farmers for a fee. In 1807, for example, Naniaba Island, which was not an actual island but a cove at the forks of the Tombigbee and Alabama Rivers, became the focus of a dispute between the Choctaws and the Upper Creeks. The Choctaws claimed the island, since it was the old homeland of the Naniaba and Tomé, both of whom had been admitted to the Choctaws as refugee groups. The Upper Creeks claimed the land through conquest, stating that the Naniaba and Tomé had fled as allies of the Choctaws in the Choctaw-Creek wars. In 1804, white farmers were cultivating the island, and the Choctaws requested that their agent, Silas Dinsmoor, ask the farmers for rent. The Upper Creeks asserted that they had rights to any rental fees. They were asking for fifty cents an acre. In this same letter, the Creeks stated their policy simply as "if you see any whites on Indian land you can ask for rent."[125]

Although many of these sorts of transactions were made by the divisional councils, several took place in the hinterlands, between individual Creeks and individual settlers. Warriors sometimes patrolled the American borders for intruders and allowed them to remain across the line if they agreed to pay for grazing and cultivation rights. The usual fee for cultivated lands goes unrecorded, but it was probably close to that for Naniaba Island. For grazing, the fee was twenty-five cents per head of cattle and fifty cents per horse.[126] Creek men and women accepted payments from white settles for the right to set fish traps in nearby streams.[127] In some cases, individual Creeks sold parcels of land to American farmers.[128]

The complexity of Creek land tenure and the decentralization of township governance meant that no national body was in a position to contest such profiteering. Besides, it was not altogether clear that such individual Creek land claims were invalid; under Creek land tenure all town citizens had use rights to the hinterlands. In 1798 the Tuckabatchee *mico* Efau Haujo implied in council that such was the case. Efau Haujo was asking Hawkins to see that white settlers would not enter agreements with individual Creeks. As Efau Haujo put it, some Creeks would go to the borders pretending to be great chiefs and, after a few drinks with the white settlers, would grant permission for the whites to graze their cattle or to settle on Indian lands.[129] He continued that only the nation, not individuals, had the right to grant grazing rights to whites, but that individuals were selling timber, grazing, and other use rights to whites and collecting the fees for themselves. Efau Haujo could not stop Creek men and women from doing so, and he was hoping that Hawkins could stop the white settlers instead.[130]

In treaty negotiations, Creek leaders often claimed that they needed all their land for themselves and for future generations to make a living. They usually couched this in terms of "hunting lands," but as we have seen, even as ranchers they did need most, if not all, of their land, given the free-ranging techniques they used. Also, the best agricultural lands were under cultivation, and people were rapidly putting the numerous small alluvial floodplains in Creek country under cultivation. In fact, Creek population was increasing, and the Creeks realized that soon "every piece of arable land will be necessary."[131] As land became a commodity, however, it took on a new economic usefulness. With the skin trade all but finished, and with a diminishing resource base for ranching, both wealthy and rank-and-file Creek men and women cast a new, appraising eye over their landscape. They now saw it as a commodity, an abstract entity to be bought and sold—something with which one could make purchases at the trading house.[132]

But this was juxtaposed with a supreme incentive to hold on to Creek country. Even if land was, as Hawkins reminded them, their "only resource"—their only source of income—the Creeks knew that their political and economic independence depended on their hold on the land.[133] Creek men and women knew that their political independence was tied to their land holdings and that increasing land sales could "lead to landlessness and even homelessness."[134] They knew that Americans, if given the chance, would take their land piece by piece and "that at last the white people will not suffer us to keep so much as will be sufficient to bury our dead."[135] They understood that the only way to stem the tide, which they still believed to be possible, was to stop the national sale of Indian lands and, perhaps more importantly, to challenge land speculators, intruders, and even the federal government in order to defuse the mounting pressure for land sales.

CHAPTER ELEVEN

THE CLOSING OF CREEK COUNTRY

The most common form of Creek resistance to land sales was raiding and harassing American settlers, especially the intruders, those American pioneers illegally settling on Indian lands. Despite their willingness to exchange natural resources with American frontier people for goods and cash, the Creeks knew that the unauthorized use of Creek lands for farming, grazing, fishing, hunting, timbering, and so on was a direct challenge to Creek land rights. Within this context, the Creeks were as quick to avenge any violations of their land rights as white settlers were to challenge them. Day-to-day life in Creek country, then, was underscored by a tension that consistently and continuously threatened to rend the fabric of life.

The physical boundaries dividing Creek country and U.S. territory marked the legitimate lines of separation, but Indians, whites, and blacks routinely penetrated far beyond these lines so that there was, in fact, no real boundary between the Creeks and the Americans. The American southern frontier settlers are barely known, but on the surface, their lives resembled those of many Creek men and women.[1] At the time of Hawkins's arrival in the Creek Confederacy, the people on the frontier were a mixed lot—Scots, English, Irish, Spanish, German, French, and American farmers migrating from Carolina, Virginia, Pennsylvania, and other more northern states—and they divided themselves along many political, social, religious, and economic lines.[2]

The demographic profile of these settlers is of young nuclear families with high birth rates.[3] They lived on single-family farmsteads consisting typically of two-room log cabins and one or two outbuildings for storage.[4] They practiced swidden agriculture and adopted Indian techniques of farming.[5] Few families used the plow. Most practiced hoe agriculture with no fertilization.[6] Their farms usually stretched along the alluvial floodplains of waterways, much like the farmsteads of Indian families who had moved out of the towns.[7] Because they practiced swidden agriculture, white frontier families were highly mobile. They stayed at their farms until the soils grew unproductive, usually after ten to fifteen years.[8] They then sold their land and moved on, usually to the West.

They grew enough to feed themselves with a minor amount of surplus to barter in the frontier exchange economy. Their crops were identical to those of the Creeks: corn was the staple, supplemented by sweet potatoes, squashes, beans, melons, peas, and so on.[9] Some families enclosed their fields with worm fences.[10] They devoted some small patches to cotton and/or tobacco, which were their main commercial agricultural crops.[11] Like the Creeks, their real commercial interests lay with ranching. And like the Creeks, most families owned a horse or two and a small herd of hogs and cows, and some families were large ranchers, reportedly owning herds in the hundreds and even thousands.[12] Their livestock were likewise free ranging. Livestock were raised primarily for the market, although pork and beef constituted some of the family's meat protein. Cows were rarely used for their milk products.[13] Basil Hall, who had taken his baby daughter on his American journey, repeatedly bemoaned the lack of milk or cheese for her.[14] In fact, most travelers who commonly took accommodations at these small farms commented on the dearth of milk products, given the preponderance of cattle in the country. Their final assessment was that these frontier ranchers mismanaged their farms and livestock and could not possibly profit from their skinny, half-wild hogs and cattle.[15] Rather, American frontier settlers usually relied on domestic fowl, hunting, and fishing for their meat protein. Domestic fowl, mostly chickens, provided eggs and Sunday dinner. Frontier people fished the streams usually by building fish traps and weirs. Fish camps stood at favored fishing spots, with crude tables and troughs for scaling and gutting fish on the spot.[16] Frontier men hunted deer, bear, rabbit, opossum, squirrel, and other wild animals for meat.[17]

The typical southern settler had few material possessions. The log cabins were sparsely furnished with handmade tables and chairs and uncomfortable feather beds. Mrs. Basil Hall, who had her aristocratic sensibilities affronted by these rough frontier families at every turn, applauded herself for her prescience in bringing linens, as she complained that she could not procure clean towels or sheets at any of these abodes. Mrs. Hall remarked that each family had only one towel that, to her trained eye, had not been washed for some time.[18]

As Mrs. Hall's visit indicates, southern frontier families did not live lives of isolation and independence, despite popular notions to the contrary. Travelers taking lodging were quite common, and they kept frontier farmsteads informed of local, regional, national, and international happenings. Husbands, wives, and children performed all of the necessary daily farming and ranching tasks, and as we have seen, they were engaged in a frontier exchange economy with Creeks and other southeastern Indians, as well as freemen and black slaves, which belies the stereotype of frontier self-sufficiency. Some families owned one or two slaves to aid in their labor, but all worked side by side.[19]

One's legal identity was associated with county citizenship. Counties were laid out as land was ceded, and each county had its local magistrates and militia, as decreed by the state. The state or territory usually required the men of a county to serve in the local militia for national and state defense as well as for local police actions.[20] Within a county, frontier families understood themselves to be part of a community, although their definition of such usually fell along lines different from those we use today. For instance, people sometimes described themselves as living in a "neighborhood," which meant a group of families living at a distance from one another but along a particular stream or in some other discernible geographic area.[21] When a town was nearby, people defined themselves as citizens of that town, even though the town center may have been miles away. The towns usually were the county or territorial seats. They were widely spaced frontier towns that could barely be called towns.[22] These small frontier towns consisted of hastily constructed taverns, stores, and the occasional county courthouse, and they usually sprang up near military forts. The streets were mud paths on which people dodged the large tree stumps that were left standing. Only a few people actually lived in the town; most of the people who claimed town citizenship lived on farms and ranches in the surrounding areas.[23] One's daily social contacts were with the people in one's neighborhood, and one could usually depend on neighbors for help with some types of heavy labor, in defense, in health matters, and in similar times of need. When an insult, death, or injury occurred to a member of the neighborhood, men banded together as "voluntary infantry" in retaliatory raids. In the face of larger threats, most frontier families sought protection at the nearest military garrison, where they also took up arms to defend the fort.[24]

In the eighteenth and nineteenth centuries the American South, perhaps more than any other region, had a rigid class structure marked by rules and laws of ownership, behavior, and etiquette. Frontier whites certainly recognized class distinctions, especially those between whites and blacks, but they did not give the typical respect and deference expected between white unequals in the American South at this time. All were accorded the same treatment, regardless of wealth or class. Southern hospitality was not yet evident on the frontier. Even though these families took in travelers for perhaps days at a time, their demeanor was obliging but aloof. Basil Hall described sitting down to dinner with a young frontier woman and her slaves, all of whom stared at him and his party as they ate, as if they "had been so many wild beast[s] feeding." Mrs. Hall was appalled to sit at table with slaves.[25]

Southern frontier families were notorious for their roughness, reputedly having no respect for law and detesting authority of any kind. As one traveler noted, "The settlers in the Georgia backcountry are lazier, and more given to drunkenness and lawlessness than backcountry people in any other state of the Union."[26] Tales of southern frontier lawlessness were legendary. The men were reportedly so mean that they would even kill or rob their neighbors, and "the deeper in the hinterlands, the meaner the men are."[27] The Georgia "crackers" held by far the worst reputation for lawlessness. Many travelers witnessed the infamous gouging fights among Georgia frontier men, wherein a seemingly goodwill wrestling match would turn into a scene of horror as the two participants went straight for each other's eyes. The idea was to gouge out an eye, and many frontier men had only one eye as a result of losing such a match.[28] In fact, Milfort insisted that the name "crackers" was a distortion of the word "gougers," the name he claimed that was usually associated with Georgia pioneers. Others related that the name came from the cracking of whips when frontier men drove their wagons.[29] Milfort, who had a low opinion of America in general, described Georgia crackers as the meanest men who ever lived. According to Milfort, they cut their hair short and painted their faces like Indians when marauding. They were ungovernable, never submitted to authority, and were "truly frightful." When Milfort told his urban friends that he was going to live among the Creeks, they warned him that the Creeks would roast and eat him. Milfort later reflected that he would have preferred that to staying among the frontier Georgians.[30]

There were also Indian haters on the southern frontier. Benjamin Harrison, the leader of the gang that attacked Padjeeligau in 1795, was a notorious and barbarous one. Harrison, apparently the loser in a past gouging, wore a patch over one eye and had "a piece out of one side of his nose."[31] Harrison, whom the Creeks detested and wanted punished, eluded the Creeks and white authorities for years. He surfaced from time to time to kill Indians, as he had sworn vengeance against every Indian he saw.[32] It is safe to say that most people on the southern frontier were not of Harrison's type, and many white settlers believed Harrison to be crazy.[33]

Urbanites traveling on the frontier typically described southern frontier men as lazy beyond words, their passions lying only with hunting, drinking, gambling, and fighting. Women, according to these writers, lived a life of abject drudgery, doing all the work while their husbands and sons whiled away the hours in lazy, unproductive pursuits. Their farms were never up to standard, and the families were poor because, according to the elite traveler, these people simply would not work and tend to their farms like they should, they had wasteful and indolent habits, they did not use their slaves like they should, and they did not use the land to its full potential. Not coincidentally, the urban elite also described the Creeks and other southern Indians in similar terms.

Clearly, Creeks and frontier Americans had much in common. Despite boundary lines and many distinctions of habit, Creeks and frontier Americans lived together in a single world composed of their interactions, shared concerns and needs, economic connections, and social affiliations (see fig. 22). This world, however, was built on an unstable foundation. Creek and American relations, no matter how cooperative, friendly, intimate, and mutually beneficial, were played out in the larger context of American westward expansion, and the Creeks looked warily on their neighbors. For they knew that American frontier families vied for the same resources: alluvial floodplains and rangelands. One way Creek men and women settled this contest was by selling natural resources to American frontier people. But despite its beauty and richness, the resources of Creek country were limited, as we have seen. The sheer number of frontier whites crowding Indian borders meant that the time for sharing was destined to be short lived. As American demands for land grew increasingly more pointed, the Creeks grew increasingly resistant.

Between 1800 and 1810 the white and black population of Georgia increased from approximately 163,000 to 250,000. After the Mississippi Territory was opened in 1803, the white and black population there rose from fewer than 10,000 to about 40,000 by 1810.[34] This growth was occurring throughout the Union. Between 1792 and 1821, ten states were admitted to the United States: Kentucky in 1792, Tennessee in 1796, Ohio in 1803, Louisiana in 1812, Indiana in 1816, Mississippi in 1817, Illinois in 1818, Alabama in 1819, Maine in 1820, and Missouri in 1821.[35]

The Creeks did not have to see the statistics; their daily experiences indi-

FIGURE 22. "Chiefs of the Creek Nation, and a Georgian Squatter" (Courtesy of the Lilly Library, Indiana University, Bloomington. This drawing is published in Captain Basil Hall, *Forty Etchings*, plate 28.)

cated only too well the increasing number of whites. For example, between October 16, 1811, and March 16, 1812, more than 3,700 white people had passed through Creek territory on the Federal Road on their way to the Mississippi Territory.[36] Westward expansion guaranteed that hostility and suspicion would characterize most dealings between Creeks and frontier Americans, and this hostility permeated regular encounters between Indians and Americans, which meant that daily life was underlaid by a contradiction: both Indians and frontier Americans knew and depended on one another, yet they fundamentally distrusted one another.

This distrust generated many tensions at all levels, tensions that could erupt in violence at unexpected times. Take the case of Appy Howard, a settler in Camden County, Georgia. On June 5, 1807, she swore a deposition describing Samuel Greene's death. According to Howard, two Creek men approached her house on the morning of May 8 and asked for breakfast. She bade them to eat, and afterward they departed "seemingly well pleased." Later that afternoon, the same men returned for dinner. She asked them to eat, and during the meal, while she had gone outside to fill a plate from the pot on the fire, the two Creeks shot her neighbor, Samuel Greene, who was dining with them. Howard fled with her two-month-old son when one of the Creeks approached her "with his gun clubbed as if to knock her down." The two men then took everything in the house.

Later, when she was asked if she knew why the two Creek men killed Greene, she swore "that there was not any offence offered the said Indians by the said Greene, or herself, or by any other person in the settlement to her knowledge, or to any other Indian whatever."[37] She believed the motive was robbery. Even so, with Greene's death, the settlers in the county were considerably alarmed because they did not know if "it was a thing done by the desire of the nation or the act of a few villains."[38]

Some of these tensions were generated from the unauthorized use of Creek lands by American border settlers. In 1796, when Hawkins moved to Creek territory, Timothy Barnard remarked that the Creeks were more peaceable than he had ever known.[39] The years before, the Creeks and Georgians had been "continually in a state of war," and border settlers had retreated to the more densely populated coastal regions.[40] By 1800, however, American westward migration had resumed apace. White settlers crowded Creek/U.S. borders. Even those whose farms were in U.S. territory and therefore legal still broke the law by crossing into Creek territory to hunt, to fish, or to graze their livestock.

Creek hunters, already facing diminishing numbers of deer, turkey, bear, and other wildlife, especially objected to whites participating in the skin trade and further depleting the game. The hunting trips of white men did not last months like those of Creek hunters, but they were fairly regular and usually ranged into Creek lands.[41] According to Creek headmen, whites "destroyed the game" and ate all of the bear when they came into Creek territory.[42] As we have seen, white hunters were not solely responsible for the dearth of whitetailed deer in the South at this time. However, Creek headmen insisted that white hunters overhunted the deer, and they pointed to the common practice of night hunting by white hunters as proof of overkill.[43]

In night hunting, hunters used torches to blind and confuse deer. According to Gosse, the deer "stand gazing on the light in utter amazement, and are shot down without fail."[44] The number of deer harvested using this method was so great that, in an early measure of conservation, some southern states had outlawed night hunting after the deer population in the coastal regions had declined.[45] A group of Creek men once threatened a group of white hunters who were hunting bear with "a great gang of dogs," something to which the Creeks steadfastly objected. The Creeks asked Timothy Barnard to pass a message to James Seagrove (Hawkins's predecessor) that they would not put up with this, "and if the white people do not decline such proceedings, they will kill some of them."[46] Creek resistance is probably one reason why the participation of frontier men in the skin trade remained nominal, at best.[47]

Frontier settlers also trespassed on Creek lands when fishing and cutting timber. They built fish traps in the rivers, hauling away large loads of fish and thus undermining another vital food source of the Creeks.[48] Timber harvesting roused complaints because it was a blatant violation of treaty stipulations and because it brought whites into Creek territory. It also meant that whites, instead of Creeks, were garnering the profits from timber sales.[49] Grazing of free-ranging livestock was, by far, the most frequently voiced Creek complaint against white settlers, and vice versa. Creek hunters killed or stole white-owned livestock that had strayed over the line, an occurrence reported so frequently that "the whites cannot count on their stock as an income."[50] White infractions against Creek-owned livestock were just as frequent.

At the talks for the Treaty of Colerain in 1796, for instance, Georgia sought compensation for its citizens for thefts at the hands of Creeks. As the Georgia commissioners were enumerating their complaints, the Creeks in attendance "rarely asserted; remained generally silent." When the Georgia commissioners began complaining about Creek hogs straying into Georgia territory, "they all laughed." Big Warrior saw some irony in Georgia settlers complaining about straying hogs. Later, while dining with the commissioners, Big Warrior asked for a roll longer than that used by the commissioners, so that he could list all of the offenses of Georgians against the Creeks.[51]

Everyone realized that "a mere mathematical line in the woods" could not prevent the livestock from ranging.[52] Much of the boundary between Creek territory and the State of Georgia was a river, the Oconee, and with the Treaty of Fort Wilkinson, the Ocmulgee River. Because livestock congregated at shallow river shoals to eat the moss, it was only natural that they strayed across the rivers. Frontier ranchers understood this, and some people even attempted, with little success, to block crossing points, although how they did so is not described.[53]

Straying livestock created problems because both Creeks and Americans crossed into each other's territory searching for strays. In both cases, the search parties went armed and, more often than not, managed a few thefts themselves while looking for their own wandering livestock. Having armed groups of Creeks and white men roving the woods was alarming on both sides and contributed to the mounting tensions. Both Hawkins and Creek headmen sought a peaceable solution to rounding up strays and to curbing the rampant thefts.[54]

In addition, white thieves as well as Creek thieves regularly moved through the hinterlands preying on hunting and traveling parties and farmsteads. Chance meetings in the woods between Creeks and whites were so dangerously explosive that many people carried vouchers of good character and/or intent from prominent frontier whites such as Hawkins or Barnard.[55] Hawkins even tried to issue hunting passes to Indians so that everyone in the woods could be accounted for.[56] But he could not enforce such decrees, as one case made clear. A group of Chehaws crossed the Oconee River (the boundary line) to steal horses. On the way back, they ambushed a militia group that had been sent to pursue them, and they killed several of the white men. As if to flaunt their exploit, the Chehaws posted on a tree a voucher written by Timothy Barnard attesting to their good character and firm friendship to America. Beneath it lay the mutilated bodies of the white men. Barnard later denied issuing the voucher and insisted that it was a forgery.[57]

Hawkins also decreed that no white was to enter Creek territory without a passport signed by him.[58] Many ignored the passport requirement or forged passes.[59] Besides, these frontier people were knowledgeable forest travelers and could evade Hawkins's watchful eye by taking one of the many "little blind paths" through Creek country.[60] When some Creeks stepped up the harassment of white travelers in 1801, Hawkins halted traffic altogether until a solution could be found.[61] He requested that military checkpoints be established along the full length of the Lower Trading Path to ensure that only legal travelers passed.[62] But his request was never honored. In 1811, after the Creeks had agreed to open the Federal Road to military personnel, Hawkins reassured the Creeks that these soldiers were under strict orders to behave correctly.[63] Neither Hawkins nor the Creeks had much faith in this promise, nor could either patrol the paths through Creek country. Even as late as 1811, Tecumseh appears to have moved into and out of Creek country quite easily.[64]

In some cases, American settlers illegally established towns in Indian territories. This form of intrusion, in which several families set up farmsteads and began a town, were limited to a few settlements; most notable in Creek country were Wofford's settlement in Georgia and Muscle Shoals in Tennessee.[65] In these cases, white settlers moved onto lands supposedly ceded by the Indians, but the deals were based on titles of dubious legality. In both of these cases, powerful land speculators such as William Blount financed the settlement and sheltered the settlers from federal legal actions. Land speculators controlled the southern state governments at this time, and therefore state governments sanctioned and abetted such illegal settlements.[66] To their way of thinking, with white settlements already established, state officials could point to the problems of removing the settlers and thus pressure the Indians for particular tracts of land.

For instance, John Chisholm, the agent of William Blount, and the Cherokee headman Doublehead oversaw and promoted the settlement of Muscle Shoals, probably according to Blount's instructions. The land was said to have been ceded by the Cherokees in the 1785 Treaty of Hopewell, but once the boundary lines were drawn, the town was still on Cherokee land. The Cherokees wanted the town removed to U.S. territory and forced the settlers to leave several times. Chisholm, however, persuaded the occupants to return after each removal. The Cherokees eventually ran Chisholm out of the country and executed Doublehead for his involvement.[67] Even so, Muscle Shoals was occupied and abandoned many times until the Cherokees finally relented and ceded the land in 1816.[68]

Wofford was settled subsequent to the 1791 Treaty of Holston between the United States and the Cherokees. But once the lines were surveyed, the town was found to be in Indian territory and in an area to which both the Creeks and the Cherokees laid claim. The Creeks and Cherokees pressed Hawkins to have the settlers removed. This proved difficult to do. For one thing, the contested Creek/Cherokee claim had to be resolved, which took more than a year. Even then it was only resolved because the Creeks, disgusted with the interminable delays, eventually renounced their claim and washed their hands of the matter.[69] The Cherokees were left pushing for the removal of the settlement. By this time Wofford, which was actually a mixed settlement of Indians, white Americans, and black slaves, was firmly entrenched, and several farms were flourishing, which made the inhabitants that much more resistant to moving. The affair came to the notice of the War Department, which conducted an investigation and found the Cherokee claims to be legitimate. Thus began a long debate as to the best way to remove the settlers.[70]

The Cherokees wanted the whole town immediately abandoned. But the War Department insisted that such a move would be ruinous to the inhabitants as they would lose that year's crops. The problem was compounded because several families were of mixed white-Indian marriages. The Cherokees agreed to let settlers stay, with no restrictions, where the marriage was between an Indian man and a white woman, but those between white men and Indian women could stay only so long as the men "behaved themselves." There was also some question regarding the "old" and "new" settlers. The Cherokees agreed to let the old settlers, presumably the original inhabitants, stay until their crops were in. The new settlers, the most recent arrivals, had to leave immediately. But all of the settlers refused to leave, even after they received stern instructions from the War Department to do so. Hawkins eventually ordered a military detachment to Wofford to dislodge the farmers, but the farmers returned later.[71] In 1804 the United States finally purchased the land on which Wofford stood, although its ownership was still in dispute as late as 1812.[72]

The Creeks apparently had similar problems with white settlements. In 1805 Hawkins reported to Secretary of War Henry Dearborn, that some white settlements were forming on Creek lands between the headwaters of the Oconee and Ocmulgee Rivers. Hawkins suggested that the settlers be immediately removed by military force because their presence would certainly pose problems in the impending negotiations for the Treaty of 1805.[73] In this case the Creeks complained about this settlement in the treaty talks, but apparently the lands were included in the 1805 cession.

More typically, intrusions onto Creek lands consisted of single families moving into disputed borders or onto Indian land. In some cases these settlers made private land sales with individual Creeks who were not authorized to do so. The settlers must have known such sales were illegal, but they pressed their claims when asked to move.[74] Again, establishing the validity of such claims was fraught with difficulties. The Creeks, as we have seen, sometimes did give land grants or lease rights to individual whites outside national treaties. This had to be sorted out, which was no easy task.

When such a situation came to Hawkins's attention, he duly submitted a report to the War Department requesting authorization for an investigation into the legality of the claim.[75] The investigations were time consuming because the information was usually faulty and imprecise and because every piece of evidence had to be verified in some way. For example, in 1803 Hawkins received information about Mrs. Durand, who had purchased some Indian lands on her own. Hawkins could not assume that this was Sophia Durant, Alexander McGillivray's sister, and his first step in this case was to find out whether she was white or an Indian. Secretary Dearborn instructed Hawkins to have her arrested if she were white, but that if she were an Indian, not to do anything as "we have no control over her."[76] It is uncertain if and how this case was resolved.

Even if one could get reliable information on the basic facts, many other things conspired to impede investigating legal titles to land. For example, when Hawkins wanted to conduct such an inquiry, he had to call a meeting of Creek town representatives, which entailed sending runners to inform men throughout Creek territory to meet at an appointed time. It also involved obtaining some sort of legal deed from the white settlers, which was nearly impossible, since most informal land deals were verbal agreements. If there was no deed, Hawkins had to go through a lengthy process of taking depositions from the white settlers and their neighbors.[77] Once all the information had been gathered, Hawkins had to sort through the conflicting claims, confer with Creek headmen, and somehow resolve the issue.[78] Because of such problems, Hawkins submitted petitions only for squatters who he believed held some justifiable claim that warranted an investigation. When white farmers and ranchers moved over the boundary in flagrant violation of the law, Hawkins refused to intercede on their behalf.[79]

Hawkins continually complained about such intrusions, and the Creeks grew restless as they saw more and more white squatters illegally crossing the line. The federal government had responded early in the proclamations of the Continental Congress by making intrusions of any sort illegal. The enforcement of such laws was always lackadaisical, however, and the budgets were always low. Those ramshackle forts in the hinterlands were all the federal government was willing to put into the effort. Although the Creeks did not want a white army in their country, Creek headmen and others welcomed a U.S. military presence on the borders because they believed only this would stop the intrusions without involving the Creeks in a general war.[80] It also meant that the Creeks, as all of the southern Indians, depended on U.S. recognition and enforcement of Indian land rights.

By treaty, Hawkins had the authority to send a military detachment to forcibly eject any intruders. The arrangements for sending such deputations are cloudy. Hawkins, as the leading U.S. military authority in Indian territory, could order such an expedition; but the costs were above ordinary expenses. For example, in 1808 Hawkins ordered Captain Boote to remove the Wofford settlers, as requested by the Cherokees. After a delay of several months, Boote sent word to Hawkins and the Cherokees that he had not yet proceeded because he had no money.[81] On another occasion Hawkins paid Capt. Timothy Freeman and his deputation two dollars a day to make the rounds of Georgia squatters and collect rental fees as the Creeks had requested.[82] The federal government never allocated the money to maintain an adequate military or police effort to stop intrusions. The southern military outposts were so few, so ill manned, and so impoverished as to be useless. The War Department, never generous to Hawkins's office anyway, did not allocate sufficient funds for military evictions. This was not lost on the Creeks, who despite treaty stipulations and promises and despite Hawkins's assertion that they "readily distinguish between intruders on their rights and the federal government," realized that the federal government was not disposed to stop the intrusions.[83]

The frontier Americans, faced with eviction from their farms, resisted forced removal even though they knew their settlements on Indian lands were illegal. They resented Hawkins. They perceived him as favoring the Creeks over themselves and increasingly questioned the Creeks' rights to the land.[84] They took their complaints to the state governments, which were laden with land speculators only too willing to question Creek rights to land. Because the subject of states' rights was so sensitive, the federal government would plead reluctance to interfere on grounds that the disputes fell within the domain of states' issues.[85]

By law, intruders could be ejected, but any claims made on Indian lands and any depredations they committed against the Creeks were state issues. The federal authorities usually opted not to interfere. Georgia and Tennessee had laws against squatting, theft, murder, and other crimes, but in those states, Indian testimony was not allowed in a court of law. Thus any Creek claims against whites were automatically invalidated. Hawkins appealed to the War Department to do something to change these state laws, since no matter how many oaths and depositions he collected from Creek complainants, the law hampered the establishment of legal proof and blocked the prosecution of white criminals.[86] In 1809 Governor Jared Irwin of Georgia finally issued a proclamation whereby anyone caught hunting, cutting cedar, building fish traps, or driving stock on Creek lands was subject to a fine of $100 or six months' imprisonment.[87] Irwin had agreed to issue the proclamation only after Hawkins and a deputation of Creeks visited the governor with the express aim of getting such an injunction. Four months later, Hawkins wrote to Secretary of War William Eustis that the proclamation was ineffectual and that it had only stopped the intrusions for about a month.[88]

The trip to see Governor Irwin was prompted by the intrusions of Capt. Roderick Easley, whose case exemplifies the legal difficulties of removing white squatters as well as the impudence and arrogance that state-supported trespassing engendered. Easley and a few other men built cow pens, cleared and farmed some land, and built a "dairy establishment" across the Creek line at High Shoals in Georgia. The Creeks sent numerous warnings to Easley, and Hawkins ordered him off the land several times.[89] For three years Easley ignored the Creeks and Hawkins. He told Hawkins he had legal title to the land, but he could not show any proof when Hawkins finally went to High Shoals to confront him.[90] Creek headmen, at Hawkins's behest, agreed to seek redress through American channels. Thus they made the trip to Governor Irwin.

Even after Irwin's proclamation was issued, Easley refused to budge. Hawkins sent Captain Smith from Fort Hawkins to arrest Easley and to destroy his establishment.[91] Easley's case was brought before William B. Bulloch, the attorney for the United States for the District of Georgia, in Milledgeville.[92] Hawkins offered to appear in court on behalf of the Creeks, since they were not allowed to do so.[93] When Hawkins arrived at Milledgeville on the court date, Easley and his partners jumped bail and "forfeited their recognizance."[94] Actually, Easley and his partners did not risk much, since under Georgia law their crime was only a misdemeanor.[95] The Easley incident, according to Hawkins, was the third time an intruder had been removed by military force and the first time one had been handed over to the civil authority.[96] This occurred in 1810 and reflects only too well the lax attitude of the federal and state governments toward intrusions.

White settlers had been squatting on Indian lands since the early years of colonization, and by the turn of the nineteenth century, the practice had become a major point of contention in Indian/white relations and was considered by the federal government to be the primary reason for Indian unrest throughout America.[97] Hawkins, with some reason, believed that Creek opposition to the plan for civilization and to America grew because white criminals went unpunished and intrusions were not controlled as promised by treaty.[98] As the intrusions continued and even increased, and with the realization that the federal government could not or would not stop them, Creek warriors increasingly took matters into their own hands by raiding and harassing border settlers, especially squatters. An indication of the tension under which these families lived occurred when Hawkins and others were tracking a group of whites. When Hawkins's party approached a farmstead, the family quickly "fled and left their house open."[99]

One of the most serious consequences of white trespassing, squatting, and Indian and white raiding was a killing. Both Creeks and frontier Americans killed one another with alarming regularity.[100] The motives for violence of this kind varied. Some killings occurred by accident. Sometimes a man or woman got caught in a spray of bullets during a robbery attempt. Some people killed for vengeance. Sometime vigilante groups, operating outside the law, executed people suspected of some offense. Some people killed out of sheer meanness and psychopathic behavior. Some killed for land. And some killed as resistance to white encroachment. Among the Creeks, every killing of a Creek required redress according to the Creek code of law.

The only truly binding Creek legal code was based on the law of blood revenge, and it was inextricably linked to their principles of balance and purity and unilineal descent. In the law of blood revenge, when someone caused the death of another person, the clan of the dead person had the duty and the right to kill the slayer or a member of the slayer's clan. Blood revenge had cos-

mological import. The Creeks understood blood revenge to be a clan responsibility that reinstated cosmic balance. Briefly, the historic southeastern Indians cognitively ordered their world into a series of opposite categories, such as
man/woman, plant/animal, war/peace, life/death, farming/hunting, and
sacred/profane.[101]

Opposites existed in a balance, and when things were in balance, the cosmos was working according to plan. The cosmos was also in good order when
things were pure; purity required categorical tidiness. In fact, things that existed between categories, like a Venus's-flytrap, for instance, were anomalous,
and because of this anomaly, they were often considered especially dangerous
and powerful medicine and magic.[102] A Venus's-flytrap, of course, is a carnivorous plant; hence, in Creek eyes it would be part animal and part plant.

So, balance and purity were part of the cosmological order; the natural and
supernatural worlds functioned well when things were pure and in balance.[103]
But according to Creek cosmology, humans existed in a place prone to pollution and imbalance, and hence unease. The Creeks understood the cosmos to
be divided into three worlds: Upper World, This World, and Under World.
The Upper World and the Under World were worlds of the supernatural, and
they were categorical opposites. The Upper World was a world of order and
purity; the Under World was one of chaos and pollution. This World, the
world of humans, existed in between. Hence, the natural human state of
affairs was a continual oscillation between balance and imbalance and purity
and impurity. Much of human life was devoted to not letting This World become too imbalanced or too impure.[104]

In the mythical past the "Master of Breath," *Hisagita misi*, revealed to humans the rituals and prayers necessary to reinstate and ensure purity and balance in This World. *Hisagita misi* was the divine creator, who the Creeks believed created all things good and who dwelled in the Upper World.[105] Many
of these rituals, prayers, and small acts were known by the layperson, who
could perform them to reinstate or ensure balance and purity as need be. In
some cases ritual specialists were required. At the annual Busk ritual, the
whole world was purified, and balance was cosmologically reinstated. In fact
the Muskogean term for Busk, *poskita*, means "to fast," or "sacred purifying";
fasting, to the Creeks, was a way to reinstate purity.[106]

Balance could be disrupted by any number of things, but humans, in particular, were clumsy beings who consistently upset balance and order. Impurity resulted from a mixing of categories. For example, being mindful of purity meant that men usually could not do the things of women, and vice versa.
This probably accounts for Creek men's long-standing refusal to farm. How-

ever, the Creeks knew that in human life categories could not always be kept separate. The Creeks believed that mixing life and death, for instance, could be especially dangerous and result in various diseases. Burying the dead, then, was a nervous task. One assigned to it would burn cedar incense, which would help keep pollution at a minimum and also scare off ghosts. Afterward, if one fell ill, there were special medicines for illness resulting from this mixing of death with life.[107]

One way to ensure purity and balance was to observe the taboos. The Creeks prohibited some behaviors during certain activities. If one broke the taboo, one could expect some misfortune, such as a poor crop that year.[108] Another way to ensure purity and balance was to be mindful of one's reciprocal obligations. Reciprocity cut two ways: one was expected to reciprocate gifts, including acts of alliance, kindness, and support, and one was expected to reciprocate acts of offense, such as injury and death. In many cases the reciprocal obligations extended far beyond one's immediate kin to the clan and also to animals, plants, and spirits. Day-to-day affairs for Creek men and women probably required one to be ever mindful of one's relations and vigilant about one's reciprocal obligations. For instance, when a hunter killed a deer, he was supposed to reciprocate the gift of the deer with a gift to the deer spirit. This gift could be a small piece of the meat thrown into the fire, or perhaps a bead buried at the place where the deer was slain. If a hunter did not do so, the deer spirit would seek revenge by afflicting the hunter or one of his kinspeople with disease.[109] If one did not pay attention to these kinds of obligations, one risked offense and imbalance and the misfortunes that resulted from these things. One also risked upsetting the cosmos.

Death and injury were strong forces of imbalance, and it was one's cosmological duty to reinstate balance through a like injury or death. The Creeks, as well as all other southeastern Indians, held so rigidly to this principle that any kinsperson who did not avenge "crying blood" was infamous throughout the nation and considered "utterly sunk in cowardice."[110] The law of blood revenge informed Creek personal and public affairs to a degree that appears almost obsessive. Revenge applied to all injuries—physical, mental, and emotional. If a little boy wounded another in play, the wounded child waited until he could inflict a similar wound on his playmate and then pronounced that "all was straight."[111] When revenge had been carried out, the matter was then at an end because both parties recognized the reinstatement of balance.

In Creek law, intent or motive did not matter, and the sole fact to be considered was the inflicting of injury or death.[112] Therefore, one could be held accountable for an accidental as well as an intentional injury. Causation was the prime concern, and causation, under Creek law, spanned a broad continuum. Indeed, if a horse tied to a post kicked a man and killed him, then the owner of the horse, or the person who tied it to the post, was responsible for the death.[113] Responsibility for a death was not strictly relegated to an individual; any of one's clan members could also be held liable. In other words, the whole clan would be considered the cause of the injury or death.[114] In matters of death, especially, this principle was so firmly adhered to that it was the acknowledged responsibility of the slayer's clan to stand aside and even to aid the avengers. This was perhaps made easier by the knowledge that if the avenging clan did not kill the slayer, they might kill one of his or her relatives, which could well be one's self.

The law of blood revenge had mechanisms for mitigating some deaths and injuries, especially those that were accidental. The clan of the injured party could accept material compensation and let the matter rest. If the clan of the person responsible for the injury could delay the revenge by avoiding the injured clan until the Busk, then all such matters were forgiven, as the Busk rituals reinstated balance and purity for everyone. In many such cases, the avenging clan would cooperate by not immediately seeking vengeance. A consequence of this principle was that within the Creek Confederacy a killing did not produce a cycle of retaliatory killings; there was one revenge, and that was the end of the affair. The slayer's clan recognized and accepted the liability of their kinsperson and the right of the dead person's kinspeople to revenge.[115]

A related principle—retaliation—was the chief motive of war between the Creeks and their neighbors, Indians and whites. Many Europeans believed that the Creeks viewed war as a sport or social necessity, waged merely for honor and status. It certainly was one of a Creek man's main occupations, but the primary motive was retaliation. Retaliation, which was based on blood revenge, was the basic principle of international law among the southeastern Indians. Retaliation had to be exacted whenever a Creek was killed by a foreigner, and it was underwritten by the same sense of cosmological duty to keep the world pure and in balance.[116] James Adair, astounded by the southeastern Indians' passion for vengeance and retaliation, wrote,

I have known the Indians to go a thousand miles, for the purpose of revenge, in pathless woods; over hills and mountains; through large cane swamps, full of grapevines and briars; over broad lakes, rapid rivers, and deep creeks; and all the way endangered by poisonous snakes, if not with the rambling and lurking enemy, while at the same time they were exposed to the extremities of heat and cold, the vicissitudes of the season; to hunger and thirst, both by chance; and their religious scanty method of living when at war; to fatigues, and other difficulties. Such is their over-boiling, revengeful temper, that they utterly condemn all these things as imaginary trifles, if they are so happy as to get the scalp of the murderer, or enemy, to satisfy the supposed craving ghost of their deceased relations.[117]

As with blood revenge, retaliation was a collective responsibility, except in this case a whole nation was liable and could be held responsible for the actions of one person.[118] The problems of national liability intensified in a frontier situation where shifting alliances and interests abounded. For one thing, a third party could instigate a war by killing members of one nation and making it appear as if members of a different nation were responsible. Since both Indians and whites typically left various symbolic items indicating who committed such acts, this was not difficult to do. Any individual could plunge his or her nation into war by maliciously or even accidentally killing a member of another nation. Likewise, a person could prevent a peace if he or she so desired and then start the war anew. Of course, the law of blood revenge meant that every death had to be avenged. Once Americans got involved, there was always a danger of uncontrolled retaliatory raids and vengeance deaths.

Hawkins states in his *Sketch* that the National Council revoked blood revenge.[119] Faced with Hawkins's insistence and the threat of spiraling vengeance raids, it fell to the town councils and to the National Council to attempt to revamp blood revenge into a system of crime and punishment based on European ideas. The National Council was now led by Creeks with pro-American sentiments, many of whom were métis and therefore knowledgeable about the fundamentals of Euro-American judicial concepts.[120] They revoked blood revenge and agreed to punish individuals responsible for assaults against Americans, and they established a warrior police to this end. They also attempted to define horse stealing and other thefts as criminal actions subject to state punishment. But such decrees were meaningless unless all the people agreed to uphold them, which they did not.

The "warriors of the nation," as Hawkins called his police force, consisted of warriors appointed by a group of towns. Hawkins described how this appointment worked for the Upper Creeks. Hawkins or perhaps the Upper Creek divisional council partitioned the Upper Creek towns into ten groups, or "classes," as Hawkins called them. Each class differed in its composition. Some had several towns, and some had only a few. Each class then appointed one to three warriors to be on the force. The first five classes were the war towns, the *Kepauyau*, or "warriors of the nation," from whence Hawkins got the name for the warrior police. The next five classes were the peace towns, or *Etallwau*. According to Hawkins, the *Etallwau* only agreed to appoint warriors after much counseling with Hawkins, who convinced them it was for the good of the nation.[121] Hawkins did not elaborate on how decisions were made among the warrior police, but it is reasonable to suppose that for the most part, the warrior police followed the institutional principles of the war and peace towns. In other words, the warriors of the nation, or the red towns, probably led the actions, since this was their proscribed role in usual affairs of blood revenge, retaliation, and war. This is not to say that men from the white towns did not participate in acts of war; they most certainly did. But the decision making was conducted by the leaders of the war towns. The warrior police were not, as some have suggested, an entirely new institution put together to execute the plans of Hawkins and the wealthy métis elite.[122] They were, however, handed a new task.

Under Creek convention, the warriors of the nation saw to blood revenge, retaliation, and any other reinstatement of balance that required the potential shedding of blood. These duties were structured along kinship, not state, lines. Under the influence of Hawkins and the elite Creeks the warriors of the nation were now charged with seeing to the enforcement of state law—those decrees made by the National Council. With this new duty, the warrior police sought men who had conducted raids or killings against Americans. Those whom they caught, they punished by whipping, disfigurement, or in one case, burning the man's house and belongings. In cases of death, the warrior police were to execute the slayer.[123]

The warrior police only conducted a handful of such actions. They only resorted to capital punishment at Hawkins's behest after the Duck River slayings and in one of the first hostile actions of the Red Stick War, and even then only after Hawkins threatened the National Council with a military invasion if nothing were done to secure the capture and punishment of those responsible for particular deeds against Americans.[124] When such punishments were meted out, however, both the warriors who conducted the punishments and the headmen who had made the decision feared for their lives.[125] Under the law of blood revenge, these men could be held accountable for the injury they had done. After one particularly brutal punishment of a horse thief, the headmen who had directed the punishment queried Hawkins on what they should say to the man's relations. Hawkins instructed them to reply that it was the nation that punished him, that stealing horses was against Creek law and subject to punishment by the nation.[126] But few Creeks accepted this explanation; most never embraced Hawkins's notions of crime and punishment, and most just ignored the warrior police. Even Hawkins admitted that neither he nor the leaders of the National Council could enforce the "laws" of the nation, except in a few towns where his influence was strong.[127] Creek headmen and warriors were reluctant to participate because they could then be subject to blood revenge. Thus blood revenge weakened any attempts to invest the headman's office or even the National Council with punitive powers; it made coercion difficult if not impossible, and it effectively thwarted any attempts the Creeks made toward centralizing their authority.[128]

Although he may not have understood the cosmological significance of retaliation and blood revenge, Hawkins knew too well their consequences in Creek and American affairs. This is one reason why he was so adamant about revoking blood revenge. On the frontier, retaliation and blood revenge made a bad situation worse. Retaliation meant that every Creek death at the hands of a white person had to be avenged with a white person's death. White frontier people operated with a similar principle of blood for blood, although their principle did not carry religious overtones. When one of their friends, family, or neighbors was killed by a Creek, they, too, sought vengeance through the death of a Creek, and not necessarily the person responsible for the slaying. According to Gosse, in the southern backcountry, "every man is his own law-maker and law-breaker, judge, jury, and executioner."[129] A few examples demonstrate the liability of such principles at this time.

In 1804 Mr. Patrick of Clarke County, Georgia, killed a Creek man and wounded another because he thought he recognized one of their horses as having been one stolen from a friend of his. The affair came to the attention of the governor of Georgia, John Milledge, because it portended serious trouble after two white men had been subsequently killed near the Flint River and a rumor was about that the deaths were in retaliation for Patrick's crime.[130] Milledge directed Lt. William Walton to proceed to Clarke County and arrest Patrick. Arriving in Clarke County, Walton could not find Patrick. The residents were apparently hiding him and refused to cooperate with Walton. They told the lieutenant that the Creeks owed them a life anyway because some Creeks had killed Mr. Moreland at some time past. They would not turn Patrick over to the authorities unless the Creeks turned over Moreland's killers. Walton reported to Milledge that if he persisted in apprehending Patrick, he feared the people of Clarke County would take to arms against the Georgia militia.[131]

In 1802 Hawkins and some Creek headmen discussed the problem of trying to settle these "debts of blood" between Creeks and whites. These were preliminary conferences concerning a land cession to Georgia as part of the

Treaty of Fort Wilkinson. After discussing several other matters, Efau Haujo commented that the Creeks had never received restitution for the murder of Davy Cornells.[132] In 1793, Cornells and a party of Creeks and whites had been en route to Colerain on the St. Mary's River in Georgia to deliver a bundle of letters to James Seagrove, the Indian agent at the time. Creek headmen were relaying, via the letters, some recent deliberations among themselves concerning a series of retaliatory raids between some Cowetas, Chehaws, and Yuchis and some white settlers on the Oconee River. Just outside Colerain, a Georgia militia group attacked the Indian party, killing Cornells, two other Creek men, and a fourteen-year-old boy who had come along to tend to the horses. The Georgia government maintained that Cornells was a known horse thief and murderer and that he was shot on sight because of his past deeds.[133] Efau Haujo told Hawkins that Cornells was not a horse thief, "but a man with a white flag."[134] Efau Haujo's reference to the white flag indicated Cornells's goodwill, since to the Creeks, white symbolized peace and good intentions. Because Georgia showed no inclination to punish Cornells's murderers, the Creeks had little faith in Georgia and saw no need to bend to the state's demands for land. Alexander Cornells, Hawkins's trusted assistant, remained bitter about his nephew's death till his dying day.

Hawkins, irritated by Efau Haujo's use of an incident that had happened almost ten years earlier to block the treaty, retorted by enumerating the many deaths of Americans at Creek hands. A black woman was murdered in Cusseta. A man in Cumberland, Tennessee, was killed without provocation. Some Cussetas had killed a white man in revenge; some Yuchis had done the same. In sum, "five debts were due the whites."[135] Tuskenehau Chapco of Cusseta countered that the black woman was killed in revenge for a white man killing a Creek hunter. Furthermore, even Hawkins acknowledged that the slayings by the Cussetas and Yuchis were in revenge for some whites killing an Indian commissioner and wounding several others, including another headman. To the Creek headmen, the Creeks owed no debt of blood to Georgia.[136]

Such harangues over the balance sheet of the "debt of blood" happened at every Creek/American treaty negotiation. The dangers in the doctrine of blood for blood were palpable. Timothy Barnard once reflected, "If people remember these old grudges we shall never have peace."[137] Barnard expressed a common sentiment. Hawkins and Creek headmen repeatedly counseled patience to agitated relations of slain Creeks on several occasions. In 1797, for example, Fusihatchee Mico reported to Hawkins that the brothers of a slain Creek man were preparing to seek vengeance among the whites. Hawkins immediately sent a runner to the brothers with a message beseeching them to calm down and let him handle the matter. Hawkins asked the brothers to come to him so that he could speak directly with them, and in so doing, he defused the situation.[138] In 1799 some Creek hunters killed a white man near the Ocmulgee River. Word of the killing quickly spread to other Creek hunting parties in the vicinity, and all feared that armed white men would flood the woods in reprisal. The women and children were sent back to town; a runner was dispatched to inform Hawkins of the affair, and the men prepared to defend themselves. In their message to Hawkins, the men asked him to assure the white people that they wished no trouble and that they would "cause justice to be done on this account."[139] Presumably this meant that the men would hand over the murderer to Hawkins or else put the man to death themselves. That same year, a Yuchi man killed a white man, Mr. Brown, and Hawkins insisted that the headmen have the Yuchi executed. The slayer fled to the Shawnees, and the executing warriors did not pursue him further. In the words of Tustunnuggee Emaultau of Tuckabatchee, one of the headmen appointed to execute the Yuchi man, "Some of us talked of killing one of his family and putting an end to the business, but were restrained by your [Hawkins] orders."[140]

American officials held the Creek Confederacy responsible for the crimes of individuals; this made it imperative for Creek headmen, now charged with preventing hostilities and punishing wrongdoers, to attempt to punish the persons responsible for such offenses. Once, Hawkins copied into his journal a letter from an unnamed relation of Sinnajijee of Tuckabatchee. Sinnajijee had scalped Mrs. Smith of Tombigbee, who survived the assault and returned to Georgia. Still, Sinnajijee's relation was fearful of retaliation. He informed Hawkins that he had convinced his family that Sinnajijee must die for the offense and that he had sent some warriors to kill him, which they had done. Sinnajijee's relation hoped Hawkins would relay the message to the white people around Tombigbee.[141] This unnamed Creek man then sent a message to the warriors of the Upper and Lower towns that "they must take heart, follow the example I have set and let us free our land from guilt to save it."[142] Sinnajijee's relation knew, as every Creek man and woman knew, that the price for killing whites could be their lands and their political sovereignty; however, the same tactics increasingly became viewed as the only way to save their lands and their political sovereignty.

One telling incident occurred in 1798 when some Creek men killed a white man on the Oconee River. When the friends and neighbors of the white men went to inspect the scene, they found a scrawled note that read, "Friends and Brothers, as we now call you and always did, we are sorry that we are obliged to take our due satisfaction ourselves; you have often promised to give satisfaction in the Likke casses, but never have done itt once. Now we have gott itt, our harts are strait, and itt is all over. We are now good friends as ever we was and can take you by the hand in friendship again."[143]

This note can be seen as a desperate effort on the part of some avenging Creek warriors to explain blood revenge, balance, purity, and straight hearts to their American neighbors. The warriors perhaps felt compelled to have the literate one among them write the note because they understood that with each killing, war with America loomed closer. It must have seemed nearly impossible to reconcile that kind of disaster with their duty to keep things in balance. The note was perhaps an effort to instruct the Americans on the distinctions between deaths due to blood revenge and deaths resulting from other causes. The principles of blood revenge and retaliation, whether the Indian or the frontier white version, spiraled in a country rife with tension and violence. But because the universe required it, Creek men and women sought vengeance and retaliation despite the fact that things seemed to be getting recklessly out of balance.

Frontier whites understood that killings portended war as well, and some hoped to use it to their own advantage. In 1803, for instance, some Creek hunters sent a runner to Hawkins with an alarming message. A white person had killed a Creek. More importantly, the whites near Ocmulgee were extremely belligerent and "threatened to kill them for their land."[144] The women and children were ordered to return home, and the warriors remained near the Ocmulgee, waiting to hear from Hawkins. Hawkins immediately dispatched a letter to Governor Milledge for information on the Ocmulgee settlers and to see if Milledge had deployed the Georgia militia for some reason and had failed to inform Hawkins. A bit later Hawkins managed to calm the situation, but obviously everyone was fearful that a war was about to begin or already had begun.[145] As Anna Vansant reported in her deposition regarding the death of her husband, Isaac, "The doctrine in her neighborhood was, let us kill the Indians, bring on a war, and we shall get land."[146]

A Creek/American war was not an unreasonable fear. Both the Creeks and the Americans knew full well that war was a real possibility. Everyone knew that the Georgia and Tennessee governments were only waiting for an excuse to invade Creek territory and drive them off their land. The Creeks faced a terrible contradiction. The Creeks knew they could never win a war with America. On one hand, then, peace was imperative. But the price for peace was high. The Creeks knew—and in case they forgot, Hawkins repeatedly reminded them—that the U.S. government held the whole Creek Confederacy accountable for crimes against whites.[147] Since the Creeks depended on the federal government to protect and acknowledge their land rights, they also feared turning the president against them by not punishing Creeks guilty of crimes against whites, and they knew friendly relations between them and the whites would keep the president (and other white officials) favorably disposed toward them.[148] Finally, and most importantly, their land was at stake.

If the headmen could not control their people, "the Creeks would be beaten and compelled to give up a portion of their land as the price for peace."[149] As Tussekia Mico of Cusseta once said, "It will not do for us to lose our land for a few mad men."[150] But the Creeks loathed intruders and saw them as the harbingers of more land cessions. If neither the U.S. federal nor the state governments could control the intruders, then the Creeks would. Many Creeks lashed out at American settlers in an attempt to terrorize the frontier, stop the intrusions, and hence stop westward expansion. Such terrorism was impossible to curb because of the principles of blood revenge and retaliation. Efau Haujo recognized this when he once pointedly observed, "I do the best I can but all I do is nothing. I look around every way and I see nothing but trouble and difficulties."[151]

Creek men and women vacillated between extremes in their opinions of Americans. Creek men and women moved easily between red, white, and black in their daily lives and, in many cases, melded their lives with those of frontier Americans as in the mixed settlement of Wofford and in their own mixed population. But in the blink of an eye, that same Creek man or woman could vow to kill every American he or she saw. For the Creeks, every frontier white in some way represented the aim of a larger America to take away their lands and to destroy them as a people; it was impossible to separate individual Americans from the larger forces working against them. By 1811 it would be impossible to separate individual Creeks from these forces as well. The result would be civil war.

Epilogue

In 1811 the Shawnee warrior Tecumseh journeyed to Creek country, his mother's homeland. Tecumseh, with his prophet brother, Tenskwatawa, advocated a return to native ways, a separation of all Indians from America, a pan-Indian confederacy, and with magical aid against American bullets and cannons, to win a war to achieve these goals. When Tecumseh talked at the Tuckabatchee square during the National Council, his words drove a wedge into the Creek Confederacy, dividing Creek society. The result was a Creek civil war, known as the Red Stick War and named after Tecumseh's followers, the Red Sticks, so called because of the red war clubs they carried.[152] In reality, Tecumseh himself did not divide the Creeks. He only gave voice to a growing conviction among many Creeks that America intended to dispossess them of their lands and to undermine their sovereignty as a people. As we have seen, this was, in fact, what America intended all along.

Prophets arose among the Creeks. The prophets traveled to the Great Lakes to meet with other followers of Tenskwatawa and to learn their magic and dances.[153] They returned to Creek country doing the "Dance of the Indians of the Lakes," full of Tenskwatawa's religious and nativistic ponderings.[154] The prophets offered a new resistance strategy to the Creeks: destroy all things American and all Americans, and then *Hisagita misi*, the Master of Breath, would shield Creek warriors with invisible, magical barricades against American armaments and troops. Anyone who followed them, so the prophets promised, would be invincible. To those for whom the religious guarantees were not enough, the prophets promised that Tecumseh's great army of northern warriors and their old allies the British were waiting with guns, ammunition, supplies, and men.[155]

The prophets' talks struck a deep chord among many Creeks that resonated with their beliefs and reverberated though their confusion over a world that was increasingly unbalanced. The Creeks were seriously divided over how their relationship with America should proceed. One side proposed cooperation and assimilation. The other side condemned compromise. Fed up and frustrated by U.S. promises, most of which had never been realized, they were defiant in the face of American threats. They believed that with the aid of Tecumseh, the prophets, the magic, and the British, the Creeks could win any war with America. The division in the Creek civil war fell along many lines. One was a pro- or anti-American axis. There also was a religious line, with the prophets' followers joining the rebellion. Most wealthy Creeks did not join the Red Sticks, but some did. Most Red Sticks were Upper Creeks, but many Lower Creeks joined the prophets. Many Red Sticks were non-Creek speakers, but many were Creek speakers. People from all clans and kinship networks joined the rebellion. Even township affiliation, one of the deepest attachments for a Creek, did not hold, and many towns divided against themselves. Towns, clans, families, and friendships were torn asunder as Creek fought against Creek.[156] As Hawkins stated at the time, there were no neutrals.[157]

Within a year after Tecumseh's first visit, the prophets had gained a strong following. But the Red Sticks did not promptly turn against the Americans. They first turned against their own. The initial targets of Red Stick wrath were pro-American headmen; once the rebellion began, however, they widened their scope to include any pro-American Creek. The Red Sticks saw as pro-American anyone who adopted the plan for civilization or expressed pro-American attitudes; any métis who preferred the ways of their white parents; friends and allies of Hawkins, such as Alexander Cornells and Timothy Barnard; and Hawkins himself. The Red Sticks set out to destroy everything American. They threw the plows and looms into the rivers. They destroyed the corn crops. They killed hogs, horses, and cattle, all symbols of America and the plan for civilization.[158]

In the spring of 1813, a contingent of Red Sticks went to Pensacola to get a load of British supplies. En route back to Upper Creek territory, a militia of the Mississippi Territory, led by Creek métis living in the Tensaw and Bigbe settlements, attacked the Red Stick party and took the supplies. In retaliation, the Red Sticks attacked Fort Mims on August 30, 1813. The battle was a ferocious Red Stick victory.[159] Tennessee and Georgia had waited for such an opportunity for years, and the southern states led the call for a Creek invasion. The leaders of the U.S. war movement were the same men who had been vying for Creek country all along—men such as William Blount and Andrew Jackson. Georgia, Tennessee, and the Mississippi Territory readied their militia and enlisted aid from the Choctaws, Cherokees, and Lower Creeks. The invasion forces were led by Andrew Jackson.

American retribution was swift and merciless. American forces invaded Creek territory and engaged the Red Sticks in numerous bloody battles. American soldiers looked on in amazement as the warriors danced and pranced in front of their cannons, believing themselves shielded from the cannonballs by the magic of their prophets.[160] Hundreds of Red Sticks died in battle. American forces burned many of the Upper towns, destroyed whatever the Red Sticks had not, drove women and children into the canebrakes and swamps, and forced the Red Sticks to move north to their refugee town, Tohopeka, at Horseshoe Bend on the Tallapoosa River. Jackson's army attacked Tohopeka on March 27, 1814.[161]

The Battle of Horseshoe Bend defeated the core of Red Sticks, and Jackson and his army routed the remaining members of the movement with little difficultly. Thousands of Red Stick women, children, and warriors fled into the Coastal Plain and into Seminole country, where they continued the resistance.[162] Refugees who did not go to the Seminoles crowded into Coweta, Cusseta, and Tuckabatchee, where the U.S. army provided them with food and shelter.[163] The Upper Creeks were ruined. As Hawkins wrote, "Look to the towns, not a living thing in them; the inhabitants scattered through the woods, dying with hunger or fed by Americans."[164] Hawkins's letters after the Red Stick War bespeak a deeply troubled man. He sank into a distracting depression. As he wrote to a colleague, "I have seen so many scenes of wretchedness since I saw you, that my feelings have been turned to commiseration and wo[e]. I often regale myself with tears."[165]

In August 1814 the Creek Confederacy was forced to meet the victors to sign the Treaty of Fort Jackson, which had been engineered by Jackson. Indeed, in a startling show of power, Jackson was the sole U.S. commissioner at the negotiations, and he forced the Creek headmen to sign under threats of renewing the war.[166] Jackson, never a friend to Hawkins, pushed the agent aside at the negotiations and prevented him from speaking or presenting any petitions on behalf of the Creeks. When Hawkins saw the land Jackson intended to take as reparation for U.S. expenses incurred in the war, Hawkins silently traced his finger along the line that cut away two-thirds of Creek country and then suggested a readjustment. Jackson only replied that "he would adhere to his first line."[167] Hawkins reported later that he was "struck forcibly" by the unfairness of the treaty.[168] The Creeks were shocked as well. Hawkins tendered his resignation as Indian agent on February 15, 1815.[169] A year later, before his resignation was effected, on June 16, 1816, Hawkins died in his home at the Creek Agency.

With the signing of the Treaty of Fort Jackson, Creek country, too, came to an end, soon to be transformed into a world of planters, slaves, and cotton. At the turn of the nineteenth century, neither the Creeks nor Hawkins could have envisioned the dramatic transformation that their world was poised to undergo. Of the original landscape that once graced Creek country, only a few small patches remain. The majestic southern forests were leveled for cotton fields and timber. Only the archaeological remains and place-names mark the former towns that once comprised the heartland of Creek country. The people of Creek country, too, are gone. The American pioneers moved west, where they would eventually spill onto the Great Plains to begin another era in American frontier history. Many of the runaway slaves and freedmen moved to Florida and joined the ranks of Creek dissidents and others who, together, became Seminoles. By 1850 the Creeks, as most of the southeastern Indians, except tiny handfuls here and there, were gone, forcibly removed west of the Mississippi. In the late eighteenth century, though, the heart of the American South was a complex whole of cultural traits, people, communities, plants, animals, landscapes, political particulars, beliefs and ideas, local situations, and larger global dynamics that made up the world of Creek country. When these things changed, Creek country changed and became something else.

SCIENTIFIC TAXONOMY FOR PLANTS AND ANIMALS MENTIONED IN THE TEXT

Plants

African watermelons	*Citrullus lanatus*
American beech	*Fagus grandifolia*
American chestnut	*Castanea dentata*
American pokeweed	*Phytolacca americana*
apples	*Malus* spp.
arrow arum	*Peltandra virginica*
ash	*Fraxinus* spp.
atamasco lily	*Zephyranthes atamasca*
barnyard grass	*Echinochloa crus-galli*
beans	*Phaseolus* spp.
beech	*see* American beech
beets	*Beta* spp.
blackberries	*Rubus* spp.
black-eyed peas	*see* cowpeas
blackgum	*Nyssa sylvatica*
blackjack oak	*Quercus marilandica*
black oak	*Quercus velutina*
black walnut	*Juglans nigra*
blue palmetto fruits	either *Serenoa* spp. or *Sabal* spp.
broomsedge	*Andropogon virginicus*
buckeye	*Aesculus* spp.
butterfly pea	*Clitoria mariana*
button snakeroot	*Eryngium yuccifolium*
cabbage	probably *Brassica oleracea* spp.
calico bush	*Kalmea* spp.
cantaloupe	*Cucumis melo*
carpetweed	*Mollugo verticillata*
cassena	*see* yaupon
cedars	*see* junipers

celery	*Apium graveolens*
chenopodium	*Chenopodium berlandieri*
cherry	*Prunus* spp.
chestnut	*see* American chestnut
Chickasaw plum	*Prunus angustifolia*
china briar	*Smilax* spp.
corn	*see* flint corn
cowpeas	*Vigna unguiculata*
cucumbers	*Cucumis* spp.
cypresses	*Taxodium* spp.
devil's shoestring	*Tephrosia virginiana*
dogwood	*see* flowering dogwood
dwarf oak	*Quercus prinoides*
eastern white pine	*Pinus strobus*
elms	*Ulmus* spp.
flint corn	*Zea mays*
flowering dogwood	*Cornus florida*
fox grape	*Vitis labrusca*
gallberry	*Ilex glabra*
giant river cane	*Arundinaria gigantea* spp. *gigantea*
ginseng	*Panax quinquefolius*
golden St. John's-wort	*Hypericum aureum*
goose grass	*Eleusine indica*
gourd	*Cucurbita pepo*
grapes	*Vitis* spp.
grass	*Gramineae*, Family
greenbriar	*see* china briar
hackberries	*Celtis* spp.
hard-shelled hickory	perhaps shagbark hickory, *Carya ovata*, or shell-bark hickory, *C. laciniosa*
hickory	*Carya* spp.
holly	*Ilex* spp.
honey locust	*Gleditsia triancanthos*
horse sugar	*Symplocos tinctoria*
Indian grass	*Sorghastrum secundum*
Indian tobacco	*Nicotiana rustica*
jack-in-the-pulpit, or Indian turnip	*Arisaema triphyllum*
junipers	*Juniperus* spp.
knotweed	*Polygonum erectum*
lady's slipper	*Cypripedium* spp.
lettuce	*Lactuca* spp.
little barley	*Hordeum pusillum*
locust	*Robinia* spp.
longleaf pine	*Pinus palustris*

magnolia	*see* southern magnolia
maples	*Acer* spp.
mayapple	*Podophyllum peltatum*
maypop	*Passiflora incarnata*
meadow spikemoss	*Selaginella apoda*
moonflower	*Ipomoea alba*
morning glories	*Ipomoea* spp.
moss	*see* meadow spikemoss
mulberry	*Morus rubra*
muscadine	*Vitis rotundifolia*
oak-leaved hydrangea	*Hydrangea quercifolia*
oaks	*Quercus* spp.
onions	*Allium* spp.
orchids	*Habenaria* spp.
panic grass	*Panicum* spp.
pawpaws	*Asimina* spp.
peach	*Prunus persica*
peas	*Pisum* spp.
peavine	unidentified
persimmon	*Diospyros virginiana*
phlox	*Phlox* spp.
pigweed	*Amaranthus* spp.
pines	*Pinus* spp.
pitcher plant	*Sarracenia* spp.
poison sumac	*Toxicodendron vernix*
pokeweed	*see* American pokeweed
poplar	*see* tulip poplar
post oak	*Quercus stellata*
pumpkins	*Cucurbita* spp.
radishes	*Raphanus* spp.
ragweed	*Ambrosia* spp.
raspberries	*Rubus* spp.
red bay	probably *Persea borbonia*
red oak	*see* southern red oak
reed	*see* switch cane
river birch	*Betula nigra*
river cane	*see* giant river cane
rosin weed	*Silphium terebinthinaceum* and *S. laciniatum*
ruellia	*Ruellia* spp.
salty moss	sea meadow spikemoss
sassafras	*Sassafras albidum*
saw palmetto	*Serenoa repens*
sedge	*Cyperaceae*, Family
shagbark hickory	*Carya ovata*
shallot	*Allium cepa* var. *ascalonicum*

shell-bark hickory	*Carya laciniosa*
shining sumac	*Rhus copallinum*
short-leaf pine	*Pinus echinata*
silver maple	*Acer saccharinum*
snakeroots	*Eryngium* spp. and *Sanicula* spp.
southern magnolia	*Magnolia grandiflora*
southern red oak	*Quercus stellata*
spider flower	*Cleome* spp.
squash	*Cucurbita pepo*
sumac	*see* poison sumac
sweetgum	*Liquidambar styraciflua*
sweet potato	*Ipomoea batatas*
switch cane	*Arundinaria gigantea* spp. *tecta*
sycamore	*Platanus occidentalis*
tobacco	*see* Indian tobacco
trumpet creeper	*Compsis radicans*
tulip poplar	*Liriodendron tulipifera*
tupelo	*Nyssa* spp.
turnips	probably *Brassica campestris*
Venus's-flytrap	*Dionaea muscipula*
verbena	*Verbena* spp.
violets	*Viola* spp.
walnut	*Juglans* spp.
watermelon	*see* African watermelon
water oak	*Quercus nigra*
white buckeye	*Aesculus parviflora*
white oak	*Quercus alba*
wild crabapple	*Malus coronaria* or *M. angustifolia*
wild plums	*Prunus* spp.
wild potato	*Ipomoea pandurata*
wild rice	*Zizania aquatica*
wild strawberry	*Fragaria* spp.
willows	*Salix* spp.
wiregrass	*Aristida* spp.
witchhazel	*Hamamelis virginiana*
yaupon	*Ilex vomitoria*

Animals

American alligator	*Alligator mississippiensis*
American Atlantic sturgeon	*Acipenser oxyrhinchus*
American beaver	*Castor canadensis*
American black bear	*Ursus americanus*

American kestrel	*Falco sparverius*
American mourning dove	*Zenaida macroura*
Bachman's sparrow	*Aimophila aestivalis*
bald eagle	*Haliaeetus leucocephalus*
beaver	*see* American beaver
black bear	*see* American black bear
bluebirds	*Sialia* spp.
bobcat	*Lynx rufus*
bobwhite quail	*Colinus virginianus*
brown-headed nuthatch	*Sitta pusilla*
Carolina parakeet	*Conuropsis carolinensis*
common raccoon	*Procyon lotor*
deer	*see* white-tailed deer
eastern cottontail	*Sylvilagus floridanus*
eastern diamondback rattlesnake	*Crotalus adamanteus*
eastern indigo snake	*Drymarchon corias* spp. *couperi*
flatwood salamander	*Ambystoma cingulatum*
gopher frog	*Rana capito*
gopher tortoise	*Gopherus polyphemus*
great horned owl	*Bubo virginianus*
grey fox	*Urocyon cinereoargenteus*
grey wolf	*Canis lupus*
horseflies	*Tabanus* spp.
ivory-billed woodpecker	*Campephilus principalis*
marsh rabbit	*Sylvilagus palustris*
mole salamander	*Ambystoma talpoideum*
mollusk	*Mollusca*, Phylum
mountain lion	*Puma concolor*
mourning dove	*see* American mourning dove
muskrat	*Ondatra zibethicus*
North American otter	*Lutra canadensis*
otter	*see* North American otter
passenger pigeon	*Ectopistes migratorius*
perch	*Perciformes*, Order
pileated woodpecker	*Dryocopus pileatus*
pine snake	*Pituophis melanoleucus*
raccoon	*see* common raccoon
red-cockaded woodpecker	*Picoides borealis*
red drum	*Sciaenops ocellatus*
red fox	*Vulpes vulpes*
red horse	*see* red drum
red wolf	*Canis rufus*

rockfish	*Sebastes* spp.
shad	*Alosa* spp. and *Dorosoma* spp.
shovelnose sturgeon	*Scaphirhynchus platorynchus*
sparrow hawk	*see* American kestrel
squirrels	*Sciurus* spp.
striped newt	*Notophthalmus perstriatus*
sturgeon	*see* American Atlantic sturgeon or shovelnose sturgeon
swamp rabbit	*Sylvilagus aquaticus*
trout	probably varieties of *Oncorhynchus* spp. or *Salmo* spp.
tufted titmouse	*Parus bicolor*
turkey vulture	*Cathartes aura*
white-tailed deer	*Odocoileus virginianus*
wild turkey	*Meleagris gallopavo*

NOTES

Abbreviations

APS   American Philosophical Society, Library, Philadelphia, Pennsylvania

GDAH   Georgia State Department of Archives and History, Atlanta

HSP   Historical Society of Pennsylvania, Philadelphia

INHP   Independence National Historical Park, Philadelphia, Pennsylvania

LC   Library of Congress, Manuscript Division, Washington, D.C.

NA   National Archives and Records Service, Washington, D.C.

NCDAH   North Carolina Department of Archives and History, Raleigh

RG 11   Record Group 11, General Records of the United States Government

RG 75   Record Group 75, Records of the Bureau of Indian Affairs

RG 77   Record Group 77, Treasure File

SI   National Anthropological Archives, Smithsonian Institution, Washington, D.C.

UNC   Southern Historical Collection, University of North Carolina Library, Chapel Hill

Introduction

1. In fact, I have found it difficult to use the conventional categories of Native American, Euro-American, and African American (Indian, white, and black) for identifying people. However, some categorization is necessary for ease of reference. I refer to specific Indian groups when they can be identified as such in the documents. In some cases, I use the terms "Indians," "southeastern Indians," or "American Indians" to refer to the more general population of American Indians or southeastern Indians in general. I use the word "white" to refer to people of European descent. I use "black" to refer to people of African descent. I use the term "métis," the French word for "cross bred" or "hybrid," to refer to people of mixed Indian and European descent, or Indian and African descent, although this applies in only the broadest way.

In using the term "métis," I am following Joel W. Martin, in *Sacred Revolt*, 79, who takes the term from the eighteenth-century French word used to refer to people of mixed descent in the Great Lakes region. Martin prefers this term because it does not carry the connotations of the English "half breed." One should note that the term "Métis" (with an upper-case M) refers to an Indian group in the Great Lakes region of Canada; their website is ‹www.metisnation.ca›. Other scholars have opted for the comparable Spanish term *mestizo*; see Wright, *Creeks and Seminoles*; Saunt, *New Order*. The term for people of mixed parentage and descent used by eighteenth-century, English-speaking white southerners was "half breed" or "mixed blood." Contemporary Indians and some contemporary scholars use the term "mixed blood"; for example, Braund uses the term in *Deerskins and Duffels* (182) but acknowledges that the genetic mixing that occurred in the eighteenth century spawned a cumbersome vocabulary of race at the time. However, as Perdue, in *"Mixed Blood Indians,"* 99–103, points out, one should not conflate a racial category with culture; not all métis were culturally Euro-American.

The French and Spanish terms in translation still imply mixing, but as Gregory Waselkov, personal communication (2001), points out, using them begins to steer us away from a common misperception that somehow blood can be ethnically pure, impure, or mixed. This question of blood purity, in fact, comes up in debates on who is or is not an Indian. Most recognized Indian nations require a "blood quantum." Blu, "Region and Recognition," documents how this misperception of basic biology and the question of "blood quantum" figures prominently into the legal disputes over state and federal recognition of Indian groups in the United States, specifically the Lumbee of North Carolina.

Perdue, *Cherokee Women*, 82–83, acknowledges that these terms reflect little on how eighteenth- and nineteenth-century Cherokees understood descent. Perdue argues that among the Cherokees one was categorized as European or Cherokee or otherwise depending on to which group one's mother belonged and regardless of the nationality of one's father. The same probably held for the Creeks as well. Categories of Indian, white, black, and métis are useful but certainly not perfect references. For a comprehensive and provocative study of how the racial category of "mixed blood" evolved, see Perdue, *"Mixed Blood Indians."* Through these essays, Perdue makes it clear that a new framework for discussing the mix of people that lived in early America is much needed. Until a newer framework is developed, however, Indian, white, black, and métis (or some comparable term) will have to suffice.

2. Charles Hudson first noted this for the southeastern Indians in his introduction to *Red, White, and Black*, 1–2, when he wrote that "the Southeastern Indians are the victims of a virtual amnesia in our historical consciousness." Hudson's comments should not be taken to mean that scholars ignored Indians altogether; rather, the historical works that included Indians as central characters, until around 1980, were limited. One reason for the small number of such works is that scholarly interest in the era of the southern frontier has been, and still is, eclipsed by interest in the antebellum era and afterward—the time after Indian Removal. Verner Crane's *Southern Frontier*, first published in 1929, was the major historical work on the frontier era and place for many years, and it has not been entirely superseded even today. Other scholars writing on the history of the southern frontier narrated the southeastern Indians' role in the political and military events of the colonial rivalry over the South; see esp. Cotterill,

Southern Indians; Corkran, *Cherokee Frontier*; Corkran, *Creek Frontier*; Wright, *William Augustus Bowles*; Wright, *Only Land They Knew*; Wright, *Creeks and Seminoles*; Wright, *Anglo-Spanish Rivalry*; Wright, *Britain and the American Frontier*; Alden, *John Stuart*; Patricia Dillon Wood, *French Indian Relations*; O'Donnell, *Southern Indians*; Henri, *Southern Indians*; Badger and Clayton, *Alabama and the Borderlands*; and Bolton and Ross, *Debatable Land*. Some scholars turned their attention to Indian Removal, most notably Foreman in *Indian Removal* and Debo in *Rise and Fall of the Choctaw Republic* and *Road to Disappearance*. Around the mid-1970s, works such as Peter H. Wood, *Black Majority*, and Nash, *Red, White, and Black*, opened new ground for colonial American history and helped launch what became known as the "new Indian history." This list of works prior to 1980 is not exhaustive but is intended to give a sampling of the works and the focus of the scholarship at that time; for a more comprehensive history of the development of southeastern Indian ethnohistory, see Usner, *American Indians in the Lower Mississippi Valley*, 1–13. Taylor, in the recent Penguin popular reader *American Colonies*, goes far in dispelling any lingering notions that American history was simply England rolling over everything in its path; *American Colonies* captures the full complexity of America's colonial years by broadening the scope to include other areas of the New World and differentiating between the various multitude of Indian groups, African groups, and European groups who made up the colonial world, and by depicting the actual contest that took place over North America. A recent volume, Gallay, *Indian Slave Trade*, brings this fine resolution to southern colonial history and emphasizes that Indian/European interactions were fundamental to the English empire building.

3. The term "new Indian history" was coined in 1971 in Berkhofer, "Political Context," 357–82. In this same article, Berkhofer proposed that the "new Indian history" should take a new direction to understanding Indian-white relations. He argued for an American history from the Indian perspective, one that would examine the connections between Indian groups; delineate the internal workings of Indian political, social, and economic structures; and then begin to investigate how Indian life intersected with Euro-American life and how each group was transformed because of this intersection. Less than fifteen years later, the new Indian history had led ethnohistorians into many new directions; for an excellent summary of these, see Calloway, *New Directions*. Two of the most influential works based on these themes have been Merrell, *Indians' New World*, and Richard White, *Middle Ground*. The scholarship on Indian life and history is more vigorous now than ever. For a sampling of monographs about the Historic Period southeastern Indians, see Braund, *Deerskins and Duffels*; Galloway, *Choctaw Genesis*; Hatley, *Dividing Paths*; Joel W. Martin, *Sacred Revolt*; Charles Hudson, *Knights of Spain*; Saunt, *New Order*; Usner, *Indians, Settlers, and Slaves*; Worth, *Timucuan Chiefdoms*; Perdue, *Cherokee Women*; Carson, *Searching for the Bright Path*; Greg O'Brien, *Choctaws in a Revolutionary Age*; and Gallay, *Indian Slave Trade*. For a modern overview of southeastern Indian history, see Perdue and Green, *Columbia Guide*. Despite such fine works as these and others, Indian history is still not a major component of American or southern history.

4. The Indians of North America are not the only people who have been left out of

Western histories; this argument is most forcefully presented in Wolf, *Europe and the People without History*, in which the author gives a sweeping overview of world history showing how all people at all times have been caught up in historical processes.

5. It has been demonstrated that such opposition constructs were part of the ideological justification behind Euro-American colonial domination. Said's *Orientalism* was one of the first in-depth looks at the construction and consequences of this binary categorization. Lewis and Wigen, *Myth of Continents*, discusses the implications of this construction on Euro-American perceptions beyond the Western/Occidental debate. Berkhofer, *White Man's Indian*, documents the early construction of American Indians as Other in the American popular mind and how this construction continues today. Deloria, *Playing Indian*, shows how the imagining of Indians by non-Indians reflects more about the identities of the non-Indians than the Indians, but Deloria shows that this imagining has a very real impact on real Indians. Deloria argues that whites imitating Indians and appropriating Indian cultural traits provided and still provide a contrasting Other in the construction of American identities.

6. Richard White, "Using the Past," 218, makes this point. Perdue, *Cherokee Women*, 3–11, notes that if Indians were depicted as changing, they were usually shown in a state of decline, wherein their "traditional ways" were interrupted and corrupted by Western cultural domination; this is known as the declension model.

7. Evans-Pritchard, "Anthropology and History," 172–73. In this essay Evans-Pritchard explores the consequences of anthropology's turning away from history. He calls for a rapprochement between the two disciplines, and he understands anthropology to be more like social history; Evans-Pritchard foresaw anthropologists doing history and historians broadening their interests to non-Western peoples (see pp. 189–90), both of which have come about in the past few decades.

8. The Smithsonian Museum of the American Indian is a long-overdue tribute to the Indian place in American history.

9. This is in contrast to the postcolonial advocacy of "native history," which is a history divested entirely of Western conceits and concepts and based on native ideas of time, the past, and myth, and on stories about the past passed along orally. The postcolonial/postmodern critique builds on the work of Michel Foucault, Clifford Geertz, Marshall Sahlins, Jacques Derrida, and other late-twentieth-century thinkers. Postmodernism today has many wrinkles, but two of its basic premises that have affected how we think of history and anthropology are the critique of the Western construction of knowledge and its intersection with imperialism and colonial domination and the idea that there are as many "histories" as there are viewpoints, and none are objectively true. For some recent essays in American Indian ethnohistory that air some of the issues raised by the postcolonial debates, see Calvin Martin, *American Indians and the Problem of History*; Mihesuah, *Natives and Academics*; Shoemaker, *Clearing a Path*; Fixico, *Rethinking American Indian History*; Thornton, *Studying Native America*; and Biolsi and Zimmerman, *Indians and Anthropologists*.

Spinning out of the postcolonial critique is a debate over who "owns" the past, with many native scholars and nonscholars claiming proprietary rights over tribal histories and writing histories that differ much, in fact and form, from traditional academic histories. One example of native history for the Creeks is Chaudhuri and Chaudhuri, *Sa-*

cred Path, a cultural insider's history of the Creeks and a chronicling of Creek values. *Sacred Path* is a different kind of history in that it is more about Creek values and the roots of these values. The authors use much oral tradition and early-twentieth-century anthropology but few primary documents to reconstruct "traditional values" of the Creeks, and many contemporary and twentieth-century oral traditions to impart contemporary Creek values. The results are some startling interpretations different from the accepted canon of the Mississippian Period mounds, Historic Period Creek relations to African Americans, and Historic Period Creek political governance, among other things.

Such native histories as the one above have come under some criticism by historians. Richard White, "Using the Past," 234–37, asserts that "native histories" subscribe to an ahistorical, passive rendering of Indian life; that these histories tend to use Europe and America as the primary focus, despite their outcries against such; and that they go on to depict American Indians as victims of colonial domination. In this article White clearly weighs in on the side of the "historicizers," or those scholars who would place American Indians into the larger narrative of American history. Richter, "Whose Indian History?" outlines competing histories as one of three problems one encounters when placing Indians into American history; the others are the indifference of many historians to American Indians and the criticism from those who still place Indians outside history.

Native histories and postcolonial interpretative histories have also raised questions about the standards of evidence used in history. I follow Cronon, "Place for Stories," that the accepted standards must adhere to certain rules of logic and contradiction, specifically that historical narrative cannot contradict known facts about the past and ecology, and that they must be read as nonfiction. Richard White, "Using the Past," 225–26, further asserts that we cannot have one set of standards for natives and cultural insiders and another set for the nonnatives and cultural outsiders.

One of the first efforts at reformulating historiography guidelines to accommodate native histories is Sioui, *Amerindian Autohistory*. A more recent exploration of how Indians use and understand their own past is Nabokov, *Forest of Time*. Linda Tuhiwai Smith, *Decolonizing Methodologies*, traces the theme of cultural domination in the history of the development of Western methods for constructing knowledge and examines the problems of both natives and nonnatives doing indigenous research. Smith also provides an innovative, insightful, and balanced beginning to reformulating our standards of evidence by taking seriously indigenous methods and ways of knowing. These efforts are just the beginning.

10. This book takes world systems theory as its basic premise. Using this model, colonial domination issues from the "core" areas of the modern world, which are those areas that control manufacturing, banking, and capital. The "peripheries" are those areas of the world from which the core extracts natural resources and labor, through either colonial or economic domination. Creek country was a periphery, and by the late eighteenth century, land was the natural resource most needed by the core areas. Hence, the Creeks were inextricably linked into the modern world system by the late eighteenth century. World systems theory was first developed by Wallerstein in *Modern World System* and has since received much scholarly attention, especially in the so-

cial sciences. In anthropology, Wolf presents the most compelling case for world systems theory in *Europe and the People without History*, which gives an overview of the impact of capitalism on a global scale, especially on the lives of indigenous people when they are incorporated into the system. For a treatment of world systems theory from the perspective of the core, see Arrighi, *Long Twentieth Century*, which tracks capitalist expansion over the past 700 years, following the changing core hegemonies and their concomitant "cycles of accumulation" that continually reproduce the structures of capital and production.

11. Historian Richard White, in *Middle Ground*, xi, notes that he could not make any sharp distinctions between the Indian and white worlds; the same can be said for Creek country.

12. Marc Bloch best defined *histoire totale* in *Historian's Craft*, in which he urged his colleagues toward a "universal history"—a history that would encompass all the aspects of a society. This later became the foundation for the framework of the *Annales* historians, later dubbed the "New History." This paradigm, formulated and epitomized by the writings of Fernand Braudel, Lucien Febvre, and Emmanuel Le Roy Ladurie, among others, is notable for its efforts to depict everyday life against the backdrop of larger historical forces. For an introduction to the *Annales* school, see Braudel, *On History*. Evans-Pritchard pointed anthropologists to the *Annaliste* as early as 1961 in his essay "Anthropology and History," 174–75, 188–91. Charles Hudson, one of the foremost proponents of using this approach in anthropology and archaeology, made a similar point in 1974 in "Historical Approach in Anthropology." Historical anthropology is still a small subset of the field. For other discussions of how the *Annales* paradigm has affected how Western historians do history, see Burke, *New Perspectives*.

13. The diaries of two Moravian missionaries who were posted at the Creek Agency refer often to the Creeks' reticence regarding discussing religious beliefs and rituals; see Mauelshagen and Davis, *Partners*, 22–23, 30, 36–37, 61–62, 67.

14. John R. Swanton compiled much ethnographic data on Creek religion in *Creek Religion*, but he failed to give a sense of the coherency of it as a belief system. Charles Hudson, *Southeastern Indians*, 120–83, provides the best effort, to date, at synthesizing the ethnographic and ethnohistorical data and placing some sense on the Historic southeastern Indian belief system. Joel W. Martin, *Sacred Revolt*, looks at the religious motives underlying the Red Stick War and comes close to Creek perceptions regarding the war. Greg O'Brien, *Choctaws in a Revolutionary Age*, examines the basis of Choctaw leadership of that era and argues that leadership could be underwritten by access to either spiritual power or Euro-American economic links. Perdue, *Cherokee Women*, 18–40, understands the basic construction of gender roles to be grounded in Cherokee ideas of balance and purity. Both Carson, *Searching for the Bright Path*, and Hill, *Weaving New Worlds*, incorporate much about Choctaw and Cherokee beliefs, respectively. Charles Hudson, *Conversations*, synthesizes much scholarship on the southeastern Indian belief system into a fictionalized account of a Coosa priest explaining his worldview to a Spanish priest during the Mississippian Period. Mostly, though, scholars have been uneven in their treatment of Historic Period southeastern Indian religion and spirituality, although most acknowledge that these elements of life were important. I, too, do not attempt a full reckoning of Creek religion.

15. Scholars framed some of the peculiar problems in doing Indian history a few decades ago; see Axtel, *European and the Indian*; Berkhofer, "Political Context"; Horsman, "Recent Trends"; and Trigger, "Ethnohistory."

16. Historians, folklorists, linguists, and anthropologists, among others, have long pondered oral traditions—their meanings, their functions, and what they can tell us about the workings of the human mind. Generally speaking, most scholars accept the uses and evaluation of oral tradition as outlined in Vansina, *Oral Tradition as History*, namely that oral traditions are cultural expressions and performances of worldviews, social systems, theoretical explanations for how the world and cosmos work, tools for social justification, and other histories. Vansina is careful to point out some of the limitations in using oral traditions as historical evidence (see 66–67, 83–91, 173–85, 186–99), and the scholarly community is not yet in agreement on how oral traditions can be used as pieces of historical evidence. Scholars of American Indian history have adopted much from Vansina's work, which was based on fieldwork in Africa, and applied it to Indian oral traditions. For instance, Cruikshank, "Oral History," demonstrates that oral traditions among the indigenous people of the Canadian Yukon are guidelines for understanding the past and change. Angela Cavender Wilson, "Power of the Spoken Word," offers oral traditions as an entry into the American Indian language for the nonnative scholar, as pieces of a coherent belief system, as interpretations of the past, and as transmissions of culture. Howe, "Story of America," understands that oral traditions and written documents exist in a dialogue with each other, each influencing the other. In contrast, Bahr, "Bad News," argues that Indian oral traditions are largely myths of Edenic pasts and parodies of ancientness and hence of little use to ethnohistorians. Keyes, "Myth and Social History," by tracking the Apalachee ball game myth through time, demonstrates that myth and oral traditions themselves change through time to accommodate, legitimate, and explain existing social conditions. Still, there is no doubt that oral traditions are important features of contemporary American Indian life. For an excellent example of the importance of oral traditions, especially as repositories of knowledge, see Lewis and Jordan, *Creek Indian Medicine Ways*.

17. Much of Hawkins's writings have been published in Hawkins, *Letters*; Hawkins, *Sketch*; and Hawkins, "Letters of Benjamin Hawkins." Hawkins was a North Carolinian who at twenty-eight years of age began a successful career in politics, serving on the North Carolina state legislature and later as a state representative to Congress for fifteen years. By the time of his appointment as Indian agent in 1796, Hawkins was around forty years old. Although he had declined to run for reelection to the North Carolina senate seat, he had an established political career. Hawkins was not born into the lap of luxury; but his family was well-to-do, and he could have taken his place at the head of this household, even though he was still a bachelor. In short, at forty years of age, with a competent if not outstanding political career and with a certain social prominence and stimulating friends and acquaintances, Hawkins could have lived out the rest of his life in relative comfort and ease; instead he opted to move to the frontier. Two biographies have been written about Hawkins. Pound, *Benjamin Hawkins*, records his full political career, while Henri, *Southern Indians*, chronicles his years as Indian agent and specifically his dealings with the southern Indians. The Hawkins family

produced many statesmen, including a governor. The Hawkins Family Papers are at UNC. Additional collections are at NCDAH.

18. That Indians and Euro-Americans lived in a mutually intelligible world was not always the case. Merrell, in *Into the American Woods*, demonstrates that during the first seventy years or so, forest diplomacy was conducted by men who continually attempted to bridge both sides of the cultural and social divide—Indian and Euro-American—with little success.

19. Environmental historians, geographers, environmental anthropologists, human ecologists, and others involved in the question of human/environment relations propose that this relationship is a dialectical one in which humans construct ideas about the natural world while simultaneously leaving their own cultural imprint on nature. These ideas were formulated by cultural geographer Yi-Fu Tuan and environmental historian Donald L. Worster, both of whom produced a wealth of scholarship; for an introduction to their works, see Tuan, *Topophilia*, and Worster, *Wealth of Nature*. The concept of nature as a construct has led to much recent discussion on how we interpret the natural world, how humans leave their imprint on it, and how this imprint, in turn, refracts back into our perceptions and interpretation. For introductions to some of these conversations, see Cronon, *Uncommon Ground*; Simmons, *Interpreting Nature*; and Spirn, *Language of Landscape*. Environmental historians and historical ecologists also argue that human and natural history cannot be separated and that they are part of a single history. Cronon best summarizes this viewpoint in *Changes in the Land*, 3–15; Krech, *Ecological Indian*, 15–28, applies this argument to Indian prehistory and history. A growing field in anthropology, dubbed "historical ecology," also takes this as its starting premise; this field, its assumptions, and its methodologies are defined in Crumley, "Historical Ecology"; Balée, "Historical Ecology"; and Whitehead, "Ecological History."

Since Cronon published *Changes in the Land* in 1983, environmental history has become a growing field of inquiry. Some fine scholars have turned an environmental lens onto the American South; see Cowdrey, *This Land*; Silver, *New Face*; Otto, *Southern Frontiers*; Miller, *Environmental History of Northeast Florida*; and Davis, *Where There Are Mountains*.

20. In compiling these maps, I used Hawkins's geographic descriptions of Creek town locations to identify these places on U.S. Geological Survey topographic maps. The inclusion of stream names and mileage allowed me to locate most of the towns with some confidence. In many cases, the locations were confirmed with archaeological excavation and survey data. Archaeologists have located some towns by name, such as Tuckabatchee, Fusihatchee, Coosada, Aubecooche, Cusseta, and Yuchi. In some cases, Hawkins's descriptions place a town at known archaeological sites, but they have not been identified by name. For example, Hawkins's description of the location of Padjeeligau on the Flint River coincides with a cluster of archaeological sites dating to the Historic Period, but these sites have not been identified as being part of Padjeeligau. In some cases, there were no known archaeological sites at the location at which I arrived using Hawkins's descriptions. Of course, archaeological investigation is needed to confirm these town locations. In a few cases I have only tentative locations

because Hawkins's descriptions did not include stream names, he estimated a long stretch of mileage that was difficult to follow, or he gave virtually no information regarding location. Lolley, "Ethnohistory and Archaeology," develops a more precise methodology to locate and to track through time historic Creek sites by using historic maps. I also remind the reader that it is illegal to take or destroy artifacts and to tamper with archaeological sites or any other cultural resources.

21. Richard White, "Indian Peoples and the Natural World," 93–94, notes that "we will never recover a pure Indian past, a purely Indian view of the natural world," but that we can use the documents to wrest something of Indian conceptions of the natural world out of them. A recent article, Carson, "Ethnogeography," argues for an integration between ethnogeography and ethnohistory in order to understand native North America as a place.

Chapter One

1. Scratching was done with a sharp-toothed comb, usually made from wood, bone, or garfish teeth. The teeth, however, were not long, and the scratches that resulted were usually superficial. The comb was drawn over the arms, legs, and torso of a person, drawing blood. Although the wounds were not serious, the procedure was painful. Not only was scratching a punishment, but it was also a ritual of purification and for restoring balance and was used in treating disease. Ballplayers often endured scratching the night before a game to ensure purity and fortitude; see Charles Hudson, *Southeastern Indians*, 232–33, 416.

2. Bartram, *Naturalist's Edition*, 164–66; Bartram, *Bartram on the Southeastern Indians*, 70–71 n. 78.

3. Much of this interpretation is taken from Waselkov and Braund; see Bartram, *Bartram on the Southeastern Indians*, 250 n. 78.

4. Crane, in *Southern Frontier*, 108–61, was the first historian to highlight the importance of the skin trade in southern colonial politics and Indian-white relations. The next sustained scholarship on the southern skin trade was Corkran's *Cherokee Frontier* and *Creek Frontier*, which detail the centrality of the trade in economic and military alliances between Indians and Europeans. Wright also gave the trade a central place in the tripartite European contest over the South; see Wright, *Anglo-Spanish Rivalry* and *Britain and the American Frontier*. Ver Steeg, in *Origins of a Southern Mosaic*, 109–14, was one of the first historians to detail the economic significance of the deerskin trade in the early history of the southern colonies, especially South Carolina. Since then, much work has been done on the skin trade in North America. The most comprehensive examination of the Anglo trade among the Creeks is Braund, *Deerskins and Duffels*. Champagne, in *Social Order*, 50–67, was one of the first scholars to discuss some of the various political mechanisms the southern Indians used in negotiating with Europeans over the trade. Much of the most recent ethnohistory for the Southeast deals with the effects of the trade era on southeastern Indian life; see Merrell, *Indians' New World*; Usner, *Indians, Settlers, and Slaves*; Perdue, *Cherokee Women*, 60–108; Hill, *Weaving New Worlds* 35–109; Carson, *Searching for the Bright Path*,

26–80; Saunt, *New Order*; and Morris, *Bringing of Wonder*. Gallay, *Indian Slave Trade*, demonstrates that the Indian trade was fundamental to the building of the English empire from its inception as a trade in Indian slaves.

5. The emergence of an assimilationist elite class among the southeastern Indians during the Removal era was first noted in Perdue, *Slavery and the Evolution*. Green, *Politics of Indian Removal*, showed a similar strata of political elites among Removal era Creeks. More recently, Joel W. Martin, *Sacred Revolt*, and Saunt, *New Order*, describe this elite class among the Creeks as market-oriented métis, whose mind-set, lifeways, and jockeying for political power were gravely disruptive and divisive forces in Creek society by the last few years of the eighteenth century. Champagne, *Social Order*, 91–92, notes that this elite class was a very thin strata among most southeastern Indians at this time.

6. Champagne, *Social Order*, 49–67.

7. The term "middle ground" is taken from Richard White, *Middle Ground*. Greg O'Brien, "Conqueror Meets the Unconquered," proposes that the middle ground was not so much a synthesizing of cultural traits as an assertion of cultural differences.

8. Braund, *Deerskins and Duffels*, 164–72.

9. Ibid., 164–88. For a history of the trading firm of Panton, Leslie, and Company, see Coker and Watson, *Indian Traders*.

10. Braund, *Deerskins and Duffels*, 164–88.

11. McGillivray's letters have been collected in McGillivray, *McGillivray*. For various aspects of McGillivray's career and life, see Green, "Alexander McGillivray"; Saunt, *New Order*, 67–89; and Wright, *Creeks and Seminoles*. McGillivray has also been the subject of several biographies; for the most recent, see Nadel, *Alexander McGillivray*. McGillivray's Scottish father is the subject of Cashin, *Lachlan McGillivray*.

12. The Creek Agency was located in present-day Crawford County, Georgia. The actual site of the agency is known and has been surveyed archaeologically.

13. Henri, *Southern Indians*, 317.

14. Ibid., 31–60.

15. Washington to Secretary of War, August 12, 1796, and "Talk to the Cherokee Nation," August 29, 1796, Washington Papers, LC. As a part of the 1790 Trade and Intercourse Act, a bill passed by the U.S. Congress to regulate Indian affairs, the Indians east of the Mississippi were divided into northern and southern districts with a federally appointed Indian agent for each district; see Washburn, *American Indians*, 4:2290. Hawkins replaced James Seagrove as agent for the southern district.

16. Jefferson was interested in the origins of the American Indians, and he believed that linguistic evidence could shed light on this question; see Sheehan, *Seeds of Extinction*, 54–58. The word list from Hawkins to Jefferson is in Benjamin Hawkins to Thomas Jefferson, "Comparative Vocabulary," APS.

17. Benjamin Hawkins to Alexander McGillivray, March 6, 1790, Washington Papers, LC.

18. Phillips, *Life and Labor in the Old South*, 21–29.

19. U.S. commissioner James White wrote to Secretary of War Henry Knox that the Creeks "look on their land as their blood and their life which they must fight for rather

than part with" (James White to Henry Knox, May 24, 1787, in Cochran, *New American State Papers*, 24).

20. Cashin, *Bartram and the American Revolution*, depicts the growing tensions during this time between the British traders and the wealthy patriots and the patriot frontier settlers; also see Braund, *Deerskins and Duffels*, 164–88. For the influences of this new leadership on Indian policy, see Prucha, *American Indian Policy in the Formative Years*, 147–87.

21. Entry No. 108, RG 11, NA.

22. Sheehan, *Seeds of Extinction*, 119–81, delineates the strands of philanthropic ideology behind the plan for civilization. Also, Joel W. Martin, *Sacred Revolt*, 94–95, presents Hawkins's ideas on what should be involved in the plan for civilization as having been influenced by Swiss reformer Johann Heinrich Pestalozzi, a contemporary of Hawkins.

23. Henri, *Southern Indians*, 81–111; Perdue, *Cherokee Women*, 109–13; Joel W. Martin, *Sacred Revolt*, 87–113; Saunt, *New Order*, 139–229, Braund, *Deerskins and Duffels*, 164–88. Perdue, *Cherokee Women*, 109–34, examines the effects of the plan for civilization on the Cherokees and especially Cherokee gender roles.

24. Cronon, *Changes in the Land*, 54–81; Kline, *First along the River*, 12–25.

25. Hawkins, *Letters*, 1:402. Such strong language is uncharacteristic of Hawkins; this letter to Henry Dearborn was also signed by James Wilkinson and Andrew Pickens.

26. President Jefferson on Indian Trading Houses, January 18, 1803, in Prucha, *Documents*, 21–22. Prucha, in *American Indian Policy in the Formative Years*, 213–49, first documented the expansionist goals behind the plan for civilization as Indian policy; for the ideology behind the civilization plan and its overt expansionist goals, see Sheehan, *Seeds of Extinction*, 119–81.

27. Scholars agree that Hawkins was a man of integrity who upheld the rights of the Creeks and sought justice in Indian affairs, but opinions are mixed regarding his agenda. Some sources, such as Joel W. Martin, *Sacred Revolt*, 87–113; Green, *Politics of Indian Removal* 36–37; and Braund, *Deerskins and Duffels*, 177–88, although testifying to his fairness, view Hawkins as condescending, ethnocentric, and a tool of expansion. Wright, *Creeks and Seminoles*, 143–53, understands Hawkins to have wielded much power in implementing the plan for civilization. Hawkins biographers Henri (*Southern Indians*) and Pound (*Benjamin Hawkins*) are sympathetic to their subject and understand Hawkins to have been concerned yet constrained in what he could accomplish by events and agendas beyond his control.

28. Jordan, *White over Black*, 162–63; Sheehan, *Seeds of Extinction*, 75–82; Henri, *Southern Indians*, 89–92. Jefferson has come to be the figurehead for the Noble Savage camp. Sheehan, *Seeds of Extinction*, documents the emergence of Jeffersonian ideology and the subsequent debates over the nature of American Indians and how these debates figured into the formulation of Indian policy. Wallace, *Jefferson and the Indians*, argues that Jefferson's ideas about Indians were merely ideological justifications for his dreams of westward expansion. For some particulars on how this debate informed Indian policy, see Prucha, *American Indian Policy in the Formative Years*, 213–49.

29. Hawkins, *Letters*, 2:780.

30. Although I cannot say definitely, I have every indication that Hawkins was fluent, or at least conversant, in Muskogean. However, he routinely used interpreters at official talks, probably to accommodate the non-Muskogean speakers who would have been present. He definitely had an interest in language, as witnessed by the word lists he sent Jefferson; see Benjamin Hawkins to Thomas Jefferson, "Comparative Vocabulary," APS.

31. The missionaries reported Hawkins's obstructions to their work in their correspondence with the officials of the Moravian Church in Salem; see Mauelshagen and Davis, *Partners*, 8, 9–10, 18, 20, 64. On the Creeks' lack of interest in their mission efforts, see ibid., 22–23, 30, 36–37, 61–62, 67. Because of these two factors, much of their work centered on the black slaves at Hawkins's plantation, and particularly on a literate slave known as Phil, who engaged in much theological debate with the brothers; see ibid., 36–40, 52–54, 56, 57, 58–59, 68, 69.

32. Stiggins, *Creek Indian History*, 80.

33. Ibid.

34. Ibid.

35. Hawkins, *Letters*, 1:193.

36. Ibid., 269.

37. Ibid., 269, 279, 281, 2:454. For more information on the infamous Bowles, see Wright, *William Augustus Bowles* and *Creeks and Seminoles*, 119–20.

38. Hawkins to Edward Price, January 8, 1801, Entry No. 42, RG 75, NA.

39. Alexander Cornells, Hawkins's good friend and confidant, for instance, may not have been as pro-American as Hawkins believed. During the Red Stick War, Cornells may have leaked information to the anti-American Red Sticks. This accusation was never proved, and there is no indication that Hawkins ever suspected Cornells, although he knew something was wrong. His friendship with Cornells did not falter; see Hawkins, *Letters*, 2:666 n. 2.

40. Hawkins, "Letters of Benjamin Hawkins," 11. The Muskogean orthography is taken from Wright, *Creeks and Seminoles*, 29. The Muskogean orthography for some terms varies tremendously in the scholarly literature, as does the spelling of historic Creek place-names and towns. In the case of town names, I have opted to use Hawkins's rendering, unless there are more-or-less modern standardized spellings. The latter, specifically, are Apalachicola, which Hawkins spelled as Patachoche and Palachocola; Chehaw, which Hawkins spelled as Cheauhau; Cusseta, which Hawkins spelled as Cussetuh; Eufaula, which Hawkins spelled as Eufaulau and Eufaufla; Fusihatchee, which Hawkins spelled as Fushatchee; Oakfuskee, which Hawkins spelled as Ocfuskee; Tuckabatchee, which Hawkins spelled as Tookaubatchee; Upatoi, which Hawkins spelled as Aupauttaue; and finally Yuchi, which Hawkins spelled as Uchee. Otherwise, all town names are as Hawkins spelled them in his *Sketch*. The place-names are taken from a variety of sources, and they are rendered as spelled in those sources. In other cases where I use the Muskogean words, either I use the word as rendered in the primary document from which the material was taken or I have cited the secondary source from which I have derived the phonetic rendering.

41. McGillivray, *McGillivray*, 55; Pound, *Benjamin Hawkins*, 163; Joel W. Martin, *Sacred Revolt*, 87.

42. Hawkins, *Letters*, 1:316–17.

43. Alexander McGillivray, however, did hold some measure of coercive power, but this appears to have been based in his close connections to Panton, Leslie, and Company; see Saunt, *New Order*, 75–80. Saunt goes on to argue that the position of power that McGillivray forged came to dominate in Creek politics. I argue later in this volume that Creek headmen were constrained by other Creek legislative principles of revenge and retaliation, and hence McGillivray's power as a Creek headman was the exception, not the rule, throughout the Historic Period.

44. For histories of these events, see Edmunds, *Shawnee Prophet*; Edmunds, *Tecumseh*; Dowd, *Spirited Resistance*; Richard White, *Middle Ground*; Joel W. Martin, *Sacred Revolt*; Saunt, *New Order*; and Halbert and Ball, *Creek War*.

45. Hawkins, *Letters*, 2:647.

46. The Muscogee (Creek) Nation and the Poarch Band of Creeks are the only federally recognized Creek groups; there are other groups seeking federal and state recognition. For information on the federally recognized Creeks, visit their websites: the Muscogee (Creek) Nation site is at ⟨http://www.ocevnet.org/creek⟩ and the Poarch Band is at ⟨http://www.poarchcreekindians.org⟩. For an introduction to scholarship on contemporary southern Indians, see Bonney and Parades, *Anthropologists and Indians*, and Parades, *Indians of the Southeastern United States*. For introductions to scholarship on and issues concerning contemporary American Indians in general, see Troy P. Johnson, *Contemporary Native American Political Issues*, and Champagne, *Contemporary Native American Cultural Issues*.

Chapter Two

1. The idea that the southeastern Indians have not always been the same has only come about in the past twenty or so years. Before that time scholarly work on the southeastern Indians, in particular, was framed by the anthropological concept of the "ethnographic present," in which non-Western, oral societies were understood to have changed little over time until many became acculturated to the twentieth-century modern world. Anthropologist John R. Swanton, who wrote in the early to mid-twentieth century, covers all of the southeastern Indians in a massive outpouring of research and synthesis. He was particularly interested in the Creeks, and he devoted several volumes explicitly to them. Although useful in many regards, Swanton's work is now considered flawed because of his use of the ethnographic present. For a sampling of Swanton's work, see his *Creek Religion*, *Indian Tribes*, *Myths and Tales*, *Indians*, "Social Significance," *Early History*, and *Social Organization*. This realization is also largely absent in Charles Hudson, *Southeastern Indians*, published in 1976.

Scholars are now aware that a profound social transformation occurred among the native people of the southeastern United States between the time of the earliest Spanish exploration and the early decades of the eighteenth century. Our contemporary awareness of this historical transformation has grown out of the research on the activities of the sixteenth-century explorers Hernando de Soto, Tristan de Luna, and Juan Pardo conducted by Charles Hudson and his colleagues; see Charles Hudson, *Juan Pardo Expedition*, "Hernando de Soto Expedition," and *Knights of Spain*; Hudson,

Smith, and DePratter, "Hernando de Soto Expedition: From Apalachee to Chiaha"; Hudson, Smith, and DePratter, "Hernando de Soto Expedition: From Mabila to the Mississippi"; and Hudson et al., "Tristan de Luna Expedition." These works and the other volumes that grew out of this project provide a kind of sixteenth-century Mississippian baseline from which scholars can now move backward and forward in time to better chronicle the changes of the southeastern Indians during and after the Mississippian Period. We now understand the European invasions into the Southeast, beginning with the Spanish explorers, to have been events that shattered the Mississippian chiefdoms and led to the reorganization of much of southeastern Indian life.

2. Anthropologist Henry F. Dobyns was one of the first to notice the impact of disease; see his "Estimating Aboriginal American Population." The question is of great interest today. Although scholars have not yet settled on specific population numbers before and after the introduction of Old World diseases into the virgin soil populations of the New World, in general, they estimate a 90 to 95 percent population loss of the indigenous peoples of the New World. Some of the best comprehensive treatments of the question are Crosby, *Ecological Imperialism* and *Columbian Exchange*; Diamond, *Guns, Germs and Steel*; Cook, *Born to Die*; and Thornton, *American Indian Holocaust*.

For the southeastern Indians, Dobyns was the first to attempt to assess the numbers. In *Their Number Become Thinned*, Dobyns arrived at an estimate in the millions for the Indians of Florida based on certain ecological factors. Dobyns's numbers were challenged by Hann in "De Soto, Dobyns, and Demography," and most scholars now agree that Dobyns's estimate was high. Since much of this work is still in progress, there is no synthesis on all the data collected and analyzed to date. Generally, though, the number at the time of contact for the entire Mississippian world hovers around 1.5 million, with a 90 to 95 percent collapse after contact. Some of these works on southeastern Indian disease epidemics are Blakley and Detweiler-Blakley, "Impact of European Disease"; Parades and Plante, "Reexamination of Creek Indian Population Trends"; Kowalewski and Hatch, "Sixteenth-Century Expansion"; Marvin Smith, *Archaeology*; Daniels, "Indian Population"; Kelton, "Not All Disappeared"; Ramenofsky, *Vectors of Death*; Thornton, *Cherokees*; Larsen, *Bioarchaeology of Spanish Florida*; Baker and Kealhofer, *Bioarchaeology of Native American Adaptation*; Spears, "European Infectious Disease"; and Worth, *Timucuan Chiefdoms*, 2:1–37.

3. For a full discussion of the archaeological evidence for the decline of the chiefdoms due to population collapse, see Marvin Smith, *Archaeology*. Marvin Smith, *Coosa*, tracks the rise and fall of a Mississippian chiefdom during the protohistoric period.

4. The term "coalescent society" was coined by Charles Hudson in Ethridge and Hudson, "Early Historic Transformations," 38–39; however, Waselkov and Cottier first recognized the process in "European Perceptions," 23. Marvin Smith also proposed a similar process in *Archaeology*, 135–37. Merrell, *Indians' New World*, was the first in-depth examination of this process.

5. Ethridge and Hudson, "Early Historic Transformations," 40–41.

6. Crane, *Southern Frontier*, 112–21, first noted that Indian slaves formed an important commodity in the early years of the English trade system. Peter H. Wood, *Black Majority*, first documented the large presence of Indian slaves on southern coastal

plantations in the early years of American chattel slavery; also see Peter H. Wood, "Indian Slavery in the Southeast." Gallay, *Indian Slave Trade*, is the first book devoted to the Indian slave trade; Gallay understands the trade to have been a crucial element in the building of the English empire but also highly disruptive of native life. For a historical novel of an Apalachee Indian slave woman during the seventeenth century, see Joyce Rockwood Hudson, *Apalachee*.

7. Ethridge and Hudson, "Early Historic Transformations," 41–42. Hahn, "Miniature Arms Race," documents the acquisition of guns among southeastern Indians in the early colonial years. The Indian slave trade first began in northeastern America. The Iroquois, seeking access to European goods and war captives whom they adopted into their kin groups to replace their dead, began doing business with English, Dutch, and French traders in the first few decades of the seventeenth century. Iroquois raiders went into the Southeast as far south as Florida and as far west as the Mississippi River. Plus, many of the northern groups suffering under Iroquois raids began to break up and move long distances west and south, seeking refuge or becoming slavers themselves. Slaving in the South, however, probably did not become fully established until sometime in the mid-seventeenth century, when Jamestown traders engaged Piedmont Indian groups like the Occaneechees and Tuscaroras as slave raiders. The most comprehensive examination of the English slave trade is Gallay, *Indian Slave Trade*. For the colonial experience of the Iroquois, see Richter, *Ordeal of the Longhouse*. For some of the effects of slaving in the Southeast, see Ethridge and Hudson, *Transformation*, 8, 19, 31–37, 43–44, 60–64, 77, 99, 108; Worth, *Timucuan Chiefdoms*, 2:140–58; Milanich, *Florida's Indians*, 171–88; Joel W. Martin, "Southeastern Indians and the English Trade," 312–13; and Hann, *Apalachee*, 264–83.

8. Ethridge, "Raiding the Remains," first characterized the disruptions of the introduction of capitalism through slaving as a "shatter zone."

9. Ethridge, "Chickasaw Factionalism," documents some of these mechanisms for the Chickasaws.

10. Ethridge and Hudson, "Early Historic Transformations," 42–48; Gallay, *Indian Slave Trade*, 315–44, makes similar points.

11. Ethridge and Hudson, "Early Historic Transformations," 42–43.

12. Ibid., 43–44. For the internal workings of this factionalism during the Historic Period, see Champagne, *Social Order*, and for the early eighteenth century, see Hahn "Invention of the Creek Nation."

13. Ethridge and Hudson, "Early Historic Transformations," 44. For Brims's political career, see Hahn, "Invention of the Creek Nation," 104–5, 115–25.

14. Hawkins, *Letters*, 1:297–98; Bartram, *Travels through North and South Carolina*, 330–31.

15. Gatschet, *Migration Legend*; Hawkins, *Letters*, 1:326–27. Scholars are beginning to reevaluate southeastern Indian migration myths for what they can tell us about the early colonial experience of the southern Indians. For instance, Jeter, "From Prehistory through Protohistory," 216–17, proposes that Quapaw migration legends that tell of an eastern migration and split at the Mississippi River may reflect Quapaw origins in the Ohio Valley and an early Historic Period migration west, as they fled Iroquois

slave raiding. Hahn, "Invention of the Creek Nation," 16–20, offers the Cusseta migration myth as a piece of historical evidence for a common origin for the Cowetas and Cussetas.

16. Knight, "Formation of the Creeks," 379–82, 386, first identified these provinces as the nucleus of the Creek coalescence. Worth, "Lower Creeks," and Waselkov and Smith, "Upper Creek Archaeology," summarize the current thought on and the archaeological evidence for the formation of the Creeks. Hahn, "Invention of the Creek Nation," picks up the story just at coalescence and tracks the beginnings of the Creek Confederacy as a political entity.

17. Ethridge and Hudson, "Early Historic Transformations," 40–41; Knight, "Formation of the Creeks," 373–92; Galloway, *Choctaw Genesis*, 393–420; Waselkov and Smith, "Upper Creek Archaeology," 244–48. For a history of the rise and fall of this protohistoric chiefdom, see Marvin Smith, *Coosa*.

18. Waselkov and Smith, "Upper Creek Archaeology," 250–55.

19. Ibid., 248–49, 255–56.

20. Hahn, "Invention of the Creek Nation," offers the first detailed history of the early years of the Creek Confederacy, from 1670–1763; Hahn chronicles the decline of Apalachicola and the ascendancy of Coweta and Cusseta.

21. Braley, *Yuchi Town*; Worth, "Lower Creeks," 268–74. Hahn, "Invention of the Creek Nation," 39–43, tentatively suggests that the people of Cusseta and Coweta were the descendants of the Late Mississippian town of Casiste on the lower Coosa River.

22. Worth, "Lower Creeks," 278–79; Crane, *Southern Frontier*, 36; Hahn, "Invention of the Creek Nation," 69–76.

23. Worth, "Lower Creeks," 286–91.

24. Swanton first attempted to put some order on our understanding of the social and political organization of the Creek Confederacy; see Swanton, *Social Organization*. Swanton, of course, did not have the benefit of understanding the origins of the Creek Confederacy or the internal factionalism characteristic of the Historic Period coalescent societies; hence, although his work offers much in identifying the various pieces that made up the Creek Confederacy, he does not place them into a historical and structural framework. Champagne, *Social Order*, shows how the internal factionalism of the Creek Confederacy during the Historic Period was largely town based, as Swanton had recognized, but Champagne further asserts that the political structure was, as a coalescent society, fluid, situational, and a highly adaptive response to European territorial demands, although Champagne understands the Upper and Lower divisions to have been important regional affiliations until Removal. Hahn, "Invention of the Creek Nation," extends Champagne's observations back into the early-eighteenth-century Creek Confederacy.

25. Muskogean is divided into Western and Eastern Muskogean. The Western Muskogean languages are Choctaw and Chickasaw. For an overview of languages among the southern Indians, see Crawford, "Southeastern Indian Languages," and Haas, "Classification." Much linguistic work has been done with contemporary Muskogean, and dictionaries are available for the some of the languages; see Sylestine, Hardy, and Montler, *Dictionary of the Alabama Language*; Jack B. Martin, *Dictionary of Creek/*

Muskogee; and Kimball et al., *Koasati Dictionary*. For an overview of Indian languages, see Mithun, *Languages of Native North America*.

26. Gatschet, *Migration Legend*, 118; Hawkins, *Letters*, 2:488; Swan, "Position and State," 259–60; Swanton, *Social Organization*, 248; Adair, *Adair's History*, 285; Woodward, *Reminiscences*, 9–16.

27. The linguistic complexity of the historic Creek Confederacy has yet to be sorted out by scholars, and we do not know what, if anything, the internal divisions between Creek and non-Creek speakers meant within the confederacy; however, there are hints that it was an important distinction. For instance, Bartram says that Creek speakers called non-Creek speakers "stinkards," a term that, according to Bartram, denoted a secondary place in Creek society; see Bartram, *Bartram on the Southeastern Indians*, 461. Stiggins states that only Creek speakers could speak in council; see Stiggins, *Creek Indian History*, 37. Hawkins states that the "remains of several tribes" seldom spoke in council and had no voice in the sale of land; see Hawkins, *Letters*, 2:488.

28. The Mobilian trade jargon was first identified in Crawford, "Southeastern Indian Languages," 45–47, and Haas, "What Is Mobilian?" The most comprehensive examination of it is Drechsel, *Mobilian Jargon*.

29. The borders between the Indians and Europeans and later Americans have been only partially examined. In 1899 Royce compiled a volume for the Bureau of American Ethnology outlining the general boundaries of Indian land cessions in the United States, including those in the South; see Royce, *Indian Land Cessions*. As part of a land claims settlement, Doster and Starrett closely examined the Creek Confederacy's southern boundary with Spain and the Seminoles; see Doster, *Creek Indians and Their Florida Lands*, and Starrett, *Appraisal Report*.

30. Territorial governor William Blount and other territorial leaders declared statehood in 1795 and began to draw up the state constitution and elect officials. The U.S. Congress did not officially admit Tennessee into the union until 1796.

31. I have chosen to refer to the people who made up the Creek Confederacy as Creeks instead of Muskogeans or Muscogulges—the latter terms have been used historically and in some writings on the Creeks—because "Creeks" is the most common reference in the historical documents, it is the term that contemporary people recognize, and it is the name contemporary Creek Indians use. On the other hand, Joel W. Martin, in *Sacred Revolt*, 6–13, argues for using the term "Muskogees" instead of "Creeks" because "Creeks" was a colonial designator that Euro-Americans used to group a diversity of people and then to rationalize violence against this group as a whole.

32. Peter H. Wood, "Changing Population," 60.

Chapter Three

1. This area is taken from the calculations in Jay Johnson, "Chickasaws," tab. 4.1, pp. 94–95.

2. Gatschet, *Migration Legend*, 58–62; Swanton, *Early History*, 215.

3. For Paleoindian and Early Archaic settlement patterns in the Southeast, see Anderson and Sassaman, *Paleoindian and Early Archaic*, 16–83. For the Woodland Period, see Anderson and Mainfort, *Woodland Southeast*.

4. Gosse, *Letters*, 109.

5. Gatschet, *Migration Legend*, 41, 131, 140; Hawkins, *Creek Country*, 31, 32; Read, *Indian Place Names*, 47.

6. The streams still exist; all except the Flint River were dammed in the twentieth century, and the eighteenth-century river valleys described here are now predominantly underwater.

7. Gatschet, *Migration Legend*, 149; Hawkins, "Letters of Benjamin Hawkins," 76; Read, *Indian Place Names*, 43.

8. Hawkins "Letters of Benjamin Hawkins," 50; Hawkins, *Letters*, 1:307; Read, *Indian Place Names*, 14.

9. Hawkins, *Letters*, 1:26.

10. Hawkins, *Creek Country*, 38.

11. Charles Hudson, *Southeastern Indians*, 324–25, 344–45.

12. Fenneman, *Physiography of Eastern United States*, 126–31.

13. Swanton, *Early History*, 270; Hawkins, *Creek Country*, 39; Gatschet, *Migration Legend*, 150.

14. Read, *Indian Place Names* 78–79; Hawkins, *Creek Country*, 54.

15. Hawkins, *Creek Country*, 47; Gatschet, *Migration Legend*, 143; Read, *Indian Place Names*, 60.

16. Read, *Indian Place Names*, 77.

17. Swanton, *Early History*, 247; Owens, "Indian Tribes and Towns," 150; Read, *Indian Place Names*, 13.

18. Hawkins, *Creek Country*, 43; Gatschet, *Migration Legend*, 140; Goff, Utley, and Hemperley, *Placenames of Georgia*, 192.

19. Read, *Indian Place Names*, 19.

20. Fenneman, *Physiography of Eastern United States*, 126–31.

21. Swan, "Position and State," 256.

22. Ibid., 257. These rivers figure in recent social histories; see Willoughby, *Flowing through Time*, and Jackson, *Rivers of History*.

23. Bartram, *Naturalist's Edition*, 258.

24. Gregory Waselkov, personal communication, 1994; Hawkins, *Letters*, 1:287–88; Swan, "Position and State," 253, 256.

25. Walsh, Burkhead, and Williams, "Southeastern Freshwater Fishes." For information on the conservation of southeastern fishes, contact Southeastern Fishes Council at ⟨http://www.flmnh.ufl.edu/fish/Organizations/SFC⟩.

26. Woodward, *Reminiscences*, 47. Parades and Plante also report that their informants from the Poarch Band related that in the 1860s and 1870s people from this group made annual fishing expeditions to the Tensaw and Alabama Rivers. These trips would last for a week or more, and they caught mostly rockfish and trout; see Parades and Plante, "Economics, Politics, and the Subjugation," 26. Shad are a saltwater fish related to herring; there are many varieties, and many spawn in freshwater rivers, which accounts for their presence in the Ocmulgee River.

27. Hawkins, *Letters*, 1:16; Gatschet, *Migration Legend*, 137.

28. Hawkins, *Letters*, 1:214.

29. Richard Thomas, "His Book," 489.

30. William Hill to Jonathan Halstead, March 21, 1805, Entry No. 42, NA, RG 75.

31. Hawkins, *Letters*, 1:8; Charles Hudson, *Southeastern Indians*, 84. The southeastern Indians also used roots of the devil's shoestring for fish poison. Parades and Plante, "Economics, Politics, and the Subjugation," 26, notes that contemporary Creeks of the Poarch Band are familiar with using fish poisons.

32. Hawkins, *Letters*, 1:307; the fishes listed here are large groupings of salt- and freshwater fish, of which there are many varieties.

33. Odum, *Ecology*, 49.

34. This idea for prehistoric southeastern Indians was first presented in Larson, "Functional Considerations."

35. Aquilani, "Bird Communities of Holly Springs National Forest."

36. Engstrom, Kirkman, and Mitchell, "Natural History of the Fire Forest."

37. Indians had been using burning as a hunting and forest management technique for perhaps millennia. In recent years, ecologists, anthropologists, environmental historians, and archaeologists have turned much scholarly attention to the use of fire by the Indians and how extensive and prolonged burning may have resulted in particular forest covers. For a good summary of the literature, see Krech, *Ecological Indian*, 101–22. For a good summary of the ecological effects of firing and other disturbances on the eastern woodlands, see Whitney, *From Coastal Wilderness*, 53–97.

38. Silver, *New Face*, 60–62.

39. Captain Basil Hall, *Travels*, 3:250. The Manuscripts Department at the Lilly Library at Indiana University holds 169 original drawings by Hall; forty of these were published in Captain Basil Hall, *Forty Etchings*.

40. Gosse, *Letters*, 118.

41. Ibid.

42. Ibid., 112.

43. Gatschet, *Migration Legend*, 131. There was a Chehaw village on Kitchofonee Creek named Otellewhoyaunau, or Hurricane Town, presumably because it marked an area hit by a tornado at some time; see Hawkins, *Creek Country*, 61.

44. Gosse, *Letters*, 179.

45. Weakley et al., "Southeastern Mixed Forests."

46. Loucks et al., "Appalachian Mixed Mesophytic Forest" and "Appalachian–Blue Ridge Forest."

47. Dinerstein et al., "Southeastern Conifer Forest."

48. Travelers' accounts of white-tailed deer are mixed. Hawkins claimed that one could pass through all of Creek territory without seeing a single deer; see Hawkins, *Letters*, 1:288. Bartram made a similar report; see Bartram, *Travels through North and South Carolina*, 135. Yet almost all people passing through Creek territory, including Bartram and Hawkins, ate fresh venison on the path, and Creek hunters still traded deerskins.

49. Gosse, *Letters*, 223; Bartram, *Naturalist's Edition*, 176–78.

50. Bartram, *Naturalist's Edition*, 181–83; Charles Hudson, *Southeastern Indians*, 128–30.

51. Bartram, *Naturalist's Edition*, 297.

52. Gosse, *Letters*, 219. Gosse was particularly interested in insects, and his writings

have some of the best descriptions of southern insects and their habitats of any eighteenth-century naturalist.

53. Bartram, *Naturalist's Edition*, 243.

54. Actually, the full environmental history of each of these regions is still incomplete. In this reconstruction, I have relied on some modern tabulations of species composition and compared those with the data gleaned largely from Hawkins, Bartram, and Gosse.

55. The paramount chiefdom of Coosa stretched into part of the Ridge and Valley province of northeast Alabama; see Marvin Smith, *Coosa*, 1–12.

56. Hunt, *Natural Regions*, 152; Delcourt et al., "Prehistoric Human Use of Fire"; Loucks et al., "Appalachian Mixed Mesophytic Forest" and "Appalachian–Blue Ridge Forest."

57. Bartram, for instance, has much information about Cherokee territory in South Carolina, eastern Tennessee, and western North Carolina.

58. Hawkins, *Letters*, 1:1–12.

59. Bartram, *Naturalist's Edition*, 211; Charles Hudson, *Southeastern Indians*, 341–42.

60. Hawkins, *Letters*, 1:1–12. Hemperley (assisted by Goff) reconstructed Hawkins's route from South Carolina to Creek Country. Hawkins traveled west along the Upper Trading Path to its intersection with the Alabama Road, where he turned south; thus he entered Creek Country from the northwest and through the southernmost portion of the Ridge and Valley province. See Hawkins, "Trip across Georgia," and Goff, "Path to Oakfuskee."

61. Hawkins, *Letters*, 1:306.

62. Ibid., 303.

63. Creek place-names also had an equal share of social as well as environmental references; see Ethridge, "Environmental Look."

64. Hawkins, *Letters*, 1:303.

65. Ibid.

66. Goff, "Great Pine Barrens."

67. Innerarity, "Creek Debtors," 72.

68. Captain Basil Hall, *Travels*, 3:175.

69. Bartram, *Naturalist's Edition*, 110.

70. Captain Basil Hall, *Travels*, 3:256; Bartram, *Naturalist's Edition*, 110.

71. Vaughan, "Apalachicola Bluffs."

72. In 1997 the longleaf pine was made the state tree of Alabama.

73. Hawkins, *Letters*, 1:286; Bartram, *Naturalist's Edition*, 119; Crofton, "Flora and Fauna," 2.

74. Bartram, *Naturalist's Edition*, 264. According to Harper, Bartram here is probably referring to the hooded pitcher plant; see ibid., 620.

75. Ibid., 108–10.

76. Dinerstein et al., "Southeastern Conifer Forest"; Joseph W. Jones Ecological Research Center, "Field Guide"; Brewer, "Current and Presettlement Tree Species," 342.

77. Bartram, *Naturalist's Edition*, 241, 242, 248, 252; Dinerstein et al., "Southeastern Conifer Forest."

78. Gosse, *Letters*, 112.

79. Hunt, *Physiography of the United States*, 103.

80. Hawkins, *Creek Country*, 21.

81. Read, *Indian Place Names*, 49; Read, "Indian Stream Names," 131.

82. Bartram, *Naturalist's Edition*, 59.

83. Ibid., 59, 199.

84. Wrens, warblers, flycatchers, and sparrows are groups of birds with a large number of varieties.

85. Dinerstein et al., "Southeastern Conifer Forest"; Joseph W. Jones Ecological Research Center, "Field Guide"; Alabama Public Television, "Long Leaf Ecosystem"; Crofton, "Flora and Fauna"; Engstrom, Kirkman, and Mitchell, "Natural History of the Fire Forest"; Dodd, "Reptiles and Amphibians."

86. Starrett, *Appraisal Report*, 47. In prehistoric times, however, the Coastal Plain was occupied; see Kirkland, "Ten Millennia of Human Land Use."

87. Starrett, *Appraisal Report*, 118.

88. Joseph W. Jones Ecological Research Center, "Field Guide"; Dinerstein et al., "Southeastern Conifer Forest"; Nelson, "Original Forests," 393–94; Hunt, *Physiography of the United States*, 101–15; Hawkins, "Benjamin Hawkins' Trip"; Hawkins, *Letters*, 1:285–316; Bartram, *Naturalist's Edition*, 248, 253–54.

89. Brewer, "Current and Presettlement Tree Species," 342.

90. Hawkins, *Letters*, 1–61; Benjamin Hawkins's Viatory, Force Collection, LC.

91. Bartram, *Travels through North and South Carolina*, 56.

92. Gosse, *Letters*, 117.

93. Bartram, *Travels through North and South Carolina*, 56.

94. G. J. N. Wilson, *Early History of Jackson County*, 36.

95. Read, *Indian Place Names*, 78; Hawkins, *Creek Country*, 38; Gatschet, *Migration Legend*, 139.

96. Hawkins, *Letters*, 1:313.

97. Ibid., 288; Bartram, *Naturalist's Edition*, 254. I have not located this grove on a modern map, but according to the descriptions, it probably occurred in or just below the Fall Line ecotone in central Alabama.

98. Bartram, *Naturalist's Edition*, 254.

99. Anniston Museum, "Oak-Hickory-Pine Forest"; Bartram, *Naturalist's Edition*, 248; Gosse, *Letters*, 115–16, 143–44; Hawkins, *Letters*, 1:285–316.

100. Bartram, *Naturalist's Edition*, 241, 242, 248, 252.

101. Hawkins, *Letters*, 1:287.

102. Fenneman, *Physiography of Eastern United States*, 102–4.

103. Bartram, *Naturalist's Edition*, 252, 626.

104. Fenneman, *Physiography of Eastern United States*, 67–71; Hunt, *Physiography of the United States*, 102–3.

105. Hawkins, *Letters*, 1:287.

106. Gatschet, *Migration Legend*, 137; USDA Forest Service, "Species."

107. Ethridge, "Southeast," 17–18; Gatschet, *Migration Legend*, 137; Charles Hudson, *Southeastern Indians*, 384–85. Hill's *Weaving New Worlds* is an intricate and compelling history of basketry among the Cherokees.

108. Swanton, *Indians of the Southeastern United States*, 296.

109. Hawkins, *Letters*, 1:301. The reed described in the historical literature was probably switch cane (*A. gigantea* spp. *tecta*), a subspecies of *Arundinaria gigantea*; there is one other recognized subspecies, *A. gigantea* spp. *macrosperma*; see USDA Forest Service, "Species."

110. Young, "Topographical Memoir," 32.

111. Read, *Indian Place Names*, 11, 23.

112. Hawkins, *Letters*, 1:297.

113. Ibid., 314.

114. Bartram, *Naturalist's Edition*, 147.

115. Gosse, *Letters*, 135; Benjamin Hawkins's Viatory, Force Collection, LC.

116. Woodward, *Reminiscences*, 24.

117. USDA Forest Service, "Species."

118. Hawkins, *Letters*, 1:25.

119. Read, *Indian Place Names*, 22.

120. Hawkins, *Letters*, 1:314.

121. Ibid., 293.

122. Ibid., 297.

123. Ibid., 291.

124. Ibid., 294–96.

125. Ibid., 296.

126. USDA Forest Service, "Species."

127. Silver, *New Face*, 22.

128. Rostlund, "Geographic Range"; Hatley, "Tallapoosa Landscape," 85–87; Chapman and Shea, "Archaeobotanical Record," 83.

129. Prehistoric period agriculture has been of primary interest to archaeologists for many years. See Scarry, *Foraging and Farming*, for information on Woodland Period agriculture. Smith, Cowan, and Hoffman, *Rivers of Change*, tracks the beginnings of intensive corn agriculture during the Early Mississippi Period.

130. This calculation is taken from a comparison of detailed day-by-day journals of Young, "Topographical Memoir"; Tatum, "Topographical Notes"; and Benjamin Hawkins's Viatory, Force Collection, LC.

131. Hawkins, *Letters*, 1:310.

132. Bartram, *Naturalist's Edition*, 247.

133. Bartram, *Travels through North and South Carolina*, 307.

134. Adair, *Adair's History*, 39.

135. Hawkins, *Letters*, 1:285.

Chapter Four

1. Hatley, "Tallapoosa Landscape," first noted that the river valleys in Creek country were landscaped.

2. The term "ecological Indian" is taken from Krech, *Ecological Indian*. Krech (pp.

15–28) also discusses the assumptions and stereotypes behind this characterization. As Krech notes (pp. 20–27), the "ecological Indian" has also been a fundamental assumption of much Indian scholarship, although a challenge to this assumption was issued as early as 1981 in Krech's argument with Calvin Martin's *Keepers of the Game*; see Krech, *Indians, Animals, and the Fur Trade*. Charles Hudson, in Krech's volume, was one of the first scholars to point out the environmental impact, at the hands of Indians, of the deerskin trade in the southeastern United States; see Charles Hudson, "Why the Southeastern Indians Slaughtered Deer." White and Cronon have also stressed the importance of dismantling this stereotype because, they have argued, it dehumanizes Indians as well as fosters an ahistorical conception of Indians; see Richard White, "Indian Peoples and the Natural World"; Cronon and White, "Indians in the Land"; and White and Cronon, "Ecological Change."

3. Shimer, *Field Guide to Landforms*, 170–82.

4. Bartram, *Travels through North and South Carolina*, 316.

5. Shimer, *Field Guide to Landforms*, 179–81. These landforms are commonly abbreviated as To for the active floodplain, T1 for the first terrace, T2 for the second terrace, and so on.

6. Hatley, "Tallapoosa Landscape," 82, 85–88; Waselkov, "Changing Strategies," 180–88.

7. Hatley, "Tallapoosa Landscape," 88; Hawkins, *Letters*, 1:21, 24, 25, 288; Bartram, *Travels through North and South Carolina*, 310–16.

8. Hatley, "Tallapoosa Landscape," 99.

9. Silver, *New Face*, 57.

10. Hawkins, *Letters*, 1:292.

11. Waselkov, "Changing Strategies," 188–90; Hally, "Overview of Lamar Culture"; Foster, "Long Term Average Rate," 118–82. The question of fuelwood has been of some interest to archaeologists since it would have been a limiting factor in town and household locations.

12. Waselkov, "Historic Creek Architectural Adaptations"; Braund, "Guardians of Tradition," 245.

13. Hawkins, *Letters*, 2:554.

14. Ibid., 1:289–316.

15. This figure is taken from a census done after the Red Stick War; see Letterbook 1814, Graham Papers, NCDAH. Joseph Graham was the quartermaster for the American army during the Red Stick War. After the war, Graham oversaw the provisioning of Creek war refugees. He tallied the number of men, women, and children for any town requesting provisions.

16. Hawkins, *Letters*, 1:307.

17. For an early report on some of the archaeological investigations of this site, see Wiley and Sears, "Kasihta Site." Since then, archaeologists have been involved in more current investigations at Cusseta, and their reports are forthcoming; Thomas Foster, personal communication, 2002.

18. Hawkins, *Letters*, 1:309–11.

19. B. Lincoln, Cyrus Griffin, and D. Humphreys to the Secretary of War, November 20, 1789, in Cochran, *New American State Papers*, 92.

20. Swan estimated that a small town had about 20 to 50 gun men and the large towns had about 200; see Swan, "Position and State," 262.

21. Hawkins, *Letters*, 1:310–11.

22. Ibid., 285–86, 307–12.

23. In the only such study done to date using witness tree data from the land plat surveys taken around the time of the Removal (1830s), Foster reconstructs, with a high resolution, the forests around ten Lower Creek towns. This is a fine microlevel study that bears replicating for other areas for which this kind of data is available; see Foster, "Long Term Average Rate," 118–73.

24. Hawkins, *Letters*, 1:307–12, 309.

25. Hatley, "Tallapoosa Landscape," 89; Hatley, "Cherokee Women Farmers," 39.

26. Bartram, however, does not explicitly state that these are maintained groves. He describes these as "clumps," which would indicate that they are discrete features; see Bartram, *Travels through North and South Carolina*, 310–17.

27. Richard Thomas, "His Book," 477.

28. Bartram, *Naturalist's Edition*, 25, 544–45. This mound site has not been found; see Bartram, *Bartram on the Southeastern Indians*, 38–39, 232. In fact, archaeologists believe that Indians may have been altering their environments to increase hickory and acorn nut masts as early as the Middle Archaic Period (5500–3000 B.C.); see Gardner, "Ecological Structure," 167, 171, 174.

29. Gremillion, "Paleoethnobotany of Native Historic Communities," 8; Hally, "Plant Preservation," 733, reports the nuts were used as a source of fuel at the protohistoric Little Egypt site in northwest Georgia.

30. Gremillion, "Fusihatchee," 111–12. The record is too incomplete to draw any conclusions as to what proportion of the overall diet each contributed.

31. Bartram, *Bartram on the Southeastern Indians*, 39.

32. Hawkins, *Letters*, 1:50.

33. Charles Hudson, *Southeastern Indians*, 301. Hawkins, *Letters*, 1:301, describes the preparation of acorn oil, and Bartram, *Bartram on the Southeastern Indians*, 39, describes the preparation of hickory oil. For a complete discussion on the southeastern Indian use of nut oil, see Battle, "Domestic Use of Oil."

34. Bartram, *Bartram on the Southeastern Indians*, 39. In fact, one can make hickory milk quite easily, and it can be used much like cream.

35. Charles Hudson, *Southeastern Indians*, 300–301.

36. Hawkins, *Letters*, 1:313.

37. Bartram, *Bartram on the Southeastern Indians*, 107, 260.

38. Hawkins, *Letters*, 1:314.

39. Bartram, *Travels through North and South Carolina*, 312.

40. Fenneman, *Physiography of Eastern United States*, 67, 68, 73, 76–77.

41. Hawkins, *Letters*, 1:315.

42. Ibid.

43. Ibid., 315–16; Swanton, *Early History*, 172–75.

44. Quoted in Swanton, *Early History*, 262.

45. Ibid., 263; Hawkins, *Letters*, 1:316.

46. Hawkins, *Letters*, 1:315–16.

47. Ibid., 313; Timothy Barnard to James Seagrove, December 18, 1798, Letters of Timothy Barnard, GDAH, 37. Barnard reported on the Harrison episode to the Indian agent James Seagrove and to Thomas Pickering of the State of Georgia War Office; see Letters of Timothy Barnard, October–December 1795, GDAH.

48. Fenneman, *Physiography of Eastern United States*, 76–77.

49. Hawkins, *Letters*, 1:313–14.

50. Ibid.

51. Ibid., 316.

52. Ibid., 314–15.

53. Ibid., 315.

54. Ibid., 314–16; Swan, "Position and State," 261.

55. Edmund Shackelford to Ann or Francis Shackelford, November 26, 1813, Manuscript No. 4911, Swanton Collection, SI.

56. Hawkins, *Letters*, 2:454; Commissioners of Indian Affairs, *Treaties*, 87–90.

57. Hawkins, *Letters*, 2:454.

58. Ibid., 2:551–52, 554.

59. The number of slaves is estimated from Benjamin Hawkins's Estate, Letters of Benjamin Hawkins, GDAH. Henri, *Southern Indians*, 317, uses the same document to derive seventy-four as the specific number. See also Hawkins, *Letters*, 2:544; Mauelshagen and Davis, *Partners*, 17, 29, 37, 57, 68. The Moravian accounts in Mauelshagen and Davis, *Partners*, give many details of the day-to-day life at the Creek Agency.

60. Hawkins, *Letters*, 2:532.

61. Ibid., 559.

62. Ibid., 543.

63. Shown on Schumann's 1810 "Plan of the Creek Agency," published in Mauelshagen and Davis, *Partners*.

64. Hawkins, *Letters*, 2:558.

65. Ibid., 1:287.

66. Fenneman, *Physiography of Eastern United States*, 67–71.

67. Stiggins, *Creek Indian History*, 36, 63; Charles Hudson, *Southeastern Indians*, 369–70; Swanton, *Indians of the Southeastern United States*, 185; Swanton, *Creek Religion*, 503–7; Hawkins, *Letters*, 1:290.

68. Fenneman, *Physiography of Eastern United States*, 66; Hawkins, *Letters*, 1:19, 291.

69. Hawkins, *Letters*, 1:291. The Tallapoosa River is dammed today; however, below the dam the falls can still be seen, although the amount of water rushing over them is regulated, of course.

70. Ibid., 19, 291.

71. The Ridge and Valley province extends into this area. The southern portion of the Appalachian Plateau enters present-day Alabama to the west.

72. Tallassee has received some archaeological attention, which is reported in Knight and Smith, "Big Tallassee."

73. Hawkins, *Letters*, 1:20, 291.

74. Ibid., 20. There are a great many varieties of perch, both freshwater and marine; red horse, or red drum, is an estuarine fish found usually in brackish or salt water, but it can live permanently in fresh water.

75. Hawkins, *Letters*, 1:290.

76. Ibid., 22–29, 290–99.

77. Ibid., 292.

78. Bartram, *Bartram on the Southeastern Indians*, 181–83.

79. Swan, "Position and State," 262.

80. Knight excavated a western portion of Tuckabatchee, where he found approximately nineteen Creek households dating to the Tallapoosa Phase (A.D. 1715–1836); see Knight, *Tukabatchee*, 59–60, 63–64, 109–68.

81. There is much documentary and archaeological evidence for this movement out of towns, but this evidence has not yet been thoroughly compared and synthesized. Some of the most fine-grained documentary evidence can be found in Tatum, "Topographical Notes"; Hawkins, *Letters*, 1:288–316; Benjamin Hawkins's Viatory, Force Collection, LC; and Hawkins, *Sketch*. The archaeological evidence can be found in Benson, *Cultural Resources Survey*; Waselkov, "Changing Strategies"; Waselkov, *Lower Tallapoosa*; Holland, "Mid-Eighteenth Century Indian Village"; Knight, *Tukabatchee*, 9–19; Ledbetter and Braley, *Archaeological and Historical Investigations*; Waselkov, *Coosa River Valley Archaeology*; Waselkov, Cottier, and Sheldon, *Archaeological Excavations*; Mistovich and Zeanah, *Intensive Phase II Survey*; Mistovich and Knight, *Excavations at Four Sites*; Marvin Smith, *Historic Period Indian Archaeology*, 78; and White et al., *Archaeological Survey at Lake Seminole*. In contrast, the archaeological evidence for sixteenth-century northwest Georgia Indians shows the towns to have been tightly nucleated; see Hally, "Little Egypt" and "King Site."

82. Romans, *Concise Natural History*, 96; Bartram, *Bartram on the Southeastern Indians*, 157. For the archaeological evidence, see Sheldon, "Historic Creek 'Summer' Houses"; Allan D. Meyers, "Household Organization"; Silvia Mueller, "Intrasite Settlement." This domestic architecture was a recent innovation, coinciding with the deerskin trade era. Around the end of the seventeenth century, Creek houses generally changed from single, semisubterranean, wattle-and-daub structures to these aboveground compounds; see Waselkov, "Macon Trading House"; Waselkov and Smith, "Upper Creek Archaeology," 253–55; Worth, "Lower Creeks," 284–85; Pluckhahn, "Tarver," 360–67; Mason, "Eighteenth Century Culture Change," 76–91.

83. The Creeks were polygamous, and occasionally a man had more than one wife. By and large, however, the Creeks practiced serial monogamy, and most men had only one wife at a time.

84. See Charles Hudson, *Southeastern Indians*, 184–97, 261–62; Knight, *Tukabatchee*, 119; Braund, "Guardians of Tradition," 240–41, 243, 250–51. Braund, "Guardians of Tradition," and Saunt, *New Order*, 139–63, explore the tensions between women and men as their social and economic roles changed with the plan for civilization; however, a comprehensive Creek gender analysis for the Historic Period has yet to be done. For a recent analysis of gender among another southeastern Indian group, see Perdue, *Cherokee Women*.

85. Charles Hudson, *Southeastern Indians*, 188–92.

86. For a full discussion of matrilineal descent among the southeastern Indians, see ibid., 194–202.

87. Ibid., 200.

88. Swan, "Position and State," 271–72. White commentators on southeastern Indian life noted the absence of deformed and crippled Indians. Perdue, *Cherokee Women*, 33, states this may have been due to selective infanticide by Cherokee women, who had the right to abandon unwanted newborns.

89. DeBrahm, *DeBrahm's Report*, 110; Bartram, *Bartram on the Southeastern Indians*, 156.

90. Waselkov, "Macon Trading House," 195; Marvin Smith, *Historic Period Indian Archaeology*, 68; Hally, "Making Sense of Aboriginal House Form," 101–9.

91. Captain Basil Hall, *Travels*, 3:290; Hodgson, *Letters*, 143–55; Levasseur, *Lafayette in America*, 73. However, few of these have been found archaeologically; see Waselkov and Smith, "Upper Creek Archaeology," 254–55.

92. Knight, *Tukabatchee*, 116–18. More recently, Allan D. Meyers, "Household Organization," examined the refuse disposal at a historic Creek site and found patterns similar to those presented by Knight. These households echo patterns revealed in Mississippi Period households. Hally intensively investigated households from the Mississippian Period King site and the Little Egypt site, both in northwest Georgia. He found ceramic and lithic concentrations and distributions, perhaps also reflecting symbolic opposition between activities that were probably gender divisions. Hally also found household compounds at the King site in northwest Georgia remarkably similar to historic Creek household compounds; see Hally, "Little Egypt Site"; Hally, "Domestic Architecture"; Hally, "King Site"; and Hally and Langford, *Mississippi Period Archaeology*. The extent of continuity of Mississippi Period traits into the Historic Period is an open question, but the evidence on households, while still tentative, is suggestive because it might be that one of the most basic, fundamental aspects of southeastern Indian life, the domestic unit, survived the upheaval of European disease and, even more interesting, could be successfully adapted to a capitalist market economic system. For a full discussion on continuity and change among Historic Period Creek households, especially as regards distribution of status items, see Wesson, "Households and Hegemony."

93. Pickett, *History of Alabama*, 96; Swan, "Position and State," 270. For archaeological confirmation, see Braley, "Historic Period Indian Archaeology," and Marvin Smith, *Historic Period Indian Archaeology*, 75.

94. Swan, "Position and State," 270. White people often remarked that Creek houses were flimsy and expedient; see DeBrahm, *DeBrahm's Report*, 110; Von Reck, *Von Reck's Voyage*, 41; Romans, *Concise Natural History*, 89, 96. Wattle and daub, as a construction material, was readily available, and these structures were easy to erect. In the southern climate, and especially in periods of heavy rainfall, Creek houses required constant repairs, such as reroofing the bark, replacing rotten or termite-eaten wooden poles, and repacking daub that washed out with the rain or cracked in the heat and fell off. Still, the repairs did not take long or require intensive labor. These structures, as well as the corncribs, storehouses, and summer structures, did eventually wear out, and fires were a daily hazard.

95. Knight, *Tukabatchee*, 41–43, 107–8.

96. Hawkins, *Letters*, 1:33, 164.

97. For a discussion of Indian countrymen among the early-nineteenth-century Cherokees, see Jurgelski, "Strangers among Them."

98. Hawkins, *Letters*, 1:316, 301, 235.

99. Ibid.

100. Ibid., 25.

101. Ibid., 186.

102. Ibid., 21.

103. Ibid., 22.

104. Ibid., 316.

105. Saunt, *New Order*, 70–75.

106. Hawkins, *Letters*, 1:298.

107. Ibid., 292–93.

108. Ibid., 17, 168.

109. Ibid., 2:603.

110. Hawkins's Journal on the Treaty of Colerain, in Cochran, *New American State Papers*, 137.

111. Hawkins, *Letters*, 2:554.

112. Timothy Barnard to Benjamin Hawkins, October 10, 1802, Letters of Timothy Barnard, GDAH.

113. October 9, 1801, Entry No. 1, RG 75, NA.

114. Hawkins, *Letters*, 2:580.

115. Ibid., 1:355, 2:554.

116. Ibid., 2:554.

117. Ibid., 554, 603.

118. Ibid., 1:355, 2:559.

119. Ibid., 1:355.

120. Ibid., 2:592.

121. Ibid., 1:293.

122. Ibid., 23, 293.

123. Ibid., 293–94.

124. Hawkins, *Creek Country*, 32; Read, "Indian Stream Names," 130; Gatschet, *Migration Legend*, 131.

125. Hawkins, *Letters*, 1:294–95.

126. Bartram, *Naturalist's Edition*, 251.

127. Hawkins, *Letters*, 1:295; Bartram, *Naturalist's Edition*, 251.

128. Hawkins, *Letters*, 1:295.

129. Ibid., 297; Waselkov, "Introduction," viii–ix; Daniel H. Thomas, *Fort Toulouse*, 1–3, 25–27.

130. Daniel H. Thomas, *Fort Toulouse*, 1–3; Waselkov, "Introduction," xx; Hawkins, *Letters*, 1:297. Fort Toulouse has had some archaeological investigations; for a summary of these, see Waselkov, "Introduction." It is also now the Fort Toulouse/Fort Jackson Park, and it has been designated a National Historic Landmark. The park has a replica of the 1751 French fort and a partial reconstruction of the fort built at the site

by Andrew Jackson during the Red Stick War, as well as other historical features. The park's website is ⟨http:\\www.wetumpka.al.us/fort.html⟩.

131. Hawkins, *Letters*, 1:297; Bartram, *Bartram on the Southeastern Indians*, 100.

132. Waselkov, "Introduction," xi.

133. Hawkins, *Letters*, 1:297.

134. Ibid., 297–98.

135. Swanton, *Early History*, 200, 274–77.

136. Ibid., 200.

137. Hawkins, *Letters*, 1:24, 25, 297, 298; Swanton, *Early History*, 242.

138. Hawkins, *Letters*, 1:24, 25.

139. Ibid., 295.

140. Ibid., 23–26, 295–98.

141. Ibid., 295–96.

142. Ibid., 50, 296.

143. According to Silver, *New Face*, 179, "peavine" referred to a wild legume.

144. Hawkins, *Letters*, 1:296.

145. Ibid.

146. For a discussion on purity and balance among the southeastern Indians, see Charles Hudson, *Southeastern Indians*, 336–51.

147. Fenneman, *Physiography of Eastern United States*, 268, 274.

148. Hunt, *Physiography of the United States*, 173; Fenneman, *Physiography of Eastern United States*, 274; Alabama Department of Archives and History, "Official Symbols and Emblems of Alabama."

149. Hawkins, *Letters*, 1:16, 17, 299, 300, 305.

150. Waselkov and Smith, "Upper Creek Archaeology," 244–48; Hawkins, *Letters*, 1:299–300.

151. Hawkins, *Letters*, 1:299.

152. Ibid.

153. Gregory Waselkov, personal communication, 2001; Waselkov also does not think this moss has been analyzed for its salt content.

154. Hawkins, *Letters*, 1:299–300, 305–6.

155. Fenneman, *Physiography of Eastern United States*, 131–32; Hunt, *Physiography of the United States*, 168–73.

156. Hawkins, *Letters*, 1:302. For a social history of Oakfuskee during the mid-eighteenth century, see Piker, "Peculiar Connections."

157. Hawkins, *Letters*, 1:301–6.

158. Ibid., 304.

159. Ibid.

160. Ibid., 301–2.

Chapter Five

1. Euro-Americans at the time understood that the Creeks were never a homogenous group, and the historical documents contain much information on which groups made up the Creek Confederacy. Euro-Americans recognized the basis of their organ-

ization as being town based. However, the internal workings of Creek politics have been long in coming to light. Swanton first identified the internal factions within Historic Period Creek and other southeastern Indian societies; much of this is compiled in Swanton, *Indians of the Southeastern United States* and *Social Organization*. Crane, *Southern Frontier*, first noted the use of these factions for the southern Indians in playing the British, French, and Spanish off one another; see esp. 254–80. Anthropologists recognized the dual organization behind the "red" and "white" towns of the Creeks and other southeastern groups, although the full scope of this dual organization remains to be investigated; see Swanton, *Social Organization*, 156–66, 286–306; Haas, "Creek Inter-Town Relations"; and Charles Hudson, *Southeastern Indians*, 234–39. Green, in *Politics of Indian Removal*, was the first scholar to understand how these factions informed intratribal Creek politics during the Removal era. Scholars then linked the factionalism among southeastern Indians to the deerskin trade and argued that it was a workable mechanism for garnering good trade agreements; see Richard White, *Roots of Dependency*, 34–65; Waselkov, "Historic Creek Indian Responses"; and Braund, *Deerskins and Duffels*, 139–63, although Braund notes that the factionalism could also be a liability in international affairs. Not until Galloway's *Choctaw Genesis* did scholars see that this factionalism may in fact have been rooted in the formation of the societies as early as the early seventeenth century. Ethridge and Hudson also understand the Historic Period factionalism to have been a product of coalescence, but following an argument first formulated in Champagne, *Social Order*, 50–55, they assert that one of the forces behind this was the British trade system that fostered decentralization and hence pulled against any efforts by the southeastern Indians to reformulate along chiefdom (centralized) lines; see Ethridge and Hudson, "Early Historic Transformations." Hahn, in "Invention of the Creek Nation," also understands internal factionalism, which he argues was town and province based, to have been a highly adaptive mechanism for dealing with Europeans at this time and that the resulting political structure was a product of Creek and European interaction. For discussions on internal factionalism as an adaptation to the trade era, see Richard White, *Middle Ground*; Galloway, *Choctaw Genesis*; Galloway, "Confederacy as a Solution"; "Ougoula Tchetoka"; Ethridge and Hudson, "Early Historic Transformations"; Ethridge, "Chickasaw Factionalism"; and Wesson, "Households and Hegemony."

Scholars have also reconstructed other internal factions in Historic Period Indian societies. Perdue, in *Slavery and the Evolution*, first explored the class division of the métis elite among the Cherokees and identified them as a powerful political entity who controlled Cherokee politics in the early nineteenth century. Green, in *Politics of Indian Removal*, also understands there to have been a class division between wealthy and poor Creeks, with the wealthy controlling Creek politics, but he does not elaborate on the rise of this class consciousness. Joel W. Martin, in *Sacred Revolt*, tracks this consciousness during the years prior to the Red Stick War and argues that class divisions lay at the foundation of that civil strife. Saunt, in *New Order*, chronicles the rise of this class division and how those wealthy Creeks who constituted the upper class adopted a capitalist ideology as they took on new ideas about property and power; Saunt also argues that these elite came to dominate Creek political and legislative life. Finally, Braund, in "Guardians of Tradition," documents the gender divisions of the Historic

Creeks, and Saunt, in *New Order*, 143–51, 266–69, argues that by the turn of the nineteenth century, gender divisions had become quite acute and even hostile, as women lost economic ground in the trade era and attempted to regain some position with the plan for civilization.

2. Some of these institutions may have even existed during the Woodland era, prior to the formation of the chiefdoms of the late prehistoric era. They would have existed as lower-level institutions within the overarching chiefdom-level political order, and they would not necessarily have been in direct competition with chiefly authority. Such lower-level institutions could have survived the disintegration of the chiefdoms, and they would have been readily adaptable to a decentralized political order; see Ethridge and Hudson, "Early Historic Transformations," 43.

3. Ibid., 42.

4. Woodward, *Reminiscences*, 60.

5. Haas, "Creek Inter-Town Relations"; Knight, "Formation of the Creeks," 374, 387; Charles Hudson, *Southeastern Indians*, 236–37; also see Swanton, *Social Organization*. For discussions on the red/white dual organization among another southeastern Indian group, see Jay Johnson, "Stone Tools" and "Chickasaws"; Galloway, "Ougoula Tchetoka"; Bushnell, "Ruling 'the Republic'"; Gleach, *Powhatan's World*, 22–60; and Ethridge, "Chickasaw Factionalism." For a discussion on how dual organization figured into Indian and European diplomatic relations and emerging race ideologies, see Shoemaker, "How Indians Got to Be Red."

6. Knight, in "Institutional Organization," 679–84, argues that the organization of religion of the Mississippian chiefdoms was comprised of three cult institutions that he characterizes as a warfare/cosmogony cult, a platform mound cult, and a temple sanctuary cult, all of which underwrote the chiefdom hierarchy. During the Historic Period after the chiefdoms fell, Knight argues, these three cults were transformed into the warrior cult and the Green Corn cult (red/white), which were the Mississippian cults reconfigured for the town-centered coalescent societies.

7. Ethridge argues this point in "Chickasaw Factionalism" and "French Connection." It is interesting to note that hunting was also associated with warfare; this does not mean that only people of the war towns could hunt, but it does mean that important decisions regarding hunting were left to the war leadership. Hence when trade was figured around deerskins, the red leadership may have still had more say.

8. Knight, "Formation of the Creeks," 387.

9. Ethridge, "Chickasaw Factionalism."

10. Hahn, "Invention of the Creek Nation," 32; Piker, "Peculiar Connections."

11. Hahn, "Invention of the Creek Nation," documents the processes that led to the idea of nationhood among the Creeks during the colonial era. Hahn argues that the Creek "nation" was a situational, frontier institution that was part European and part Creek and not a typical politically centralized nation. Hahn also asserts that the Creeks only began to think in terms of nationhood when their land became an issue with the British, and hence, nation was defined in terms of territory and not polity.

12. At least this is the conventional wisdom, but as noted above, the red/white moiety division among the Creeks has not been thoroughly investigated. Champagne, *Social Order*, 66, 72, presents a strong case for the moiety division as holding significance

into the nineteenth century. For the history of the provincial polities among the Upper and Lower divisions, see Waselkov and Smith, "Upper Creek Archaeology," and Worth, "Lower Creeks." Hahn, "Invention of the Creek Nation," 33–35, also only briefly addresses the red/white division among the Creeks, concentrating instead on the polity divisions.

13. Hawkins listed the Upper Creek war and peace towns when he was describing how the warrior police were formed. In this list the whole of the Upper Creek towns were divided into war (red) and peace (white) towns; see Hawkins, *Letters*, 1:306–7.

14. Ibid., 2:612. Saunt, *New Order*, 241–43, argues that this incident indicates a breaking with Creek conventions by the warrior police, who were directed by pro-American, market-oriented Creek elites. I argue later in this volume that the warrior police may have been conforming to the red/white institutional rules, albeit under new circumstances.

15. Knight, "Formation of the Creeks," 387–88. This idea is central to Hahn's argument in "Invention of the Creek Nation," 380.

16. Hawkins, *Letters*, 1:322.

17. Most collections of Creek myths and legends are sorted according to township/province affiliations such as Alabama, Yuchi, Hitchiti, and so on; see Grantham, *Creation Myths*; Lankford, *Native American Legends*; and Swanton, *Myths and Tales*.

18. Hawkins, *Letters*, 1:295, 296, 321.

19. Ibid., 298.

20. Ibid., 313.

21. Gatschet, *Migration Legend*, 156.

22. Knight, "Formation of the Creeks," 386–88; Wright, *Creeks and Seminoles*, 30–31; Joel W. Martin, *Sacred Revolt*, 11, 50.

23. I have not been able to identify the *talwa* affiliation for each *talofa* for the late eighteenth century; this listing, then, is just a sampling of those that I have been able to determine.

24. Bartram, *Travels through North and South Carolina*, 315. Albert S. Gatschet, a late-nineteenth-century anthropologist, believed a splinter group migrated due to over-population of a town and the subsequent stress on agricultural fields or competition for firewood; see Gatschet, *Migration Legend*, 56. Recent archaeological investigations show soil depletion, not firewood, to have been the primary determining factor in Creek residential mobility; see Foster, "Temporal Trends" and "Long Term Average Rate."

25. Charles Hudson, *Southeastern Indians*, 229, 233.

26. Elliott et al., "Up on the Upatoi," 261, 262; Hawkins, *Letters*, 1:315, 313.

27. Charles Hudson, *Southeastern Indians*, 218; Hawkins, *Letters*, 1:319. Hawkins spells it *choochofauthlucco*, which glosses as "big hot house."

28. Waselkov, "Historic Creek Architectural Adaptations"; Waselkov and Smith, "Upper Creek Archaeology," 254–55; Sheldon, "Historic Creek 'Summer' Houses." For a summary of the changing house patterns of southeastern Indians from the protohistoric into the Historic Period, see Hally, "Making Sense of Aboriginal House Form."

29. Sheldon, "Upper Creek Architecture at Fusihatchee," 59–73.

30. Huscher, "Historic Lower Creek Sites," 41.

31. The archaeological remains of the Fusihatchee council houses are described in Sheldon, "Upper Creek Architecture at Fusihatchee." Okfuskenena was located on the upper Chattahoochee River; see Huscher, "Historic Lower Creek Sites."

32. Bartram describes a similar rotunda used by the Cherokees; see Bartram, *Travels through North and South Carolina*, 297–98.

33. Hawkins, *Letters*, 1:319–20.

34. Drooker proposes that the Shawnees were a seventeenth-century product of Iroquois predations and European conflicts who adapted to the tumultuous times by becoming highly mobile and adopting a very fluid social structure; see Drooker, "Ohio Valley," 124–28.

35. Hawkins, *Letters*, 1:23, 296.

36. Pope, *Tour*, 36; Romans, *Concise Natural History*, 41; Swan, "Position and State," 277.

37. Hawkins, *Letters*, 1:1–7.

38. Ibid., 2:553.

39. Ibid., 1:319; Pope, *Tour*, 56; Romans, *Concise Natural History*, 93.

40. Hawkins, *Letters*, 1:319; Charles Hudson, *Southeastern Indians*, 221–22. For a discussion on chunky and other games, see Charles Hudson, *Southeastern Indians*, 421–26.

41. Bartram, *Bartram on the Southeastern Indians*, 101.

42. Innerarity's stay at Tuckabatchee is recorded in Innerarity, "Creek Debtors."

43. Hawkins, *Letters*, 1:148.

44. Ibid., 88–89.

45. Captain Basil Hall, *Travels*, 3:296.

46. Charles Hudson, *Southeastern Indians*, 408–13.

47. Romans, *Concise Natural History*, 79.

48. For a discussion on southeastern Indian ball games, see Charles Hudson, *Southeastern Indians*, 408–21.

49. Captain Basil Hall, *Travels*, 3:297–98.

50. Ibid., 300.

51. Ibid., 305.

52. Ibid., 296–307.

53. Speck, "Taskigi Town," 112; Charles Hudson, *Southeastern Indians*, 221. The Muskogean orthography is taken from Hudson.

54. Pickett, *History of Alabama*, 98; Milfort, *Sojourn*, 95.

55. Sheldon, "Upper Creek Architecture at Fusihatchee," 71.

56. Hawkins, *Letters*, 1:320.

57. Ibid., 319; Swanton, *Social Organization*, 101, 297. The term *mico* is a degraded Mississippian term.

58. Stiggins, *Creek Indian History*, 48; Wright, *Creeks and Seminoles*, 29. The Muskogean orthography is taken from Wright.

59. Speck, "Taskigi Town," 114; Wright, *Creeks and Seminoles*, 29. The Muskogean orthography is taken from Wright.

60. Stiggins, *Creek Indian History*, 49.

61. List compiled by the chiefs and submitted to Hawkins, 1802, in "Benjamin Hawkins's Journal of Occurrences," APS.

62. Hewitt, *Notes*, 133; Speck, "Taskigi Town," 113; Woodward, *Reminiscences*, 19.

63. Stiggins, *Creek Indian History*, 49.

64. Richard White, in his historical analysis of the Choctaw headmanship in *Roots of Dependency*, 34–68, was one of the first scholars to link the headmanship to European trade. White showed headmen to have had absolute authority in the early years of European colonization. Once the deerskin trade was under way, however, Europeans undermined accession to the office by giving presents and medals and by dealing with preferred men who were not always headmen. This bolstered a man's prestige and eroded the headmen's authority. According to White, headmanship changed from a hereditary office of control to one in which a headman may have come from a particular clan, but he retained leadership only by consensus. Hahn, in "Invention of the Creek Nation," documents something similar among the Creeks during the colonial era but emphasizes the role of diplomatic skills among Creek leaders. In contrast, Greg O'Brien, in *Choctaws in a Revolutionary Age*, argues for two avenues of power for Choctaw headmen: spirituality and Euro-American economic contacts.

65. Stiggins, *Creek Indian History*, 50.

66. Woodward, *Reminiscences*, 45.

67. Swanton, *Social Organization*, 297; Wright, *Creeks and Seminoles*, 29–30; Charles Hudson, *Southeastern Indians*, 225. The Muskogean orthography is taken from Wright.

68. Hawkins, *Letters*, 1:319.

69. Speck, "Taskigi Town," 114; Swanton, *Social Organization*, 96–104, 201; Wright, *Creeks and Seminoles*, 29–30. The Muskogean orthography is taken from Wright.

70. Braund, "Classification"; Perdue, *Cherokee Women*, 126; Saunt, *New Order*, 98; Carson, *Searching for the Bright Path*, 63–64.

71. Stiggins, *Creek Indian History*, 56.

72. Hawkins, *Letters*, 1:317–18; Milfort, *Sojourn*, 95.

73. Pickett, *History of Alabama*, 99; Adair, *Adair's History*, 32.

74. Milfort, *Sojourn*, 94.

75. Hawkins, *Letters*, 1:314; Milfort, *Sojourn*, 93–95; Romans, *Concise Natural History*, 93.

76. Bartram, *Bartram on the Southeastern Indians*, 103.

77. Charles Hudson, *Southeastern Indians*, 226–29; Milfort, *Sojourn*, 92. For a thorough discussion of the beliefs about and the ceremonial use of black drink among the southeastern Indians, see Charles Hudson, *Black Drink*.

78. Charles Hudson, *Southeastern Indians*, 223–29; Bartram, *Bartram on the Southeastern Indians*, 102–5.

79. Saunt, in *New Order*, 186–204, argues that many Creeks began to devalue oratory by the late eighteenth century and understood writing to be the more powerful form of political and social persuasion. Still, the Creeks remained largely an oral society until the twentieth century.

80. For a modern interpretation of the Indian/Euro-American language of diplo-

macy and treaties, see Merritt, "Metaphor, Meaning, and Misunderstanding," and Greg O'Brien, "Conqueror Meets the Unconquered."

81. Hawkins, *Letters*, 1:88–89, 152.

82. Ibid., 152.

83. Bossu, *Travels*, 154; Gatschet, *Migration Legend*, 170; Hawkins, *Letters*, 1:317. Green, *Politics of Indian Removal*, 21–22, and Champagne, *Social Order*, 33, place the beginnings of the National Council in the early eighteenth century. Wright, in *Creeks and Seminoles*, 116, writes that the National Council was "as much a product of the whites as the Indians" and that it existed as a body politic when dealing with whites, who insisted on some form of centralized governance; Wright also attributes McGillivray with strengthening the councils as a governing body.

84. Milfort, *Sojourn*, 93; Pickett, *History of Alabama*, 96–97.

85. Hawkins, *Letters*, 1:232, 2:430.

86. Ibid., 1:186.

87. Ibid., 2:505.

88. Ibid., 1:350, 2:419.

89. Ibid., 1:352.

90. Ibid., 355; Woodward, *Reminiscences*, 4.

91. Bossu, *Travels*, 154.

92. Ibid.

93. Hawkins, *Letters*, 1:352.

94. Hawkins recorded several National Council meetings, and he sent minutes to the secretary of war; see ibid., 184–91, 2:468–80, 753–61.

95. Ibid., 1:338, 2:524.

96. Ibid., 2:488, 564–65.

97. Ibid., 601.

98. The punishments are documented in ibid., 1:275, 273, 268, 317. The characterization of the leadership of the National Council as presented here is from Saunt, *New Order*. Saunt's conclusion has recently been called into question by Richter, in "Review of a New Order," 679, wherein he notes that Saunt does not adequately chronicle exactly who made up the National Council or how the council worked.

99. Hawkins, *Letters*, 1:86, 269, 273, 2:458.

100. Champagne, in *Social Order*, 113–14, first made this observation. This is in contrast to Saunt, *New Order*, 1, 164–85, who argues that the National Council, controlled by a métis elite, could exert its control "over every Creek person." Other scholars also question the central authority of the National Council and the political Creek elite; see Richter, "Review of a New Order," 679, and Hahn, "Invention of the Creek Nation," 378–80.

101. Hawkins, *Letters*, 1:261, 272, 359, 2:467.

102. Charles Hudson, *Southeastern Indians*, 223, 232. Green, *Politics of Indian Removal*, 21–28, first noted that factions acted independently within the Creek Confederacy and with no overarching authority.

103. Bossu, *Travels*, 139; Adair, *Adair's History*, 5.

104. Von Reck, *Von Reck's Voyage*, 48.

105. Ibid., 41; Swan, "Position and State," 273–74; Adair, *Adair's History*, 163.

106. Bossu, *Travels*, 146.

107. Bartram, *Bartram on the Southeastern Indians*, 90, 100.

108. Stiggins, *Creek Indian History*, 52.

109. Bossu, *Travels*, 131; Stiggins, *Creek Indian History*, 52.

110. Timothy Barnard to James Seagrove, October 18, 1793, Letters of Timothy Barnard, 220, GDAH.

111. Stiggins, *Creek Indian History*, 51–52.

112. Ibid., 51.

113. Swan, "Position and State," 280.

114. For discussions on how these kinship metaphors clashed in Euro-American and southeastern Indian diplomacy, see Galloway, "'Chief Who Is Your Father,'" and Greg O'Brien, "Conqueror Meets the Unconquered." Perdue *Cherokee Women*, 135–58, discusses the role of kinship in the formation of the Cherokee Republic of the early nineteenth century.

115. Swan, "Position and State," 273.

116. Charles Hudson, *Southeastern Indians*, 191–94.

117. Saunt, *New Order*, 19–21. Saunt also makes the point that clan obligations in political affairs may have been breaking down by the late eighteenth century; see ibid., 81–82.

118. Stiggins, *Creek Indian History*, 64–65.

119. Ibid., 65.

120. This list is taken from Swanton's compilation in *Indians of the Southeastern United States*, 654–61. Gatschet, *Migration Legend*, 155, lists twenty-eight.

121. Gatschet first noted the connection in 1884 when he mused that the numerous clans in the Muskogee Nation pointed to "either a long historic development of the tribe or internal dissensions" (Gatschet, *Migration Legend*, 154). See Knight, "Formation of the Creeks," and Galloway, *Choctaw Genesis*, for discussions of the complexity of the origins of a coalescent society.

122. Charles Hudson, *Southeastern Indians*, 236–39.

123. Hawkins, *Letters*, 1:341.

124. Ibid., 218; Richard Thomas, "His Book," 497.

125. Hawkins, *Letters*, 1:340, 2:494.

126. Swan, "Position and State," 63.

127. Hawkins, *Letters*, 1:26. Hawkins lists the resident traders by name for many of the Upper Creek towns; see ibid., 16–17.

128. Parades and Plante, "Economics, Politics, and the Subjugation," 41–42.

129. Braund, *Deerskins and Duffels*, 86.

130. Archaeologists believe they found some evidence for one at Fusihatchee (see Waselkov and Smith, "Upper Creek Archaeology," 253) and at Upatoi (see Elliott et al., "Up on the Upatoi," 258).

131. Bartram, *Bartram on the Southeastern Indians*, 100.

132. Richard Thomas, "His Book," 475.

133. Hawkins, "Letters of Benjamin Hawkins," 103.

134. Hawkins, *Letters*, 1:187; Benjamin Hawkins to Edward Price, May 29, 1798, Entry No. 42, RG 75, NA.

135. Hawkins, *Letters*, 1:187–89.

136. Ibid., 63.

137. Ibid., 2:457.

138. Ethridge, "Horse Stealing."

139. Swan, "Position and State," 273.

140. Hawkins, *Letters*, 1:47–48.

141. Grant and Davis, "Wedding"; Henri, *Southern Indians*, 317, 334; Mauelshagen and Davis, *Partners*, 36 n. 21.

142. Hawkins, *Letters*, 1:47, 239, 2:455–56.

143. Swan, "Position and State," 272; Charles Hudson, *Southeastern Indians*, 198.

144. Milfort, *Sojourn*, 137.

145. Hawkins, "Letters of Benjamin Hawkins," 340.

146. Ibid.; Hawkins to Samuel Alexander, January 21, 1799, Benjamin Hawkins's Letterbook, INHP.

147. Hawkins, "Letters of Benjamin Hawkins," 340.

148. Entry for May 2, 1799, and Benjamin Hawkins to Samuel Alexander, May 21, 1799, Benjamin Hawkins's Letterbook, INHP; Benjamin Hawkins to Edward Price, November 19, 1798, Entry No. 42, RG 75, NA.

149. Benjamin Hawkins to S. Alexander, January 21, 1799, Benjamin Hawkins's Letterbook, INHP.

150. Hawkins, *Letters*, 1:300.

151. Cherokee Reply, June 27, 1802, Entry No. 1, RG 75, NA.

152. We still have no full scholarly treatment of the lives of blacks living among the southern Indians at this time. One of the most recent and thorough for the Creeks is in Saunt, *New Order*, 111–35, 273–90. Other examinations are offered in Braund, "Creek Indians, Blacks, and Slavery"; Perdue, *Slavery and the Evolution*; Littlefield, *Africans and Creeks*; Willis, "Divide and Rule"; Porter, *Negro on the American Frontier*; and Wright, *Creeks and Seminoles*, 73–100. May, *African Americans and Native Americans*, examines Indian and African American interactions after Removal.

153. This characterization comes from Braund, "Creek Indians, Blacks, and Slavery," 623–31, although Braund notes that there were cases in which Creek owners considered their black slaves chattel property.

154. Saunt, *New Order*, 111–35; Littlefield, *Africans and Creeks*, 38, 49; Woodward, *Reminiscences*, 108.

155. Saunt, *New Order*, 116–17.

156. Hawkins, *Letters*, 1:15, 22, 24, 292.

157. Barnard has many references to his slaves and to freedmen he occasionally hired for various tasks around his ranch or trading business; see Letters of Timothy Barnard, GDAH.

158. Estate of Benjamin Hawkins, Inventory and Sale, Letters of Benjamin Hawkins, GDAH.

159. Saunt, *New Order*, 111–35; Littlefield, *Africans and Creeks*, 17–46.

160. Saunt, *New Order*, 111–35, 273–90. Saunt also discusses the roles of blacks among the Seminoles in ibid., 205–29.

161. Perdue makes this observation for the Cherokees in *Cherokee Women*, 82–83, and for southeastern Indians in general in "Mixed Blood Indians," 90–95. With all of this genetic mixing, color or race was a complicated concept in the eighteenth-century South; see also Saunt, *New Order*, 111–35, and Braund, "Creek Indians, Blacks, and Slaves." For a history of racial terminology and changing Euro-American perceptions on people of color, see Forbes, *Africans and Native Americans*.

162. Braund, "Guardians of Tradition," 248–50. For studies of how southeastern Indian women acted as cultural brokers, see Perdue, *Cherokee Women*, and Morris, *Bringing of Wonder*, 13–70.

163. Hawkins, *Letters*, 1:21.

164. Ibid., 28.

165. Ibid., 21, 28.

166. Ibid., 22.

167. Ibid., 200.

168. Timothy Barnard to the Honorable Edward Telfair, Governor, August 22, 1786, Letters of Timothy Barnard, GDAH.

169. Bartram, *Bartram on the Southeastern Indians*, 100.

170. Saunt, *New Order*, 129–33.

171. Richard Thomas, "His Book," 494.

172. Hawkins, *Letters*, 2:768.

173. Ibid., 1:293.

174. Ibid.

Chapter Six

1. This is not to say that southern Indians did not use waterways as communication and travel routes. For a summary of communication and travel routes used by the southeastern Indians, see Tanner, "Land and Water Communication." The comprehensive study of southern Indian trails, to date, is Meyer, *Indian Trails*.

2. Hawkins, *Letters*, 2:706.

3. Ibid., 1:295.

4. Bossu, *Travels*, 129.

5. James McIntosh Affidavit, 1809, and McIntosh Passport, February 27, 1809, Entry No. 1, RG 75, NA.

6. James McIntosh Affidavit, 1809, Entry No. 1, RG 75, NA.

7. Tustunnuggee Thlucco to Benjamin Hawkins, May 1, 1805; E. Parson to Benjamin Hawkins, May 28, 1810; Tustunnuggee Thlucco to Pathmaker, May 1, 1809, Entry No. 1, RG 75, NA. There is also ample evidence that land speculator John Chisholm and Cherokee Indian agent Return J. Meigs were involved in this incident and that the real purpose was to make fraudulent land deals with some Lower Creek Indians.

8. The history of the Federal Road is in Southerland and Brown, *Federal Road*.

9. Tanner, "Land and Water Communication," 8–9.

10. Meyer, *Indian Trails*; Tanner, "Land and Water Communication." Goff, "Path to Oakfuskee," reconstructs the Upper Trading Path and many of the connecting paths through Georgia.

11. Hawkins, *Letters*, 1:141, 2:405–9. Goff, "Path to Oakfuskee," also locates several such smaller routes; many such trails are shown in Miscellaneous No. 11, Map of General Jackson's campaign against the Creek Indians, 1813, RG 77, NA.

12. Hawkins, *Letters*, 2:409.

13. Ibid., 409, 585.

14. Gatschet, *Migration Legend*, 129.

15. Goff, Utley, and Hemperley, *Placenames of Georgia*, 199, 203–4; Hawkins, "Letters of Benjamin Hawkins," 172. The Muskogean orthography is taken from Hawkins.

16. Romans, *Concise Natural History*, 65.

17. Hawkins, *Letters*, 1:141; Lane, *Rambler in Georgia*, 60, 69.

18. Hawkins, *Letters*, 1:307–11.

19. Gatschet, *Migration Legend*, 131; Swanton, *Early History*, 286.

20. Read, *Indian Place Names*, 20, 32; Gatschet, *Migration Legend*, 130.

21. Bartram, *Naturalist's Edition*, 281.

22. Hawkins, *Letters*, 1:51.

23. Bartram, *Naturalist's Edition*, 280–81.

24. Captain Basil Hall, *Travels*, 3:266–70.

25. Hawkins, *Letters*, 2:602.

26. Captain Basil Hall, *Travels*, 3:266.

27. Hawkins, *Letters*, 2:494, 602.

28. Hodgson, *Letters*, 110.

29. Swan, "Position and State," 253; Bartram, *Naturalist's Edition*, 289.

30. Romans, *Concise Natural History*, 281; Hawkins, *Letters*, 1:51.

31. Hawkins, *Letters*, 1:10–11.

32. Pope, *Tour*, 63–64.

33. Hawkins, *Letters*, 1:51–52.

34. Goff, Utley, and Hemperley, *Placenames of Georgia*, 152–53.

35. Swanton, *Creek Religion*, 487, 631, 638.

36. Captain Basil Hall, *Travels*, 3:249.

37. Bartram, *Naturalist's Edition*, 177.

38. Romans, *Concise Natural History*, 189, 316.

39. Hawkins, *Letters*, 2:467.

40. Hodgson, *Letters*, 120–21.

41. Hawkins, *Letters*, 1:281.

42. Ibid., 2:497, 563, 587.

43. The Creek trading houses are described in Mattison, "Creek Trading House"; Harmon, "Benjamin Hawkins and the Federal Factory System"; and Chambers, "Creek Indian Factory at Fort Mitchell." For examinations of the U.S. Factory System as a whole, see Peake, *History of the United States Indian Factory System*, and Way, "United States Factory System."

44. Mattison, "Creek Trading House," 184; Superintendent of Indian Trade to Dan Hughes, August 16, 1819, and to Dinkins, November 23, 1815, Entry No. 4, RG 75, NA.

45. For the most part, U.S. officials and businessmen were more interested in the northern fur trade, which was still vigorous; see General Remarks, 1807–1830, Entry No. 4, RG 75, NA.

46. William Harris to Edward Wright, March 10, 1801, Entry No. 42, RG 75, NA.

47. William Davy to Jonathan Halstead, June 17, 1806, Entry No. 42, RG 75, NA.

48. Superintendent of Indian Trade to Jonathan Halstead, June 26, 1812, Entry No. 4, RG 75, NA.

49. Braund, *Deerskins and Duffels*, 72.

50. Ibid., 178–80; Coker and Watson, *Indian Traders*.

51. Doster, *Creek Indians and Their Florida Lands*, 2:217; Henry Dearborn to Jonathan Halstead, September 14, 1802, Entry No. 42, RG 75, NA.

52. Braund, *Deerskins and Duffels*, 98–99.

53. Benjamin Hawkins to Edward Wright, Christmas 1799, Entry No. 42, RG 75, NA.

54. Hawkins, *Letters*, 1:280; November 1799, Benjamin Hawkins's Letterbook, INHP.

55. Permit for Dealers in Stock, November 1799, Benjamin Hawkins's Letterbook, INHP.

56. April 1, 1816, Entry No. 47, RG 75, NA.

57. Hawkins, *Letters*, 1:280, 2:560.

58. Henry Dearborn to Jonathan Halstead, September 14, 1802, Entry No. 42, RG 75, NA.

59. Hawkins, *Letters*, 1:280, 2:560; Benjamin Hawkins to Edward Wright, October 26, 1799, Entry No. 42, RG 75, NA.

60. Benjamin Hawkins to Edward Wright, Christmas 1799, Entry No. 42, RG 75, NA.

61. Hawkins, *Letters*, 1:355, 2:503; Benjamin Hawkins to Edward Wright, August 2, 1799, Entry No. 42, RG 75, NA.

62. Entry No. 42 and Entry No. 52, RG 75, NA.

63. These records can be found in the Records of the Office of Indian Trade, Creek Factory; see Entry No. 5, Entry No. 6, Entry No. 9, Entry No. 42, Entry No. 43, Entry No. 47, Entry No. 49, Entry No. 50, Entry No. 52, Entry No. 53, and Entry No. 1065, RG 75, NA.

64. Henry Dearborn to Jonathan Halstead, January 9, 1804, Entry No. 42, RG 75, NA.

65. For an accounting of a southern frontier military garrison, see Entry No. 53, RG 75, NA.

66. Prucha, *American Indian Policy in the Formative Years*, 145–47.

67. For a listing of Alabama forts built before and during the Red Stick War, see Halbert and Ball, *Creek War*, 105–19. For a listing of frontier forts in Georgia during the eighteenth and early nineteenth centuries, see Wilcox, *Fort Hawkins*, 13–29. Fort Hawkins is now a small state park in Macon, Ga. Part of the fort has been reconstructed; especially impressive is the lookout tower, from which one can get a grand vista of the Ocmulgee River and beyond for miles. The website for Old Fort Hawkins is ⟨http:\\www.hollidaydental.com/forthawk.htm⟩.

68. The site of Fort Mims, in northern Baldwin County, Ala., is on the National Register of Historic Places. There is an annual reenactment of the Red Stick Battle

there in August hosted by the Fort Mims Restoration Association; their website is ‹http://home.att.net/~fortmims/home.htm›.

69. We know somewhat more about colonial frontier military life, since some of the colonial frontier forts in the South have been excavated by archaeologists; see Waselkov, "Introduction"; Daniel H. Thomas, *Fort Toulouse*; Williams, *Memoir*; and Higginbotham, *Old Mobile*.

70. For a look at some of the daily activities at a frontier fort, see Wilcox's compilation of much of the primary materials relating to Fort Hawkins in present-day Macon, Ga., in Wilcox, *Fort Hawkins*.

71. Orders from Secretary of War to Captain Eaton, November 16, 1795, and Pickering to Eaton, 1795, Entry No. 42, RG 75, NA.

72. John Webb to Edward Price, February 4, 1798; Henry Dearborn to Jonathan Halstead, September 14, 1802; and Pickering to Eaton, 1795, Entry No. 42, RG 75, NA; Hawkins, *Letters*, 2:502.

73. Orders from Secretary of War to Captain Eaton, November 16, 1795, Entry No. 42, RG 75, NA.

74. Price letters, 1799–1801, Entry No. 42, RG 75, NA.

75. Hawkins, *Letters*, 2:511; Superintendent of Indian Trade to Jonathan Halstead, 1810, Entry No. 4, RG 75, NA.

76. Hawkins, *Letters*, 2:560.

77. Harmon makes this point in "Benjamin Hawkins and the Federal Factory System," 151, although he views the factories as running more smoothly and successfully than depicted here. Harmon, however, based his description on a handful of published primary sources; he did not review the unpublished factory records. The nature of the factories as presented here derives from the unpublished factory records that contain much about the financial affairs of the trading houses; these are Entry No. 5, Entry No. 6, Entry No. 9, Entry No. 42, Entry No. 43, Entry No. 47, Entry No. 53, and Entry No. 1065, RG 75, NA.

78. Hawkins, *Letters*, 1:141.

79. Braley, "Historic Period Indian Archaeology," 49. Braley's figures are based on late-eighteenth-century population estimates for the Lower Creeks. He notes that a hunting party more than likely had more than one camp a season, and he also calls for more archaeological attention to these kinds of sites.

80. Hawkins, *Letters*, 1:135.

81. Braley, "Historic Period Indian Archaeology," 49; Braund, "Guardians of Tradition," 244; Wright, *Creeks and Seminoles*, 65. The full composition of a Creek hunting party is not known. Braund, *Deerskins and Duffels*, 67, suggests that the nuclear family was the basic economic unit during the deerskin trade era and that this helped to erode the role of the matriline. I suggest elsewhere (Chapter 8) that the matriline may have stayed intact through both the trade and ranching eras. For an examination of how the deerskin trade changed Cherokee gender roles and kinship, see Perdue, *Cherokee Women*, 65–87.

82. Von Reck, *Von Reck's Voyage*, 116–17.

83. Hawkins, "Letters of Benjamin Hawkins," 44; Hawkins, *Letters*, 1:303; Braund, *Deerskins and Duffels*, 67.

84. Braund, *Deerskins and Duffels*, 65–66.

85. Braund, "Guardians of Tradition," 245.

86. Braund, *Deerskins and Duffels*, 66–68.

87. Hawkins, *Letters*, 1:275.

88. Braund, *Deerskins and Duffels*, 61.

89. Hawkins, *Letters*, 2:448, 449, 565; June 6, 9, 13, 1802, "Benjamin Hawkins's Journal of Occurrences," APS.

90. June 6, 10, 13, 1802, "Benjamin Hawkins's Journal of Occurrences," APS.

91. June 13, 1802, ibid.

92. Hawkins, *Letters*, 2:448–49.

93. Creek Chiefs to Commissioners, June 6, 1802, and Tupulueh Micco and Efau Haujo to Benjamin Hawkins, June 10, 1802, "Benjamin Hawkins's Journal of Occurrences," APS.

94. Hawkins, *Letters*, 2:448.

95. Hopithle Micco to President, May 15, 1811, Entry No. 1, RG 75, NA.

96. Stiggins, *Creek Indian History*, 77. Bartram states that the non–Muskogean speakers (whom he said the Creeks called the "Stinkards") were assigned specific hunting grounds given by the Creek Confederacy, and only Muskogean speakers had free access to all other lands. I find it unlikely that just the non–Muskogean towns were assigned hunting grounds (Creek land tenure is more fully discussed in Chapter 10), and even Bartram equivocates on this point; see Bartram, *Bartram on the Southeastern Indians*, 155–56.

97. Hawkins, *Letters*, 1:288.

98. Bartram, *Bartram on the Southeastern Indians*, 58.

99. Sales of Peltries Received from Coleraine Store, August 24, 1796; Sales of Furs, received by Andrew Tybout, 1799; and Sales of Furs and Peltries received from Georgia Factory in 1799 by Andrew Tybout, February 16, 1801, Entry No. 52, box 1, 1795–1803, Miscellaneous Papers, RG 75, NA.

100. Charles Hudson argues that the southern deer population was so seriously diminished as to be the major cause of the decline of the deerskin trade; see Charles Hudson, "Why the Southeastern Indians Slaughtered Deer." Waselkov, in "Anglo-Indian Trade," 202–5, argues that because white-tailed deer are so fecund, rebounding so quickly to population depletion, shortages of deer for commercial purposes were short-lived pulses. He further argues that one should examine the decline of the trade in light of the changes in the European market and the increasing interest of the southeastern Indians in economic alternatives such as ranching, rather than solely attributing it to a decline in the deer population. Haan, "'Trade do's not Flourish,'" argues that the deer population in coastal Carolina began to decline early in the skin trade and was a primary factor in the Yamassee War of 1715.

101. Waselkov, "Evolution of Deer Hunting," first noted this changing pattern in the archaeological evidence.

102. Henry Drinker, Thomas Wintson, and Thomas Stewardson to Henry Dearborn, December 31, 1801, Entry No. 1, RG 75, NA.

103. Hahn, "Invention of the Creek Nation," 224, argues just this point.

Chapter Seven

1. Gremillion, "Paleoethnobotany of Native Historic Communities," 5–8, also makes this point. Prehistoric southern farming has been extensively studied on a site-by-site basis by archaeologists for many decades. However, Charles Hudson's chapter on subsistence in *Southeastern Indians*, 258–316, is still the best synthesis to date. For more up-to-date archaeological discussions on Woodland and Mississippian agriculture, see Harris and Hillman, *Foraging and Farming*; Scarry, *Foraging and Farming*; Gremillion, *People, Plants, and Landscapes*; Gremillion, "Development and Dispersal of Agricultural Systems"; and Cobb, *From Quarry to Cornfield*. Bruce Smith has created a broad-ranging body of work on the beginnings of southern agriculture; for an introduction to some of this literature, see Smith, Cowan, and Hoffman, *Rivers of Change*. For a recent discussion on Lower Creek agriculture, methods, and soil depletion, see Foster, "Long Term Average Rate."

2. Cowdrey, *This Land*, 3.

3. Hunt, *Natural Regions*, 127–33.

4. Starrett, *Appraisal Report*, 45–47. The classification systems varied by region and state. For a general discussion on the use of trees as soil indicators, see Whitney, *From Coastal Wilderness*, 135–43.

5. Foster, "Long Term Average Rate," offers an in-depth, local-level analysis of soils, associated tree types, soil depletion rates, and agricultural productivity around five Lower Creek towns; for the soils and forest cover, see esp. 188–273.

6. Hawkins, *Letters*, 1:290–98.

7. Ibid., 307.

8. Ibid., 309.

9. In 1942 anthropologist Ralph Linton surveyed Native American land tenure and found that each group he studied divided their lands differently and that they recognized varying rights to tenure. Linton offers this generalization: "In the background of all assertions of individual rights to land there lie certain economic factors deriving both from the ecology of the region and from the current techniques of land exploitation" (Linton, "Land Tenure," 42). Much of Creek township land tenure patterns falls within Linton's generalization.

10. Waselkov, "Changing Strategies," 189, located agricultural fields and their dividing lines for the towns of the Tallapoosa River valley; also see Hawkins, *Letters*, 1:293–95, 297, 314.

11. Waselkov, "Changing Strategies" 237; Adair, *Adair's History*, 435.

12. Bartram, *Bartram on the Southeastern Indians*, 54; Adair, *Adair's History*, 435.

13. Hawkins, *Letters*, 1:296.

14. Bartram, *Bartram on the Southeastern Indians*, 165.

15. Doolittle, "Agriculture in North America," 396–97.

16. Bartram, *Bartram on the Southeastern Indians*, 54, 127, 158; Milfort, *Sojourn*, 104.

17. Bartram, *Bartram on the Southeastern Indians*, 158.

18. Milfort, *Sojourn*, 104.

19. Bartram, *Bartram on the Southeastern Indians*, 158.

20. Milfort, *Sojourn*, 104.

21. Romans, *Concise Natural History*, 87–88.

22. Foster, "Long Term Average Rate," 96.

23. Hewitt, *Notes*, 127. I do not presume that Hewitt's information necessarily reflects early-nineteenth-century practices; I include it only as a possibility.

24. Hawkins, *Letters*, 1:309.

25. Ibid., 42.

26. Swan, "Position and State," 282.

27. Hawkins, *Letters*, 2:542.

28. Ibid., 1:293–94.

29. Gremillion, "Paleoethnobotany of Native Historic Communities," 5. Cobb, *From Quarry to Cornfield*, argues that during the Mississippian Period, hoe production was a task done by specialists and that hoes made of especially good stone entered a large exchange network.

30. Hawkins, *Letters*, 2:552.

31. Bartram, *Bartram on the Southeastern Indians*, 165.

32. Bonner, *History*, 95.

33. Pope, *Tour*, 62.

34. Gremillion, "Paleoethnobotany of Native Historic Communities," 5.

35. Doolittle, "Agriculture in North America," 392–93, categorizes the agriculture of the Eastern Woodlands as annual cultivation rather than swidden because of the long cultivation (twelve years) and the short fallow (one or two years). I use swidden here to distinguish this type of cultivation from monocropping, because of the simple technology characteristic of swidden agriculture, because they did not use fertilizer, and because of the field rotations.

36. The amount of fallow time and the length of time a southern field could be cultivated with eighteenth-century Creek agricultural techniques is not known. Undoubtedly it varied from place to place, depending on soil quality. In his study of Mississippian Period agriculture floodplains on the Little Tennessee River in eastern Tennessee, archaeologist William Baden estimates that a field could be cultivated for approximately fifteen years before the amount of corn produced diminished to the point that it was not worth the investment of time and labor to cultivate the field; see Baden, "Stability and Change," 107–20. Foster takes his rotation cycle from Baden; see Foster, "Long Term Average Rate," 193–208. Richard White, in *Roots of Dependency*, 24, estimates that eighteenth-century Choctaw fields for the town of Tala were cultivated for approximately ten years and left fallow for fifty, although he admits that these estimates are taken from New England fallow times. Doolittle, in "Agriculture in North America," 392–93, supports a long cultivation rotation for Eastern Woodland Indian agriculture, suggesting fields were kept in active cultivation for about twelve years. However, Doolittle argues that the fallow times were short, perhaps only one or two years. One can also get some idea of field rotation by examining the agricultural practices of the first wave of frontier farmers to the South. They usually bought only enough land for a single farmstead; they were not the large landholders and planters who came later; see Hilliard, *Hog Meat*, 65, 107–20, and Ver Steeg, *Origins of a Southern Mosaic*, 114–16. When their fields began producing less and less, these frontier farmers, who were highly mobile, sold their lands to new arrivals and moved on. The

timing of these moves would perhaps indicate the life span of an agricultural field. Jordan-Bychkov and Kaups estimate that in the Middle Colonies a frontier family moved after twelve to fifteen years because of soil exhaustion; see Jordan-Bychkov and Kaups, *American Backwoods*, 105. To date no such study exists for the southern frontier farmers, but anecdotal evidence suggests that southern frontier whites also began looking for new farms after about fifteen years.

37. Hawkins, *Letters*, 1:1–61; Benjamin Hawkins's Viatory, Force Collection, LC; Hatley, "Tallapoosa Landscape," 85–86; Waselkov, "Changing Strategies," 233. Foster demonstrates that with field rotations, Creek farmers utilized the floodplain soils within at least a two-kilometer catchment until they showed signs of strain, at which point a whole town would then relocate; see Foster, "Long Term Average Rate," 183–208.

38. Richard Thomas, "His Book," 478.

39. Mood, "Winthrop," 127; Romans, *Concise Natural History*, 120.

40. Bossu, *Travels*, 127.

41. Baden questions the amount of nutrient replenishment from this ash. Since there is no evidence that the southeastern Indians turned the ash into the soil, Baden concludes that firing left only a thin layer of ash that would have quickly run off in a rainstorm. Baden further states that firing itself increased nutrient depletion because even a low-level fire over a whole field was hot enough to damage the soil; see Baden, "Stability and Change," 56–58. However, Arianoutsou and Margaris, "Fire-Induced Nutrient Loss," estimates that fire releases 96 percent of the nitrogen stored in plant remains in gaseous form.

42. Hawkins, *Letters*, 2:548.

43. Ibid.

44. Charles Hudson, *Southeastern Indians*, 295.

45. Doolittle, "Agriculture in North America," 393; Whitney, *From Coastal Wilderness*, 133. The amount of time it took a tree to fall varied; oaks took about four years.

46. Hurt, *Indian Agriculture*, 39; Silver, *New Face*, 50.

47. Gosse, *Letters*, 88.

48. Ibid.; Whitney, *From Coastal Wilderness*, 133.

49. Bartram, *Bartram on the Southeastern Indians*, 165; Bossu, *Travels*, 127; Mood, "Winthrop," 128; Romans, *Concise Natural History*, 119; Hawkins, *Letters*, 1:23. We do not know for certain which supplemental cultigens Creek women planted in the communal fields and which they planted in their gardens. The Creeks dried and stored squashes and pumpkins, which would indicate a high yield that probably required large acreage.

50. Hatley, "Cherokee Women Farmers," 40; Silver, *New Face*, 49.

51. J. Gregory Keyes, personal communication, 1997. Keyes led an agriculture experiment using southeastern Indian hoe technology on the floodplain of the Oconee River at the State Botanical Garden of Georgia in Athens.

52. Hurt, *Indian Agriculture*, 30.

53. For instance, Cronon, in *Changes in the Land*, 73–81, argues that the fence and fenced fields represented European ideas of "improvements," which, in turn, indicated the value of land property and the industriousness of the owner.

54. Jordan-Bychkov and Kaups, *American Backwoods*, 105.

55. Hawkins, *Letters*, 1:285–327.

56. Saunt, *New Order*, 171–74; Joel W. Martin, *Sacred Revolt*, 142–43.

57. The Busk as it was performed by Creeks in the eighteenth and early nineteenth centuries was described by many literate observers; see Hawkins, *Letters*, 1:322–26; Swan, "Position and State," 267–68; Stiggins, *Creek Indian History*, 60–64; Bartram, *Bartram on the Southeastern Indians*, 124–27, 149; Payne, "Green-Corn Dance"; and Milfort, *Sojourn*, 98. Also see Witthoft, *Green Corn Ceremonialism*; Swanton, *Creek Religion*, 546–611; and Charles Hudson, *Southeastern Indians*, 365–75.

58. We do not know which specific varieties. Archaeological remains of corn can rarely be identified beyond the species level, and the evidence from Historic Period sites is particularly inadequate and sparse. White observers in Creek territory attempted to describe different types, but their descriptions of corn are not complete enough to specify variety.

59. Gosse, *Letters*, 134.

60. Romans, *Concise Natural History*, 118.

61. Ibid., 326.

62. Ibid., 118.

63. Hawkins, "Letters of Benjamin Hawkins," 323; Hawkins, *Letters*, 1:21. In a calculation for Choctaw production, White settles on 40 bushels per acre as the average corn production on southern alluvial soils because modern agricultural scientists are skeptical of anything more being possible on pre-nitrogen-fertilized soils; see Richard White, *Roots of Dependency*, 23. This figure also conforms more closely to the corn production of white farmers. In 1840, per capita corn production for Georgia was 30.2 bushels, and for Alabama it was 35.5 bushels; Hilliard, *Hog Meat*, 156. For a detailed analysis of antebellum southern farm and plantation production and consumption, see Hilliard, *Hog Meat*.

64. Foster, "Long Term Average Rate," 14–25, 54–68, 183–208, has a fine-grained analysis of correlations between soil types, corn production, and depletion rates around some Lower Creek towns during the late eighteenth century. Also see Baden, "Stability and Change," and Schroeder, "Understanding Variation."

65. Richard Thomas, "His Book," 484.

66. Hawkins, *Letters*, 1:22, 88, 163, 193, 2:455, 583, 557.

67. Ibid., 1:35.

68. The archaeological evidence for the slow adoption of Old World crops is documented in Gremillion, "Adoption of Old World Crops." Also see Hatley, *Dividing Paths*, 8–9, 160–63, 233–34; Bartram, *Bartram on the Southeastern Indians*, 236; and Hawkins, *Letters*, 1:294–96.

69. Hawkins, *Letters*, 1:350, 353, 2:522, 534, 552, 553, 555, 621; Hawkins, "Letters of Benjamin Hawkins," 322.

70. Bartram, *Bartram on the Southeastern Indians*, 244 n. 52.

71. Romans, *Concise Natural History*, 163; Gremillion, "Fusihatchee."

72. Bartram, *Bartram on the Southeastern Indians*, 165, 274 n. 48.

73. Ibid., 165.

74. Ibid.

75. Hawkins, *Letters*, 1:314.

76. Ibid.

77. Ibid., 353. Hawkins's references to the swamps and rice cultivation along the Flint suggest that the Creeks were engaged in wet-rice rather than dry-rice cultivation, but this cannot be firmly established.

78. Kristen J. Gremillion, personal communication, 2002.

79. Bartram, *Bartram on the Southeastern Indians*, 165; Pope, *Tour*, 60.

80. Romans, *Concise Natural History*, 93.

81. Sweet potatoes were present in prehistoric Mesoamerica; however, there is no archaeological evidence for sweet potato cultivation in the prehistoric Southeast. For a discussion on the origin and diffusion of sweet potato cultivation, see Patricia O'Brien, "Sweet Potato."

82. Romans, *Concise Natural History*, 123.

83. Hilliard, *Hog Meat*, 175; Romans, *Concise Natural History*, 163–64.

84. Von Reck, *Von Reck's Voyage*, 37; Lane, *Rambler in Georgia*, 4.

85. Hawkins, *Letters*, 1:43; Romans, *Concise Natural History*, 173.

86. Hawkins, *Letters*, 1:21; Pope, *Tour*, 62.

87. According to Kristen Gremillion, because they are tubers, sweet potatoes would not be identifiable in carbonized form, except perhaps under high magnification; however, seeds of *Ipomoea* are found at Historic Period sites, but these probably represent the morning glory, which is a common weed in southeastern agricultural fields; Kristen J. Gremillion, personal communication, 2002.

88. Bartram, *Bartram on the Southeastern Indians*, 180.

89. Hatley, "Cherokee Women Farmers," 42.

90. Hawkins, *Letters*, 2:552; Hawkins, "Letters of Benjamin Hawkins," 322.

91. Hawkins, *Letters*, 2:522, 621.

92. Ibid., 534, 560.

93. Jordan-Bychkov and Kaups, *American Backwoods*, 115.

94. Richard Thomas, "His Book," 477. See Chapter 11 for a more complete discussion of reciprocity.

95. Bartram, *Bartram on the Southeastern Indians*, 236.

96. Hawkins, *Letters*, 1:15.

97. Ibid.

98. Black drink is discussed at length in Charles Hudson, *Black Drink*.

99. Hawkins, *Letters*, 1:288.

100. Ibid.

101. Swanton describes *coonti* in "Coonti." Also see Hawkins, *Letters*, 1:286, and Bartram, *Bartram on the Southeastern Indians*, 237.

102. Hawkins, *Letters*, 1:50; Romans, *Concise Natural History*, 145.

103. Gremillion, "Paleoethnobotany of Native Historic Communities," 9; Hatley, "Tallapoosa Landscape," 85.

104. Bartram, *Bartram on the Southeastern Indians*, 165–66, 232, 239.

105. Swanton, *Indians of the Southeastern United States*, 285.

106. Ibid., 289–93.

107. Charles Hudson, *Southeastern Indians*, 289. For an examination of prehistoric

domestication of chenopodium, see Gremillion, "Crop and Weed." In one of his journals, Bartram described some methods of food preparation among the Seminoles; see Bartram, *Bartram on the Southeastern Indians*, 236–39.

108. Hawkins, *Letters*, 1:300; Bartram, *Bartram on the Southeastern Indians*, 270–71 n. 26. Also see Jakes and Ericksen, "Prehistoric Use of Sumac."

109. There are many works on American Indian use of herbal medicines, but little specifically on the Creeks. For an introduction to this topic, see Vogel, *American Indian Medicine*; Moerman, *Native American Ethnobotany*; and Erichsen-Brown, *Medicinal and Other Uses*. Swanton, *Creek Religion*, 639–70; Canouts, "Towards a Reconstruction," 146–48, 156–64; and Grantham, *Creation Myths*, 55–62, have short sections on Creek herbal medicines. Bartram, *Bartram on the Southeastern Indians*, 161–64, gives some details on a few Creek medicinals. It is also likely that many of the folk medicines of white southerners were based on Indian recipes; for a recent discussion on white folk medicines from 1750 to 1820, see Moss, *Southern Folk Medicine*. For an essay detailing the complete ethnohistorical sources for Creek medicine, see Lewis and Jordan, *Creek Indian Medicine Ways*, 122–66. There are, of course, medicine men and women among contemporary Creeks who know the uses of various herbal remedies and the incantations that are just as important in medicine and magic. In *Creek Indian Medicine Ways*, David Lewis Jr., a contemporary Creek medicine man, collaborates with anthropologist Ann Jordan in relating contemporary medicine ways as passed down in the oral traditions of his family's long history of medicine people (Jackson Lewis, David Lewis's great-grandfather, was John R. Swanton's well-known collaborator on Creek medicine and oral traditions in the early twentieth century); see esp. 78–89 for various plants used in healing and 90–105 for the procedures in "making medicine."

110. Swan, "Position and State," 270; Swanton, *Creek Religion*, 614–29. Little scholarly work has been devoted to Creek medicine and magic, and that which has been done uses the methods of the ethnographic present, which combine sources of information from the eighteenth, nineteenth, and twentieth centuries to construct some sense of Creek practices. For instance, Swanton combines contemporary twentieth-century Creek accounts with historic accounts in *Creek Religion*, and Grantham also uses the ethnographic present to summarize some aspects of Creek medicine and magic in *Creation Myths*. Although ideas about the supernatural world are perhaps some of the most enduring structures of a society, one should use Grantham and Swanton with caution.

111. Richard White, *Roots of Dependency*, 28, makes this point in regard to hunting and subsistence agriculture for the eighteenth-century Choctaws. Anthropologists have done much work looking at various peoples who have a mixed economy of foraging and subsistence agriculture; for a general introduction to this literature, see Cashdan, *Risk and Uncertainty*. Scholars of the southeastern Indians have focused largely on the mixed economy that resulted with the domestication of plants during the Woodland Period; see Scarry, *Foraging and Farming*; Winterhalder and Goland, "Diet Choice, Risk, and Plant Domestication"; Winterhalder and Goland, "On Population, Foraging Efficiency, and Plant Domestication"; and Smith, Cowan, and Hoffman, *Rivers of Change*.

112. Hawkins, *Letters*, 2:521.

113. Hunt, *Physiography of the United States*, 59; Charles Hudson, *Southeastern Indians*, 20–21.

114. Pope, *Tour*, 62.

115. Ibid., 60.

116. Hawkins, *Letters*, 1:254.

117. Ibid., 38, 254.

118. Ibid., 294, 297–98.

119. Ibid., 24, 297–98.

120. Ibid., 2:521, 550, 553, 569; Timothy Barnard to Edward Price, December 17, 1797, Entry No. 42, RG 75, NA.

121. Bartram, *Bartram on the Southeastern Indians*, 127.

122. Hawkins, *Letters*, 2:521; Mauelshagen and Davis, *Partners*, 55.

123. Joel W. Martin, *Sacred Revolt*, 102–8, first noted this growing rift among the Creeks in regard to the plan for civilization; Martin proposes that those who favored the plan were mostly the wealthy métis elite. Saunt, *New Order*, 205–29, further argues that it was the métis elite who demonstrated this change in attitude during the drought.

124. Hawkins, *Letters*, 1:14, 103, 129; Hawkins, "Letters of Benjamin Hawkins," 322–23.

125. Pope, *Tour*, 60; Swanton, *Creek Religion*, 629–31; Bartram, *Bartram on the Southeastern Indians*, 69, 118–19.

126. Hawkins, *Letters*, 1:292, 302, 310.

127. Ibid., 311.

128. Ibid.

129. Bartram, *Travels through North and South Carolina*, 305.

130. This is the basic argument in Baden, "Stability and Change." Foster also offers archaeological evidence from Historic Period Creek sites to support this; see Foster, "Long Term Average Rate" and "Evolutionary Ecology."

131. Foster, "Long Term Average Rate," 183–92, 217–18.

132. Cowdrey, *This Land*, 77.

133. Baden, "Stability and Change," 56–58.

134. Ibid., 58. Russell, in "Soil Conditions and Plant Growth," asserts that the denitrification process is actually encouraged by waterlogged conditions, and alluvial soils are, therefore, not necessarily nitrogen rich.

135. Meyers, in examining the alluvial soils in the Ridge and Valley province of northwest Georgia, also found that the friability of the soils, which is increased by flooding, is more important than nitrogen replenishment as a factor in influencing Mississippian Period site locations; see Maureen Elizabeth Siewert Meyers, "Natural Factors."

136. Baden, "Stability and Change," 57.

137. Hatley, "Tallapoosa Landscape," 83.

138. Gremillion, "Fusihatchee"; Knight, *Tukabatchee*, 112–13; Gremillion, "Paleoethnobotany of Native Historic Communities," 9. Some of these weeds (chenopodium, knotweed, and little barley) were prehistoric cultigens, but archaeologists believe that by the mid-eighteenth century, their use as food had declined and that the weeds

at Fusihatchee, in particular, were just weeds; see Gremillion, "Paleoethnobotany of Native Historic Communities," 6, 10. Gremillion, "Human Ecology at the Edge of History," 25–26, proposes that many of the weeds found during the Historic Period were introduced varieties that either edged out native weeds or colonized other disturbed habitats.

139. Gregory Waselkov, personal communication, 2001; Hatley, "Tallapoosa Landscape," 85–87.

140. Mood, "Winthrop," 127; Romans, *Concise Natural History*, 119.

141. Pope, *Tour*, 60.

142. DeBrahm, *DeBrahm's Report*, 994.

143. Hawkins, *Letters*, 1:291, 296, 297.

144. Again, Foster shows soil depletion and low corn production to have been a primary factor in some Historic Period Creek residential mobility; however Foster's study does not cover the ranching era (ca. 1780–1830). See Foster, "Long Term Average Rate."

Chapter Eight

1. Parades and Plante, in a 1975 National Park Service report, were the first to recognize the importance of ranching in the changing economy of the Creeks with the end of the deerskin trade; see Parades and Plante, "Economics, Politics, and the Subjugation," 12–22. Since then, many scholars have documented the ranching complex among southern Indians during the Historic Period. Usner, *Indians, Settlers, and Slaves*, 149–90, documents the importance of ranching as part of the frontier exchange system in the lower Mississippi Valley during the eighteenth century. For a discussion of ranching among the late-eighteenth-century Choctaws, see Carson, *Searching for the Bright Path*, 70–85. Saunt, *New Order*, 46–50, 159–60, 171–74, documents the part that livestock played in dividing the wealthy from the poor among late-eighteenth-century Creeks. Archaeologists generally acknowledge the important transforming effects of ranching on the Indian lifestyles, especially settlement patterns; see Waselkov, "Changing Strategies"; Worth, "Lower Creeks," 286–91; and Jay Johnson, "Chickasaws," 107–15. For a look at the use of introduced vertebrates in the early eighteenth century, see Pavao-Zuckerman, "Vertebrate Subsistence." Ver Steeg, *Origins of a Southern Mosaic*, 114–16, first noted the importance of ranching for the economy of the South Carolina colony during its early years (1690–1715). Still, the role of domesticated animals, especially herd animals such as cows, pigs, and sheep, in the early southern colonial experience has received only the most cursory scholarly attention, despite the proposition by Reitz that the ability of these animals to survive very much affected the success or failure of some early colonies; see Reitz, "Spanish Colonial Experience" and "Morphometric Data." Southern ranching during the Federal era and the antebellum years has received a bit more attention, and it is generally acknowledged that ranching was integral to the economies of both eras; see Clark and Guice, *Old Southwest*, 99–116; Guice, "Cattle Raisers"; Hilliard, *Hog Meat*, 92–140; and McDonald and McWhiney, "Antebellum Southern Herdsman."

2. Swanton, *Indians of the Southeastern United States*, 299; Bartram, *Bartram on the Southeastern Indians*, 164.

3. Hawkins, *Letters*, 1:203.

4. Bartram, *Bartram on the Southeastern Indians*, 59.

5. Bartram, *Travels through North and South Carolina*, 136.

6. Adair, *Adair's History*, 340.

7. Hawkins, *Letters*, 2:554.

8. Adair, *Adair's History*, 138–39.

9. Hawkins, *Letters*, 1:352.

10. This conclusion and the archaeological evidence supporting it are presented in Pavao-Zuckerman, "Vertebrate Subsistence."

11. Jordan-Bychkov and Kaups, *American Backwoods*, 120.

12. Hawkins, *Letters*, 2:553.

13. Ibid., 511, 553.

14. Ibid., 553.

15. Reitz, "Spanish Colonial Experience," 84.

16. Hawkins, *Letters*, 2:511, 553.

17. Ibid., 1:296.

18. Ibid., 2:525.

19. Ibid., 631.

20. Ibid., 530; Bartram, *Travels through North and South Carolina*, 121; Richard Thomas, "His Book," 475; Benjamin Hawkins to Edward Price, December 12, 1798, Benjamin Hawkins's Letterbook, INHP; Timothy Barnard to Edward Price, April 27, 1797, Entry No. 42, RG 75, NA.

21. Knight, *Tukabatchee*, 181.

22. Hawkins, "Letters of Benjamin Hawkins," 328–38.

23. Using the data in Hawkins, *Sketch*, Parades and Plante, in "Economics, Politics, and the Subjugation," 13–14, tallied the cattle, hogs, horses, and chickens and found them in almost all Upper and Lower Creek towns. My research, too, indicates that most Creeks were involved in ranching to some extent, although the amount of profit from it certainly varied. This is in contrast to Joel W. Martin, who asserts in *Sacred Revolt*, 80–81, that the ranching complex was spearheaded by the métis elite, and to Saunt, in *New Order*, 47–50, 159–61, 171–74, who follows Martin and argues that the métis elite were mostly involved, although he acknowledges that the nonelite were involved as well. Saunt further argues that ranching generated deep anxieties among the Creeks because it was a kind of wealth that could be accumulated and hence underwrote the emerging class divisions; he further explores the divisive effects of livestock raising on Creek gender roles and inheritance rules.

24. Hawkins, *Letters*, 2:583.

25. Joel W. Martin, *Sacred Revolt*, 80–81; Saunt, *New Order*, 47–50.

26. Most of Barnard's business ventures are recorded in Letters of Timothy Barnard, GDAH; Timothy Barnard to Jonathan Halstead, November 6, 1802, Entry No. 42, RG 75, NA; Swan, "Position and State," 261; Starrett, *Appraisal Report*, 116.

27. Hawkins, *Letters*, 1:316.

28. Ibid., 24–25, 2:556.

29. Historians are divided over the effects of the plan for civilization on the southeastern Indians, especially its effects on gender roles. Braund, in "Guardians of Tradition," 252–53, concludes that the new economic ventures offered in the plan for civilization, such as ranching, contributed to a growing separation between market-oriented Creeks and "traditional" Creeks, but that women tended to be culturally conservative. Likewise, Saunt, in *New Order*, 139–63, argues that Creek women's new economic pursuits increased gender tensions among the Creeks because it was an entirely new way of gaining wealth and understanding property. On the other hand, Perdue, in *Cherokee Women*, 115–34, argues that the Cherokees folded much about the plan for civilization into existing cultural patterns and that the result was both a change in context for those patterns and a persistence of those patterns. In this argument, Perdue asserts that ranching was never important to Cherokee women because it "fulfilled no cultural function." Instead, ranching appealed more to men because it was analogous to hunting; see Perdue, *Cherokee Women*, 124, 121–23. Carson, likewise, argues that Choctaw women linguistically glossed cows as fruit trees, which was a cognitive trick for keeping ranching within their defined roles as gatherers; see Carson, *Searching for the Bright Path*, 77–79. My research indicates that ranching was, in fact, very integral to Creek women at the turn of the nineteenth century and that many women were deeply involved in it. I understand this to be a new role for women, but one that was not altogether foreign or that needed to be glossed into purely Indian terms. In other words, by the end of the eighteenth century, Creek women and men were quite familiar with ranching, either through their own participation in it or through the participation of their white and black friends, family, and neighbors. Plus, that most families were involved in ranching tends to indicate that involvement did not divide along class lines, although the wealth generated from it probably did, as Saunt and Braund indicate.

30. Hawkins, *Letters*, 1:353, 387, 2:553.

31. Ibid., 1:298, 299, 2:556.

32. Ibid., 1:35.

33. Ibid., 2.

34. Gosse, *Letters*, 223–24, 271–72. Gosse is describing a white wrangler here, but I assume that Creek wranglers would have acquired the same skills. Waselkov's compilation of British trade items does not show European-made whips to have been in much demand, but this list stops at 1799, when ranching was still ascending; plus, Creek wranglers may have made their own version of a whip. See Waselkov, "Anglo-Indian Trade," 196–97, 209.

35. Hawkins, *Letters*, 2:530.

36. Ibid., 1:15, 302; Bartram, *Bartram on the Southeastern Indians*, 53; Gosse, *Letters*, 223–24, 271–72.

37. Hawkins, "Letters of Benjamin Hawkins," 46; Gatschet, *Migration Legend*, 144; Swanton, *Early History*, 249.

38. Bartram, *Bartram on the Southeastern Indians*, 53, 77, 82, 164, 198; Hawkins, *Letters*, 1:288–316; Richard Thomas, "His Book," 475.

39. Read, *Indian Place Names*, 130.

40. Hawkins, *Letters*, 1:248.

41. Ibid., 2:553.

42. Ibid., 1:352.

43. Timothy Barnard to James Seagrove, July 13, 1792, Letters of Timothy Barnard, GDAH.

44. Hilliard, *Hog Meat*, 129; for a comprehensive discussion of antebellum herding, see 92–140.

45. Ibid., 95.

46. Gosse, *Letters*, 63.

47. Hilliard, *Hog Meat*, 102.

48. Reitz, "Spanish Colonial Experience," 87–89; Reitz, "Morphometric Data," 706–9.

49. Silver, *New Face*, 179.

50. Hilliard, *Hog Meat*, 95–96, 129; Bonner, *History*, 29.

51. Benjamin Hawkins to Colonel David Henley, November 23, 1798, Hawkins Family Papers, UNC.

52. Hilliard, *Hog Meat*, 136; Silver, *New Face*, 180.

53. Silver, *New Face*, 173.

54. Ibid., 177; Starrett, *Appraisal Report*, 117.

55. Hawkins, *Letters*, 1:296, 300–305.

56. Hilliard, *Hog Meat*, 137.

57. Silver, *New Face*, 179.

58. Romans, *Concise Natural History*, 16, 23; Starrett, *Appraisal Report*, 117.

59. Jordan-Bychkov and Kaups, *American Backwoods*, 70; Starrett, *Appraisal Report*; USDA Forest Service, "Species."

60. Silver, *New Face*, 180.

61. Ibid., 180; USDA Forest Service, "Species."

62. USDA Forest Service, "Species."

63. Silver, *New Face*, 177; Gosse, *Letters*, 135.

64. Hawkins, *Letters*, 1:291.

65. Young, "Topographical Memoir," 32; Silver, *New Face*, 64.

66. Representatives of the Creek Lands to Commissioners of Georgia, in Cochran, *New American State Papers*, 140; Timothy Barnard to Edward Price, March 27, 1797, Entry No. 42, RG 75, NA.

67. Indian Petitions to Thomas Jefferson, Parker Papers, HSP; Timothy Barnard to Edward Price, March 27, 1797, Entry No. 42, RG 75, NA.

68. Hawkins, *Letters*, 2:524; Timothy Barnard to Edward Price, March 27, 1797, Entry No. 42, RG 75, NA.

69. For a good discussion of this U.S./Creek contention, see Saunt, *New Order*, 46–50. In the mid-nineteenth century, after Removal, when the southern livestock population was reaching its peak, overgrazing by free-range livestock led many southern ranchers to grow pasturage for their cattle and corn for their hogs. Also, antebellum livestock production was primarily in areas north and south of Creek country—in areas of plentiful grasses. For a discussion on antebellum ranching, see Guice, "Cattle Raisers," 184–85; Hilliard, *Hog Meat*, 92–140; and McDonald and McWhiney,

"Antebellum Southern Herdsman," 147–66. Another reason for this discrepancy was the opening of the Coastal Plain longleaf forest to development in the mid-nineteenth century. Some southern herders who still practiced free-ranging husbandry began moving into the longleaf forests when much of the South went into cotton production; see Starrett, *Appraisal Report*, 118.

70. Canouts, "Towards a Reconstruction," 107.

71. Hatley, "Tallapoosa Landscape," 95.

72. Newsom, "History of Deer"; Silver, *New Face*, 24–26; Hatley, "Tallapoosa Landscape," 89, 91, 93–94.

73. McDonald and McWhiney, "Antebellum Southern Herdsman," 158–59.

74. Haan, in "'Trade do's not Flourish," 349–50, first made the same observation for coastal South Carolina as early as 1715.

75. Henry Dearborn to Benjamin Hawkins, January 24, 1803, Entry No. 2, RG 75, NA; Henry Dearborn to William R. Davie, July 3, 1801, in Cochran, *New American State Papers*, 180; Hawkins' Journal on the Treaty of Colerain, June 24, 1796, in Cochran, *New American State Papers*, 139; Creek Chiefs to Thomas Jefferson, November 3, 1805, Parker Papers, HSP; June 9, 1802, "Benjamin Hawkins's Journal of Occurrences," APS; Hawkins, *Letters*, 2:608.

76. Hatley, "Tallapoosa Landscape," 95.

77. Ibid.

78. Doster, *Creek Indians and Their Florida Lands*, 2:215.

79. Charles Hudson, *Southeastern Indians*, 139; Swanton, *Creek Religion*, 527, 598–99. Bears also appear in many Creek oral traditions and myths; see Grantham, *Creation Myths*, 167–73, 181–86, 231–32, 237–39, 266–67; Swanton, *Myths and Tales*, 82, 87, 149–50, 192; and Lankford, *Native American Legends*, 69, 118, 123. Bears were also mythical creatures to the Cherokees; see Mooney, *Myths of the Cherokees*, 239, 250.

80. Hawkins, *Letters*, 1:294.

81. Silver, *New Face*, 176–77.

82. Benjamin Hawkins to Jonathan Halstead, February 20, 1805, Entry No. 42, RG 75, NA.

83. Gosse, *Letters*, 222.

84. Waselkov, "Anglo-Indian Trade," 196–97.

85. Von Reck, *Von Reck's Voyage*, 37.

86. Silver, *New Face*, 177.

87. Gosse, *Letters*, 221–22.

88. Hawkins, *Letters*, 1:292.

89. Hawkins, "Letters of Benjamin Hawkins," 88; Hawkins, *Letters*, 1:50; Goff, Utley, and Hemperley, *Placenames of Georgia*, 43; Read "Indian Stream Names," 129. Read and Goff spell it *echeconnee*.

90. Adair, *Adair's History*, 121–22; Romans, *Concise Natural History*, 94.

91. Waselkov, "Anglo-Indian Trade," 198–99.

92. Hawkins, *Letters*, 1:285–327; Pope, *Tour*, 62.

93. Hawkins, *Letters*, 1:21.

94. Cowdrey, *This Land*, 3; Jordan-Bychkov and Kaups, *American Backwoods*, 170; Romans, *Concise Natural History*, 23.

95. Silver, *New Face*, 50.

96. Newsom, "History of Deer"; Silver, *New Face*, 111–12.

97. Cowdrey, *This Land*, 3; Hatley, "Tallapoosa Landscape," 99; Silver, *New Face*, 180.

98. Again, Parades and Plante first observed this shift in "Economics, Politics, and the Subjugation," 18–24.

99. Benson, *Cultural Resources Survey*, 464; Elliott et al., "Up on the Upatoi," 255.

100. Hawkins, *Letters*, 1:290, 301, 302, 304.

101. Ibid., 290–314.

102. Worth, "Lower Creeks," 286–91.

103. Hawkins, *Letters*, 1:290–314. A similar pattern has been established for the late-eighteenth-century Chickasaws as they moved from their nucleated settlements near present-day Tupelo and spread throughout present-day northern Mississippi; see Jay Johnson, "Chickasaws," 107–9.

104. This pattern resembles that of the Removal era Cherokee town of Sixes Old Town, where twenty-six families lived along a twenty-six-mile section of the Etowah River; see Ledbetter et al., "Cultural Resources Survey," 274–92.

105. The settlement patterns are shown in several survey and excavation reports on Historic Creek sites; see Benson, *Cultural Resources Survey*; Holland, "Mid-Eighteenth Century Indian Village"; Knight, *Tukabatchee*, 9–19; Ledbetter and Braley, *Archaeological and Historical Investigations*; Mistovich and Knight, *Excavations at Four Sites*; Mistovich and Zeanah, *Intensive Phase II Survey*; Marvin Smith, *Historic Period Indian Archaeology*; Waselkov, *Coosa River Valley Archaeology*; Waselkov, *Lower Tallapoosa*; Waselkov, "Changing Strategies"; Waselkov, Cottier, and Sheldon, *Fusihatchee*; Waselkov, Cottier, and Sheldon, *Archaeological Excavations*; and White et al., *Archaeological Survey at Lake Seminole*. The chronology of the historic Creek archaeological sites is at present not refined enough to determine how many of these sites date to the late eighteenth and early nineteenth centuries.

106. The archaeological work done at Upatoi is reported in Elliott et al., "Up on the Upatoi."

107. Hawkins, *Letters*, 1:311.

108. Ibid., 42–43, 311–12.

109. Ibid., 302–3.

110. Ibid., 88.

111. Anthropologists studying late-nineteenth- and twentieth-century Creeks have shown the towns to be a particularly salient social and political entity; see Speck, "Taskigi Town"; Swanton, *Indians of the Southeastern United States*, 629–41; and Champagne, *Social Order*, 238–40.

112. Hawkins, *Letters*, 1:95; Henry Drinker, Thomas Wintson, and Thomas Stewardson to Henry Dearborn, December 31, 1801, Entry No. 1, RG 75, NA.

113. Hawkins, *Letters*, 1:95, 2:520.

114. Henry Drinker, Thomas Wintson, and Thomas Stewardson to Henry Dearborn, December 31, 1801, Entry No. 1, RG 75, NA.

115. Hawkins, *Letters*, 2:531.

116. Braund, *Deerskins and Duffels*, 184; Waselkov, "Changing Strategies," 239;

Saunt, *New Order*, 159–61. It is important to note here that Mississippian Period farmers also sometimes lived on individual farmsteads, and there is no indication that the matrilineage was affected by this type of settlement pattern.

117. This argument follows Braund, *Deerskins and Duffels*, 131–32, 184, which notes that women provided much cultural continuity during the deerskin trade era, although Braund suggests that the plan for civilization supplanted the matrilineage. Perdue, *Cherokee Women*, 174–77, 190–91, states that matrilineality was a persisting cultural feature among the Cherokees, despite economic forces to the contrary and the many efforts by American government officials and Christian missionaries to change Cherokee kinship to a bilateral, patriarchal system. This is a refinement of an earlier argument Perdue presented in "Cult of True Womanhood"; see esp. 46–47.

118. A Cherokee farmstead near present-day Canton, Georgia, dating to the same time period had one or two log cabins with storage basements. This site is reported in Webb, "Hickory Log."

119. Elliott et al., "Up on the Upatoi," 44, 47, 69, 81, 82–86, 262.

120. Hawkins, *Letters*, 1:4, 8, 24, 28, 42–43. Also, at the Removal era Cherokee town of Sixes Old Town on the Etowah River in present-day Georgia, each family had approximately three houses (which may or may not have been log cabins), a corncrib, and approximately seventeen acres in cultivation. Although it is by no means certain, the presence of three houses per family suggests a household compound. At Sixes Old Town, the average number of people per household was seven. Since most Indian women only had two to three children with any marriage, seven people in a household may imply that the matrilineage composition of a household was still intact on the individual farmsteads. At Sixes Old Town, each household had an average of two farmers older than eighteen years, one weaver, and two spinsters (cotton spinners). This also suggests a matrilineage, since each household contained more than one adult male (the farmers?) and perhaps two or three adult females, although adolescent girls also wove and spun; see Ledbetter et al., "Cultural Resources Survey," 274–92.

121. Hawkins, *Letters*, 1:88.

Chapter Nine

1. This is not to say that all manufactured goods came through the British and French trade system. Waselkov, "Seventeenth-Century Trade," documents that goods also traveled to Creek country via the Spanish in La Florida during the seventeenth century. It was the British trade, however, that proved transforming.

2. Usner, *Indians, Settlers, and Slaves*, first identified the mixed economy of hunting, farming, gathering, and trading as a coherent system of frontier exchanges. Usner tracked the numerous exchanges of goods and services among whites, blacks, and Indians living in the Lower Mississippi Valley before 1783, and he discovered the exchanges helped to define the region and were a cohesive element in its development. He dubbed the whole a "frontier exchange economy"; I use the term here as he defines it. Unlike the Lower Mississippi Valley, where the plantation economy was the dominant economic activity, however, in Creek country the deerskin trade had been the dominant economic activity until the late eighteenth century. The frontier exchange

economy of the interior Southeast, therefore, was somewhat different from what Usner describes for the Lower Mississippi Valley. In *American Indians in the Lower Mississippi Valley*, Usner extends his analysis through the nineteenth century. Carson, *Searching for the Bright Path*, 51–69, discusses the Choctaw frontier exchange economy of the eighteenth century.

3. Hill, *Weaving New Worlds*, chronicles the movement of and subsequent changes in Cherokee basketry from prehistoric and protohistoric utilitarian and ritual objects for community consumption to eighteenth-century utilitarian objects for exchange in the frontier economy to twentieth-century decorative items for exchange in the tourist industry. Hill shows how changes in Cherokee basketry are tied to changes in Cherokee history, society, and ecology.

4. Hawkins, *Letters*, 1:230.

5. Creek chiefs to Thomas Jefferson, November 3, 1805, Parker Papers, HSP; Entry No. 108, RG 11, NA; Henry Dearborn to Benjamin Hawkins, February 11, 1804, Entry No. 2, RG 75, NA; Hawkins, *Letters*, 2:592.

6. Creek Chiefs to Thomas Jefferson, November 3, 1805, Parker Papers, HSP.

7. Hawkins, *Letters*, 1:11, 230.

8. These exchanges are not recorded in any formal accounting methods. The Creek Factory records list transactions by day, and exchanges such as those discussed here occur in almost all entries and hence are too numerous to list. These records are Entry No. 5, Entry No. 6, Entry No. 9, Entry No. 42, Entry No. 43, Entry No. 47, Entry No. 49, Entry No. 50, Entry No. 52, Entry No. 53, and Entry No. 1065, RG 75, NA. Other good sources for exchanges between Georgians and Creeks are the depositions in Creek Indian Letters, Talks, and Treaties, 1705–1839, and Indian Letters, 1782–1839, GDAH.

9. May 14, 1799, Benjamin Hawkins's Letterbook, INHP.

10. Richard Thomas, "His Book," 484.

11. For a discussion of the preparation and cooking of corn, see Charles Hudson, *Southeastern Indians*, 303–7.

12. Romans, *Concise Natural History*, 93.

13. Hawkins, "Letters of Benjamin Hawkins," 328–39.

14. Timothy Barnard to Edward Price, Sept. 22, 1797, Entry No. 42, RG 75, NA; July 31, 1798, Benjamin Hawkins's Letterbook, INHP.

15. Hawkins, *Letters*, 1:235.

16. Ibid., 2:753.

17. Benjamin Hawkins's Estate, Sales and Inventory, Letters of Benjamin Hawkins, GDAH.

18. There are several such entries in both Entry No. 49, RG 75, NA, and Benjamin Hawkins's Letterbook, INHP.

19. Letters of Benjamin Hawkins, GDAH, 352, 354.

20. Ibid.

21. Ibid., 503.

22. Permit for Order in Dealing in Stock, November 1799, Benjamin Hawkins's Letterbook, INHP.

23. Swan, "Position and State," 282.

24. These sorts of transactions are recorded throughout Richard Thomas, "His Book."

25. The records from the Creek Factory are contained in several entries; for a list of items routinely bought and sold at the factory, see Entry No. 42, Entry No. 52, and Entry No. 1065, RG 75, NA. The southeastern Indians understood button snakeroot, in particular, to have not only powerful medicinal value but also powerful ritual and magical value; see Ethridge, "Button-snakeroot."

26. Fort Hawkins, July 8, 1816, Entry No. 52, box 3, 1809–1816, RG 75, NA.

27. The Commissioners to the Secretary of War, November 20, 1789, in Cochran, *New American State Papers*, 92–94.

28. The literature on Mississippian Period chiefdoms and chiefly power is quite large and cannot be enumerated here. However, Wesson, "Households and Hegemony," tracks the changing role of prestige items among the southeastern Indians and in particular the Historic Period Creeks.

29. This is the basis of Wesson's argument in "Creek and Pre-Creek Revisited"; see esp. 99–100, 101, 103–5. Wesson goes on to say that because the elite could not control access to such prestige items, the result was an erosion of "traditional elite authority" and a standardization of the political economy to the household level. As this occurred, the Creek elite sought to strengthen their position by accumulating more and more prestige items. Wesson concludes that "the Creek were not dependent upon Euro-American trade goods because these were functionally superior, or because the Creek were becoming acculturated to Euro-American lifeways, but because Euro-American prestige goods were essential capital for developing social status and prestige. In the end, these items became necessary for social reproduction" (ibid., 105). This take is quite different from that of Saunt, who argues in *New Order* that during the eighteenth century, the elite Creeks accumulated items because they came to understand property as capitalistic wealth and acted accordingly. This difference between Saunt and Wesson can be situated within the large debate on continuity and change. See n. 32 below.

30. Bartram, *Travels through North and South Carolina*, 319.

31. Waselkov, "Anglo-Indian Trade," 196–97, 207–11. Waselkov has tallied trade items from trade lists covering 1702–99; this tally shows the purchasing trends of southeastern Indians during the eighteenth century.

32. The question of persistence and change is important for determining the full effects of colonization on native peoples. Most scholars agree that once Indian life became entwined with that of Europeans and Africans, it was changed, but exactly what was changed and what stayed the same is contested. There is also the question of what old patterns were adapted to new circumstances. Scholars acknowledge that the blending of European/African/Indian cultural elements produced a new world made up of elements from all three as well as elements particular to this new world. Likewise, most scholars agree that entering the capitalist economy changed much about Indian life, but again, they are not always in agreement as to the degree of this change. However, this question rests on tracking Mississippian Period continuities through time with some degree of certainty. Some scholars, most notably Charles Hudson and his students, argue for collapse with European contact; see Charles Hudson, *Knights of*

Spain; Hudson and Tesser, *Forgotten Centuries*; and Ethridge and Hudson, *Transfor-mation*. Others argue against collapse from various angles; see esp. Galloway, *Choctaw Genesis*, and Muller, *Mississippian Political Economy*. Addressing the question of Mississippian continuities first entails sifting through some serious methodological problems in moving from archaeological source material and concepts to historical source material and concepts, which has yet to be done; for some beginnings in tackling these methodological issues, see Galloway, *"Conjoncture* and *Longue Durée"*; Galloway, "Archaeology of Ethnohistorical Narrative"; Krech, "State of Ethnohistory"; Knapp, *Archaeology, Annales, and Ethnohistory*; Lightfoot, "Culture Contact Studies"; Pauketat, *Archaeology of Traditions*; and Rogers and Wilson, *Ethnohistory and Archaeology*.

33. Both Joel W. Martin, *Sacred Revolt*, 104–7, and Champagne, *Social Order*, 54, 92, make this point. Martin identifies this tension between acquisitive and nonacquisitive Creeks as the beginnings of a disruptive class division. Saunt, *New Order*, examines the emergence and effects of the acquisitive ideology among the elite Creeks.

34. Saunt, *New Order*, 175.

35. Anthropologists have long recognized reciprocity as a form of economic exchange among pre-state, kinship-based societies. For an introduction to the concept, see Sahlins, *Stone Age Economics*. For a discussion of the transformation from reciprocity to capitalist dependency among various Indian groups, see Richard White, *Roots of Dependency*. For a discussion of the persistence and adaptation of reciprocity among Creeks during the Historic Period, see Wesson, "Households and Hegemony."

36. Stiggins, *Creek Indian History*, 52.

37. Hawkins, *Letters*, 1:196; Benjamin Hawkins to Edward Price, May 29, 1799, Entry No. 42, RG 75, NA. On chalks, see Braund, *Deerskins and Duffels*, 264–65. A chalk was a medium of currency worth about forty cents.

38. Saunt, *New Order*, 175–77.

39. This is in contrast to Saunt, who in *New Order* argues that the elite Creeks adopted the rational, capitalist mind-set and that this created a widening economic, ideological, and cultural gap between the rich and the poor, which he attributes as the reason for the Red Stick War and for the Seminole resistance.

40. Stiggins, *Creek Indian History*, 78.

41. Richard Thomas, "His Book," 489.

42. Hawkins, *Letters*, 2:535.

43. May 18, 1814, and February 21, 1815, Entry No. 47, RG 75, NA.

44. Timothy Barnard to Edward Price, October 15, 1798, Entry No. 42, RG 75, NA.

45. Henry Dearborn to William R. Davie, James Wilkinson, and Benjamin Hawkins, July 3, 1801, in Cochran, *New American State Papers*, 180; Dexter to R. Davies, General Wilkinson, Benjamin Hawkins, July 22, 1801, Entry No. 2, RG 75, NA.

46. Waselkov, "Anglo-Indian Trade," 196–97, 209.

47. Hawkins, *Letters*, 2:553.

48. Manuscript No. 4914, from the Notebook of Michael Johnstone Kenan (grandfather of Mrs. Walter A. Harris of Macon), Swanton Collection, SI.

49. Romans, *Concise Natural History*, 59, 94.

50. Hawkins, *Letters*, 1:45.

51. Ibid., 2:508.

52. Ibid., 435.

53. Hawkins, "Letters of Benjamin Hawkins," 231.

54. See esp. Entry No. 1065, RG 75, NA, and July 3, August 2, 1798, Benjamin Hawkins's Letterbook, INHP.

55. Inventory of Public Property, January 19, 1808, Entry No. 1065, RG 75, NA.

56. Braund, *Deerskins and Duffels*, 89.

57. Hawkins, *Letters*, 1:134, 146.

58. Ibid., 197.

59. Ibid., 275, 317.

60. Ibid., 189, 262.

61. Ibid., 111, 130.

62. Ibid., 185.

63. August 10, 1798, Benjamin Hawkins's Letterbook, INHP.

64. Hawkins, *Letters*, 2:457; August 10, 1798, Benjamin Hawkins's Letterbook, INHP.

65. Benjamin Hawkins to William Hawkins, Hawkins Family Papers, UNC.

66. January 31, 1798, February 4, March 19, July 11, 1799, Benjamin Hawkins's Letterbook, INHP.

67. March 19, 1799, ibid.

68. This is the price Hawkins recorded in Hawkins, *Letters*, 1:213, and in various entries in Entry No. 49, RG 75, NA.

69. Braund, *Deerskins and Duffels*, 89, 264, takes Florette Henri's estimate that 1 chalk was worth 25 cents, or one deerskin; see Henri, *Southern Indians*, 118–20. However, a 1799 voucher from the Creek Factory lists 40 chalks as being equivalent to $10.00; see voucher for George Cornells, Entry No. 42, RG 75, NA. Henri admits that the chalk system was quite irregular and subject to inflation.

70. In the Creek Factory papers at the National Archives for this time period there are many loose-leaf vouchers from various people for various people; most of the people listed on these vouchers remain unknown. See Entry No. 42, Entry No. 43, Entry No. 47, Entry No. 49, Entry No. 50, Entry No. 52, Entry No. 53, and Entry No. 1065, RG 75, NA.

71. September 5, 1816, Entry No. 47, RG 75, NA.

72. Hawkins, *Letters*, 2:578.

73. Ibid., 511, 528, 592–93.

74. Hawkins, "Letters of Benjamin Hawkins," 324–38.

75. Ibid.

76. Hawkins, *Letters*, 2:606.

77. Von Reck, *Von Reck's Voyage*, 40.

78. Hawkins, *Letters*, 2:507–8.

79. Ibid., 606.

80. Ibid., 494, 606.

81. Ibid., 1:281.

82. Benjamin Hawkins to Edward Wright, July 7, 1807, Entry No. 42, RG 75, NA.

83. Timothy Barnard to General Blackshear, January 14, 1815, Letters of Timothy Barnard, GDAH.

84. Hawkins, *Letters*, 2:406, 537, 773.

85. James Robertson to Pitman Colbert and his company of spies, June 1, 1814, Entry No. 1, RG 75, NA.

86. May 10, 1799, Benjamin Hawkins's Letterbook, INHP.

87. Hawkins, *Letters*, 1:92, 274, 283, 389, 2:526, 589; Indian Department to U.S. Factory, 1797, Entry No. 52, box 1, 1795–1803, RG 75, NA.

88. William Hill to Edward Wright, October 15, 1801, Entry No. 42, RG 75, NA.

89. July 1, 1809, Entry No. 52, RG 75, NA.

90. Indian Department to U.S. Factory, 1797, Entry No. 52, RG 75, NA.

91. August 11, 1817, Entry No. 47, RG 75, NA.

92. October 9, 1817, Entry No. 47, RG 75, NA.

93. July 8, 1816, Entry No. 52, RG 75, NA.

94. Fort Hawkins, July 8, 1816, Entry No. 52, RG 75, NA.

95. January 19, 1808, Entry No. 49, RG 75, NA.

96. Hawkins, *Letters*, 2:559; Timothy Barnard to Benjamin Hawkins, October 10, 1801, Entry No. 1, RG 75, NA.

97. Timothy Barnard to Benjamin Hawkins, October 10, 1801, Entry No. 1, RG 75, NA.

98. Hawkins, *Letters*, 1:355.

99. Ibid., 2:531, 553.

100. Ibid., 552, 554.

101. Bossu, *Travels*, 131.

102. Hawkins, *Letters*, 2:412.

103. Hawkins, "Letters of Benjamin Hawkins," 328–36; Entry No. 49, RG 75, NA.

104. Hawkins, *Letters*, 1:246.

105. Ibid., 14.

106. Braund, *Deerskins and Duffels*, 122–24; Waselkov, "Anglo-Indian Trade," 194–96, 205–8.

107. Point Blankets, George Sibley, Entry No. 6, RG 75, NA.

108. Waselkov, "Anglo-Indian Trade," 194–96, 207–8.

109. Hawkins, *Letters*, 1:238; Timothy Barnard to Benjamin Hawkins, October 10, 1802, Letters of Timothy Barnard, GDAH.

110. Hawkins, *Letters*, 1:238; Timothy Barnard to Benjamin Hawkins, October 10, 1802, Letters of Timothy Barnard, GDAH.

111. Hawkins to Edward Price, November 19, 1798, Entry No. 42, RG 75, NA.

112. Benjamin Hawkins, "Letters of Benjamin Hawkins," 200, 228.

113. Hawkins, *Letters*, 1:238.

114. Ibid., 2:407, 557.

115. Ibid., 411–12.

116. Timothy Barnard to Benjamin Hawkins, October 10, 1801, Entry No. 1, RG 75, NA.

117. Hawkins, *Letters*, 2:531.

118. Ibid., 1:329.

119. Ibid., 2:580.

120. Ibid., 633.

121. Ibid., 562.

122. Ibid., 523, 531.

123. Ibid., 583–85.

124. Ibid., 562–63.

125. Ibid., 1:35, 238.

Chapter Ten

1. Romans, *Concise Natural History*, 142.

2. James White to Henry Knox, May 24, 1787, in Cochran, *New American State Papers*, 24.

3. In "Invention of the Creek Nation" Hahn persuasively argues that land issues lay at the heart of the Creek idea of nationhood and, in fact, that the Creek nation was a situational, frontier institution that, when land was not at issue, disappeared, "phantom-like, when those talks ended" (257–314, 380).

4. Prucha's extensive works on the history of American Indian policy still stand as the most definitive; see Prucha, *American Indian Policy, American Indian Policy in the Formative Years*, and *Great Father*.

5. De Vorsey, *Indian Boundary*, 3, 35, first noted the importance of the Proclamation of 1763 as a primary focus of Anglo-Indian relations during the pre-Revolution period. This work also chronicles the drawing of the boundary lines in the southern colonies and the consequences for Anglo-Indian political and economic relations. Champagne, *Social Order*, 68–74, argues that the Proclamation of 1763 ushered British hegemony into the Southeast, which diminished the Indian strategy of playing the Europeans off one another and thereby divesting them of an important negotiating tool. Hahn, "Invention of the Creek Nation," 368–80, likewise depicts the Proclamation of 1763 as an important turning point in Anglo-Indian relations. Here Hahn documents that the proclamation divvied up the North American colonies among England, Spain, and France, with little, if any, concern for Indian claims to the territories. The most famous Indian contest for these lands was Pontiac's Rebellion (1763–66); but the Creeks, too, were apprehensive about the proclamation because of the land claims in it and because the European rivalry that they had used to their benefit was ending. According to Hahn, the subsequent Creek difficulties with other southern Indian groups, the British, and later, Americans were based in their opposition to the proclamation and, after the American Revolution, in their efforts to resuscitate the old imperial rivalries.

6. Proclamation of the Continental Congress, September 22, 1781, in Prucha, *Documents*, 3.

7. Prucha, *American Indian Policy*, 30–33.

8. Proclamation of the Continental Congress, September 22, 1783, in Prucha, *Documents*, 3 (emphasis added).

9. Although scholars of the colonial South and southeastern Indian history acknowledge that land speculators played an important role in Indian affairs, the role of land speculators in Indian and American history has not received comprehensive scholarly attention. De Vorsey, *Indian Boundary*, 53, notes the role of land speculation

in the drawing of the southern boundary lines as issued in the Proclamation of 1763. Prucha, *American Indian Policy in the Formative Years*, 137–87, documents the heavy hand that land speculators and their sponsored squatting on Indian lands had in the federal government's formation of American Indian policy. Henri, *Southern Indians*, provides an excellent treatment of the influence of land speculation on southern Indian affairs during Hawkins's tenure among the Creeks. Champagne, *Social Order*, 68–69, 125, 146, 159, notes that land speculation and illegal intrusions were a source of contention and hostility between the southern Indians and the Euro-American governments until Indian Removal, and that land speculators were instrumental in pushing Removal through the federal and state governments. Clark and Guice, *Old Southwest*, 67–82, acknowledges the importance of speculation in the formulation of national land policies. Dunaway, *First American Frontier*, 51–86, examines the role of speculation in the formation of agrarian capitalism in southern Appalachia and the powerful effect this enterprise had in America.

10. Henri, *Southern Indians*, 64.

11. Ibid. For a discussion of the effects of the Yazoo land fraud on American policy and in the history of American settlement in the Mississippi Territory, see Clark and Guice, *Old Southwest*, 67–82.

12. Henri, *Southern Indians*, 62–63.

13. McGillivray, *McGillivray*, 259; Henri, *Southern Indians*, 67.

14. Milfort, *Sojourn*, 90.

15. Hawkins, *Letters*, 1:146.

16. Trade and Intercourse Act, July 22, 1790, in Prucha, *Documents*, 15; Prucha, *American Indian Policy in the Formative Years*, 45–46.

17. Prucha, *American Indian Policy in the Formative Years*, documents the role of land speculators in undermining the Trade and Intercourse Acts passed throughout the late eighteenth century and the reformulation of Indian policy along lines to benefit their land schemes.

18. Henri, *Southern Indians*, 39–60.

19. Ibid., 52–53.

20. Hawkins, *Letters*, 2:425–31, 446–49.

21. Henry Dearborn to Benjamin Hawkins, June 28, 1805, Entry No. 2, RG 75, NA.

22. Henri was the first to recognize this when she wrote, "Little by little, treaty by treaty, the acre replaced the deerskin as the unit of trade"; see Henri, *Southern Indians*, 134, 137–264.

23. Several scholars have investigated the changing role of gift giving among southeastern Indians during the colonial era. For the Creeks, see Wesson, "Creek and Pre-Creek Revisited"; Wesson, "Households and Hegemony"; and Braund, *Deerskins and Duffels*, 26–39. For the Choctaws, see Richard White, *Roots of Dependency*, 1–148. For various Piedmont Indians, see Merrell "'Our Bond of Peace.'" For the Catawbas, see Merrell, *Indians' New World*, 49–91. For the Virginia Algonquians, see Potter, "Early English Effects." For the Cherokees, see Hatley, *Dividing Paths*. For discussions of the Indian perspective of southeastern Indian/European diplomacy, see Galloway, "'Chief Who Is Your Father'"; Greg O'Brien, "Conqueror Meets the Unconquered"; and Merrell, *Indians' New World*, 134–66.

24. Corkran, *Creek Frontier*, 237–41, 247–52, 259–62, 278–81; Green, *Politics of Indian Removal*, 30.

25. Most U.S. treaties with the southeastern Indians can be found in Entry No. 108, RG 11, NA. However, the records of the negotiations are not included in this collection; some of those can be found in Cochran, *New American State Papers*, and Commissioners of Indian Affairs, *Treaties*.

26. Crutchfield, "Shoes and Feathers," 23.

27. Hawkins, *Letters*, 1:207, 209, 225, 346, 388, 2:555.

28. Commissioners of Indian Affairs, *Treaties*, 62.

29. Treaty of New York, August 1790, Entry No. 108, RG 11, NA.

30. Commissioners of Indian Affairs, *Treaties*, 65–69.

31. Ibid., 88–89.

32. Ibid., 127; Entry No. 108, RG 11, NA.

33. Commissioners of Indian Affairs, *Treaties*, 159–63.

34. Instructions to Commissioners, August 29, 1789, in Cochran, *New American State Papers*, 75; Creek Talks, Hawkins's Journal on the Treaty of Colerain, June 24, 1796, in Cochran, *New American State Papers*, 139–40.

35. Hawkins, *Letters*, 2:481, 483.

36. Ibid., 468–84.

37. Ibid., 404; Henry Dearborn to Benjamin Hawkins, February 12, 1805, Entry No. 1, RG 75, NA.

38. Dearborn to Hawkins, February 12, 1805, Entry No. 2, RG 75, NA.

39. Hawkins, *Letters*, 2:484.

40. Creek Chiefs to Thomas Jefferson, November 3, 1805, Parker Papers, HSP.

41. Jefferson to Creek Chiefs, November 2, 1805, Parker Papers, HSP.

42. Return J. Meigs to William Eustis, December 20, 1811, Entry No. 1, RG 75, NA.

43. Creek Chiefs to Thomas Jefferson, November 3, 1805, Parker Papers, HSP.

44. Commissioners of Indian Affairs, *Treaties*, 127; Entry No. 108, RG 11, NA.

45. Hawkins, *Letters*, 2:513, 544, 547, 561, 581, 600, 635, 697, 751.

46. Benjamin Hawkins to Edward Wright, October 20, 1799, Entry No. 42, RG 75, NA.

47. Ibid., December 5, 1799.

48. Hawkins, *Letters*, 2:411.

49. Ibid., 751, 775.

50. Ibid., 635.

51. Ibid., 525.

52. The financial situation between the Creeks and the United States cannot be precisely reckoned because of the fragmentary nature of the documents. The Creek Factors, until the patient and methodical Jonathan Halstead was appointed in 1800, were notoriously lax in detailing their accounts. Furthermore, the records of the War Department burned in 1800, leaving large gaps in the historical record.

53. Commissioners of Indian Affairs, *Treaties*, 34.

54. Ibid., 67.

55. Ibid., 89.

56. Ibid., 127; Entry No. 108, RG 11, NA.

57. Hawkins, *Letters*, 2:603.

58. Ibid., 538; Hawkins, "Letters of Benjamin Hawkins," 326–33. The most complete set of the financial records for the Creek Agency can be found in Entry No. 49, RG 75, NA.

59. Hawkins, *Letters*, 2:584; Superintendent of Indian Trade to Benjamin Hawkins, September 22, 1812, Entry No. 4, RG 75, NA.

60. Hawkins, *Letters*, 1:156. The Records of the Office of the Indian Trade have numerous examples of this; see esp. Entry No. 42, Entry No. 47, Entry No. 50, Entry No. 52, and Entry No. 1065, RG 75, NA.

61. Commissioners of Indian Affairs, *Treaties*, 88–89.

62. Fort Wilkinson Garrison, Account of Payments Made since July 1, 1809, Entry No. 52, RG 75, NA.

63. January 9, 1799, Benjamin Hawkins's Letterbook, INHP.

64. Hawkins, *Letters*, 1:156.

65. March 27, 1813, Entry No. 47, RG 75, NA.

66. Coker and Watson, *Indian Traders*, 364–65.

67. Forbes, in fact, pressured Seminole and Lower Creek headmen to pay trade debts by ceding to the company large tracts of land around Pensacola in 1804 and 1811. See Hawkins, *Letters*, 586; Saunt, *New Order*, 221–22; and Coker and Watson, *Indian Traders*, 251–55.

68. General Wilkinson to Henry Dearborn, October 1, 1803, Entry No. 1, RG 75, NA; Coker and Watson, *Indian Traders*, 227, 234.

69. Innerarity, "Creek Debtors," 80.

70. Ibid., 87.

71. Ibid.

72. Ibid., 81.

73. Ibid., 81–82.

74. Ibid., 83.

75. Benjamin Hawkins to Edward Wright, October 20, 1799, and Benjamin Hawkins to Jonathan Halstead, March 13, 1806, Entry No. 42, RG 75, NA.

76. Hawkins, *Letters*, 2:655; Innerarity, "Creek Debtors," 74.

77. Innerarity, "Creek Debtors," 85.

78. Ibid., 86.

79. Henri, *Southern Indians*, 134.

80. The best example of this exchange in an account book is Entry No. 42, RG 75, NA.

81. General Wilkinson to Creek Chiefs, May 23, 1802, "Benjamin Hawkins's Journal of Occurrences," APS.

82. Hawkins, *Letters*, 2:411.

83. Voucher No. 11, Benjamin Labbree's Receipt for the Creek Nation Annuities for the Year 1797, Entry No. 52, RG 75, NA.

84. Benjamin Hawkins to Jonathan Halstead, March 13, 1806, Entry No. 42, RG 75, NA.

85. Hawkins, *Letters*, 1:325.

86. Ibid., 2:580–85.

87. Ibid., 583.

88. In fact, Hawkins avoided interfering in the annuity distributions among the

Creeks, and he was not instructed by the War Department to intercede. So, other than the money allotted to the medal chiefs and other headmen as stipulated by treaty, the United States did not see a need to oversee the intra-Creek division of the annuity. See Hawkins, *Letters*, 2:584–85, and Henry Dearborn to Benjamin Hawkins, December 31, 1805, Entry No. 2, RG 75, NA.

89. Hawkins, *Letters*, 2:525, 562.

90. Saunt, *New Order*, 215–29.

91. Old Fields, March 17, 1808, and Fort Wilkinson, Account of Payments Made since July 1, 1809, Entry No. 52, RG 75, NA.

92. Fort Wilkinson, Account of Payments Made since July 1, 1809, Entry No. 52, RG 75, NA.

93. Ibid.

94. Ibid.

95. Misc. Papers, Indian Department to U.S. Factory, 1797, Entry No. 52, RG 75, NA.

96. July 26, 1811, Entry No. 49, RG 75, NA.

97. Hawkins, *Letters*, 2:599.

98. Timothy Barnard to Edward Price, December 21, 1797, Entry No. 42, RG 75, NA.

99. Seagrove to James Jordan, August 10, 1796, Entry No. 42, RG 75, NA.

100. This stereotype also finds its way into the scholarship; see Henri, *Southern Indians*, 141–42; Hurt, *Indian Agriculture*, 65; and Snyderman, *Concepts of Land Ownership*, 15–17.

101. See Charles Hudson, *Knights of Spain*, for the definitive route of DeSoto and his encounters with Mississippian chiefdoms.

102. DeBrahm, *DeBrahm's Report*, 255; Waselkov, "Indian Maps." Most map requests came from whites, and there is no evidence that any southern Indian group kept territorial maps for themselves. However, De Vorsey's investigation of Euro-American colonial maps shows that many of these were drafted according to what Indians, not the colonizers, knew about the geography; see De Vorsey, "American Indians and the Early Mapping of the Southeast."

103. Braund, "'Like a Stone Wall,'" 17, 27–30.

104. Ibid., 31–38.

105. Bartram, *Bartram on the Southeastern Indians*, 156.

106. Snyderman, *Concepts of Land Ownership*, 21; Wallace, "Political Organization and Land Tenure," 306.

107. Creek headmen affidavit on Creek and Cherokee line, January 22, 1816, Entry No. 1, RG 75, NA.

108. N. Casey, March 15, 1816, Entry No. 1, RG 75, NA.

109. Hawkins, *Letters*, 2:772; William Cocke to the Secretary of War, May 12, 1816, Entry No. 1, RG 75, NA.

110. General Coffee to James Monroe, March 15, 1816, Entry No. 1, RG 75, NA.

111. Return J. Meigs to Benjamin Hawkins, September 19, 1815, Entry No. 1, RG 75, NA.

112. General Coffee to James Monroe, March 15, 1816, Entry No. 1, RG 75, NA.

113. Lanning, "Oglethorpe's Treaty," 6–8.

114. Braund, "'Like a Stone Wall,'" makes this point. Braund examines the Creeks' understanding of their national borders and the forging of a national identity by examining land negotiations between the British and the Creeks in the mid-eighteenth century. Hahn, in "Invention of the Creek Nation," likewise understands the building of a Creek national identity to have involved consolidating Creek-European compacts of alliance, trade, and territory, although he is explicit that the government was not centralized. Studies on land tenure among eastern American Indians during the Historic Period point out that land speculation was a primary factor in how an Indian group divided the land among its members, although they do not explore this deeply; see Linton, "Land Tenure"; Provinse, "Tenure Problems"; Snyderman, *Concepts of Land Ownership*; and Wallace, "Political Organization and Land Tenure." Some scholars generalize that most American Indian groups had both communal and private land tenure, but that with the increasing pressure for land sales, communal control grew more important; see Hurt, *Indian Agriculture*, 68, and Provinse, "Tenure Problems," 421.

115. McGillivray, *McGillivray*, 220–81; Hawkins, *Letters*, 1:371, 2:433.

116. John Chisholm to Henry Dearborn, January 25, 1807, Entry No. 1, RG 75, NA.

117. Ibid.

118. Waselkov, in "Changing Strategies," 190–92, makes the point about exclusive rights, but he does not conclude that these planters had rights of alienation. Saunt, in *New Order*, 40–42, also states that land did not become private property.

119. Hawkins, *Letters*, 1:206, 380, 2:480; Richard Thomas, "His Book," 493.

120. Hawkins, *Letters*, 381. Many scholars feel that the idea of private property was foreign to the Creeks and thus the plan for civilization as envisioned by Hawkins undermined Creek beliefs; see Braund, *Deerskins and Duffels*, 185; Henri, *Southern Indians*, 96; and Joel W. Martin, *Sacred Revolt*, 92.

121. Abstract of Provisions, Fort Wilkinson Treaty, 1802, Entry No. 52, RG, NA.

122. Hawkins, *Letters*, 1:336; Innerarity, "Creek Debtors," 76.

123. Hawkins, *Letters*, 1:336–37.

124. Ibid., 2:434.

125. Creek Chiefs to Choctaw Nation, October 3, 1804, Parker Papers, HSP. For a full discussion of the origins of this Choctaw-Creek land dispute, see Braund, "'Like a Stone Wall,'" 31–38.

126. Hawkins, *Letters*, 2:556.

127. Chiefs of National Council to Hawkins, May 30, 1810, in Doster, *Creek Indians and Their Florida Lands*, 2:18–19.

128. Henry Dearborn to Benjamin Hawkins, January 24, 1803, Entry No. 2, RG 75, NA.

129. Hawkins, *Letters*, 1:184.

130. Ibid., 183.

131. Hawkins's Journal on the Treaty of Colerain, in Cochran, *New American State Papers*, 140. Foster, "Temporal Trends," discusses the consequences of this population increase in terms of town size and fissioning.

132. Joel W. Martin, in *Sacred Revolt*, 97–99, 102–5, first recognized that a segment of Creek society, the elite métis, was beginning to understand natural resources as commodities. However, he contrasts this with those Creeks who held to their "tra-

ditional culture" and "ancestral ways," instead of becoming "market-oriented, money-mongering individuals." My argument is that not just the elite but many rank-and-file Creeks also came to understand natural resources as commodities.

133. Hawkins reply to Creek Chiefs, June 6, 1802, "Benjamin Hawkins's Journal of Occurrences," APS.

134. Snyderman, *Concepts of Land Ownership*, 29.

135. Hawkins's Journal on the Treaty of Colerain, in Cochran, *New American State Papers*, 140.

Chapter Eleven

1. In the early twentieth century, Turner typified the American frontiersperson as a rugged individualist, averse to authority of any kind, fiercely independent, and democratically minded. For Turner, American pioneers embodied the American spirit, and indeed they gave birth to it. According to Turner, as these people entered the eastern woodlands, their European habits of mind were exorcized by the sheer necessities and hardships of settling a remote and untamed wilderness. In Turner's frontier, European immigrants were impelled to reconfigure much about their Old World social, political, and economic structures once they were faced with the immensity of settling North America. The American frontiersperson was premarket, individualistic, and isolated; American Indians barely figure in Turner's scenario. Two of Turner's most famous works are *Frontier in American History* and *Frontier and Section*. Turner's thesis about the frontier and the American pioneer have become the basis of much stereotyping and myth making as well as scholarly debate. The frontier thesis has been alternately validated and invalidated by frontier historians; for a summary of these early debates, see Billington, *Frontier Thesis*, 1–8. In the 1970s, historians attempted again to evaluate the frontier thesis and its components. For introductions to some of these early debates, see Billington, *Genesis of the Frontier Thesis* and *Frontier Thesis*.

Scholars now understand frontiers to be places of multicultural interactions, mutual dependency, and connections to the larger world, specifically the global economy. Indian history, in particular, has done much to reformulate our ideas on what constitutes a frontier. Richard White's *Middle Ground* is one of the seminal volumes documenting this version of the American frontier. For the South, Peter H. Wood, *Black Majority*, first proposed that the colonial southern frontier, despite those forces to the contrary, required mutual cooperation between Indians, whites, and blacks. Recent works about the southern frontier during the eighteenth and early nineteenth centuries concur with Wood's assessment and further argue that southern whites were decidedly market-oriented; see esp. Otto, *Southern Frontiers*; Clark and Guice, *Old Southwest*; Dunaway, *First American Frontier*; and Chaplin, *Anxious Pursuit*. Cashin has produced an impressive body of work on the southern frontier that also belies Turner's characterization of the American pioneer as isolated, independent, and noncapitalist. Instead, Cashin's southern frontier is a place of intense political maneuvering; Indian, white, and black interactions; market-oriented decision making; and so on. See esp. Cashin's biographies, *King's Ranger*, *Lachlan McGillivray*, and *William Bartram and the Amer-*

ican Revolution, which contextualize the lives of frontier personalities in this complex history.

Regarding the myth of the frontier and history, Slotkin's groundbreaking and comprehensive trilogy, *Regeneration through Violence, Fatal Environment*, and *Gunfighter Nation*, chronicles the rise of the myth of the American frontier (particularly as it figures in the story of the American West) in the American imagination and how it has shaped American identity, ideology, perceptions, and sense of moral mission. Most recently, Richter, *Facing East*, explores the overtones of imperialism in the idea of the American frontier by reconstructing Euro-American expansion from the viewpoint of historic Indian personalities.

2. Perkins, "Distinctions and Partitions," 205–9; Dunaway, *First American Frontier*, 249–86; Clark and Guice, *Old Southwest*, 183–206; Usner, *Indians, Settlers, and Slaves*, 180.

3. Jordan-Bychkov and Kaups, *American Backwoods*, 66.

4. Captain Basil Hall, *Travels*, 3:271. Gosse, *Letters*, 150–56, gives a detailed description of an early-eighteenth-century log cabin.

5. Hilliard, *Hog Meat*, 1–20; Jordan-Bychkov and Kaups, *American Backwoods*, 94–100.

6. Bonner, *History*, 95.

7. Benson, *Cultural Resources Survey*; Jordan-Bychkov and Kaups, *American Backwoods*, 123; Hurt, *Indian Agriculture*, 39; Starrett, *Appraisal Report*, 46–47.

8. Jordan-Bychkov and Kaups, *American Backwoods*, 105 Hilliard, *Hog Meat*, 65, 107–20.

9. Hilliard, *Hog Meat*, 9–16.

10. Jordan-Bychkov and Kaups, *American Backwoods*, 105.

11. Reidy, *From Slavery*, 20–21.

12. Lane, *Rambler in Georgia*, 61.

13. Hilliard, *Hog Meat*, 13, 120.

14. Captain Basil Hall, *Travels*, 3:270.

15. This assessment is found in many such travelogues. For a sampling, see Captain Basil Hall, *Travels*, vol. 3; Hodgson, *Letters*; Lane, *Rambler in Georgia*; Romans, *Concise Natural History*; Milfort, *Sojourn*.

16. William Hill to Jonathan Halstead, March 21, 1805, Entry No. 42, RG 75, NA.

17. Hilliard, *Hog Meat*, 38–40.

18. Mrs. Basil Hall, *Aristocratic Journey*, 236, 237.

19. Jordan-Bychkov and Kaups, *American Backwoods*, 19; Dunaway, *First American Frontier*, 108–11.

20. Clark and Guice, *Old Southwest*, 202.

21. The frontier neighborhood was especially obvious in Wilkes County, Georgia, which has been the subject of various historical investigations during its frontier era; see Warren, *Chronicles of Wilkes County*; Coulter, *Old Petersburg*; and Saggus, *Agrarian Arcadia*.

22. For a compilation of historic travelogues about the American South from the era of Spanish exploration through the nineteenth century, see Gallay, *Voices of the Old*

South. Clark, *Travels in the Old South*, provides an annotated bibliography of travelogues pertaining to the American South.

23. Gosse, *Letters*, 156–57. Captain Basil Hall, *Travels*, has several colorful descriptions of frontier towns. For a detailed narrative of a late-eighteenth-century southern frontier town, see Coulter, *Old Petersburg*. Captain Basil Hall drew a picture of Columbus, Georgia as a frontier town; see his *Forty Etchings*, plate 26. Gosse drew a picture of Pleasant Hill, Alabama, as a frontier town; see Gosse, *Letters*, 157.

24. The file on Georgia Indian affairs and "depredations" contains numerous references to neighborhood forts and voluntary militia; see Creek Indian Letters and Indian Letters, GDAH. Wilcox compiled a list of frontier forts in *Fort Hawkins*, 13–29. Of course the most famous case of the use of a southern frontier fort occurred with the Fort Mims battle; see Halbert and Ball, *Creek War*, 105–19, and Hawkins, *Letters*, 2:663–73.

25. Captain Basil Hall, *Travels*, 3:274–75; Mrs. Basil Hall, *Aristocratic Journey*, 236.

26. Lane, *Rambler in Georgia*, 12.

27. Milfort, *Sojourn*, 29. This conception was not formed out of nothing; the file on so-called Indian depredations for Georgia contains as many crimes committed by whites against whites as by Indians against whites; see Creek Indian Letters and Indian Letters, GDAH.

28. Lane, *Rambler in Georgia*, xviii, 42; Milfort, *Sojourn*, 87.

29. Milfort, *Sojourn*, 87; John Lambert, "Travels through Lower Canada and the United States of America, 1810," quoted in Lane, *Rambler in Georgia*, 49.

30. Milfort, *Sojourn*, 23, 88–89. Milfort's observation was not unusual, as many American white and black frontier people donned Indian garb. For a more general discussion of frontier Americans' use of dress as a cultural marker, see Perkins, "Distinctions and Partitions," 211–19. Whites imitating Indians was not confined to the eighteenth-century South. Deloria, *Playing Indian*, documents this imitation over several hundred years; Deloria understands the imitating to be a part of the process of constructing the American identity.

31. Hawkins, *Letters*, 1:313; Timothy Barnard to James Seagrove, December 18, 1798, Letters of Timothy Barnard, GDAH, 37; Major Jacob Kingsberry to Governor John Milledge, May 6, 1803, Creek Indian Letters, GDAH, 672–73; Timothy Barnard to George Mathews, October 9, 1795, Letters of Timothy Barnard, GDAH. Timothy Barnard reported on the Harrison episode to Indian agent James Seagrove and to Thomas Pickering of the State of Georgia War Office; see Letters of Timothy Barnard for October through December 1795, Letters of Timothy Barnard, GDAH.

32. Major Jacob Kingsberry to Governor John Milledge, May 6, 1803, Creek Indian Letters, GDAH, 672–73.

33. Ibid.

34. Horsman, *Frontier*, 58.

35. Doster, *Creek Indians and Their Florida Lands*, 1:85.

36. Hawkins, *Letters*, 2:602.

37. James Seagrove to Governor Jared Irwin, June 3, 1807, and Appy Howard's deposition, June 3, 1807, Creek Indian Letters, GDAH, 716–18, 719.

38. James Seagrove to Governor Jared Irwin, June 3, 1807, Creek Indian Letters, GDAH, 716.

39. Timothy Barnard to Edward Price, March 27, 1799, Entry No. 42, RG 75, NA.

40. Robert Woodruff, Journal of a Trip, INHP; T. Barnard to James Seagrove, June 20, 1793; Jacob Townsend to James Jackson; James Kirby's deposition; and Court of Inquiry into death of Davy Cornells, October 1793, Creek Indian Letters, GDAH, 325–26, 327–28, 344–48, 338–39; Barnard to James Seagrove, July 2, 3, 1793, and Barnard to Major Henry Gaither, July 7, 1793, Letters of Timothy Barnard, GDAH, 188, 192b, 197. This had been McGillivray's campaign against Georgia, although people at the time blamed the aggressive American settlers and their intrusions for the unrest. Creek hostilities during this time were fearsome and widespread. McGillivray's warriors robbed and killed settlers and destroyed their farms. After McGillivray's death, the hostilities subsided so that by 1796, the year of Hawkins's appointment, the southern frontier was relatively peaceful, as Barnard stated. The earlier years of terror, however, had left their imprint on the psyches of both the Creeks and the white settlers.

41. For a detailed description of frontier American hunting, see Aron, "Pigs and Hunters."

42. James White to Thomas Pickney, May 24, 1787, in Cochran, *New American State Papers*, 24; June 9, 1802, "Benjamin Hawkins's Journal of Occurrences," APS.

43. Hawkins, *Letters*, 2:608; Hawkins's Journal on the Treaty of Colerain, June 24, 1796, in Cochran, *New American State Papers*, 119–54; Creek Chiefs to Jefferson, November 3, 1805, Parker Papers, HSP.

44. Gosse, *Letters*, 269.

45. Cowdrey, *This Land*, 57; Silver, *New Face*, 94–97. Night hunting is still illegal in most southern states.

46. Timothy Barnard to James Seagrove, March 26, 1793, Letters of Timothy Barnard, GDAH, 135.

47. Stephen Aron makes a similar argument for the white Kentucky frontier hunters' lack of participation in the skin trade; see Aron, "Pigs and Hunters."

48. June 9, 1802, "Benjamin Hawkins's Journal of Occurrences," APS; Chiefs of National Council to Benjamin Hawkins, May 30, 1810, in Doster, *Creek Indians and Their Florida Lands*, 1:18–19.

49. Hawkins's Journal on the Treaty of Colerain, June 24, 1796, in Cochran, *New American State Papers*, 119–54; Hawkins, *Letters*, 2:460, 529, 608.

50. Prucha, *American Indian Policy in the Formative Years*, 158, first noted the illegal grazing of white-owned livestock to be a serious issue for the southeastern Indians. Also see Early County to the Governor of Georgia and Benjamin Hawkins, 1808, Entry No. 1065, RG 75, NA.

51. Report on Negotiations with Indians in Georgia, in Cochran, *New American State Papers*, 133.

52. Henry Dearborn to Benjamin Hawkins, February 19, 1803, Entry No. 2, RG 75, NA.

53. Richard Thomas, "His Book," 491.

54. Hawkins, *Letters*, 1:184, 2:496; Richard Thomas, "His Book," 491.

55. Hawkins, *Letters*, 1:137; June 7, 1798, Benjamin Hawkins's Letterbook, INHP.

56. Hawkins, *Letters*, 1:169, 275.

57. James Adams, Affidavit Respecting Indian 1794, and Report of Dr. Frederick Dalcho to the Troops of the U.S. in Georgia, May 10, 1794, Letters of Timothy Barnard, GDAH, 236, 233.

58. Hawkins, *Letters*, 1:126.

59. Ibid., 2:550; Henry Dearborn to William DaVies, James Wilkinson, and Benjamin Hawkins, July 22, 1801, and William Eustis to Benjamin Hawkins, July 20, 1811, Entry No. 2, RG 75, NA.

60. Creek Chiefs to Jefferson, November 3, 1805, Parker Papers, HSP.

61. Hawkins, *Letters*, 2:409.

62. Henry Dearborn to William DaVies, James Wilkinson, and Benjamin Hawkins, July 22, 1801, Entry No. 2, RG 75, NA.

63. William Eustis to Benjamin Hawkins, July 20, 1811, Entry No. 2, RG 75, NA.

64. Hawkins, *Letters*, 2:591, 604.

65. Prucha, *American Indian Policy in the Formative Years*, 158–62, documents another such case for the Chickasaws in 1809–10.

66. Ibid., 137–47; Henri, *Southern Indians*, 43, 194–95, 305; James Wilkinson to Governor Josiah Tatnell, June 10, 1802, Entry No. 1, RG 75, NA; June 9, 1802, "Benjamin Hawkins's Journal of Occurrences," APS.

67. Hawkins, *Letters*, 2:525.

68. Henri, *Southern Indians*, 43, 194–95, 305.

69. James Wilkinson to Governor Josiah Tatnell, June 10, 1802, Entry No. 1, RG 75, NA.

70. June 9, 1802, "Benjamin Hawkins's Journal of Occurrences," APS.

71. Hawkins, *Letters*, 2:542; General Wilkinson to a Deputation of the Cherokee Nation, June 10, 1802; Amahuskasata (Dreadful Water), Calauesta (Hatchet), and Coatahu (Badger's Son) reply, June 27, 1802; Return J. Meigs to William Eustis, December 20, 1811; W. R. Carnes, Roderick Easley, B. Harris, and Howell Cobb, June 29, 1802; and Cherokee Reply, June 27, 1802, Entry No. 1, RG 75, NA.

72. Henri, *Southern Indians*, 224, 229, 252; Meigs to Secretary of War, December 20, 1811, August 25, 1812, Entry No. 1, RG 75, NA.

73. Henry Dearborn to Benjamin Hawkins, June 28, 1805, Entry No. 2, RG 75, NA.

74. Hawkins, *Letters*, 2:460, 767; Henry Dearborn to Benjamin Hawkins, January 24, 1803, June 28, 1805, Entry No. 2, RG 75, NA.

75. Hawkins, *Letters*, 2:460, 529, 767.

76. Henry Dearborn to Benjamin Hawkins, January 24, 1803, Entry No. 2, RG 75, NA.

77. Hawkins, *Letters*, 2:460, 529, 767; Henry Dearborn to Benjamin Hawkins, January 24, 1803, June 28, 1805, Entry No. 2, RG 75, NA. Creek Indian Letters and Indian Letters, GDAH, also contain many such depositions.

78. Hawkins, *Letters*, 2:504.

79. Ibid., 767.

80. Barnard to James Seagrove, May 12, 1793, Letters of Timothy Barnard,

GDAH, 165; Hawkins, *Letters*, 2:499; June 11, 16, 1802, "Benjamin Hawkins's Journal of Occurrences," APS.

81. Hawkins, *Letters*, 2:542.

82. Ibid., 556; Entry No. 49, RG 75, NA.

83. Hawkins, *Letters*, 1:107, 2:409.

84. Ibid., 1:148.

85. Report on Negotiations with Indians of Georgia, 1797; Message on Negotiations with the southern Indians, 1801; and Message on Negotiations of Creek Treaty and Compact, 1812, in Cochran, *New American State Papers*, 118–62, 178–84, 184–201. In fact, federal jurisdiction over whites in Indian country was always cloudy, and most cases fell within the territorial or state jurisdiction; see Prucha, *American Indian Policy in the Formative Years*, 198–99.

86. Proclamation, July 19, 1790, Letters of Timothy Barnard, GDAH, 109–10; Hawkins, *Letters*, 2:504.

87. Hawkins, *Letters*, 2:555.

88. Ibid., 556.

89. Ibid., 574.

90. Ibid., 560.

91. Ibid., 574.

92. Ibid., 574, 601.

93. Ibid., 574.

94. Ibid., 578.

95. Ibid.

96. Ibid.

97. Prucha, *American Indian Policy in the Formative Years*, 139–87, chronicles the problem of white intrusions on Indian lands just after the American Revolution, the various prohibitions of such as decreed in the Trade and Intercourse Acts of the late eighteenth century, and the problems of enforcement faced by the federal government.

98. Hawkins, *Letters*, 2:462, 504, 548.

99. Ibid., 1:143.

100. Prucha, *American Indian Policy in the Formative Years*, 188–212, first made this point for the eastern Indians in general and delineated the problems of federal and state jurisdiction, the lax criminal code for whites, and the reluctance of Indians to participate in the American judicial system.

101. Charles Hudson, *Southeastern Indians*, 120–83, first pieced together the patterns of categorical opposites that comprise much of the historic southeastern Indian belief system. In *Conversations*, Hudson presents a more recent formulation of these ideas as they may have been presented from the viewpoint of a Mississippian Period Coosa priest. For discussions on how balance and opposites organized other aspects of southeastern Indian life, see Perdue, *Cherokee Women*, 13–40, and Joel W. Martin, *Sacred Revolt*, 17–45.

102. Charles Hudson, *Southeastern Indians*, 139–40.

103. Ibid., 350–51.

104. Ibid., 122–30.

105. Hawkins, *Letters*, 1:325, 2:665; Joel W. Martin, *Sacred Revolt*, 24–25; Swanton,

Creek Religion, 514, 584; Swan, "Position and State," 269–70. The Muskogean orthography is taken from Swanton. Swan also wrote that the Creeks believed in the deity *Stefuts Áségó*, which was a "bad spirit" that dwelt in the underworld.

106. Stiggins, *Creek Indian History*, 60; Charles Hudson, *Southeastern Indians*, 338–39.

107. Swanton, *Creek Religion*, 651–53; Charles Hudson, *Southeastern Indians*, 343.

108. Swanton, *Creek Religion*, 517–21, 629–31.

109. Adair, *Adair's History*, 124; Charles Hudson, *Southeastern Indians*, 340.

110. Adair, *Adair's History*, 157.

111. Ibid.

112. Reid, *Law of Blood*, 76. The principle of blood revenge among the Creeks has not been thoroughly investigated; however, they probably followed those of the Cherokees, which Reid reconstructed in *Law of Blood*.

113. Adair, *Adair's History*, 156.

114. Ibid., 156; Saunt, *New Order*, 101–2. In fact, Saunt points out that the English concept of guilt and innocence was so foreign to the Creeks that they did not have a word for "guilt" and translated it into *mu'tte*, or "fault" or "cause."

115. Reid, *Law of Blood*, 78.

116. Ibid., 154; Charles Hudson, *Southeastern Indians*, 239–40.

117. Adair, *Adair's History*, 158.

118. Charles Hudson, *Southeastern Indians*, 239–40.

119. Hawkins, *Letters*, 1:317.

120. Saunt, *New Order*, 90–110.

121. Hawkins, *Letters*, 1:306–7.

122. Parades and Plante, "Economics, Politics, and the Subjugation," 132–34. Saunt, *New Order*, 180–85, states that the warrior police paid little heed to the principle of blood revenge and acted primarily on the new Euro-American "social compact" of crime and punishment as instituted by the wealthy elite Creeks; however, Saunt also acknowledges that most Creeks did not pay attention to the warrior police.

123. Hawkins, *Letters*, 1:218, 221, 2:609, 610, 612, 613, 615, 616. Saunt, *New Order*, 180–84, 241–43, 251–52, credits the warriors of the nation with other actions as well as these; however, Saunt does not adequately demonstrate whether these actions were done by the warriors of the nation or some other group, or if the men involved were indeed "annonymous" (241) to the party being punished.

124. Hawkins, *Letters*, 1:120, 186, 194, 218, 221–22, 2:609, 613; Saunt, *New Order*, 251–52.

125. Hawkins, *Letters*, 1:246, 262, 2:540.

126. Report of Tustunee Haujo and Robert Walton to Benjamin Hawkins, November 4, 1799, Benjamin Hawkins's Letterbook, INHP.

127. Hawkins, *Letters*, 1:245.

128. Champagne, *Social Order*, 73, 113–14, also understands blood revenge not to have been revoked among the Creeks during this time and that the principle worked against any attempts at centralization. Perdue, *Cherokee Women*, 13, also makes the point that the significance of balance among the Cherokees made hierarchy untenable. All of this is in contrast to Saunt, who in *New Order*, 90–110, argues that wealthy,

market-oriented Creeks worked diligently to dismantle blood revenge and to construct a new social compact based on Euro-American ideas of guilt and innocence. But Saunt also acknowledges that this endeavor merely created more tensions in the Creek Confederacy, as most Creeks held to blood revenge. Other scholars also argue that many things, both internal to Creek culture and external forces, conspired to inhibit the centralization of authority; see Wesson, "Households and Hegemony," and Champagne, *Social Order*.

129. Gosse, *Letters*, 250.

130. Joseph Phillips to E. Park, December 8, 1804, Creek Indian Letters, GDAH, 705.

131. Ibid., 704. For another similar incident involving Colonel Clarke of Georgia, see James Seagrove to Governor Mathews of Georgia, May 26, 1794; Report of Dr. Frederick Dalcho to the troops of the U.S. in Georgia, May 10, 1794; Alick Cornal to Timothy Barnard, September 14, 1794; and George Washington to Senate and House, June 2, 1794, Letters of Timothy Barnard, GDAH. For one involving Adam Carson, see Captain Jonas Fauche to Governor Mathews, October 19, 1794, Creek Indian Letters, GDAH, 406–18.

132. Efau Haujo, in "Benjamin Hawkins's Journal of Occurrences," APS.

133. Hawkins, *Letters*, 1:314; Barnard to James Seagrove, July 2, 3, 1793, and Barnard to Major Henry Gaither, July 7, 1793, Letters of Timothy Barnard, GDAH, 188, 192b, 197; Court of Inquiry into death of Davy Cornells, October 1793, Creek Indian Letters, GDAH, 344–48. Cornells's murder is documented in Timothy Barnard to James Seagrove, June 20, 1793; James Kirby's deposition, July 22, 1793; and Court of Inquiry into death of Davy Cornells, October 26, 1793, Creek Indian Letters, GDAH, 325–28, 338–39, 344–48.

134. Efau Haujo, in "Benjamin Hawkins's Journal of Occurrences," APS.

135. June 12, 1802, "Benjamin Hawkins's Journal of Occurrences," APS.

136. Ibid.

137. Barnard to Patrick Carr, April 13, 1784, Letters of Timothy Barnard, GDAH, 28.

138. Hawkins, *Letters*, 1:145.

139. Ibid., 280.

140. Ibid., 140.

141. Ibid., 2:422.

142. Ibid.

143. Hawkins, "Letters of Benjamin Hawkins," 286.

144. Hawkins, *Letters*, 2:452.

145. Ibid.

146. Hawkins, "Letters of Benjamin Hawkins," 102.

147. Hawkins, *Letters*, 1:120.

148. Ibid., 2:478.

149. Ibid., 1:263.

150. Richard Thomas, "His Book," 491.

151. Hawkins, *Letters*, 2:417.

152. Tecumseh, Tenskwatawa, and their pan-Indian unification efforts are covered in many scholarly works; see Dowd, *Spirited Resistance*; Edmunds, *Shawnee Prophet*

and *Tecumseh*; and Richard White, *Middle Ground*. There are many biographies on Tecumseh; one of the most scholarly and thorough is Sugden, *Tecumseh*. The Red Stick War has figured in several works on the late-eighteenth-century Creeks; the most recent are Joel W. Martin, *Sacred Revolt*; Saunt, *New Order*; and Dowd, *Spirited Resistance*. For earlier treatments, see Owsley, *Struggle for the Gulf Borderlands* and "Prophet of War," and Griffith, *McIntosh and Weatherford*. Halbert and Ball, *Creek War*, published in 1895, is the earliest full history of the war and was written from firsthand accounts of participants. Stiggins, *Creek Indian History*, 83–136, gives the only Creek account of the war, although Stiggins probably did not witness it firsthand.

153. Hawkins, *Letters*, 2:632.

154. Joel W. Martin, *Sacred Revolt*, 114–32.

155. Ibid., 132–49. For an in-depth look at the prophet Josiah Francis, see Owsley, "Prophet of War."

156. Halbert and Ball, *Creek War*, 99–100, following Gatschet, *Migration Legend*, 189–90, states that it was largely an Upper/Lower Creek split, but later when enumerating the battles, the authors point out that this may be an overgeneralization. Most scholars concur with this latter assessment; see Parades and Plante, "Economics, Politics, and the Subjugation," 143–45; Wright, *Creeks and Seminoles*, 162–71; Joel W. Martin, *Sacred Revolt*, 34–39, 132–35, 137–38; Waselkov and Wood, "Creek War," 7–8; Saunt, *New Order*, 249–51; and Champagne, *Social Order*, 119. That the lines were drawn otherwise is also indicated by Hawkins; see Hawkins, *Letters*, 2:668, and "Sketch of the Creek Country," APS. Still, scholars do not agree on the specific dividing lines in the Creek civil war. Wright, in *Creeks and Seminoles*, 162–71, underscores the complexity of the political, social, and economic lines within Creek country at this time but believes that the majority of rebels were mostly non-Muskogean speakers who resented the plan for civilization, Hawkins, and America. Champagne, in *Social Order*, 110, posits that it was mostly an Upper and Lower division and that regional affiliation determined one's position in the conflict. Joel W. Martin, in *Sacred Revolt*, 133–39, believes the prophets' message "powerfully and authentically" addressed deep concerns for the Creeks "at a critical juncture in their history" (133). His assessment is that the motive to join the movement was largely cultural and religious and that most believers were traditionalists in Upper Creek towns, but he acknowledges that the lines are difficult to decipher and that some nontraditionalist Upper Creeks and some disaffected Lower Creeks joined as well. He understands that those who did not join the prophets were under the influence of Hawkins and pro-American headmen. On the other hand, Saunt, in *New Order*, 249–59, understands the line to have been largely a class division. According to Saunt, the market-oriented Creeks, many of whom were wealthy métis, comprised the bulk of those fighting against the Red Sticks, and the Red Sticks were those dissidents who had opposed the reforms of the pro-American Creeks for several decades. Although he does not state it explicitly, Saunt indicates that these divisions of rich/poor, pro-American/anti-American did not follow any conventional Creek social lines and were, in fact, entirely new. Ethridge, in "Contest for Land," 414–30, sees the dividing line as basically pro-American/anti-American and cutting across many of the internal divisions within Creek country, even the

class lines denoted by Saunt and Martin. This assessment is in line with Hassig's in "Internal Creek Conflict." Haussig does not assess the lines of division as falling along any structural lines of Creek society but states, rather, that "there were no clearcut rules" (268). Hassig also points out that the reintegration of the Red Sticks into Creek society after the outbreak was rapid.

157. Hawkins, *Letters*, 2:673.

158. Halbert and Ball, *Creek War*, covers the war mostly after America got involved. Stiggins, *Creek Indian History*, 83–186, gives much on the intra-Creek hostilities. Also see Joel W. Martin, *Sacred Revolt*, 142, and Saunt, *New Order*, 249–59.

159. Halbert and Ball, *Creek War*, 143–76; Stiggins, *Creek Indian History*, 107–14; Hawkins, *Letters*, 2:664–65; Owsley, "Fort Mims Massacre"; Joel W. Martin, *Sacred Revolt*, 157.

160. Transcript of letter from Edmond Shackelford to Frances Shackelford, November 26, 1813, Swanton ms. 4911, Swanton Collection, SI.

161. The Battle of Horseshoe Bend as well as other American/Creek battles during the war are covered in Halbert and Ball, *Creek War*, 105–286, and Stiggins, *Creek Indian History*, 97–136. Also see Hawkins, *Letters*, 2:681, 748, 757; Owsley, *Struggle for the Gulf Borderlands*, 30–86; Joel W. Martin, *Sacred Revolt*, 161–62; and Saunt, *New Order*, 259–72. Tohopeka has been excavated; see Boyd, *Historic Sites*; Dickens, "Archaeological Investigations at Horseshoe Bend"; and Fairbanks, "Excavations at Horseshoe Bend." For a drawing of the breastworks done by an American soldier who was there, see Letterbook 1814, Graham Papers, NCDAH.

162. Saunt, *New Order*, 273–90; Boyd, *Historic Sites*.

163. Hawkins, *Letters*, 2:681, 748; Letterbook 1814, Graham Papers, NCDAH.

164. Hawkins, *Letters*, 2:687.

165. Ibid., 741.

166. Ibid., 744.

167. Ibid.

168. Ibid.

169. Ibid., 717.

BIBLIOGRAPHY

Manuscript Collections

American Philosophical Society Library, Philadelphia, Pennsylvania
  "Benjamin Hawkins's Journal of Occurrences in the Creek Agency," 1802
  Benjamin Hawkins to Thomas Jefferson, "A Comparative Vocabulary of the
    Muskogee or Creek, Chickasaw, Choctaw, and Cherokee Languages," 1800
  "A Sketch of the Creek Country in the Years 1798 and 1799," addenda
Georgia State Department of Archives and History, Atlanta
  Creek Indian Letters, Talks, and Treaties, 1705–1839, typescript by Louise F.
    Hays, 1939
  Indian Letters, 1782–1839, typescript by Louise F. Hays, 1940
  Letters of Benjamin Hawkins, 1797–1815, typescript by Louise F. Hays, 1939
  Unpublished Letters of Timothy Barnard, 1784–1820, typescript by Louise F.
    Hays, 1939
Historical Society of Pennsylvania, Philadelphia
  Daniel Parker Papers
Independence National Historical Park, Philadelphia, Pennsylvania
  Benjamin Hawkins's Letterbook, May 1798–September 1801, 1802, 1810
  Robert Woodruff, Journal of a Trip Through New York, New Jersey, Pennsyl-
    vania, Delaware, Maryland, Virginia, North Carolina, Rhode Island, Massa-
    chusetts, South Carolina, Georgia, as Clerk to John Ansley, December 17,
    1785–May 1, 1788
Library of Congress, Manuscript Division, Washington, D.C.
  Peter Force Collection, Benjamin Hawkins's Viatory or Journal of Distances and
    Observations, 1797–1802
  Thomas Jefferson Papers
  James Madison Papers
  George Washington Papers
National Anthropological Archives, Smithsonian Institution, Washington D.C.
  J. Woodbridge Davis Collection
  John R. Swanton Collection

National Archives and Records Service, Washington, D.C.

Record Group 11, General Records of the United States Government

Entry No. 108, Ratified Indian Treaties, 1722–1869

Record Group 75, Records of the Bureau of Indian Affairs

Entry No. 1, Records of the Office of the Secretary of War Relating to Indian Affairs, Letters Received, 1800–1823

Entry No. 2, Records of the Office of the Secretary of War Relating to Indian Affairs, Letters Sent, 1800–1824

Entry No. 3, Records of the Superintendent of Indian Trade, Letters Received, 1806–1824

Entry No. 4, Records of the Superintendent of Indian Trade, Letters Sent, 1807–1830

Entry No. 5, Records of the Office of Indian Trade, Creek Factory, Invoice and Letterbook, 1803–1804, 1816–1822

Entry No. 6, Records of the Office of Indian Trade, Creek Factory, Memorandum Book, 1807–1813

Entry No. 9, Records of the Office of Indian Trade, Creek Factory, Journals, 1805–1824

Entry No. 42, Records of the Office of Indian Trade, Creek Factory, Creek Factory Correspondence, 1795–1814

Entry No. 43, Records of the Office of Indian Trade, Creek Factory, Creek Factory, Letters Sent, 1795–1816

Entry No. 47, Records of the Office of Indian Trade, Creek Factory, Creek Factory Journals, 1801–1820

Entry No. 49, Records of the Office of Indian Trade, Creek Factory, Journal of Transactions with Benjamin Hawkins, 1808–1814

Entry No. 50, Records of the Office of Indian Trade, Creek Factory, Ledger of Hawkins's Accounts, 1808–1814

Entry No. 52, Records of the Office of Indian Trade, Creek Factory, Miscellaneous Accounts, 1795–1816

Entry No. 53, Records of the Office of Indian Trade, Creek Factory, Records of the Fort Wilkinson Garrison, 1795–1801

Entry No. 1065, Records of the Office of Indian Trade, Field Office Records, Records of the Creek Agency, East, Correspondence and Other Records, 1794–1818

Record Group 77, Treasure File

North Carolina Department of Archives and History, Raleigh

Joseph Graham Papers, 1782, 1813–1836

Joseph Graham Papers, 1782, 1813–1836, Letterbook 1814

Benjamin Hawkins Papers

Southern Historical Collection, University of North Carolina Library, Chapel Hill

Hawkins Family Papers

Published Sources

Adair, James. *Adair's History of the American Indians.* Edited by Samuel Cole Williams. 1775. Reprint, Johnson City, Tenn.: Watauga Press, 1930.

Alabama Department of Archives and History. "Official Symbols and Emblems of Alabama." ⟨http://www.archives.state.al.us/emblems/st_miner.html⟩ (July 12, 2002).

Alabama Public Television. "Long Leaf Ecosystem." Discovering Alabama Series. Produced by the Alabama Museum of Natural History, Tuscaloosa, 1998.

Alden, John R. *John Stuart and the Southern Colonial Frontier: A Study of Indian Relations, War, Trade, and Land Problems in the Southern Wilderness, 1754–1775.* University of Michigan Publications in History and Political Science, no. 15. Ann Arbor: University of Michigan Press, 1944.

Anderson, David G., and Rolbert C. Mainfort Jr., eds. *The Woodland Southeast.* Tuscaloosa: University of Alabama Press, 2002.

Anderson, David G., and Kenneth E. Sassaman. *The Paleoindian and Early Archaic Southeast.* Tuscaloosa: University of Alabama Press, 1996.

Anniston Museum. "The Oak-Hickory-Pine Forest of Alabama." ⟨http://www.annistonmuseum.org/bio301.html⟩.

Aquilani, Steven M. "Bird Communities of Holly Springs National Forest: Past and Present Habitat Considerations for Forest Songbird Conservation." Ph.D. diss., University of Mississippi, 2002.

Arianoutsou, M., and N. Margaris. "Fire-Induced Nutrient Loss in a Phyrganic (East Mediterranean) Ecosystem." *International Journal of Biometeorology* 25 (1981): 341–47.

Aron, Stephen. "Pigs and Hunters: 'Rights in the Woods' on the Trans-Appalachian Frontier." In *Contact Points: American Frontiers from the Mohawk Valley to the Mississippi, 1750–1830,* edited by Andrew R. L. Cayton and Fredrika J. Teute, 175–204. Chapel Hill: University of North Carolina Press for the Omohundro Institute of Early American History and Culture, 1998.

Arrighi, Giovanni. *The Long Twentieth Century: Money, Power, and the Origins of Our Times.* New York: Verso Press, 1994.

Axtel, James. *The European and the Indian: Essays in the Ethnohistory of Colonial North America.* New York: Oxford University Press, 1981.

Baden, William W. "A Dynamic Model of Stability and Change in Mississippian Agricultural Systems." Ph.D. diss., University of Tennessee, Knoxville, 1987.

Badger, Reid R., and Lawrence A. Clayton, eds. *Alabama and the Borderlands, from Prehistory to Statehood.* University: University of Alabama Press, 1985.

Bahr, Donald. "Bad News: The Predicament of Native American Mythology." *Ethnohistory* 48 (2001): 587–612.

Baker, Brenda J., and Lisa Kealhofer. *Bioarchaeology of Native American Adaptation in the Spanish Borderlands.* Gainesville: University Press of Florida, 1996.

Balée, William. "Historical Ecology: Premises and Postulates." In *Advances in Historical Ecology,* edited by William Balée, 1–29. Historical Ecology Series. New York: Columbia University Press, 1998.

Bartram, William. *The Travels of William Bartram: Naturalist's Edition.* Edited by
Francis Harper. New Haven: Yale University Press, 1958. Reprint, Athens: University of Georgia Press, 1998.

―――. *Travels through North and South Carolina, Georgia, East and West Florida,
the Cherokee Country, the Extensive Territories of the Muscogulges, or Creek Confederacy, and the Country of the Chactaws.* 1791. Reprint, New York: Penguin, 1988.

―――. *William Bartram on the Southeastern Indians.* Edited by Gregory A.
Waselkov and Kathryn E. Holland Braund. Lincoln: University of Nebraska
Press, 1995.

Battle, Herbert B. "The Domestic Use of Oil among the Southern Aborigines."
American Anthropologist 24 (1992): 171–82.

Benson, Robert W. *Cultural Resources Survey for FY91 / FY92 Timber Harvesting
Compartments and Testing Site MTA-2, Fort Benning, Alabama and Georgia.* Final
report. U.S. Army Corps of Engineers, Savannah District and Fort Benning.
Athens, Ga.: Southeastern Archaeological Services, 1994.

Berkhofer, Robert F., Jr. "The Political Context of a New Indian History." *Pacific
Historical Review* 40 (1971): 357–82.

―――. *The White Man's Indian: Images of the American Indian from Columbus to the
Present.* New York: Alfred A. Knopf, 1978.

Billington, Ray Allen, ed. *The Frontier Thesis: Valid Interpretation of American History?* New York: Krieger, 1977.

―――. *The Genesis of the Frontier Thesis: A Study in Historical Creativity.* San Ma-
rino, Calif.: H. E. Huntington Library and Art, 1971.

Biolsi, Thomas, and Larry J. Zimmerman, eds. *Indians and Anthropologists: Vine Deloria, Jr., and the Critique of Anthropology.* Tucson: University of Arizona Press,
1997.

Blakley, Robert, and Bettina Detweiler-Blakley. "The Impact of European Disease in
the Sixteenth Century Southeast: A Case Study." *Midcontinental Journal of Archaeology* 14 (1989): 62–89.

Bloch, Marc. *The Historian's Craft.* New York: Vintage, 1953.

Blu, Karen I. "Region and Recognition: Southern Indians, Anthropologists, and
Presumed Biology." In *Anthropologists and Indians in the New South*, edited by
Rachel A. Bonney and J. Anthony Parades, 71–85. Contemporary American
Indian Studies. Tuscaloosa: University of Alabama Press, 2001.

Bolton, Herbert E., and Mary Ross. *The Debatable Land: A Sketch of the Anglo-
Spanish Contest for the Georgia Country.* Berkeley: University of California Press,
1925.

Bonner, James C. *A History of Georgia Agriculture, 1732–1860.* Athens: University
of Georgia Press, 1964.

Bonney, Rachel A., and J. Anthony Parades, eds. *Anthropologists and Indians in the
New South.* Contemporary American Indian Studies. Tuscaloosa: University of
Alabama Press, 2001.

Bossu, Jean-Bernard. *Travels in the Interior of North America, 1751–1762.* Edited by
Seymour Feiler. Norman: University of Oklahoma Press, 1962.

Boyd, Mark F. *Historic Sites in and around the Jim Woodruff Reservoir Area, Florida-*

Georgia. River Basin Surveys Paper, no. 13. Bureau of American Ethnology Bulletin, no. 169, pp. 195–318. Washington, D.C.: Government Printing Office, 1958.

Braley, Chad. *Archaeological Data Recovery at Yuchi Town, 1Ru63, Ft. Benning, Alabama*. U.S. Army Corps of Engineers, Savannah District and Environmental Management Division, Fort Benning, Ga. Athens, Ga.: Southeastern Archaeological Services, 1991.

――――. "Historic Period Indian Archaeology of the Georgia Coastal Plain." Georgia Archaeological Context Report, no. 26. Georgia Department of Natural Resources, Historic Preservation Division, Atlanta, 1994.

Braudel, Fernand. *On History*. Chicago: University of Chicago Press, 1980.

Braund, Kathryn E. Holland. "The Classification of Eighteenth-Century Creek Towns." Paper presented at the Annual Meeting of the Society for American Archaeology, April 2–6, 1997, Nashville, Tenn.

――――. "The Creek Indians, Blacks, and Slavery." *Journal of Southern History* 57 (1991): 601–36.

――――. *Deerskins and Duffels: The Creek Indian Trade with Anglo-America, 1685–1815*. Lincoln: University of Nebraska Press, 1993.

――――. "Guardians of Tradition and Handmaidens to Change: Women's Roles in Creek Economic and Social Life during the Eighteenth Century." *American Indian Quarterly* 14 (1990): 329–58.

――――. "'Like a Stone Wall Never to be Broke': The British Indian Boundary Line with the Creek Indians, 1763–1773." Paper presented at the Porter L. Fortune History Symposium, University of Mississippi, Oxford, 2001.

Brewer, J. Stephen. "Current and Presettlement Tree Species Composition of Some Upland Forests in Northern Mississippi." *Journal of the Torrey Botanical Society* 128, no. 4 (2001): 332–49.

Burke, Peter. *New Perspectives on Historical Writing*. 2nd ed. University Park: Pennsylvania State University Press, 2001.

Bushnell, Amy. "Ruling 'the Republic of Indians' in Seventeenth-Century Florida." In *Powhatan's Mantle: Indians in the Colonial Southeast*, edited by Peter H. Wood, Gregory A. Waselkov, and Thomas M. Hatley, 134–50. Lincoln: University of Nebraska Press, 1989.

Calloway, Colin G. *New Directions in American Indian History*. Norman: University of Oklahoma Press, 1988.

Canouts, Veletta Kay. "Towards a Reconstruction of Creek and Pre-Creek Cultural Ecology." M.A. thesis, University of North Carolina, Chapel Hill, 1971.

Carson, James Taylor. "Ethnogeography and the Native American Past." *Ethnohistory* 49 (2000): 769–88.

――――. *Searching for the Bright Path: The Mississippi Choctaws from Prehistory to Removal*. Indians of the Southeast. Lincoln: University of Nebraska Press, 1999.

Cashdan, Elizabeth, ed. *Risk and Uncertainty in Tribal and Peasant Economies*. Boulder, Colo.: Westview Press, 1990.

Cashin, Edward J. *The King's Rangers: Thomas Brown and the American Revolution on the Southern Frontier*. New York: Fordham University Press, 1999.

————. *Lachlan McGillivray, Indian Trader: The Shaping of the Southern Colonial Frontier*. Athens: University of Georgia Press, 1992.

————. *William Bartram and the American Revolution on the Southern Frontier*. Columbia: University of South Carolina Press, 2000.

Chambers, Nella J. "The Creek Indian Factory at Fort Mitchell." *Alabama Historical Quarterly* 21 (1959): 15–53.

Champagne, Duane. *Contemporary Native American Cultural Issues*. Contemporary Native American Communities, no. 2. New York: Altamira Press, 1999.

————. *Social Order and Political Change: Constitutional Governments among the Cherokee, the Choctaw, the Chickasaw, and the Creek*. Stanford, Calif.: Stanford University Press, 1992.

Chaplin, Joyce E. *An Anxious Pursuit: Agricultural Innovation and Modernity in the Lower South, 1730–1815*. Chapel Hill: University of North Carolina Press for the Institute of Early American History and Culture, Williamsburg, Va., 1993.

Chapman, Jefferson, and Andrea Brewer Shea. "The Archaeobotanical Record: Early Archaic Period to Contact in the Lower Little Tennessee River Valley." *Tennessee Anthropologist* 6 (1981): 81–84.

Chaudhuri, Jean, and Joyotpaul Chaudhuri. *A Sacred Path: The Way of the Muscogee Creeks*. Los Angeles: University of California at Los Angeles American Indian Studies Center, 2001.

Clark, Thomas D., ed. *Travels in the Old South: A Bibliography*. Vol. 1, *The Formative Years, 1527–1783: From the Spanish Explorations through the American Revolution*. American Exploration and Travel Series. Norman: University of Oklahoma Press, 1956.

Clark, Thomas D., and John D. W. Guice. *The Old Southwest: Frontiers in Conflict, 1795–1830*. Norman: University of Oklahoma Press, 1996.

Cobb, Charles R. *From Quarry to Cornfield: The Political Economy of Mississippian Hoe Production*. Tuscaloosa: University of Alabama Press, 2000.

Cochran, Thomas C., ed. *The New American State Papers: Indian Affairs*. Wilmington, Del.: Scholarly Resources, 1972.

Coker, William S., and Thomas Watson. *Indian Traders of the Southeastern Spanish Borderlands: Panton, Leslie and Company, 1783–1847*. Pensacola: University of West Florida Press, 1986.

Commissioners of Indian Affairs. *Treaties between the United States of America and the Several Indian Tribes from 1778–1837*. 1837. Reprint, Millwood, N.Y.: Kraus, 1975.

Cook, Noble David, *Born to Die: Disease and New World Conquest, 1492–1650*. New York: Cambridge University Press, 1998.

Corkran, David H. *The Cherokee Frontier: Conflict and Survival, 1740–1762*. Norman: University of Oklahoma Press, 1962.

————. *The Creek Frontier, 1540–1783*. Norman: University of Oklahoma Press, 1967.

Cotterill, R. S. *The Southern Indians: The Story of the Civilized Tribes before Removal*. Norman: University of Oklahoma Press, 1964.

Coulter, Ellis Merton. *Old Petersburg and the Broad River Valley of Georgia: Their Rise and Decline*. Athens: University of Georgia Press, 1965.

Cowdrey, Albert E. *This Land, This South: An Environmental History*. Lexington: University Press of Kentucky, 1983.

Crane, Verner W. *The Southern Frontier, 1670–1732*. Ann Arbor: University of Michigan Press, 1929.

Crawford, James M. "Southeastern Indian Languages." In *Studies in Southeastern Indian Languages*, edited by James M. Crawford, 1–120. Athens: University of Georgia Press, 1975.

Crofton, Elizabeth W. "Flora and Fauna of the Longleaf Pine-Grassland Ecosystem." ⟨http:www.sherpaguides.com/georgia/fire_forest/wildnotes/index.html⟩.

Cronon, William. *Changes in the Land: Indians, Colonists, and the Ecology of New England*. New York: Hill and Wang, 1983.

———. "A Place for Stories: Nature, History, and Narrative." *Journal of American History* 78 (1992): 1347–76.

———, ed. *Uncommon Ground: Rethinking the Human Place in Nature*. New York: W. W. Norton, 1996.

Cronon, William, and Richard White. "Indians in the Land." *American Heritage* 37 (1986): 18–25.

Crosby, Alfred W. *The Columbian Exchange: Biological and Cultural Consequences of 1492*. Contributions in American Studies, no. 2. Westport, Conn.: Greenwood, 1972.

———. *Ecological Imperialism: The Biological Expansion of Europe, 900–1900*. Studies in Environment and History. New York: Cambridge University Press, 1986.

Cruikshank, Julie. "Oral History, Narrative Strategies, and Native American Historiography: Perspectives from the Yukon Territory, Canada." In *Clearing a Path: Theorizing the Past in Native American Studies*, edited by Nancy Shoemaker, 2–28. New York: Routledge, 2002.

Crumley, Carole. "Historical Ecology: A Multidimensional Ecological Orientation." In *Historical Ecology: Cultural Knowledge and Changing Landscapes*, edited by Carole Crumley, 1–16. School of American Research Advanced Seminar Series. Santa Fe: School of American Research Press, 1994.

Crutchfield, Lisa Laurel. "From Shoes and Feathers to Cash and Power: The Transformation of the Cherokee Annuity System and Its Role in the Emergence of Cherokee Nationalism, 1791–1835." M.A. thesis, University of Georgia, 1995.

Daniels, John D. "The Indian Population of North America in 1492." *William and Mary Quarterly*, 3rd ser., 49 (1992): 298–320.

Davis, Donald Edward. *Where There Are Mountains: An Environmental History of the Southern Appalachians*. Athens: University of Georgia Press, 2000.

Debo, Angie. *The Rise and Fall of the Choctaw Republic*. Norman: University of Oklahoma Press, 1961.

———. *Road to Disappearance: A History of the Creek Indians*. 1941. Reprint, Norman: University of Oklahoma Press, 1985.

DeBrahm, John Gerar William. *DeBrahm's Report of the General Survey in the Southern District of North America*. Edited by Louis De Vorsey Jr. Columbia: University of South Carolina Press, 1971.

Delcourt, Paul, Hazel Delcourt, Cecil Ison, William Sharp, and Kristen J. Gremillion. "Prehistoric Human Use of Fire, the Eastern Agricultural Complex, and Appalachian Oak-Chestnut Forests: Paleoecology of Cliff Palace Pond, Kentucky." *American Antiquity* 63 (1998): 263–78.

Deloria, Philip J. *Playing Indian.* New Haven: Yale University Press, 1998.

De Vorsey, Louis, Jr. "American Indians and the Early Mapping of the Southeast." In *The Southeast in Early Maps*, edited by William P. Cumming. 1958. 3rd ed., rev. and enl. by Louis De Vorsey Jr., Chapel Hill: University of North Carolina Press, 1998.

————. *The Indian Boundary in the Southern Colonies, 1763–1775.* Chapel Hill: University of North Carolina Press, 1966.

Diamond, Jared. *Guns, Germs, and Steel: The Fates of Human Societies.* New York: W. W. Norton, 1997.

Dickens, Roy S., Jr. "Archaeological Investigations at Horseshoe Bend, National Military Park, Alabama." Special Publications of the Alabama Archaeological Society, no. 3. Auburn: Alabama Archaeological Society, 1979.

Dinerstein, E., A. Weakley, R. Noss, R. Snodgrass, K. Wolfe. "Southeastern Conifer Forest (NA0529)." World Wildlife Fund and National Geographic Society. Wild World Website. ⟨http://worldwildlife.org/wildworld/profiles/terrestrial/na/na0529_full.html⟩.

Dobyns, Henry F. "Estimating Aboriginal American Population: An Appraisal of Techniques with a New Hemispheric Estimate." *Current Anthropology* 6 (1966): 395–416.

————. *Their Number Become Thinned: Native American Population Dynamics in Eastern North America.* Knoxville: University of Tennessee Press, 1983.

Dodd, C. Kenneth, Jr. "Reptiles and Amphibians in the Endangered Longleaf Pine Ecosystem." U.S. Geological Survey. ⟨http.biology.usgs.gov/stt/frame/d272.htm⟩.

Doolittle, William E. "Agriculture in North America on the Eve of Contact: A Reassessment." *Annals of the Association of American Geographers* 82 (1992): 386–401.

Doster, James F. *The Creek Indians and Their Florida Lands, 1740–1823.* 2 vols. New York: Garland, 1974.

Dowd, Gregory Evans. *A Spirited Resistance : The North American Indian Struggle for Unity, 1745–1815.* Johns Hopkins University Studies in Historical and Political Science. Baltimore: Johns Hopkins University Press, 1993.

Drechsel, Emanuel J. *Mobilian Jargon: Linguistic and Sociohistorical Aspects of a Native American Pidgin.* New York: Oxford University Press, 1997.

Drooker, Penelope B. "The Ohio Valley, 1550–1750: Patterns of Sociopolitical Coalescence and Dispersal." In *The Transformation of the Southeastern Indians, 1540–1760*, edited by Robbie Ethridge and Charles Hudson, 115–34. Jackson: University Press of Mississippi, 2002.

Dunaway, Wilma A. *The First American Frontier: Transition to Capitalism in Southern Appalachia, 1700–1860.* Fred W. Morrison Series in Southern Studies. Chapel Hill: University of North Carolina Press, 1996.

Edmunds, R. David. *The Shawnee Prophet.* Lincoln: University of Nebraska Press, 1985.

————. *Tecumseh and the Quest for Indian Leadership*. New York: Little, Brown, 1984.

Elliott, Daniel T., Karen G. Wood, Rita Folse Elliott, and W. Dean Wood. "Up on the Upatoi: Cultural Resources Survey and Testing of Compartments K-6 and K-7, Fort Benning Military Reservation, Georgia." Environmental Management Division, Fort Benning, Ga., 1996.

Engstrom, R. Todd, L. Katherine Kirkman, and Robert J. Mitchell. "The Natural History of the Fire Forest." ⟨http:www.sherpaguides.com/georgia/fire_forest/wildnotes/index.html⟩.

Erichsen-Brown, Charlotte. *Medicinal and Other Uses of North American Plants*. New York: Dover, 1989.

Ethridge, Robbie. "Button-snakeroot: Symbolism among the Southeastern Indians." *Tennessee Anthropologist* 4 (1979): 160–66.

————. "Chickasaw Factionalism." Paper presented at the Annual Meeting of the Southeastern Archaeological Conference, November 14–17, 2001, Chattanooga, Tenn.

————. "A Contest for Land: The Creek Indians on the Southern Frontier, 1796–1816." Ph.D. diss. University of Georgia, Athens, 1996.

————. "An Environmental Look at Creek Indian Place Names in Georgia and Alabama." Paper presented at the Annual Meeting of the Southern Anthropological Society, March 23–26, 1993, Savannah, Ga.

————. "The French Connection." Paper presented at the Annual Meeting of the Southeastern Archaeological Conference, November 8–11, 2000, Macon, Ga.

————. "Horse Stealing as an Informal Economic Strategy on the Late Eighteenth Century Southern Frontier." Paper presented at the Annual Meeting of the American Society for Ethnohistory, November 3–6, 1993, Bloomington, Ind.

————. "Raiding the Remains: Indian Slave Traders and the Collapse of the Southeastern Chiefdoms." Paper presented at the Annual Meeting of Southeastern Archaeological Conference, November 14–17, 2001, Chattanooga, Tenn.

————. "The Southeast." In *Native Americans: Arts and Crafts*, Colin F. Taylor, editorial consultant, 12–21. London: Salamander, 1995.

Ethridge, Robbie, and Charles Hudson. "Early Historic Transformations of the Southeastern Indians." In *Cultural Diversity in the U.S. South: Anthropological Contributions to a Region in Transition*, edited by Carole E. Hill and Patricia D. Beaver, 34–50. Southern Anthropological Society Proceedings, no. 31. Athens: University of Georgia Press, 1998.

————, eds. *The Transformation of the Southeastern Indians, 1540–1760*. Chancellor Porter L. Fortune Symposium in Southern History Series. Jackson: University Press of Mississippi, 2002.

Evans-Pritchard, E. E. "Anthropology and History." In *Social Anthropology and Other Essays*, 172–91. Glencoe, N.Y.: Free Press, 1962.

Fairbanks, Charles H. "Excavations at Horseshoe Bend, Alabama." *Florida Anthropologist* 15 (1962): 41–56.

Fenneman, Nevin M. *Physiography of Eastern United States*. New York: McGraw-Hill, 1938.

Fixico, Donald Lee, ed. *Rethinking American Indian History*. Albuquerque: University of New Mexico Press, 1997.

Forbes, Jack D. *Africans and Native Americans: The Language of Race and the Evolution of Red-Black Peoples*. 2nd ed. Urbana: University of Illinois Press, 1993.

Foreman, Grant. *Indian Removal: The Emigration of the Five Civilized Tribes*. Norman: University of Oklahoma Press, 1972.

Foster, Thomas. "Evolutionary Ecology of Creek Indian Residential Mobility." Paper presented at the Annual Meeting of the Southeastern Archaeological Conference, November 8–11, 2000, Macon, Ga.

———. "Long Term Average Rate Maximization of Creek Indian Residential Mobility: A Test of the Marginal Value Theorem." Ph.D. diss., Pennsylvania State University, 2001.

———. "Temporal Trends in Paleodemography of the Late Historic Creek Indians." Paper presented at the Annual Meeting of the Southeastern Archaeological Conference, November 14–17, 2001, Chattanooga, Tenn.

Gallay, Alan. *The Indian Slave Trade: The Rise of the English Empire in the American South, 1670–1717*. New Haven: Yale University Press, 2002.

———, ed. *Voices of the Old South: Eyewitness Accounts, 1528–1861*. Athens: University of Georgia Press, 1994.

Galloway, Patricia. "The Archaeology of Ethnohistorical Narrative." In *The Spanish Borderlands in Pan-American Perspective*, edited by D. H. Thomas, 453–70. Columbian Consequences, vol. 3. Washington, D.C.: Smithsonian Institutions Press, 1991.

———. "'The Chief Who Is Your Father': Choctaw and French Views of the Diplomatic Relation." In *Powhatan's Mantle: Indians in the Colonial Southeast*, edited by Peter H. Wood, Gregory A. Waselkov, and Thomas M. Hatley, 254–78. Lincoln: University of Nebraska Press, 1989.

———. *Choctaw Genesis, 1500–1700*. Lincoln: University of Nebraska Press, 1996.

———. "Confederacy as a Solution to Chiefdom Dissolution: Historical Evidence in the Choctaw Case." In *The Forgotten Centuries: Indians and Europeans in the American South, 1521–1704*, edited by Charles Hudson and Carmen Chaves Tesser, 393–420. Athens: University of Georgia Press, 1994.

———. "*Conjoncture* and *Longue Durée*: History, Anthropology, and the Hernando de Soto Expedition." In *Historiography of the Hernando de Soto Expedition*, edited by Patricia K. Galloway, 283–94. Norman: University of Nebraska Press, 1997.

———. "Ougoula Tchetoka, Ackia, and Bienville's First Chickasaw War: Whose Strategy and Tactics?" *Journal of Chickasaw History* 2, no. 1 (1996): 3–10.

Gardner, Paul S. "The Ecological Structure and Behavioral Implications of Mast Exploitation Strategies." In *People, Plants, and Landscapes: Studies in Paleoethnobotany*, edited by Kristen J. Gremillion, 161–78. Tuscaloosa: University of Alabama Press, 1997.

Gatschet, Albert S. *A Migration Legend of the Creek Indians*. 1884. Reprint, Millwood, N.Y.: Kraus, 1969.

Gleach, Frederic W. *Powhatan's World and Colonial Virginia: A Conflict of Cultures*. Lincoln: University of Nebraska Press, 1997.

Goff, John H. "The Great Pine Barrens." *Emory University Quarterly* 5 (1949): 20–31.

―――. "The Path to Oakfuskee Upper Trading Route in Georgia to the Creek Indians." *Georgia Historical Quarterly* 39 (1955): 1–36.

Goff, John H., Francis Lee Utley, and Marion R. Hemperley, eds. *Placenames of Georgia: Essays of John Goff.* Athens: University of Georgia Press, 1975.

Gosse, Philip Henry. *Letters from Alabama (U.S.), Chiefly Relating to Natural History.* 1859. Reprint, Tuscaloosa: University of Alabama Press, 1973.

Grant, C. L., and Gerald H. Davis. "The Wedding of Col. Benjamin Hawkins." *North Carolina Historical Review* 54 (1977): 308–16.

Grantham, Bill. *Creation Myths and Legends of the Creek Indians.* Gainesville: University Press of Florida, 2002.

Green, Michael D. "Alexander McGillivray." In *American Indian Leaders: Studies in Diversity*, edited by R. David Edmunds, 41–63. Lincoln: University of Nebraska Press, 1980.

―――. *The Politics of Indian Removal: Creek Government and Society in Crisis.* Lincoln: University of Nebraska Press, 1982.

Gremillion, Kristen J. "Adoption of Old World Crops and Processes of Cultural Change in the Historic Southeast." *Southeastern Archaeology* 12 (1993): 15–20.

―――. "Comparative Paleoethnobotany of Three Native Historic Southeastern Communities of the Historic Period." *Southeastern Archaeology* 14 (1995): 1–16.

―――. "Crop and Weed in Prehistoric Eastern North America: The Chenopodium Example." *American Antiquity* 58 (1993): 496–509.

―――. "The Development and Dispersal of Agricultural Systems in the Woodland Period Southeast." In *The Woodland Southeast*, edited by David G. Anderson and Rolbert C. Mainfort Jr., 483–501. Tuscaloosa: University of Alabama Press, 2002.

―――. "Human Ecology at the Edge of History." In *Between Contacts and Colonies: Archaeological Perspectives on the Protohistoric Southeast*, edited by Cameron B. Wesson and Mark A. Rees, 12–31. Tuscaloosa: University of Alabama Press, 2002.

―――. "Preliminary Report on Plant Remains from Fusihatchee Village (1EE191)." In *Archaeological Excavations at the Early Historic Creek Indian Town of Fusihatchee (Phase I, 1988–1989)*, edited by Gregory A. Waselkov, John W. Cottier, and Craig T. Sheldon Jr., 109–28. Report to the National Science Foundation. Auburn, Ala.: University of Auburn Department of Sociology and Anthropology, 1990.

―――, ed. *People, Plants, and Landscapes: Studies in Paleoethnobotany.* Tuscaloosa: University of Alabama Press, 1997.

Griffith, Benjamin W., Jr. *McIntosh and Weatherford, Creek Indian Leaders.* Tuscaloosa: University of Alabama Press, 1988.

Guice, John D. W. "Cattle Raisers of the Old Southwest: A Reinterpretation." *Western Historical Quarterly* 8 (1977): 167–87.

Haan, Richard L. "The 'Trade do's not Flourish as Formerly': The Ecological Origins of the Yamassee War of 1715." *Ethnohistory* 28 (1982): 341–58.

Haas, Mary R. "The Classification of the Muskogean Languages." In *Language*,

Culture, and Personality: Essays in Memory of Edward Sapir, edited by Leslie Spier, A. Irving Hallowell, and Stanley S. Newman, 41–56. Menasha, Wisc.: Sapir Memorial Publication Fund, 1941.

———. "Creek Inter-Town Relations." *American Anthropologist* 42 (1940): 479–89.

———. "What is Mobilian?" In *Studies in Southeastern Indian Languages*, edited by James M. Crawford, 257–61. Athens: University of Georgia Press, 1975.

Hahn, Steven Christopher. "The Invention of the Creek Nation: A Political History of the Creek Indians in the South's Imperial Era, 1540–1763." Ph.D diss., Emory University, 2000.

———. "A Miniature Arms Race: The Role of the Flintlock in Initiating Indian Dependency in the Colonial Southeastern United States, 1656–1730." M.A. thesis, University of Georgia, 1995.

Halbert, Henry Sale, and T. H. Ball. *The Creek War of 1813 and 1814.* 1895. Reprint, Tuscaloosa: University of Alabama Press, 1969.

Hall, Captain Basil. *Forty Etchings, from Sketches made with the Camera Lucida, in North America, in 1827 and 1828.* 4th ed. Edinburgh: Cadell & Co.; London: Simpkin & Marshall, and Moon, Boys & Graves, 1830.

———. *Travels in North America in the Years 1827 and 1828.* 3 vols. Edinburgh: Cadell & Co., 1829.

Hall, Mrs. Basil. *The Aristocratic Journey, Being the Outspoken Letters of Mrs. Basil Hall.* Edited by Una Pope-Hennessy. London: G. P. Putnam's Sons, 1931.

Hally, David J. "Archaeological Investigation of the Little Egypt Site (9Mu102), Murray County, Georgia, 1970–72 Seasons." Heritage Conservation and Recreation Service, U.S. Department of the Interior, 1980.

———. "Archaeology and Settlement Plan of the King Site." In *The King Site: Continuity and Contact in Sixteenth-Century Georgia*, edited by Robert L. Blakley, 3–16. Athens: University of Georgia Press, 1988.

———. "'As Caves below the Ground': Making Sense of Aboriginal House Form in the Protohistoric and Historic Southeast." In *Between Contacts and Colonies: Archaeological Perspectives on the Protohistoric Southeast*, edited by Cameron B. Wesson and Mark A. Rees, 90–109. Tuscaloosa: University of Alabama Press, 2002.

———. "Domestic Architecture and Domestic Activities in the Native South." *Early Georgia* 10 (1982): 40–52.

———. "An Overview of Lamar Culture." In *Ocmulgee Archaeology, 1936–1986*, edited by David J. Hally, 144–74. Athens: University of Georgia Press, 1994.

———. "Plant Preservation and Content of Paleobotanical Samples: A Case Study." *American Antiquity* 46 (1981): 723–42.

Hally, David J., and James B. Langford Jr. *Mississippi Period Archaeology of the Georgia Valley and Ridge Province.* University of Georgia Laboratory of Archaeology Series, no. 25. Athens: University of Georgia Laboratory of Archaeology, 1988.

Hann, John H. *Apalachee: The Land between the Rivers.* Ripley P. Bullen Monographs in Anthropology and History, no. 7. Gainesville: University Press of Florida, 1988.

———. "De Soto, Dobyns, and Demography." *Florida Anthropologist* 48 (1990): 3–12.

Harmon, George D. "Benjamin Hawkins and the Federal Factory System." *North Carolina Historical Review* 9 (1932): 138–52.

Harris, D., and Gordon Hillman, eds. *Foraging and Farming: The Evolution of Plant Exploitation.* London: Allen and Unwin, 1989.

Hassig, Ross. "Internal Creek Conflict in the Creek War of 1813–1814." *Ethnohistory* 21 (1974): 251–71.

Hatley, M. Thomas. "Cherokee Women Farmers Hold Their Ground." In *Appalachian Frontiers*, edited by Robert D. Mitchell, 37–61. Lexington: University Press of Kentucky, 1991.

———. *The Dividing Paths: Cherokees and South Carolinians through the Era of Revolution.* New York: Oxford University Press, 1992.

———. "The Eighteenth-Century Tallapoosa Landscape Re-visited." In *Archaeological Excavations at the Early Historic Creek Indian Town of Fusihatchee (Phase I, 1988–1989)*, edited by Gregory A. Waselkov, John W. Cottier, and Craig T. Sheldon Jr., 77–108. Report to the National Science Foundation. Auburn, Ala.: University of Auburn Department of Sociology and Anthropology, 1990.

Hawkins, Benjamin. "Benjamin Hawkins' Trip across Georgia in 1796." Annotated by Marion B. Hemperley. *Georgia Historical Quarterly* 56 (1972): 415–31.

———. *The Creek Country, Being a Reprint of Vol. Three, Part One of the Georgia Historical Society Publications.* Americus, Ga.: Americus Book Co., 1938.

———. *The Letters, Journals, and Writings of Benjamin Hawkins.* 2 vols. Edited by C. L. Grant. Savannah: Beehive Press, 1980.

———. "Letters of Benjamin Hawkins, 1796–1806." *Collections of the Georgia Historical Society*, vol. 11. 1916.

———. *A Sketch of the Creek Country in the Years 1798 and 1799. Collections of the Georgia Historical Society*, vol. 3. 1848. Reprint, New York: Kraus, 1971.

Henri, Florette. *The Southern Indians and Benjamin Hawkins, 1796–1816.* Norman: University of Oklahoma Press, 1986.

Hewitt, J. N. B. *Notes on the Creek Indians.* Edited by John R. Swanton. Bureau of American Ethnology Bulletin, no. 123, pp. 119–59. Washington, D.C.: Government Printing Office, 1939.

Higginbotham, Jay. *Old Mobile: Fort Louis de la Louisianne, 1702–1711.* 1977. Reprint with a new introduction by the author. Tuscaloosa: University of Alabama Press, 1991.

Hill, Sarah H. *Weaving New Worlds: Southeastern Cherokee Women and Their Basketry.* Chapel Hill: University of North Carolina Press, 1997.

Hilliard, Sam Bowers. *Hog Meat and Hoecake: Food Supply in the Old South, 1840–1860.* Carbondale: Southern Illinois University Press, 1972.

Hodgson, Adam. *Letters from North America, Written during a Tour in the United States and Canada.* London: Hurst, Robinson, and Co., 1824.

Holland, C. G. "A Mid-Eighteenth Century Indian Village on the Chattahoochee River." *Florida Anthropologist* 27 (1974): 31–46.

Horsman, Reginald. *The Frontier in the Formative Years, 1783–1815.* New York, Holt, Rinehart and Winston, 1970.

———. "Recent Trends and New Directions in Native American History." In *The

American West: New Perspectives, New Dimensions, edited by Jerome O. Steffen, 124–51. Norman: University of Oklahoma Press, 1979.

Howe, LeAnne. "The Story of America: A Tribalography." In *Clearing a Path: Theorizing the Past in Native American Studies*, edited by Nancy Shoemaker, 29–48. New York: Routledge, 2002.

Hudson, Charles. *Conversations with the High Priest of Coosa*. Chapel Hill: University of North Carolina Press, 2003.

———. "The Hernando de Soto Expedition, 1539–1543." In *Forgotten Centuries: Indians and Europeans in the American South, 1521–1704*, edited by Charles Hudson and Carmen Chaves Tesser, 74–103. Athens: University of Georgia Press, 1994.

———. "The Historical Approach in Anthropology." In *Handbook of Social and Cultural Anthropology*, edited by John J. Honnogmann, 111–41. New York: Rand McNally College Publishing Co., 1974.

———. *The Juan Pardo Expedition: Exploration of the Carolinas and Tennessee, 1566–1568*. Washington, D.C.: Smithsonian Institution Press, 1990.

———. *Knights of Spain, Warriors of the Sun: Hernando de Soto and the South's Ancient Chiefdoms*. Athens: University of Georgia Press, 1998.

———. *The Southeastern Indians*. Knoxville: University of Tennessee Press, 1976.

———. "Why the Southeastern Indians Slaughtered Deer." In *Indians, Animals, and the Fur Trade: A Critique of Keepers of the Game*, edited by Shepard Krech III, 168–70. Athens: University of Georgia Press, 1981.

———, ed. *Black Drink: A Native American Tea*. Athens: University of Georgia Press, 1979.

———. *Red, White, and Black: Symposium on Indians in the Old South*. Athens: University of Georgia Press, 1971.

Hudson, Charles, Marvin Smith, and Chester DePratter. "The Hernando de Soto Expedition: From Apalachee to Chiaha." *Southeastern Archaeology* 8 (1989): 65–77.

———. "The Hernando de Soto Expedition: From Mabila to the Mississippi." In *Towns and Temples along the Mississippi*, edited by David Dye and Cheryl Anne Cox, 181–207. Tuscaloosa: University of Alabama Press, 1990.

Hudson, Charles, Marvin Smith, Chester DePratter, and Emilia Kelly. "The Tristan de Luna Expedition, 1559–1561." *Southeastern Archaeology* 8 (1989): 31–45.

Hudson, Joyce Rockwood. *Apalachee: A Novel*. Athens: University of Georgia Press, 2000.

Hunt, Charles B. *Natural Regions of the United States and Canada*. A Series of Books in Geology. San Francisco: W. H. Freeman and Co., 1974.

———. *Physiography of the United States*. A Series of Books in Geology. San Francisco: W. H. Freeman and Co., 1967.

Hurt, R. Douglas. *Indian Agriculture in America: Prehistory to the Present*. Lawrence: University Press of Kansas, 1987.

Huscher, Harold A. "Historic Lower Creek Sites." Georgia State Archaeological Site Manuscript Files, no. 182. University of Georgia, Athens, 1958.

Innerarity, John. "The Creek Debtors to John Forbes & Company, Successors to

Panton, Leslie & Company: A Journal of John Innerarity, 1812." *Florida Historical Quarterly* 9 (1930): 67–89.

Jackson, Harvey H., III. *Rivers of History: Life on the Coosa, Tallapoosa, Cahaba, and Alabama.* Tuscaloosa: University of Alabama Press, 1995.

Jakes, Kathryn A., and Annette G. Ericksen. "Prehistoric Use of Sumac and Bedstraw as Dye Plants in Eastern North America." *Southeastern Archaeology* 20 (2001): 56–66.

Jeter, Marvin D. "From Prehistory through Protohistory to Ethnohistory in and near the Northern Lower Mississippi Valley." In *The Transformation of the Southeastern Indians, 1540–1760*, edited by Robbie Ethridge and Charles Hudson, 177–224. Jackson: University Press of Mississippi, 2002.

Johnson, Jay. "The Chickasaws." In *Indians of the Greater Southeast: Historical Archaeology and Ethnohistory*, edited by Bonnie G. McEwan, 85–121. Gainesville: University Press of Florida for the Society for Historical Archaeology, 2000.

———. "Stone Tools, Politics, and the Eighteenth-Century Chickasaw in Northeast Mississippi." *American Antiquity* 62 (1997): 215–30.

Johnson, Troy P. *Contemporary Native American Political Issues.* Contemporary Native American Communities, no. 3. New York: Altamira Press, 1999.

Jordan-Bychkov, Terry G., and Matti Kaups. *The American Backwoods Frontier: An Ethnic and Ecological Interpretation.* Baltimore: Johns Hopkins University Press, 1989.

Jordan, Winthrop D. *White over Black: American Attitudes toward the Negro, 1550–1812.* Chapel Hill: University of North Carolina Press for the Institute of Early American History and Culture at Williamsburg, Virginia, 1968.

Joseph W. Jones Ecological Research Center at Ichuaway. "Field Guide." ⟨http://www.jonesctr.org/fieldguide/geograph_app.html⟩.

Jurgelski, Bill. "Strangers among Them: The Indian Countrymen of Western North Carolina and Their Place in Early Nineteenth Century Cherokee Society." Paper presented at the Annual Meeting of the Southeastern Archaeological Society, November 14–17, 2001, Chattanooga, Tenn.

Kelton, Paul. "Not All Disappeared: Disease and Southeastern Indian Survival, 1500–1800." Ph.D. diss., University of Oklahoma, 1998.

Keyes, Greg. "Myth and Social History in the Early Southeast." In *Perspectives on the Southeast: Linguistics, Archaeology, and Ethnohistory*, edited by Patricia B. Kwachka, 106–15. Athens: University of Georgia Press, 1994.

Kimball, Geoffrey D., Bel Abbey, Martha John, and Ruth Poncho. *Koasati Dictionary.* Studies in the Anthropology of North American Indians. Lincoln: University of Nebraska Press, 1994.

Kirkland, Dwight Servey. "Ten Millennia of Human Land Use on the Interior Coastal Plain of Georgia." M.A. thesis, University of Georgia, 1994.

Kline, Benjamin. *First along the River: A Brief History of the U.S. Environmental Movement.* San Francisco: Acada Books, 1997.

Knapp, Arthur Bernard. *Archaeology, Annales, and Ethnohistory.* New Directions in Archaeolgoy Series. London: Cambridge University Press, 1992.

Knight, Vernon James, Jr. "The Formation of the Creeks." In *The Forgotten Cen-*

turies: Indians and Europeans in the American South, 1521–1704, edited by Charles Hudson and Carmen Chaves Tesser, 373–92. Athens: University of Georgia Press, 1994.

———. "The Institutional Organization of Mississippian Religion." *American Antiquity* 51 (1986): 675–87.

———. *Tukabatchee: Archaeological Investigations at an Historic Creek Town*. Report of Investigations, no. 45. Moundville: University of Alabama Office of Archaeological Research, 1985.

Knight, Vernon J., and Marvin T. Smith. "Big Tallassee: A Contribution to Upper Creek Site Archaeology." *Early Georgia* 8 (1980): 59–74.

Krech, Shepard, III. *The Ecological Indian: Myth and History*. New York: W. W. Norton, 1999.

———. "The State of Ethnohistory." *Annual Review of Anthropology* 20 (1991): 345–75.

———, ed. *Indians, Animals, and the Fur Trade: A Critique of Keepers of the Game*. Athens: University of Georgia Press, 1981.

Kowalewski, Stephen A., and James W. Hatch. "The Sixteenth-Century Expansion of Settlement in the Upper Oconee Watershed, Georgia." *Southeastern Archaeology* 10 (1991): 1–17.

Lane, Mills. *The Rambler in Georgia*. Savannah: Beehive Press, 1973.

Lankford, George E. *Native American Legends, Southeastern Legends: Tales from the Natchez, Caddo, Biloxi, Chickasaw, and Other Nations*. Little Rock, Ark.: August House, 1987.

Lanning, John Tate, ed. "Oglethorpe's Treaty with the Lower Creek Indians." *Georgia Historical Quarterly* 4 (1920): 3–16.

Larsen, Clark Spencer. *Bioarchaeology of Spanish Florida: The Impact of Colonialism*. Gainesville: University Press of Florida, 2001.

Larson, Lewis H. "Functional Considerations of Warfare in the Southeast during the Mississippian Period." *American Antiquity* 37 (1971): 383–92.

Ledbetter, R. Jerald, and Chad O. Braley. *Archaeological and Historical Investigations at Florence Marina State Park, Walter F. George Reservoir, Stewart County, GA*. Atlanta: Georgia Department of Natural Resources, 1989.

Ledbetter, R. Jerald, W. Dean Wood, Karen G. Wood, and Robbie Ethridge. "Cultural Resources Survey of Allatoona Lake Area Georgia." U.S. Army Engineer District, Mobile, Ala., 1987.

Levasseur, A. *Lafayette in America in 1824 and 1825; or, Journal of a Voyage to the United States*. Philadelphia: Carey and Lea, 1829.

Lewis, David, and Ann Jordan. *Creek Indian Medicine Ways: The Enduring Power of Mvskoke Religion*. Albuquerque: University of New Mexico Press, 2002.

Lewis, Martin W., and Kären E. Wigen. *The Myth of Continents: A Critique of Metageography*. Berkeley: University of California Press, 1997.

Lightfoot, Kent G. "Culture Contact Studies: Redefining the Relationship between Prehistoric and Historical Archaeology." *American Antiquity* 60 (1995): 199–217.

Linton, Ralph M. "Land Tenure in Aboriginal America." In *The Changing Indian*, edited by Oliver La Farge, 42–54. Norman: University of Oklahoma Press, 1942.

Littlefield, Daniel F., Jr. *Africans and Creeks from the Colonial Period to the Civil War*. Westport, Conn.: Greenwood, 1979.

Lolley, Terry L. "Ethnohistory and Archaeology: A Map Method for Locating Historic Upper Creek Indian Towns and Villages." *Journal of Alabama Archaeology* 42 (1996): 1–96.

Loucks, C., D. Olson, E. Dinerstein, A. Weakley, R. Noss. J. Striholt, and K. Wolfe. "Appalachian–Blue Ridge Forest (NA0403)." World Wildlife Fund and National Geographic Society. Wild World Website. ⟨http://worldwildlife.org/wildworld/profiles/terrestrial/na/na0403_full.html⟩.

———. "Appalachian Mixed Mesophytic Forest (NA0402)." World Wildlife Fund and National Geographic Society. Wild World Website. ⟨http://worldwildlife.org/wildworld/profiles/terrestrial/na/na0402_full.html⟩.

Martin, Calvin. *The American Indians and the Problem of History*. New York: Oxford University Press, 1987.

———. *Keepers of the Game: Indian-Animal Relationships and the Fur Trade*. Berkeley: University of California Press, 1978.

Martin, Jack B. *A Dictionary of Creek/Muskogee with Notes on the Florida and Oklahoma Seminole Dialects of Creek*. Lincoln: University of Nebraska Press, 2000.

Martin, Joel W. *Sacred Revolt: The Muskogee's Struggle for a New World*. Boston: Beacon Press, 1991.

———. "Southeastern Indians and the English Trade in Skins and Slaves." In *The Forgotten Centuries: Indians and Europeans in the American South, 1521–1704*, edited by Charles Hudson and Carmen Chaves Tesser, 304–24. Athens: University of Georgia Press, 1994.

Mason, Carol L. "Eighteenth Century Culture Change among the Lower Creeks." *Florida Anthropologist* 16 (1963): 65–80.

Mattison, Ray H. "The Creek Trading House: From Colerain to Fort Hawkins." *Georgia Historical Quarterly* 30 (1946): 169–84.

Mauelshagen, Carl, and Gerald H. Davis, eds. *Partners in the Lord's Work: The Diary of Two Moravian Missionaries in Creek Country*. School of Arts and Sciences Research Papers, no. 21. Atlanta: Georgia State College, 1969.

May, Katja. *African Americans and Native Americans in the Creek and Cherokee Nations, 1830s to 1920s: Collision and Collusion*. Studies in African American History and Culture. New York: Garland, 1996.

McDonald, Forrest, and Grady McWhiney. "The Antebellum Southern Herdsman: A Reinterpretation." *Journal of Southern History* 41 (1975): 147–66.

McGillivray, Alexander. *McGillivray of the Creeks*. Edited by John Walton Caughey. Norman: University of Oklahoma Press, 1938.

Merrell, James H. *The Indians' New World: Catawbas and Their Neighbors from European Contact through the Era of Removal*. Chapel Hill: University of North Carolina Press, 1989.

———. *Into the American Woods: Negotiators on the Pennsylvania Frontier*. New York: Norton, 1999.

———. "'Our Bond of Peace': Patterns of Intercultural Exchange in the Carolina

Piedmont, 1650–1750." In *Powhatan's Mantle: Indians in the Colonial Southeast*, edited by Peter H. Wood, Gregory A. Waselkov, and Thomas M. Hatley, 196–222. Lincoln: University of Nebraska Press, 1989.

Merritt, Jane T. "Metaphor, Meaning, and Misunderstanding: Language and Power on the Pennsylvania Frontier." In *Contact Points: American Frontiers from the Mohawk Valley to the Mississippi, 1750–1830*, 60–87, edited by Andrew R. L. Cayton and Fredrika J. Teute. Chapel Hill: University of North Carolina Press for the Omohundro Institute of Early American History and Culture, 1998.

Meyer, William E. *Indian Trails of the Southeast*. Forty-second Annual Report of the Bureau of American Ethnology. Washington, D.C.: Government Printing Office, 1928.

Meyers, Allan D. "Household Organization and Refuse Disposal at a Cultivated Creek Site." *Southeastern Archaeology* 15 (1996): 132–44.

Meyers, Maureen Elizabeth Siewert. "Natural Factors Affecting the Settlement of Mississippian Chiefdoms in Northwestern Georgia." M.A. thesis, University of Georgia, Athens, 1995.

Mihesuah, Devon A., ed. *Natives and Academics: Researching and Writing about American Indians*. Lincoln: University of Nebraska Press, 1998.

Milanich, Jerald T. *Florida's Indians from Ancient Times to the Present*. Gainesville: University Press of Florida, 1998.

Milfort, Louis LeClerc de. *Louis LeClerc de Milfort, Memoir or a Cursory Glance at My Different Travels and My Sojourn in the Creek Nation*. Edited by John Francis McDermott. 1802. Reprint, Chicago: Donnelley, 1956.

Miller, James J. *An Environmental History of Northeast Florida*. Gainesville: University Press of Florida, 1998.

Mistovich, Tim S., and Vernon James Knight Jr. *Excavations at Four Sites on Walter F. George Lake, Alabama and Georgia*. Report of Investigations, no. 49. Moundville: University of Alabama Office of Archaeological Research, 1986.

Mistovich, Tim S., and David W. Zeanah. *An Intensive Phase II Survey of Selected Areas of the Coosa River Navigation Project*, vols. 3 and 4. Report of Investigations, nos. 35 and 38. Moundville: University of Alabama Office of Archaeological Research, 1983.

Mithun, Marianne. *The Languages of Native North America*. Cambridge Language Surveys. Cambridge: Cambridge University Press, 1999.

Moerman, Daniel E. *Native American Ethnobotany*. Portland, Ore.: Timber Press, 1998.

Mood, Fulmer, ed. "John Winthrop, Jr., on Indian Corn." *New England Quarterly* 10 (1937): 121–33.

Mooney, James. *Myths of the Cherokees and Sacred Formulas of the Cherokees from the 19th and 7th Annual Reports of the Bureau of American Ethnology*. Nashville: Charles and Randy Elder, 1982.

Morris, Michael P. *The Bringing of Wonder: Trade and the Indians of the Southeast, 1700–1783*. Contributions in Comparative Colonial Studies, no. 36. Westport, Conn.: Greenwood, 1999.

Moss, Kay K. *Southern Folk Medicine, 1750–1820*. Columbia: University of South Carolina, 1999.

Muller, Jon. *Mississippian Political Economy*. New York: Plenum Press, 1997.

Nabokov, Peter. *A Forest of Time: American Indian Ways of History*. Cambridge: Cambridge University Press, 2002.

Nadel, Stanley. *Alexander McGillivray*. American National Biography. New York: Oxford University Press, 1999.

Nash, Gary B. *Red, White, and Black: The Peoples of Early America*. Englewood Cliffs, N.J.: Prentice-Hall, 1974.

Nelson, Thomas C. "The Original Forests of the Georgia Piedmont." *Ecology* 38 (1957): 390–97.

Newsom, John D. "History of Deer and Their Habitat in the South." In *White-tailed Deer in Southern Forest Habitat: Proceedings of a Symposium at Nacogdoches, Texas, March 25–26, 1969*. Nacogdoches, Tex.: Southern Forest Experiment Station, 1969.

O'Brien, Greg. *Choctaws in a Revolutionary Age, 1750–1830*. Lincoln: University of Nebraska Press, 2002.

———. "The Conqueror Meets the Unconquered: Negotiating Cultural Boundaries on the Post-Revolutionary Southern Frontier." *Journal of Southern History* 67 (2001): 39–72.

O'Brien, Patricia. "The Sweet Potato: Its Origin and Dispersal." *American Anthropologist* 74 (1972): 342–65.

O'Donnell, James H., III. *Southern Indians in the American Revolution*. Knoxville: University of Tennessee Press, 1973.

Odum, Eugene P. *Ecology and Our Endangered Life Support Systems*. Sunderland, Mass.: Sinauer Associates, 1989.

Otto, John Solomon. *Southern Frontiers, 1607–1860: The Agricultural Evolution of the Colonial and Antebellum South*. Contribution in American History, no. 133. Westport, Conn.: Greenwood, 1989.

Owens, Thomas M. "Indian Tribes and Towns in Alabama." *Alabama Historical Quarterly* 12 (1950): 118–241.

Owsley, Frank Lawrence, Jr. "The Fort Mims Massacre." *Alabama Review* 24 (1971): 192–204.

———. "Prophet of War: Josiah Francis and the Creek War." *American Indian Quarterly* 9 (1985): 273–93.

———. *Struggle for the Gulf Borderlands: The Creek Wars and the Battle of New Orleans*. Gainesville: University Press of Florida, 1981. Paperback ed., Tuscaloosa: University of Alabama Press, 2000.

Parades, J. Anthony, ed. *Indians of the Southeastern United States in the Late Twentieth Century*. Tuscaloosa: University of Alabama Press, 1992.

Parades, J. Anthony, and Kenneth J. Plante. "Economics, Politics, and the Subjugation of the Creek Indians." Report submitted to the Southeast Archaeological Center, National Park Service, Tallahassee, Fla., 1975.

———. "A Reexamination of Creek Indian Population Trends, 1738–1832." *American Indian Culture and Research Journal* 6, no. 4 (1982): 3–28.

Pauketat, Timothy R., ed. *The Archaeology of Traditions: Agency and History before and after Columbus*. Gainesville: University Press of Florida, 2001.

Pavao-Zuckerman, Barnet. "Vertebrate Subsistence in the Mississippian-Historic Transition." *Southeastern Archaeology* 19 (2000): 135–44.

Payne, John Howard. "The Green-Corn Dance." *Continental Monthly* 1 (1862): 17–29.

Peake, Ora Brooks. *A History of the United States Indian Factory System, 1795–1822.* Denver: Sage Books, 1954.

Perdue, Theda. *Cherokee Women: Gender and Culture Change, 1700–1835.* Lincoln: University of Nebraska Press, 1998.

———. *"Mixed Blood Indians": Racial Construction in the Early South.* Mercer University Lamar Memorial Lectures, no. 45. Athens: University of Georgia Press, 2003.

———. *Slavery and the Evolution of Cherokee Society, 1540–1866.* Knoxville: University of Tennessee Press, 1979.

———. "Southern Indians and the Cult of True Womanhood." In *The Web of Southern Social Relations: Women, Family, and Education,* edited by Walter J. Fraser Jr., R. Frank Saunders Jr., and Jon L. Wakelyn, 35–51. Athens: University of Georgia Press, 1985.

Perdue, Theda, and Michael D. Green. *The Columbia Guide to American Indians of the Southeast.* Columbia Guides to American Indian History and Culture. New York: Columbia University Press, 2001.

Perkins, Elizabeth A. "Distinctions and Partitions amongst Us: Identity and Interactions in the Revolutionary Ohio Valley." In *Contact Points: American Frontiers from the Mohawk Valley to the Mississippi, 1750–1830,* edited by Andrew R. L. Cayton and Fredrika J. Teute, 205–34. Chapel Hill: University of North Carolina Press for the Omohundro Institute of Early American History and Culture, 1998.

Phillips, Ulrich B. *Life and Labor in the Old South.* New York: Little and Brown, 1929.

Pickett, James Albert. *History of Alabama and Incidentally of Georgia and Mississippi from the Earliest Period.* Charleston, S.C.: Walker and James, 1851.

Piker, Joshua. "Peculiar Connections: The Creek Town of Oakfuskee and the Study of Colonial America." Manuscript on file with author, 2002.

Pluckhahn, Thomas J. "Archaeological Investigation of the Tarver (9Jo6) and Little Tarver (9Jo98) Sites, Jones County, Georgia." Report submitted to the Federal Emergency Management Agency, Region IV, Atlanta, by Southeastern Archaeological Services, Athens, Ga., 1997.

Pope, John A. *A Tour through the Southern and Western Territories of the United States of North America; the Spanish Dominion on the River Mississippi and the Floridas; the Countries of the Creek Nation and Many Uninhabited Parts.* 1791. Reprint, New York: Charles L. Woodward, 1888.

Porter, Kenneth Wiggins. *The Negro on the American Frontier.* New York: Arno Press and the New York Times, 1971.

Potter, Stephen R. "Early English Effects on Virginia Algonquian Exchange and Tribute in the Tidewater Potomac." In *Powhatan's Mantle: Indians in the Colonial Southeast,* edited by Peter H. Wood, Gregory A. Waselkov, and Thomas M. Hatley, 151–72. Lincoln: University of Nebraska Press, 1989.

Pound, Merritt B. *Benjamin Hawkins, Indian Agent.* Athens: University of Georgia Press, 1951.

Provinse, John. "Tenure Problems of the American Indian." In *Land Tenure: Proceedings of the International Conference on Land Tenure and Related Problems in World Agriculture Held in Madison, Wisconsin, 1951,* edited by Kenneth H. Parsons, Raymond J. Penn, and Philip M. Raup, 420–29. Madison: University of Wisconsin Press, 1956.

Prucha, Francis Paul. *American Indian Policy.* Lincoln: University of Nebraska Press, 1981.

―――. *American Indian Policy in the Formative Years: The Indian Trade and Intercourse Acts, 1790–1834.* Cambridge: Harvard University Press, 1962.

―――. *The Great Father: The United States Government and the American Indians.* 2 vols. Lincoln: University of Nebraska Press, 1984.

―――, ed. *Documents of United States Indian Policy.* 2nd ed., expanded. Lincoln: University of Nebraska Press, 1990.

Ramenofsky, Ann. *Vectors of Death: The Archaeology of European Contact.* Albuquerque: University of New Mexico Press, 1987.

Read, William A. *Indian Place Names in Alabama.* Rev. ed. Foreword, Appendix, and Index by James B. Macmillan. Tuscaloosa: University of Alabama Press, 1984.

―――. "Indian Stream Names in Georgia." *International Journal of American Linguistics* 15 (1949): 128–30.

Reid, John Phillip. *A Law of Blood: The Primitive Law of the Cherokee Nation.* New York: New York University Press, 1970.

Reidy, Joseph P. *From Slavery to Agrarian Capitalism in the Cotton Plantation South.* Fred W. Morrison Series in Southern Studies. Chapel Hill: University of North Carolina Press, 1992.

Reitz, Elizabeth J. "Morphometric Data for Cattle from North America and the Caribbean prior to the 1850s." *Journal of Archaeological Science* 21 (1994): 699–713.

―――. "The Spanish Colonial Experience and Domestic Animals." *Historical Archaeology* 26 (1992): 84–91.

Richter, Daniel K. *Facing East from Indian Country: A Native History of Early America.* Cambridge: Harvard University Press, 2002.

―――. *The Ordeal of the Longhouse: The Peoples of the Iroquois League in the Era of European Colonization.* Chapel Hill: University of North Carolina Press for the Institute of Early American History and Culture, Williamsburg, Va., 1992.

―――. "Review of a New Order of Things: Property, Power, and the Transformation of the Creek Indians, 1733–1816." *Journal of Southern History* 68 (2002): 678–79.

―――. "Whose Indian History?" *William and Mary Quarterly* 50 (1993): 379–93.

Rogers, J. Daniel, and Samuel M. Wilson. *Ethnohistory and Archaeology: Approaches to Post Contact Change in the Americas.* New York: Plenum Press, 1993.

Romans, Bernard. *A Concise Natural History of East and West Florida.* Edited by Kathryn E. Holland Braund. Tuscaloosa: University of Alabama Press, 1999.

Rostlund, Erhard. "The Geographic Range of the Historic Bison in the Southeast." *Annals of the Association of American Geographers* 50 (1960): 395–407.

Royce, Charles C., comp. *Indian Land Cessions in the United States*. Eighteenth Annual Report of Bureau of American Ethnology, no. 2, pp. 521–997. Washington,
D.C.: Government Printing Office, 1899.

Russell, E. *Soil Conditions and Plant Growth*. New York: John Wiley and Sons, 1966.

Saggus, Charles Danforth. *Agrarian Arcadia: Anglo-Virginian Planters of Wilkes
County, Georgia, in the 1850s*. Washington, Ga.: Mary Willis Library, 1996.

Sahlins, Marshall. *Stone Age Economics*. New York: Aldine de Gruyter, 1972.

Said, Edward. *Orientalism*. New York: Random House, 1979.

Saunt, Claudio. *A New Order of Things: Property, Power, and the Transformation of
the Creek Indians, 1733–1816*. Cambridge: Cambridge University Press, 1999.

Scarry, C. Margaret. *Foraging and Farming in the Eastern Woodlands*. Gainesville:
University Press of Florida, 1993.

Schroeder, Sissel. "Understanding Variation in Prehistoric Agricultural Productivity: The Importance of Distinguishing among Potential, Available, and Consump-
tive Yields." *American Antiquity* 66 (2001): 512–25.

Sheehan, Bernard W. *Seeds of Extinction: Jeffersonian Philanthropy and the American
Indian*. Chapel Hill: University of North Carolina Press, 1973.

Sheldon, Craig T. "Historic Creek 'Summer' Houses of Central Alabama." Paper
presented at the Annual Meeting of the Society for American Archaeology, April
4, 1997, Nashville, Tenn.

———. "Upper Creek Architecture at Fusihatchee." In *Archaeological Excavations
at the Early Historic Creek Indian Town of Fusihatchee (Phase I, 1988–1989)*, edited by Gregory A. Waselkov, John W. Cottier, and Craig T. Sheldon Jr., 45–76.
Report to the National Science Foundation. Auburn, Ala.: University of Auburn
Department of Sociology and Anthropology, 1990.

Shimer, John A. *Field Guide to Landforms in the United States*. New York: Macmillan, 1972.

Shoemaker, Nancy. "How Indians Got to Be Red." *American Historical Review* 102
(1997): 625–44.

———, ed. *Clearing a Path: Theorizing the Past in Native American Studies*. New
York: Routledge, 2002.

Silver, Timothy. *A New Face on the Countryside: Indians, Colonists, and Slaves in
South Atlantic Forests, 1500–1800*. Cambridge: Cambridge University Press,
1990.

Silvia Mueller, Diane. "Intrasite Settlement at the Historic Creek Town of Hickory
Ground (1EE89), Elmore County, Alabama (1990–1991)." *Journal of Alabama
Archaeology* 41 (1995): 107–34.

Simmons, I. G. *Interpreting Nature: Cultural Constructions of the Environment*. New
York: Routledge, 1993.

Sioui, Georges E. *For an Amerindian Autohistory: An Essay on the Foundations of a
Social Ethic*. Montreal: McGill-Queen's University Press, 1992.

Slotkin, Richard. *The Fatal Environment: The Myth of the Frontier in the Age of In-
dustrialization, 1800–1890*. Tulsa: University of Oklahoma Press, 1998.

———. *Gunfighter Nation: The Myth of the Frontier in Twentieth Century America*.
Tulsa: University of Oklahoma Press, 1998.

————. *Regeneration through Violence: The Mythology of the American Frontier, 1600–1860.* Tulsa: University of Oklahoma Press, 2000.

Smith, Bruce D., C. Wesley Cowan, and Michael P. Hoffman. *Rivers of Change: Essays on Early Agriculture in Eastern North America.* Washington, D.C.: Smithsonian Institution Press, 1992.

Smith, Linda Tuhiwai. *Decolonizing Methodologies: Research and Indigenous Peoples.* New York: Zed Books, 1999.

Smith, Marvin. *Archaeology of Aboriginal Culture Change in the Interior Southeast: Depopulation during the Early Historic Period.* Ripley P. Bullen Monographs in Anthropology and History, no. 6. Gainesville: University Press of Florida, 1987.

————. *Coosa: The Rise and Fall of a Southeastern Mississippian Chiefdom.* Florida Museum of Natural History Ripley P. Bullen Series. Gainesville: University Press of Florida, 2000.

————. *Historic Period Indian Archaeology of Northern Georgia.* University of Georgia Laboratory of Archaeology Series, no. 30. Athens: University of Georgia Laboratory of Archaeology, 1994.

Snyderman, George S. *Concepts of Land Ownership among the Iroquois and Their Neighbors.* Bureau of American Ethnology Bulletin, no. 149, pp. 13–34. Washington, D.C.: Government Printing Office, 1951.

Southerland, Henry DeLeon, Jr., and Jerry Elijah Brown. *The Federal Road through Georgia, the Creek Nation, and Alabama, 1806–1836.* Tuscaloosa: University of Alabama Press, 1989.

Spears, Carrie Weir. "European Infectious Disease and the Depopulation of Southeastern American Indians." Ph.D. diss., University of Southern Mississippi, 1999.

Speck, Frank G. "The Creek Indians of Taskigi Town." *Memoirs of the American Anthropological Association* 2 (1907): 99–164.

Spirn, Anne Whiston. *The Language of Landscape.* New Haven: Yale University Press, 1998.

Starrett, Paul. *Appraisal Report: Lands in Southern Georgia and Southeastern Alabama Ceded by the Creek Nation, before the Indian Claims Commission, Docket No. 21, Valued as of August 9, 1814.* U.S. Department of Justice. Washington, D.C.: Government Printing Office, 1957.

Stiggins, George. *Creek Indian History: A Historical Narrative of the Genealogy, Traditions, and Downfall of the Ispocoga or Creek Indian Tribes of Indians by One of the Tribe, 1788–1845.* Edited by Virginia Pounds Brown. Birmingham, Ala.: Birmingham Public Library Press, 1989.

Sugden, John. *Tecumseh: A Life.* New York: Henry Holt, 1999.

Swan, Caleb. "Position and State of Arts and Manufactures, with the Creek Indians, in 1791." In *Information Respecting the History, Condition and Prospects of the Indian Tribes of the United States,* pt. 5, edited by Henry Rowe Schoolcraft, 251–83. Philadelphia: J. B. Lippincott, 1855.

Swanton, John R. "Coonti." *American Anthropologist* 15 (1913): 141–42.

————. *Creek Religion and Medicine.* Bison Book ed. Lincoln: University of Nebraska Press, 2000. Originally published as *Religious Beliefs and Medical Practices* of the Creek Indians. Forty-second Annual Report of the Bureau of American Ethnology. Washington, D.C.: Government Printing Office, 1928.

———. Early History of the Creek Indians and Their Neighbors. Bureau of American Ethnology Bulletin, no. 73. Washington, D.C.: Government Printing Office, 1922.

———. The Indians of the Southeastern United States. Bureau of American Ethnology Bulletin, no. 137. Washington, D.C.: Government Printing Office, 1946.

———. Indian Tribes of the Lower Mississippi Valley and Adjacent Coast of the Gulf of Mexico. Bureau of American Ethnology Bulletin, no. 43. Washington, D.C.: Government Printing Office, 1911.

———. Myths and Tales of the Southeastern Indians. Bureau of American Ethnology Bulletin, no. 88. Washington, D.C.: Government Printing Office, 1928.

———. Social Organization and Social Usages of the Indians of the Creek Confederacy. Forty-second Annual Report of the Bureau of American Ethnology. Washington D.C.: Government Printing Office, 1928.

———. "The Social Significance of the Creek Confederacy." Proceedings of the Nineteenth International Congress of Americanists. Washington, D.C.: Government Printing Office, 1915.

Sylestine, Cora, Heather Hardy, and Timothy Montler. A Dictionary of the Alabama Language. Austin: University of Texas Press, 1993.

Tanner, Helen Hornbeck. "The Land and Water Communication Systems of the Southeastern Indians." In Powhatan's Mantle: Indians in the Colonial Southeast, edited by Peter H. Wood, Gregory A. Waselkov, and Thomas M. Hatley, 6–20. Lincoln: University of Nebraska Press, 1989.

Tatum, Major Howell. "Topographical Notes and Observation on the Alabama River, August 1814." Edited by Peter J. Hamilton and Thomas M. Owen. In Transactions of the Alabama Historical Society, vol. 2, 1897–1898, 130–77. Tuscaloosa: Alabama Historical Society, 1898.

Taylor, Alan. American Colonies. Penguin History of the United States, vol. 5. New York: Penguin, 2002.

Thomas, Daniel H. Fort Toulouse: The French Outpost at the Alabamas on the Coosa. 1960. Reprint with a new Introduction by Gregory A. Waselkov, Tuscaloosa: University of Alabama Press, 1989.

Thomas, Richard. "His Book, Begun November 21, 1796." In "Letters of Benjamin Hawkins, 1796–1806," Collections of the Georgia Historical Quarterly 11 (1916): 448–500.

Thornton, Russell. American Indian Holocaust and Survival: A Population History since 1492. Civilization of the American Indian Series, vol. 186. Norman : University of Oklahoma Press, 1987.

———. The Cherokees: A Population History. Lincoln: University of Nebraska Press, 1990.

———, ed. Studying Native America: Problems and Prospects. Madison: University of Wisconsin Press, 1998.

Trigger, Bruce G. "Ethnohistory: Problems and Prospects." Ethnohistory 29 (1982): 1–19.

Tuan, Yi-Fu. *Topophilia: A Study of Environmental Perception, Attitudes, and Values.* New York: Columbia University Press, 1990.

Turner, Frederick Jackson. *Frontier and Section: Selected Essays of Frederick Jackson Turner.* Englewood Cliffs, N.J.: Prentice-Hall, 1961.

———. *The Frontier in American History.* New York: Hold and Co., 1920.

USDA Forest Service. "Species: Arundinaria gigantea." ⟨http://www.fs.fed.us/database/feis...graminoid/arugig/introductory.html⟩.

Usner, Daniel H., Jr. *American Indians in the Lower Mississippi Valley: Social and Economic Histories.* Indians of the Southeast Series. Lincoln: University of Nebraska Press, 1998.

———. *Indians, Settlers, and Slaves in a Frontier Exchange Economy: The Lower Mississippi Valley before 1783.* Chapel Hill: University of North Carolina Press, 1992.

Vansina, Jan. *Oral Tradition as History.* Madison: University of Wisconsin Press, 1985.

Vaughan, Elizabeth. "The Apalachicola Bluffs and Ravines Preserve in Northern Florida: A Longleaf Pine and Wiregrass Restoration Project." University of Minnesota Horticultural Science website. ⟨http://www.hort.agri.umn.edu/h5015/01/papers/vaughan.htm⟩.

Ver Steeg, Clarence L. *Origins of a Southern Mosaic: Studies of Early Carolina and Georgia.* Athens: University of Georgia Press, 1975.

Von Reck, Philip Georg Friedrich. *Von Reck's Voyage: Drawings and Journal of Philip Georg Friedrich von Reck.* Edited by Kristian Hvidt. Savannah: Beehive Press, 1980.

Vogel, Virgil J. *American Indian Medicine.* Civilization of the Americas Series, vol. 95. Norman: University of Oklahoma Press, 1970.

Wallace, Anthony F. C. *Jefferson and the Indians: The Tragic Fate of the First Americans.* Cambridge: Harvard University Press, 2001.

———. "Political Organization and Land Tenure among the Northeastern Indians, 1600–1830." *Southwestern Journal of Anthropology* 13 (1957): 301–21.

Wallerstein, Immanuel. *The Modern World System: Capitalist Agriculture and the Origin of the European World Economy in the Sixteenth Century.* New York: Academic Press, 1974.

Walsh, Stephen J., Noel M. Burkhead, and James D. Williams. "Southeastern Freshwater Fishes." In "Our Living Resources: A Report to the Nation on the Distribution, Abundance, and Health of U.S. Plants, Animals, and Ecosystems," edited by E. T. LaRoe, G. S. Farris, E. E. Puckett, P. D. Doran, and M. J. Mac, 144–47. Report submitted to the U.S. Department of the Interior, National Biological Service, Washington D.C., 1995. Reprinted on the Southeastern Fishes Council website ⟨http://www.flmnh.ufl.edu/fish/Organizations/SFC/Walsh/sff.htm⟩.

Warren, Mary Bondurant, ed. *Chronicles of Wilkes County, Georgia, from Washington's Newspapers, 1889–1898.* Danielsville, Ga.: Heritage Papers, 1978.

Waselkov, Gregory A. "Changing Strategies of Indian Field Location in the Early Historic Southeast." In *People, Plants, and Landscapes: Studies in Paleoethno-*

botany, edited by Kristen J. Gremillion, 179–94. Tuscaloosa: University of Alabama Press, 1997.

————. *Coosa River Valley Archaeology: Results of a Cultural Resources Reconnaissance*. 2 vols. Report to the U.S. Army Corps of Engineers, Mobile District. Auburn, Ala.: Auburn University Department of Sociology and Anthropology, 1980.

————. "The Eighteenth-Century Anglo-Indian Trade in Southeastern North America." In *New Faces of the Fur Trade: Selected Papers of the Seventh North American Fur Trade Conference, Halifax, Nova Scotia, 1995*, edited by Jo-Anne Fiske, Susan Sleeper-Smith, and William Wicken, 193–222. East Lansing: Michigan State University Press, 1998.

————. "Evolution of Deer Hunting in the Eastern Woodlands." *Midcontinental Journal of Archaeology* 3 (1978): 15–34.

————. "Historic Creek Architectural Adaptations to the Deerskin Trade." Paper presented at the Southeastern Archaeological Conference, October 22, 1988, New Orleans, La.

————. "Historic Creek Indian Responses to European Trade and the Rise of Political Factions." In *Ethnohistory and Archaeology: Approaches to Postcontact Change in the Americas*, edited by J. Daniel Rogers and Samuel M. Wilson, 123–31. New York: Plenum Press, 1993.

————. "Indian Maps of the Colonial Southeast." In *Powhatan's Mantle: Indians in the Colonial Southeast*, edited by Peter H. Wood, Gregory A. Waselkov, and Thomas M. Hatley, 292–343. Lincoln: University of Nebraska Press, 1989.

————. "Introduction: Recent Archaeological and Historical Research." In *Fort Toulouse: The French Outpost at the Alabamas on the Coosa*, by Daniel H. Thomas, vi–xli. 1960. Reprint, Tuscaloosa: University of Alabama Press, 1989.

————. *Lower Tallapoosa River Cultural Resources Survey, Phase I Report*. Auburn, Ala.: Auburn University Department of Sociology and Anthropology, 1981.

————. "The Macon Trading House and Early European-Indian Contact in the Colonial Southeast." In *Ocmulgee Archaeology, 1936–1986*, edited by David J. Hally, 190–96. Athens: University of Georgia Press, 1994.

————. "Seventeenth-Century Trade in the Colonial Southeast." *Southeastern Archaeology* 8 (1989): 117–33.

Waselkov, Gregory A., and John W. Cottier. "European Perceptions of Eastern Muskogean Ethnicity." In *Proceedings of the Tenth Meeting of the French Colonial Historical Society, April 12–14, 1984*, edited by Philip Boucher, 23–45. Lanham, Md.: University Press of America, 1985.

Waselkov, Gregory A., and Marvin T. Smith. "Upper Creek Archaeology." In *Indians of the Greater Southeast: Historical Archaeology and Ethnohistory*, edited by Bonnie G. McEwan, 242–64. Gainesville: University Press of Florida for the Society for Historical Archaeology, 2000.

Waselkov, Gregory A., and Brian M. Wood. "The Creek War of 1813–1814: Effects on Creek Society and Settlement Pattern." *Journal of Alabama Archaeology* 32 (1986): 1–24.

Waselkov, Gregory A., John W. Cottier, and Craig T. Sheldon Jr. *Archaeological Excavations at the Early Historic Creek Indian Town of Fusihatchee (Phase I,*

1988–1989). Report to the National Science Foundation. Auburn, Ala.: University of Auburn Department of Sociology and Anthropology, 1990.

Washburn, Wilcomb E. *The American Indians and the United States: A Documentary History*. 4 vols. 1973. Reprint, Westport, Conn.: Greenwood, 1979.

Way, Royal B. "The United States Factory System for Trading with the Indians, 1796–1822." *Mississippi Valley Historical Review* 6 (1919): 220–35.

Weakley, A., E. Dinerstein, R. Noss, and K. Wolfe. "Southeastern Mixed Forests (NA0413)." World Wildlife Fund and National Geographic Society. Wild World Website. ⟨http://worldwildlife.org/wildworld/profiles/terrestrial/na/na0413_full.html⟩.

Webb, Paul A. "Hickory Log: Investigations at a Cherokee Homestead in North Georgia." Paper presented at the Fifty-second Annual Meeting of the Southeastern Archaeological Conference, November 1995, Knoxville, Tenn.

Wesson, Cameron B. "Creek and Pre-Creek Revisited." In *The Archaeology of Traditions: Agency and History before and after Columbus*, edited by Timothy R. Pauketat, 94–106. Gainesville: University Press of Florida, 2001.

———. "Households and Hegemony: An Analysis of Historic Creek Culture Change." Ph.D. diss., University of Illinois, Urbana-Champaign, 1997.

White, Nancy, Stephanie J. Belovich, and David S. Rose. *Archaeological Survey at Lake Seminole*. Cleveland Museum of Natural History Archaeological Research Report, no. 29, for the U.S. Army Corps of Engineers, Mobile District, Mobile, Ala., 1981.

White, Richard. "Indian Peoples and the Natural World: Asking the Right Questions." In *Rethinking American Indian History*, edited by Donald L. Fixico, 87–100. Albuquerque: University of New Mexico Press, 1997.

———. *The Middle Ground: Indians, Empires, and Republics in the Great Lakes Region, 1650–1815*. Cambridge: Cambridge University Press, 1991.

———. *The Roots of Dependency: Subsistence, Environment, and Social Change among the Choctaws, Pawnees, and Navajos*. Lincoln: University of Nebraska Press, 1983.

———. "Using the Past: History and Native American Studies." In *Studying Native America: Problems and Prospects*, edited by Russell Thornton, 217–43. Madison: University of Wisconsin Press, 1998.

White, Richard, and William Cronon. "Ecological Change and Indian-White Relations." In *Handbook of North American Indians*, vol. 4, *History of Indian-White Relations*, edited by Wilcomb Washburn, 417–29. Washington, D.C.: Smithsonian Institution, 1988.

Whitehead, Neil J. "Ecological History and Historical Ecology: Diachronic Modeling Versus Historical Explanation." In *Advances in Historical Ecology*, edited by William Balée, 30–41. Historical Ecology Series. New York: Columbia University Press, 1998.

Whitney, Gordon G. *From Coastal Wilderness to Fruited Plain: A History of Environmental Change in Temperate North America, 1500 to the Present*. Cambridge: Cambridge University Press, 1994.

Wilcox, Dianne Dent. *Fort Hawkins and Frontier Georgia: A Research Guide*. Milledgeville, Ga.: Boyd, 1999.

Wiley, Gordon R., and William H. Sears. "The Kasihta Site." *Southern Indian Studies* 4 (1952): 3–18.

Williams, Marshall W. *A Memoir of the Archaeological Excavation of Fort Prince George, Pickens County, South Carolina, along with Pertinent Historical Documentation.* Research Manuscript Series, no. 226. Columbia: South Carolina Institute of Archaeology and Anthropology, University of South Carolina, 1998.

Willis, William S., Jr. "Divide and Rule: Red, White, and Black in the Southeast." In *Red, White, and Black: Symposium on Indians in the Old South*, edited by Charles M. Hudson, 99–115. Athens: University of Georgia Press, 1971.

Willoughby, Lynn. *Flowing through Time: A History of the Lower Chattahoochee River.* Chattahoochee Valley Legacy Series. Tuscaloosa: University of Alabama Press, 1999.

Wilson, Angela Cavender. "Power of the Spoken Word: Native Oral Traditions in American Indian History." In *Rethinking American Indian History*, edited by Donald L. Fixico, 101–16. Albuquerque: University of New Mexico Press, 1997.

Wilson, G. J. N. *The Early History of Jackson County, Georgia.* Atlanta: Foote and Daves, 1914.

Winterhalder, Bruce, and Carol Goland. "An Evolutionary Ecology Perspective on Diet Choice, Risk, and Plant Domestication." In *People, Plants, and Landscapes: Studies in Paleoethnobotany*, edited by Kristen J. Gremillion, 123–60. Tuscaloosa: University of Alabama Press, 1997.

———. "On Population, Foraging Efficiency, and Plant Domestication." *Current Anthropology* 34 (1993): 710–15.

Witthoft, John. *Green Corn Ceremonialism in the Eastern Woodlands.* University of Michigan, Museum of Anthropology, Occasional Contributions, no. 13. Ann Arbor: University of Michigan Press, 1949.

Wolf, Eric. *Europe and the People without History.* Berkeley: University of California Press, 1982.

Wood, Patricia Dillon. *French Indian Relations on the Southern Frontier, 1699–1762.* Ann Arbor: UMI Research Press, 1980.

Wood, Peter H. *Black Majority: Negroes in Colonial South Carolina from 1670 through the Stono Rebellion.* New York: Alfred A. Knopf, 1974.

———. "The Changing Population of the Colonial South: An Overview by Race and Region, 1685–1790." In *Powhatan's Mantle: Indians in the Colonial Southeast*, edited by Peter H. Wood, Gregory A. Waselkov, and Thomas M. Hatley, 434–43. Lincoln: University of Nebraska Press, 1989.

———. "Indian Slavery in the Southeast." In *Handbook of North American Indians*, vol. 4, *History of Indian-White Relations*, edited by Wilcomb Washburn, 407–90. Washington, D.C.: Government Printing Office, 1988.

Woodward, Thomas S. *Woodward's Reminiscences of the Creek, or Muscogee Indians.* 1859. Reprint, Tuscaloosa: Alabama Book Store; Birmingham: Birmingham Book Exchange, 1939.

Worster, Donald. *The Wealth of Nature: Environmental History and the Ecological Imagination.* New York: Oxford University Press, 1993.

Worth, John. "The Lower Creeks: Origins and Early History." In *Indians of the*

Greater Southeast: Historical Archaeology and Ethnohistory, edited by Bonnie G. McEwan, 265–98. Gainesville: University Press of Florida for the Society for Historical Archaeology, 2000.

————. *The Timucuan Chiefdoms of Spanish Florida*. 2 vols. Gainesville: University Press of Florida, 1998.

Wright, J. Leitch, Jr. *Anglo-Spanish Rivalry in North America*. Athens: University of Georgia Press, 1971.

————. *Britain and the American Frontier, 1783–1815*. Athens: University of Georgia Press, 1975.

————. *Creeks and Seminoles: The Destruction and Regeneration of the Muscogulge People*. Lincoln: University of Nebraska Press, 1986.

————. *The Only Land They Knew: The Tragic Story of the American Indians in the Old South*. New York: Free Press, 1981.

————. *William Augustus Bowles: Director General of the Creek Nation*. Athens: University of Georgia Press, 1967.

Young, Captain Hugh. "A Topographical Memoir on East and West Florida with Itineraries of General Jackson's Army, 1818, by Captain Hugh Young, Corps of Topographical Engineers, U.S.A." Edited by Mark F. Boyd and Gerald M. Ponton. *Florida Historical Quarterly* 13 (1934): 16–50.

INDEX

Abihka, 26–27, 28, 87, 88, 193. *See also* Towns, Upper Creek—Aubecooche

Agricultural fields: and river valley floodplains, 55–60, 271 (n. 5); of Chattahoochee River valley, 57–60; and soil exhaustion, 58–60, 97, 144, 155–56, 216, 293 (n. 41), 294 (n. 64); of Flint River valley, 64–66; of Tallapoosa River valley, 71, 80–84, 90–91; of Alabama River valley, 82–87; of Coosa River valley, 88–89; soils of, 140–41; and town communal fields, 141–43; clearing of, 144–46; rotation of, 144–45, 292 (n. 36); and weed infestation, 156–57, 297 (n. 138); and livestock foraging, 164, 168–69. *See also* Agriculture; Land tenure, Creek

Agriculture: reform of, 67, 148–49, 155; and market economy, 131, 141; methods of, 143–48, 292 (nn. 35, 36); and introduced crops, 149–52; risks in, 153–57. *See also* Agricultural fields; Domesticated plants

Alabama River valley, 32, 266 (n. 26), 82, 85, 122, 149–50, 154, 209; landscape of, 36, 82–84, 85. *See also* Towns, Upper Creek

Alabamas: and formation of Creek Confederacy, 27, 28, 82, 94, 95; language of, 30; towns of, 83–87; oral traditions of, 84–85; hunting range of, 136. *See also* Towns, Upper Creek

Alcohol: Creek use of, 99, 100, 106, 160; and Creek Factory, 131, 134; exchange of, 177, 184, 305 (n. 3)

American Indian policy. *See* United States Indian policy

American Indians: in American history, 2–9, 250 (n. 2), 251 (n. 3), 261 (n. 1); and "ecological Indian," 54–55, 270 (n. 2)

Animals. *See* Birds; Domesticated animals; Fish; Horses; Livestock; Pests; Ranching; Reptiles and amphibians; Wild animals

Annuities: and Treaty System, 196–200; as payment for land, 198–200; payments of, 201–2; as payment for debts, 203–6; allocation of, 206–8, 313 (n. 88); and land tenure, 207–11; spending of, 207–8

Apalachicola province, 25, 27–30, 135, 264 (n. 20); and Apalachicola Old Fields, 52. *See also* Towns, Lower Creek—Patachoche

Appalachian–Blue Ridge Mixed Mesophytic Forest. *See* Mixed mesophytic forest

Appalachian Mixed Mesophytic Forest. *See* Mixed mesophytic forest

Coosa, chiefdom of, 26–27. *See also* Towns, Upper Creek—Coosa

Coosa River valley, 32, 33, 35, 50, 51, 79, 82, 87, 120, 121–22, 154, 209; landscape of, 87–89. *See also* Towns, Upper Creek

Corn. *See* Domesticated plants

Cornells, Alexander, 16, 189, 205, 207, 240, 260 (n. 39); household of, 79

Cotton. *See* Domesticated plants

Coweta. *See* Towns, Lower Creek—Coweta

Creek Agency, 12, 17, 155, 160, 182, 192, 241, 258 (n. 121); landscape of, 66–68; and frontier exchange economy, 178–79. *See also* Hawkins, Benjamin; Plan for civilization

Creek Confederacy: as coalescent society, 25–26, 92–95, 277 (n. 1); formation of, 25–31, 264 (nn. 16, 24), 265 (n. 31), 279 (n. 11); provinces of, 26–31; map of, 29; languages of, 30, 111, 265 (n. 27), 324 (n. 156); population of, 31, 57, 58, 64, 66, 71, 84, 85, 88, 90, 91, 213; political organization of, 94–96; non-Creeks living in, 111–19. *See also* Creeks; Lower Creeks; Towns, Lower Creek; Towns, Upper Creek; Upper Creeks

Creek Factory, 212, 287 (n. 43), 312 (n. 52); and U.S. Factory System, 11, 129–30, 134; and livestock trading, 130; and Panton, Leslie, and Company, 130–31; and Benjamin Hawkins, 131–32, 134; and military, 132–33; and thefts, 132, 185; and frontier exchange economy, 178–79, 186, 189–90; and annuities, 199, 201–2, 203, 205

Creek place-names, 32–35, 163, 268 (n. 63); of waterways, 32–35; of wetlands, 45–46; of groves, 48; of fords and bridges, 123–24

Creeks: and confrontation, 107–8; hospitality of, 108–9, 176; and hostility with American frontier people, 220–21, 222–23, 228–38, 239–41; and Red Stick War, 239–41, 324 (n. 156). *See also* Lower Creeks; Upper Creeks

Cusseta. *See* Towns, Lower Creek—Cusseta

Deer. *See* Wild animals

Deerskin trade: and "middle ground," 9–11; and transformation of southeastern Indians, 9–10, 23; decline of, 10–13, 137–39, 259 (n. 20); and European alliances, 10, 257 (n. 4). *See also* Frontier exchange economy; Plan for civilization; Property

Disease. *See* Old World disease

Dogs. *See* Domesticated animals

Domesticated animals: cattle, 50, 164–67, 168; sheep, 79, 159–60; dogs, 158; in Creek diet, 159–60; goats, 159–60; yard fowl, 159, 177, 216; hogs, 164–67, 168. *See also* Horses; Livestock; Ranching; Wild animals

Domesticated plants: cotton, 15, 149, 150, 151–52; varieties of, 67–68, 78, 79, 81, 95, 142, 146–47, 149–51, 191, 192, 200, 216, 216, 293 (n. 49), 295 (n. 77); sweet potatoes, 82, 149, 150–51, 174, 216, 295 (nn. 81, 87); corn, 142, 146, 147–48, 150–51, 156, 216, 294 (n. 63); rice, 149–50, 177, 295 (n. 77); and frontier exchange economy, 177–78. *See also* Agriculture; Black drink; Wild plants

Downs, Lavina, 12, 66, 113, 192

Durant, Sophia, 84–85, 116, 225; as ranchers, 161–62

Eastern Muskogean language: and formation of Creek Confederacy, 28, 30, 95; linguistic classification of, 30, 264 (n. 25); Hawkins as speaker of, 260 (n. 30); orthography of, 260 (n. 40)

Euro-American frontier settlers, 120–21, 126; communities of,

River, 69–71, 82–83, 90–91; on Alabama River, 85, 87; on Coosa River, 88–89. *See also* Switch cane; Wild plants
Gift giving. *See* Reciprocity
Goats. *See* Domesticated animals
Great Pine Barren. *See* Longleaf pine forest
Green Corn Ceremony. *See* Busk
Guns, 135; and Indian slave trade, 23–24, 263 (n. 7); as trade item, 131, 178, 184, 193

Hall, Basil, 39, 43, 75, 100, 109, 218; etchings by, 39, 44, 77, 220; at Creek ballgame, 101–2; at water crossing, 124–25
Harrison, Benjamin, 64, 218–19, 318 (n. 31)
Hawkins, Benjamin: as historical source, 3–6, 255 (n. 17), 256 (n. 20); appointment of as U.S. Indian Agent, 12, 258 (n. 15); and Indian languages, 12, 17, 260 (n. 30); and plan for civilization, 12, 13–16, 18, 19, 148–49, 191–93; and Thomas Jefferson, 12; and Creek Indians, 16–20; and land speculators, 16, 196, 211–12; as *isti atcagagi*, 18–20; and Creek Factory, 131–32, 185; and frontier exchange economy, 178–79; and thefts, 182, 183–85, 189; and Creek law reforms, 232–38; and Red Stick War, 240–41; death of, 241
Hinterlands: definition of, 120–21; travel through, 120–26; trading houses in, 129–34; military forts in, 132–34; and hunting ranges, 134–37
Hitchiti province, 27–28; language of, 28. *See also* Towns, Lower Creek—Hitchiti
Hogs. *See* Domesticated animals
Horses: for travel, 123; in hunting, 135; other uses of, 158–59; branding of, 183–84; prices of, 184; for postal services, 187–88; renting of, 187. *See*

also Domesticated animals; Livestock; Ranching; Thefts: and horse stealing
Horseshoe Bend: Creek place-name of, 35; battle of, 240
Horse stealing. *See* Thefts: and horse stealing
Households, Creek: economy of, 25, 306 (n. 29); dispersed settlements of, 71–73, 169–74; description of, 74–77, 97, 274 (n. 82), 275 (n. 94), 280 (n. 28); and gender divisions, 74–75, 76, 99, 275 (n. 92); and log cabins, 75–77, 78, 173, 216, 317 (n. 4); abandonment of, 76–77; of Indian countrymen, 78–79; of métis, 78–80, 211. *See also* Agriculture; Gender roles; Households, Creek; Men, Creek; Women, Creek
Hunting: camps, 134–35; methods of, 134–35; ranges of, 135–37, 290 (n. 96); and land claims, 137, 200, 213; among Euro-American frontier settlers, 216, 221. *See also* Deerskin trade; Men, Creek

Indian countrymen, 77–78, 111–12, 276 (n. 97); ranches of, 78–79, 117–18, 161; use rights of, 78; Creek wives of, 117–18
Indian policy. *See* United States Indian policy
Indians. *See* American Indians; Southeastern Indians
Indian slave trade, 23; and formation of coalescent societies, 23–26; and global economy, 23–24, 262 (n. 6), 263 (nn. 7, 8); and Yamasee War, 24–25
Insects. *See* Pests
Interior Low Plateaus, 33, 34; ecoregions of, 37
Intruders, 199, 215, 321 (n. 97); military protection against, 132, 224, 225, 226–27, 321 (n. 100); illegal use of Creek resources by, 221; illegal settle-

ments of, 223–25, 226–28; and land speculators, 223–25; and threats of war, 236–38. *See also* Euro-American frontier settlers; Land speculation
Iroquois, 209, 263 (nn. 7, 15), 281 (n. 34)

Jackson, Andrew, 21; and land speculation, 196, 240, 241
Jefferson, Thomas: and Benjamin Hawkins, 12, 148; and ideas on Indians, 13, 15–16, 259 (n. 28); and Treaty of 1805, 201
John Forbes and Company. *See* Panton, Leslie, and Company

Kinship: clans, 17, 109–11, 284 (n. 117); matrilineal, 25, 74–75, 109, 110, 113, 275 (n. 86); and *huti*, 74–75, 134, 143; and diplomacy, 93–94, 109–10; and Creek social structure, 109–10, 113; and political leadership, 110; and adoption, 115; and dispersed settlement patterns, 173–74, 304 (n. 117); erosion of, 289 (n. 81)

Land, Creek: and cotton economy, 12–13; and use rights, 84, 212–13, 225; and Treaty System, 199–200; and monetary values, 200–201, 203–5, 315 (n. 132); and national sovereignty, 213–14. *See also* Land speculation; Land tenure, Creek
Land speculation, 286 (n. 7); and U.S. Indian policy, 13, 196–200, 310 (n. 9); and Benjamin Hawkins, 16, 196, 211–12; and Andrew Jackson, 196, 240, 241; and land companies, 196–97, 311 (nn. 11, 17); and William Blount, 196, 197, 199, 223, 240; and Tennessee and Georgia, 219, 222, 227, 237–38, 240; and intruders, 223–25. *See also* Land, Creek; Land tenure, Creek
Land tenure, Creek, 120–21, 208–11,

291 (n. 9); and leasing to Euro-Americans, 17, 78, 84, 143, 200, 212; and National Council, 106–7, 108; and hunting ranges, 135–39, 200, 213, 290 (n. 96); and agricultural fields, 141–43; and rights of alienation, 208, 211–12; and land speculators, 210–12; and national ownership, 210–11, 310 (n. 3), 315 (n. 14); and use rights, 223–24. *See also* Agriculture; Hunting; Land, Creek; Land Speculation; Ranching
Languages. *See* Eastern Muskogean language
Leadership, Creek, 19–20, 198, 282 (n. 64); and *micos*, 102–4; and Hawkins's influence on, 103; and consensus, 107–8; and clans, 110; and blood revenge, 232–34. *See also* Creek Confederacy; Men, Creek; National Council; Towns, Creek: town councils of
Livestock: and plan for civilization, 13; in Coastal Plain, 46; in Flint River valley, 64, 66; ranging patterns of, 64, 164–67; and salt, 68; in Tallapoosa River valley, 68–69, 70–71, 79–81, 84, 90–91; in Alabama River valley, 85–87; in Coosa River valley, 88–89; and land rights, 137; and wild animal habitats, 137–38, 166–67, 169; and agricultural fields, 146–47; as food, 160; as trade item, 160–61; wild predators of, 160, 167–68; owners of, 161–62; health of, 163–64; and frontier exchange economy, 177–78, 200, 212. *See also* Cattle; Hogs; Horses; Land Tenure, Creek; Ranching
Longleaf pine forest, 36, 40, 46, 171; and Coastal Plain, 37; as fire-dependent ecosystem, 37–39; description of, 43–46; singing of, 43–44; hammocks in, 45, 141; fauna of, 47–51; and Chattahoochee River valley, 60, 62–64; and Flint River valley, 64–66; and Tallapoosa River valley, 70–71, 83;

and livestock foraging, 164, 302
(n. 71). *See also* Coastal Plain; Wild
animals; Wild plants
Lower Creeks, 68, 80, 280 (n. 12); and
formation of Creek Confederacy, 27–
30; towns of, 32, 33, 46; landscape of,
57–68. *See also* Towns, Lower Creek
Lower Trading Path. *See* Trails: and
Lower Trading Path

Matrilineality. *See* Kinship
McGillivray, Alexander, 12, 18, 84, 162,
199, 225, 258 (n. 11), 319 (n. 40); as
Creek leader, 11, 105, 110, 261 (n. 43);
household of, 79
Men, Creek: town activities of, 98–100;
and ball games, 100–102; ranks of,
102–4; and town councils, 102–5;
and sex, 113–14; as guides, 123, 125;
as postmen, 128; as runners, 128; and
commercial hunting, 134
Métis: market orientation of, 10, 181,
258 (n. 5); lives of, 118–19; as ranchers, 161, 299 (n. 23); and land rights,
201, 315 (n. 32); and National Council, 232–33, 322 (n. 128); and Red
Stick War, 240; definition of, 249
(n. 1); and class divisions, 278 (n. 1),
283 (n. 100). *See also* Class divisions,
Creek; Indian countrymen
Middle ground: and deerskin trade, 9–
11; erosion of, 10–13; definition of,
258 (n. 7)
Military forts, 132–33, 217, 218, 288
(n. 67); Fort Toulouse, 82, 121, 132,
276 (n. 130); Fort Mitchell, 129; Fort
Wilkinson, 129, 165, 222, 197, 218;
and intruders, 132, 224, 225, 226–27;
Fort Hawkins, 133, 227, 288 (n. 67),
289 (n. 70); Fort Mims, 133, 240, 288
(n. 68); soldiers at, 133–34
Missionaries, Moravian, 17, 66, 254
(n. 13), 260 (n. 31)
Mississippian Period chiefdoms, 42,
100, 156, 304 (n. 116), 306 (n. 28); de-

cline of, 22–26, 262 (nn. 2, 3); and
formation of coalescent societies, 22–
26, 261 (n. 1), 275 (n. 92), 279 (nn. 2,
6), 306 (n. 32); and formation of
Creek Confederacy, 26–31; and
earthen mounds, 60, 81, 82, 85, 154
Mississippi River, 33, 34
Mississippi Territory, 30–31, 125, 176,
219, 220
Mixed mesophytic forest: ecology of,
37–38, 46; fauna of, 37–41; description of, 41–43. *See also* Longleaf pine
forest; Southeastern mixed forest;
Wild animals; Wild plants
Mobilian lingua franca, 30, 265 (n. 28)
Modern world system, 2, 253 (n. 10);
and deerskin trade, 9–10; and cotton
economy, 12–13; and Indian slave
trade, 23–24; and transformation of
southeastern Indians, 23–26; and
Euro-American frontier settlers, 316
(n. 1)
Muscogee (Creek) Nation, 21, 261
(n. 46). *See also* Creek Confederacy;
Poarch Band of Creeks
Muskogean language. *See* Eastern Muskogean language
Myths. *See* Oral traditions

Natchez, 23, 27, 30. *See also* Towns,
Upper Creek—Nauchee
National Council, 18, 19, 178, 190, 238,
283 (nn. 98, 100); and Benjamin
Hawkins, 105, 106, 107; description
of, 105–8; duties of, 106–7; and
Speaker of the Nation, 106; authority
of, 107–8; and horse stealing, 185;
and "laws of the nation," 232–38
Native Americans. *See* American Indians; Southeastern Indians
Nuts: masts of, 48, 91, 172; uses of, 56,
60–62, 135, 272 (nn. 26, 28, 29, 30,
33, 34); and livestock foraging, 166;
and frontier exchange economy, 179.
See also Mixed mesophytic forest;

Southeastern mixed forest; Wild plants

Oak-hickory-pine forest. *See* Southeastern mixed forest
Ocfuskee province, 27–28. *See also* Towns, Upper Creek—Oakfuskee
Oche Haujo. *See* Cornells, Alexander
Ocmulgee River valley, 28, 209, 222, 236; and town of Ocmulgee, 33; and fishing, 36; and Ocmulgee Old Fields, 52
Old fields. *See* Agricultural fields
Old World disease, 24, 28, 80, 275 (n. 92); introduction of, 22–23, 262 (nn. 2, 3)
Oral traditions, 4, 255 (n. 16), 296 (n. 109), 300 (n. 29); and migration myths, 26, 68, 263 (n. 15); of Alabamas, 84; and Creek towns, 95, 280 (n. 17)

Panton, Leslie, and Company, 11, 100, 112, 189, 212; and Creek Factory, 130–31; and livestock trade, 130, 160, 161–62; and Creek annuities, 202, 203–5; Creek debts to, 204
Pests, 40–41, 267 (n. 52); varieties of, 41, 46, 163; and agriculture, 146; scientific taxonomy of, 246–48
Physiographic Provinces. *See* Appalachian Plateau; Coastal Plain; Fall Line; Interior Low Plateaus; Piedmont province; Ridge and Valley province
Piedmont province, 33, 34, 37, 87, 171; ecoregions of, 37, 46–49; landscape of, 89–91. *See also* Southeastern mixed forest; Wild animals; Wild plants
Place-names. *See* Creek place-names
Plan for civilization, 12, 19; formulation of, 13–16, 173, 259 (nn. 22, 26); and Hawkins's assistants, 36, 111, 112, 113, 179; and public establishments,

56, 66, 68, 79–80, 190, 202; and Creek Agency, 66, 67–68; and Creek gender roles, 98, 138, 193–94, 274 (n. 84), 300 (n. 29); resistence to, 143, 228, 240; and agricultural reforms, 144, 148–49; and Creek women, 148–49; and ranching, 160; and private property, 173; and the frontier exchange economy, 178–79; and Creek annuities, 202, 206. *See also* Agriculture; Hawkins, Benjamin
Plants. *See* Agriculture; Domesticated plants; Wild plants
Poarch Band of Creeks, 21, 261 (n. 46), 266 (n. 26)
Postal routes. *See* Communication: and postal service
Property: and black slaves, 116–17, 185–86; and trade goods, 175–77, 304 (n. 1); as status indicator, 179–80; Creek ideas on, 180–81, 307 (n. 39); and reciprocity, 180–81. *See also* Land Tenure, Creek; Métis; Reciprocity; Thefts
Public establishments. *See* Plan for civilization: and public establishments
Purity. *See* Religious beliefs

Ranching, 15; and settlement patterns, 64–66, 71–72, 80–81, 169–74; and Indian countrymen, 78, 117; and métis, 78–79, 84; and trade, 130–31, 161, 163; and plan for civilization, 149; methods of, 162–63; ecology of, 164–67, 301 (n. 69); and competition with Euro-American frontier settlers, 165–66, 174, 216, 219, 222, 319 (n. 52); and wage labor, 189. *See also* Cattle; Domesticated animals; Frontier exchange economy; Hogs; Horses; Land Tenure, Creek; Livestock
Reciprocity, 152, 307 (n. 35); and gift giving, 25, 198–99, 311 (n. 23); and thefts, 180–82; and treaties, 198–99;

and purity and balance, 230; and blood revenge, 230–32

Red Stick War, 20–21, 50, 81, 121, 126, 133, 147, 187, 188, 260 (n. 39), 271 (n. 15), 307 (n. 39); and Creeks, 238–41, 323 (n. 152), 324 (n. 156); and plan for civilization, 240

Reed. *See* Switch cane

Religious beliefs, 3, 4, 17, 254 (nn. 13, 14); and "scratching," 8–9, 108, 257 (n. 1); and "going to water," 33, 118; and purity, 33, 87, 147, 228–32; and ghosts, 52, 76–77, 126, 230; and lightning, 127; and agriculture, 155; and blood revenge, 228–32; and categorial opposites, 229–30, 321 (n. 101); and Master of Breath, 229; and Red Stick War, 239–40

Reptiles and amphibians, 7–9; varieties of, 38, 41, 46, 127; scientific taxonomy of, 246–48

Retaliation. *See* Blood revenge

Revenge. *See* Blood revenge

Rice. *See* Domesticated plants: rice

Ridge and Valley province, 33, 34, 90, 273 (n. 71); ecoregions of, 37; landscape of, 87–89. *See also* Mesophytic mixed forest; Southeastern mixed forest; Wild animals; Wild plants

Salt, 171; and meadow spikemoss, 68–69, 88–89, 90, 91, 162, 168; and salt licks, 89, 162, 168; as trade item, 131, 168, 177–78, 207

Savananahs, 36, 44, 48–49. *See also* Longleaf pine forest; Southeastern mixed forest

Seminoles, 7–8, 18, 22, 30, 120, 209, 240, 296 (n. 107), 307 (n. 39); and black slaves, 117, 286 (n. 160)

Settlement patterns. *See* Towns, Creek

Shatter zone, 24, 263 (n. 8)

Shawnees, 21, 27, 30, 82, 97, 236, 281 (n. 34). *See also* Towns, Upper Creek—Sawanogi

Sheep. *See* Domesticated animals

Slaves. *See* Black slaves

Soils. *See* Agricultural fields

Southeastern conifer forest. *See* Longleaf pine forest

Southeastern Indians: transformation of, 22–31, 261 (n. 1), 306 (n. 32); as coalescent societies, 22–26; and Indian slave trade, 23–25; and land claims, 30–31, 265 (n. 29)

Southeastern mixed forest: and physiographic provinces, 37; as fire-dependent ecosystem, 37–38, 47; description of, 46–49; and Chattahoochee River valley, 60–64; and Flint River valley, 64; and Tallapoosa River valley, 71; and Alabama River valley, 85–87; and Coosa River valley, 88; and Upper Tallapoosa River valley, 90–91; and livestock foraging, 164, 171. *See also* Fall Line; Longleaf pine forest; Mixed mesophytic forest; Piedmont province; Ridge and Valley province; Wild animals; Wild plants

Squatters. *See* Intruders

Stiggins, George, 17, 103, 110, 181, 324 (n. 152)

Stipends. *See* Annuities

Swamps. *See* Wetlands

Sweet potatoes. *See* Domesticated Plants: sweet potatoes

Switch cane, 43, 49–50, 64, 171, 172, 246, 270 (n. 109); in Flint River valley, 64–66. *See also* Giant river cane; Wild plants

Tallapoosa province, 26–27, 28. *See also* Towns, Upper Creek—Tuckabatchee

Tallapoosa River valley, 27, 32, 35, 50, 54, 82, 87, 120, 141, 149–50, 154, 167, 209, 273 (n. 69); and Fall Line, 35, 68–69; and fishing, 36; landscape of, 68–71, 87–88; and settlement patterns, 71–72, 169–70; uplands of, 171–72. *See also* Towns, Upper Creek

Tallassee. *See* Towns, Upper Creek—
Tallassee
Tecumseh, 21, 107, 205, 223, 323
(n. 152); and Red Stick War, 238–39
Tennessee, State of, 31, 121, 265 (n. 30);
and land speculation, 219, 227,
237–38, 240
Tenskwatawa, 21, 323 (n. 152); and Red
Stick War, 238–39
Thefts: and banditti, 46, 112–13, 128,
183, 187, 189; and horse stealing,
112–13, 182–85, 203, 207, 223, 233–
34, 235; and travel, 125, 128; and
Creek Factory, 132, 182, 185; of livestock, 160, 222–23; and reciprocity,
180–82; and frontier exchange economy, 182–85; and Creek annuities,
202–3, 207
Thomas, Richard, 36, 112, 179, 148,
152, 179
Towns, Creek: and civic affiliations, 93,
94–96; and red and white (war and
peace) towns, 93–94, 232–33, 278
(n. 1), 279 (nn. 5, 6, 12); and *talofas*,
95–96; and *talwas*, 95–96, 280
(n. 23); and soil exhaustion, 96, 155,
170–71, 280 (n. 24); description of,
96–102; and fuelwood, 96; square
grounds of, 96, 102; town plazas of,
96, 97–100; rotundas of, 97–98; ball
fields of, 100; town councils of, 102–
5, 142, 178; hunting ranges of, 135–
37, 209; agricultural fields of, 141–
43, 209. *See also* Creek Confederacy;
Towns, Lower Creek; Towns, Upper
Creek
Towns, Lower Creek
—Aumucullee, 150; Creek place-name
of, 33; landscape of, 65–66
—Cheauhooche: landscape of, 63; as
Hitchiti *talofa*, 96
—Chehaw, 141, 143, 223; *talofas* of, 50,
55, 64–66, 267 (n. 43); landscape of,
62; as Hitchiti *talofa*, 62, 96; hunting

range of, 136; and plan for civilization, 143
—Coweta, 55, 68, 79, 141, 170, 240, 264
(n. 20); people of, 28, 264 (n. 15); and
fishing rights, 37; landscape of, 57–
58; as capital of Lower Creeks, 68, 94,
105, 106; hunting ranges of, 135–36
—Coweta Tallahassee, 12, 18, 55, 62,
141, 143, 148, 191; landscape of, 58,
60
—Cusseta, 55, 155, 170, 240, 264
(n. 20), 271 (n. 17); and fishing rights,
37, 141; and Cusseta Old Fields, 52;
landscape of, 58–60; people of, 28,
63, 264 (n. 15); *talofas* of, 96; hunting
range of, 135–36
—Eufaula, 169; landscape of, 63–64;
people of, 63–64
—Hitchiti: landscape of, 62–63; *talofas*
of, 64–66, 96
—Hitchetoochee: landscape of, 65–66;
as Hitchiti *talofa*, 96
—Intuchculgau: landscape of, 64–66;
as Yuchi *talofa*, 96
—Oconee: landscape of, 63–64
—Okfuskenena: rotunda of, 97
—Okteyoconnee: landscape of, 63–64;
black slaves in, 64
—Ooseoochee, 50, 55, 141; landscape
of, 62
—Otellewhoyaunau: landscape of, 65–
66; Creek place-name of, 267 (n. 43)
—Padjeeligau, 218; landscape of, 64
—Patachoche: landscape of, 63
—Sauwoogelo: landscape of, 63–64
—Sauwoogelooche: landscape of, 63–
64
—Toccogulegau: landscape of, 64–66
—Tuttallosee: landscape of, 65–66; as
Hitchiti *talofa*, 96; hunting range of,
136
—Upatoi: landscape of, 173–74, 284
(n. 130); as Cusseta *talofa*, 96
—Wetumcau: Creek place-name of, 34

126–28; and camps, 126–27; and lodging, 126, 176, 217; and passports, 222–23. *See also* Communication; Hinterlands; Trails

Treaty of Colerain (1796), 12, 13, 80, 129, 199, 200, 202

Treaty of Coweta (1739), 210

Treaty of 1805 (Treaty of Washington), 13, 199, 202; negotiations of, 200–201

Treaty of Fort Jackson (1814), 21, 46, 129, 200, 210, 241

Treaty of Fort Wilkinson (1802), 13, 66, 197, 199, 201, 202, 203, 222, 235

Treaty of Holston (1791), 197, 199, 224

Treaty of Hopewell (1785), 12, 199, 224

Treaty of New York (1790), 12, 13, 129, 199, 201, 202

Treaty of Washington. *See* Treaty of 1805

Treaty System. *See* Annuities

Trees, 42, 45, 47–48, 56, 60, 64, 66, 87, 88, 90, 141, 150, 153, 171, 172, 179, 230; glades and groves of, 40, 48, 60, 269 (n. 97), 272 (nn. 26, 28); hickories, 42, 47, 60, 62, 63, 66, 70, 71, 82, 87, 141, 171, 172; oaks, 42, 43, 45, 47, 48, 49, 60, 62, 63, 66, 70, 71, 82, 87, 88, 90, 141, 171, 172, 201; pines, 42, 48, 60, 62, 63, 70, 71, 90, 141, 171, 172, 268 (n. 72); and soil quality, 141; and use rights, 200, 201, 212, 221; scientific taxonomy of, 243–46. *See also* Black drink; Domesticated plants; Flowers, shrubs, and grasses; Giant river cane; Longleaf pine forest; Mixed mesophytic forest; Nuts; Southeastern mixed forest; Switch cane; Wild plants

Tuckabatchee. *See* Towns, Upper Creek—Tuckabatchee

Turkey. *See* Birds: wild turkey

Turkey Town. *See* Cherokees: and Turkey Town

United States Factory System. *See* Creek Factory

United States Indian policy: and westward expansion, 12–15, 195, 310 (n. 5); and land speculators, 13; and Treaty System, 196–200; and intruders, 226–28

Upper Creeks: formation of, 27–30, 280 (n. 12); landscape of, 68–91. *See also* Towns, Upper Creek

Upper Trading Path. *See* Trails: Upper Trading Path

Warfare, 279 (n. 6); and male ranking, 102–4; and travel, 127–28; and blood revenge, 228–32

Warrior police, 18, 232–34, 322 (nn. 122, 123). *See also* Blood revenge; National Council; Towns, Creek: town councils of

Waterways: Creek place-names of, 32–35; and purity, 33; as feature of Creek country, 35–37; and fishing, 36–37; and use rights, 37; and travel, 121–22; crossings of, 123–25, 176, 186–87. *See also* Trails; Travel; Wetlands

Weaving. *See* Cloth

Wetlands, 45–46; and cypress swamps, 64, 80–82; in Flint River valley, 64–66; in Tallapoosa River valley, 71, 80–82; in Alabama River valley, 87; and travel, 127; and rice cultivation, 149–50. *See also* Coastal Plain; Waterways

Wild animals: white-tailed deer, 9, 10, 38, 41, 137–38, 216, 217, 248, 267 (n. 48), 290 (n. 100); American black bear, 38, 41, 127, 216, 221, 246, 300 (n. 29); varieties of, 38, 41, 127, 137, 216; and livestock foraging, 137–38, 166–67, 169; wolf, 160, 167; and "bear reserves," 167; scientific taxonomy of, 246–48. *See also* Birds; Domesticated animals; Fish; Pests; Reptiles and amphibians

Wild plants: as foods, 152–54, 295

(nn. 87, 107), 296 (n. 111), 297
(n. 138); and nuts, 60–62, 152; as
dyes, 153; as medicines, 110, 153, 179,
296 (n. 109); and livestock foraging,
164–65, 169. *See also* Flowers,
shrubs, and grasses; Nuts; Trees
Wolves. *See* Wild animals
Women, Creek, 102, 286 (n. 162); activities of, 99–100; and Benjamin Hawkins, 99, 113, 148–49, 190–93; and
town councils, 104; and sex, 113–14;
and Indian countrymen, 117–18; and
commercial hunting, 134–35; and
farming, 142–43; and ranching, 149,
160, 161–62; and plan for civilization,
173; and frontier exchange economy,
176, 190–94. *See also* Agriculture;
Cloth; Gender roles; Kinship; Men,
Creek; Women, Euro-American
Women, Euro-American: in Creek Confederacy, 114–15, 191–92. *See also*
Euro-American frontier settlers
World systems theory. *See* Modern
world system

Yamassee War, 24–25, 28, 290 (n. 100)
Yard fowl. *See* Domesticated animals
Yuchi, 28, 30. *See also* Towns, Lower
Creek—Yuchi